MEDIEVAL
TOWN WALLS

AN ARCHAEOLOGY AND SOCIAL
HISTORY OF URBAN DEFENCE

MEDIEVAL TOWN WALLS

AN ARCHAEOLOGY AND SOCIAL HISTORY OF URBAN DEFENCE

OLIVER CREIGHTON &
ROBERT HIGHAM

TEMPUS

Dedicated to the memories of Ann Hamlin and Andrew Houghton, two influential teachers

Cover illustration: One of the many mural towers on the city wall of Canterbury, including a gun-port; the masonry in the background forms part of the town wall at King's Lynn, incorporating some re-used ship ballast derived from the Baltic.

First published 2005

Tempus Publishing Ltd
The Mill, Brimscombe Port
Stroud, Gloucestershire GL5 2QG
www.tempus-publishing.com

British Library Cataloguing in Publication Data.
A catalogue record for this book is available from the British Library.

ISBN 0 7524 1445 3

Typesetting and origination by Tempus Publishing.
Printed and bound in Great Britain.

CONTENTS

'All these buildings serve to indicate the lamentable state of society in which our ancestors lived, and which is delightfully contrasted with that in which it is our good fortune to be placed.'

From John Britton's paper 'On Ancient Gate-Houses: castellated, domestic and ecclesiastical, with particular reference to those in the city of Norwich', read at the Norwich meeting of the Archaeological Institute of Great Britain and Ireland, 3 August 1847

ACKNOWLEDGEMENTS

For academic advice on specific items, or for supplying illustrations, we are grateful to the following: John Allan (on Exeter); Richard Avent (on Caernarfon); Brian Ayers (on Norwich); Stuart Blaylock (on Exeter); David Bruce (on Bristol); C. Calmettes and V. Graves (on the bastides of south-west France); John Chandler (on Salisbury); Neil Christie (on Southern Europe); George Demidowicz (on Coventry); Dave Evans (on Beverley and Hull); Harold Fox (on Bridgwater); Derek Gore (on York and the Danelaw); Will Fletcher (on Bridgnorth); Salvatore Garfi (on Tenby); Anthony Garrett (on Kingswear); Martin Gillard (on Christchurch); Avril Henry (on Canterbury); Gill Hey (on Oxford); David Hinton (on Southampton); Tom James (on Winchester); John Kenyon (on Caernarfon); Maryanne Kowaleski (on Exeter); Penny Ledbury (on Brecon); Robert Liddiard (on King's Lynn and Norwich); Keith Lilley (on Coventry); Julian Munby (on Oxford); Richard Oram (on Scotland); Stephen Price (on Worcester) and the City of Bristol Museum and Art Gallery (on Bristol); Andy Russel (on Southampton Bargate); Liz Sheppard-Popescu (on Norwich); Derek Renn (on Caernarfon and Oxford); Bob Silvester and Clwyd-Powys Archaeological Trust (on New Radnor); Geoffrey Stell (on Scotland); Mark Stoyle (on Exeter); L. Thomas (on Westminster); P. Thomas and Exeter Cathedral Library (on early modern Exeter); Simon Ward (on Chester); Alan Vince (on London, and *wics* and *burhs*); Bill Woodburn (on Chichester); and Barbara Yorke (on Winchester).

We are indebted to Mrs E. Foster-Smith, widow of the late Mr A.H. Foster-Smith for the donation in 1991 to the (then) Department of History and Archaeology of Exeter University, of an extensive collection of notes, photographs and other extracts compiled during research over many years into the history of medieval town defences. Tom Franklin (New College, Oxford) is also thanked for granting access to parts of the wall of Oxford.

Help from the staff of the following libraries and archives is also gratefully acknowledged: Exeter University Library; National Army Museum Library (Chelsea); National Monuments Record (Swindon); National Monuments Record of Wales (Aberystwyth); National Monuments Record of Scotland (Edinburgh).

Thanks on technical matters are due to Mike Rouillard and Sal Garfi (for line drawings), Marcus Horsfall of Realise Designs (for computer imaging), and Suzie Creighton (for work on the manuscript).

We also thank the publisher's academic reader for providing many helpful comments on our draft text.

The British Academy is also gratefully acknowledged for a research grant enabling much supporting research and fieldwork to be carried out.

LIST OF ILLUSTRATIONS

COLOUR PLATES

BLACK AND WHITE FIGURES

projecting machicolations and arrow loops facing into the gate passage

39   Bury St Edmunds: the Great Gate, a late medieval gate into the monastic precinct

40   Bury St Edmunds: the Norman gate into the monastic precinct, featuring fine Romanesque detailing

41   Canterbury: precinct gate of St Augustine's Priory

42   Exeter: engraving of Broadgate, one of the gates into the cathedral precinct, demolished in 1825

43   Wells: gate into the bishop's palace

44   Wells: gate into the cathedral precinct

45   Leicester: as depicted by John Speed in the early seventeenth century

46   Canterbury: 'keyhole' type gun port in West Gate; the circular opening is 25cm across

47   Southampton: blocked arcades on the south-west side of the medieval circuit

48   Southampton: detail of blocked arcade, showing a 'keyhole' type gun port; the circular opening is 15cm across

49   Southampton: Catchcold Tower, a late medieval addition to the circuit for the provision of gunpowder artillery

50   Southampton: West Gate, showing rectangular gunports

51   Tenby: late medieval gun loops in a mural tower

52   Norwich: Cow Tower

53   Southampton: God's House Tower

54   Kingswear: artillery tower opposite Dartmouth Castle

55   York: Lendal Tower, located on the bank of the River Ouse opposite the North Street Postern Tower, to which it was connected with a chain

56   Part of the London wall at St Giles, Cripplegate, from an etching published in 1812

57   Recording of Exeter's city wall

58   An elevation of Exeter's city wall, with interpretative phasing

59   Detailed recording of an elevation of the town wall of Tenby, with annotations

60   Conwy: detail of crenellations and arrow loops on the west side of the circuit, showing the levelled masonry courses on the wall and the inclined masonry courses of the parapet

61   Conwy: Upper Gate, showing features of military architecture including traces of a barbican and a drawbridge recess

62   Rye: Landgate, viewed from within the town

63   Excavated section through Coventry town wall

64   Warkworth: medieval bridge-gate over the River Coquet

65   Chepstow: medieval Portwall, viewed from the landward side, showing a rounded mural tower

66   Colchester: Balkerne Gate, showing surviving Roman masonry

INTRODUCTION

The subject of the medieval town defences of Britain is one that has often been neglected by historians and archaeologists. In particular, their study did not benefit from the same sort of groundwork carried out on the architecture and history of castles in the late nineteenth and early twentieth centuries by early authorities such as Alexander Hamilton Thompson, George Clark and Ella Armitage. And while the second half of the twentieth century saw much attention devoted to the archaeology of Anglo-Saxon and Anglo-Scandinavian town defences, those of the later period did not receive the same level of scrutiny, despite the general growth of urban archaeology. Overall, compared to the vast literature available on castles, or for that matter abbeys, cathedrals, palaces and many other classes of major medieval monument or building, the available body of literature relating to town defences is unbalanced. Frequently, town walls have been overlooked entirely or else treated as a mere footnote in studies of medieval architecture, fortification and castles. Only two general works dealing specifically with the town walls of England and Wales were published in the twentieth century: Harvey's *The Castles and Walled Towns of England* (which also dealt with Wales) in 1911; and Turner's *Town Defences in England and Wales* in 1970. In a British context must also be noted Thomas's valuable two-volume work *The Walled Towns of Ireland*, published in 1992, while at a broader level still Tracy has edited a collection of papers examining urban defence from a global perspective: *City Walls: The Urban Enceinte in Global Perspective* (2000).

We might also note that systematic studies of the defences of individual towns are rare in fully published form. Notable exceptions include the RCHME's *Inventory of the Historical Monuments in the City of York, Volume II, The Defences* (1972) and Stoyle's document-based study *Circled with Stone: Exeter's City Walls, 1485-1660* (2003), while Kenyon, in *Medieval Fortifications* (1990), devoted a chapter to the archaeological evidence for town defences. In addition, very few detailed guidebooks exist to aid the visitor in finding, exploring and unravelling extant remains of town defences. This relative paucity of general works is in contrast to the great amount of archaeological work carried out on the defences of individual towns, especially from the 1960s onwards, which has added substantially to our understanding of defence across the full spectrum of urban settlements, as the sizeable bibliography at the end of this book testifies. It is hoped, therefore, that this bibliography provides a useful tool to readers and researchers in its own right.

But why have Britain's medieval town walls remained the poor relation to castles in terms of scholarship? We can identify five factors that, combined, explain this relative lack of study. First, town walls have been perceived as lacking the glamour often associated with castles. Being 'communal' rather than 'private' enterprises, urban defences perhaps lack some of the associations with prominent historical figures, families and related events that have added to the fascination of castles for many generations. Second, the physical fabric of town walls is often discontinuous and vestigial, presenting considerable challenges for study, to the extent that a great number of formerly walled towns preserve little or nothing of these features. Third, it has commonly been thought that the physical remains of town walls and gates are second-rate examples of medieval architecture. In studies of medieval buildings, town walls have often been considered as utilitarian structures lacking the investment, elaboration and experimentation commonly seen in major secular and ecclesiastical buildings. Fourth, studies of town defences have often been biased towards the study of documentary sources, and in particular the 'murage grants' through which kings permitted communities to raise funds for wall-building, with insufficient attention paid to the physical evidence of archaeology, architecture and urban topography. Fifth and finally, when the subject of town walls is examined from a European perspective, it rapidly becomes obvious that the urban defences of British towns compare poorly with many of their counterparts across the English Channel in terms of their scale, planning and legacy to present townscapes. This is especially true with regard to European town defences in the post-medieval era exemplified by the many well-known fortified towns (places fortes) established in France by Marshall Vauban in the seventeenth century, or the Italian city states of the Renaissance period. Seen to fall somewhere in between architecture and archaeology and carrying something of a military stigma, town walls in the British Isles have thus unfortunately remained a relatively neglected and unfashionable branch of scholarship.

SCOPE AND APPROACH

This book is an attempt to provide an up to date study of medieval town defences that seeks to question and, indeed, aims to overturn many of these preconceptions. Its focus is on the period c.1050-1650 — roughly from the Norman Conquest to the English Civil Wars. Among its aims is the need to revise the topic of town walls by paying particular attention to their often underestimated social and symbolic values, putting emphasis on the growth of information derived from urban excavation, and enhancing our understanding of the defences of smaller towns. It also attempts to re-examine the common assumption that town walls were communal defences, by investigating the roles of different types of interest groups, including lords, burgesses, secular oligarchies and ecclesiastical authorities, that contributed in different ways to their development. In short, its purpose is to restore medieval urban defence to the position it deserves in broader academic study.

This volume is not a replacement for Turner's 1970 book *Town Defences in England and Wales*, to which the reader should still refer, and which arose from an Oxford DPhil thesis. We have not systematically revisited murage grants, local civic financial records and other such sources through the primary data, but have drawn on Turner's and others' published studies of this material. However, we have expanded the scope of the subject, as defined by Turner, placing more emphasis on archaeology, topography and other aspects that reflect the growth of the subject in the last thirty years. However, although we have visited most places where walls survive, making our own observations, neither is this volume primarily a work of independent fieldwork, nor a compendium of chronological and physical data. Finally, it is not a study of the place of the medieval town in contemporary warfare. Rather, it is a work of commentary, reflection and interpretation, and readers should consult individual publications cited here for details of particular places as well as general inventories, histories and bibliographies, such as the *Victoria County Histories of England* and the inventories of the various *Royal Commissions*. Thus, *the* study of town walls in England, Scotland and Wales, with comprehensive physical and documentary data on all places, remains to be written (and many volumes it would occupy). But we hope our treatment lays out the framework of the subject as it can be understood at the beginning of the twenty-first century.

A central aim of this book is to give full recognition to the diverse range of sources available for the study of town walls: architectural, archaeological, documentary, pictorial, topographical, and cartographical. The quantity and quality of these data vary immensely between different towns, making the judicious use of different types of information a major challenge. But it seems manifestly wrong to assume that documentary sources alone can provide definitive accounts of the construction and maintenance of town walls and reveal the motivation of those responsible. A further aim is to highlight, but also to go some way towards redressing, previous imbalances within the study of town walls. Perhaps most important of all, while the defences of major medieval towns and cities have much to tell us, it would be wrong to examine the archaeology and social history of town walls simply through their scrutiny alone. While the smaller towns of medieval Britain have been, until recently, neglected in research, many were enclosed. Furthermore, the question of how and why traditions of defence spread a long way down the urban hierarchy in some contexts yet remained a privilege of more powerful communities in others, is an interesting one. Likewise, it is important that a treatment of medieval town defences is not restricted to the places where physical remains are more substantial, impressive and obvious, including such photogenic gems as Caernarfon, Canterbury, Chester, Conwy, Southampton, Tenby and York. Also deserving of attention are towns, both large and small, with more vestigial walls or gates – sites such as Brecon, Coventry, King's Lynn, Launceston, Ludlow, Norwich, Stirling and Winchelsea, as well as places where only earth-works of defences survive, such as Montgomery, Salisbury and Wallingford, and others still which preserve no tangible above-ground remains at all, such as Aberystwyth, Arundel and Nottingham, where defences are known only through archives, illustrations and excavation.

The book thus draws together a wide variety of evidence to further our understanding of the chronologies, functions, structures and social significance of British town walls, and to emphasise their fascinating and under-exploited potential for research by archaeologists, historians and historical geographers. The chronological focus of this work is the period from the eleventh to the seventeenth centuries, though earlier and later developments are examined more briefly to set the developments of the period in question in a wider historical context. The town walls of medieval England and Wales are the principal focus of this work, although it is essential that this material is set within a wider geographical context. As town defences in Ireland have been the subject of a detailed two-volume study by Thomas, *The Walled Towns of Ireland* (1992), important sites and trends in this part of the British Isles are examined at a lower level of detail, as are the handful of known defended medieval towns in Scotland, while some reference to examples from further afield in Western Europe is also made for comparative purposes. Yet in recog-nition of the fact that it is artificial to sever town walls from their townscapes, this is also a book that, in its wider context, touches upon the study of walled towns and their associated communities. This emphasises a crucial point: in truth, the study of town walls is not a discrete field of study in its own right, but a component part of the study of the urban phenomenon.

The text of this book is structured to strike a balance between a chronolog-ical and thematic treatment of the topic of town defences. The first part of Chapter 1 is a self-contained introductory essay exploring some crucial themes and concepts in the study of town walls; the second outlines traditions of town defence in the first millennium AD as background to the later medieval period that is the main focus. Given the broad-ranging nature of this scene-setting chapter, readers should note that referencing has been kept to a minimum, while in subsequent chapters full references to works consulted are provided in the form of endnotes, as well as summaries of recommended further reading that identify key books of interest. Chapter 2 traces the development of town walls from the time of the Norman Conquests of England, Ireland, Scotland

and Wales into the beginnings of gunpowder artillery fortification in the four-teenth and fifteenth centuries. The interpretation of different types of source material is the focus of Chapter 3, which examines in turn the role of archae-ological, architectural and topographical evidence in illuminating medieval town walls and associated structures. Chapter 4 is intended to provide the framework of an explanation for the phenomenon of town walls that weighs up the relative significance of the crucial factors of military requirements, symbolism and economic necessity. Examining the legacies of urban defences from the Tudor period onwards, the concluding Chapter 5 draws attention to the various fates of town walls up to the twentieth and twenty-first centuries. Finally, Chapter 6 provides a reflective conclusion that identifies some central themes of significance. An annotated gazetteer is also provided at the back of the book. Comprising a series of summary entries for towns in England and Wales where some physical remains of urban defences survive, this is intended as a starting point for readers who wish to discover and experience a little more of Britain's walled heritage at first hand.

Despite the inevitable search for patterns and trends in the process of academic writing, we should not overlook that wall-building shared an important feature in common with the contemporary world of castle-building. Although it is possible to define influences that have a general bearing on the phenomenon of town defence, the overall distribution map of effort accumu-lated over many centuries was also the result of large numbers of particular events in individual places. Thus, in an idealised enquiry into the world of medieval walled towns, each would be subjected to a very detailed examina-tion of its own circumstances. From this theoretical position, individual data sets would be paramount. At a slightly lesser level of enquiry, as pursued in a book of this sort, we have inevitably (from time to time) relied upon what is (to some extent) a traditional process – namely, of allowing some examples to speak for the larger whole. We must not, however, forget that, as beautifully expressed by the eminent social and economic historian Maurice Beresford in *The New Towns of the Middle Ages* (1967, 413), analogy is 'the last resort of the perplexed'.

Note on places mentioned in the text
Readers should note that throughout the text, names of towns are not accom-panied by the counties in which they lie, partly for brevity and partly due to reorganisations of local government that have sometimes made such juxtapo-sition of names historically misleading. Full references to counties/unitary authorities are provided in the index.

I

FOUNDATIONS: UNDERSTANDING URBAN DEFENCE

In the long-term history of European fortification, a particular characteristic of the medieval period – comprising the millennium following the collapse of the Western Roman Empire – was the degree to which traditions of fortification were not confined to what we would now call 'government'. Whereas in the Roman and post-medieval periods fortification was very much the prerogative and responsibility of the ruling authority, in the medieval period defensive traditions permeated more widely through the upper echelons of society as a whole. The most widely recognised tradition of medieval defence is, of course, the castle (*1*). This institution represented simultaneously the status, wealth, power and defensive needs of the landowning classes and also occurred in different forms, often slightly further down the social hierarchy, in the form of moated manor houses, peles, bastles and tower houses. All these types of sites represented, in essence, 'private' forms of defence, under an umbrella of imperial, royal or princely authority. Members of ecclesiastical society also enjoyed this privilege, so that monasteries, cathedrals and the residences of clerical magnates were often furnished with trappings of 'military architecture' such as crenellated precinct walls and gatehouses. The other major type of defensive tradition in the medieval period was the walled town (*2*). While town defences were more obviously communal than private in nature, they represented a response to the needs of social elites as much as other forms of medieval fortification, with rulers, lords, wealthy merchants and urban authorities being a major driving force behind the construction of town walls. Thus the town wall, like the defences of a castle or bishop's palace, was an expression not only of a perceived need for protection, but also a perceived need to express status and identity. Notably, while 'private' traditions of defence, as represented by the castle, were a peculiarity of the medieval period, the defended town had

1 Rochester: the royal castle, located in the corner of a walled circuit of Roman origin. *Authors' collection*

2 Carcassonne: the reconstructed concentric defences of the medieval cité. *Authors' collection*

both pre-medieval ancestry and a post-medieval future. For this reason, the study of medieval town defences can benefit from a longer-term view of the subject.

An extremely diverse range of towns of all shapes, sizes and origins were walled or defended (*3-7*). But just as in the countryside, not every lord had the resources or motivation to build a castle, so not every urban community was provided with defences. Thus, in order to understand why certain towns were walled, it is also important to consider those that were not. From a European perspective, and even sometimes in a British context, an enclosing wall is often seen as one of the essential qualities that defined an urban as opposed to a rural settlement.[1] Yet in the British context many medieval towns – indeed the majority – were established and prospered without the need for defences. Where they were built, walls were clearly symbols of corporate identity as well as defensive features, but they were not, in contrast, simply badges of communities

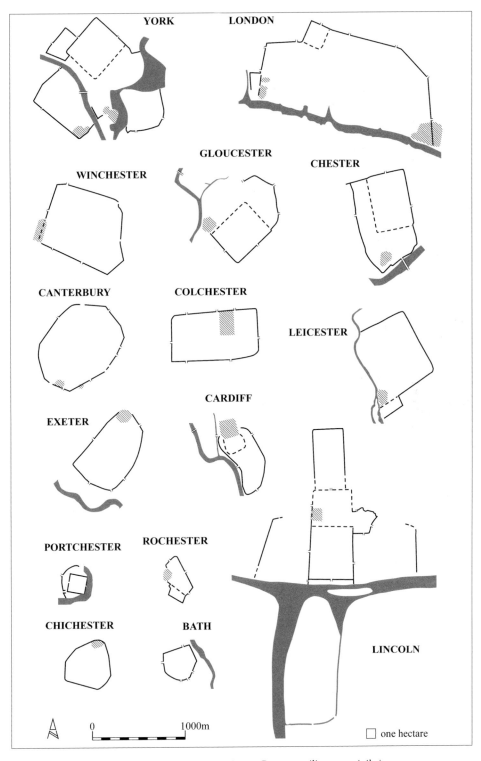

3 Plans of medieval walled towns originating as Roman military or civil sites

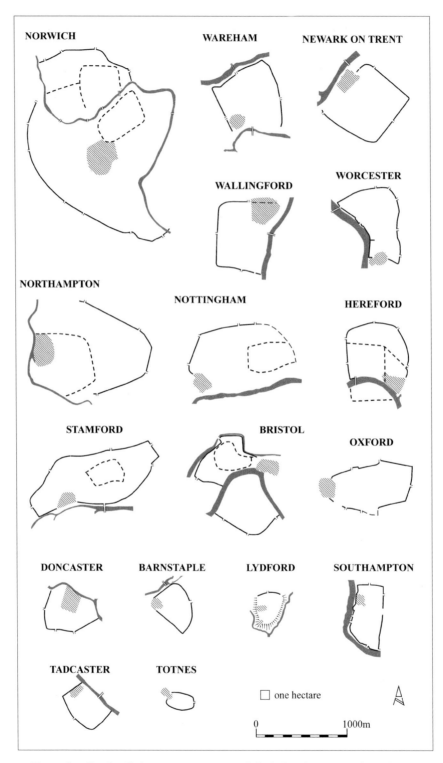

4 Plans of medieval walled towns originating as defended settlements in the early medieval period

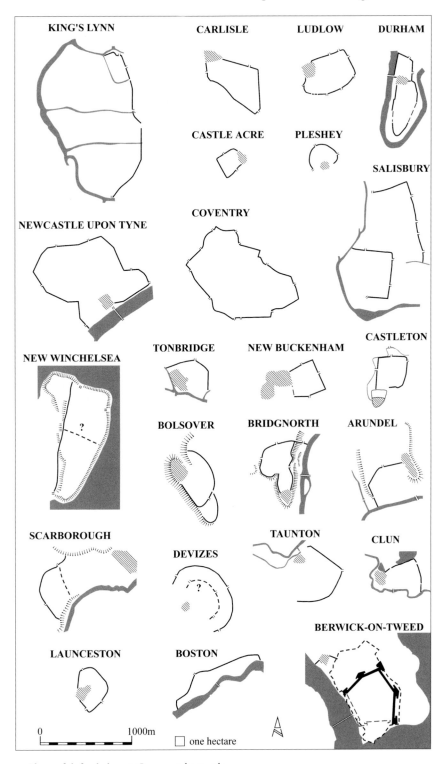

5 Plans of defended post-Conquest boroughs

that had attained borough status — i.e. they were not 'automatically' built around settlements that had attained a given level of independence.

Contrary to the popular view of medieval defended towns, it was not always the case that a completely enclosed perimeter was achieved or even intended. In some places there is good evidence for gateways but no enclosing wall, and these structures were largely jurisdictional features controlling access and defining the physical limits of the urban zone without being defensible in any real sense. In such cases it is tempting to assume from the negative evidence of apparently 'missing' features such as walls that schemes of a grander design were never completed. But excepting cases where there may be clear evidence to this effect, we should also allow for the possibility that a more fragmentary approach to enclosure and defence was all that was required. A great many towns were partially or entirely enclosed with ditches or other earthworks rather than masonry structures. Thus, while gates or bars of some sort were essential components in the topography of any developed town, walls were clearly not. This highlights the role of gateways in controlling traffic and people, the exaction of tolls, and the imposition of curfews. Gates too were the most obvious expressions of urban status through fine architecture (see page 139).

Urban centres of various sorts were capable of flourishing without defence, pointing to our eventual explanation of town defences being more than simply protective. Yet it is clear that it was not simply the physical size or prosperity of a town that determined whether or not it was walled. In post-Conquest England, for instance, important shire towns such as Bedford and Hertford and prestigious cathedral cities such as Ely and Wells appear not to have possessed fully developed urban defences, while tiny boroughs that grew up outside Norman castles such as Castle Acre and Richard's Castle were embraced within fortifications. In attempting to explain which towns within the urban hierarchy were provided with defences, it is therefore necessary to consider a far wider range of social, political and economic, as well as demographic and geographical, factors. At the centre of this debate is the pivotal question: why did towns have walls?[2] But it is also instructive to turn this question back to front. In the light of the fact that in certain periods and certain areas non-enclosed commercial centres could exist separately from fortifications of various types, we should not neglect to consider, also: why did walls have towns?

Overall, therefore, it is hoped that the study of town walls may enhance our understanding of precisely what did or did not define a town to contemporaries. To move towards this aim it is crucial that town walls and related structures should not be seen as isolated and crumbling fragments of the past, but as components within living and evolving townscapes. The holistic study of town walls within their wider contexts can open windows into the communities who built and rebuilt them and lived and died within and around them. Town walls clearly have much to tell us about communities, identities and structures of power within the societies that built and maintained them.

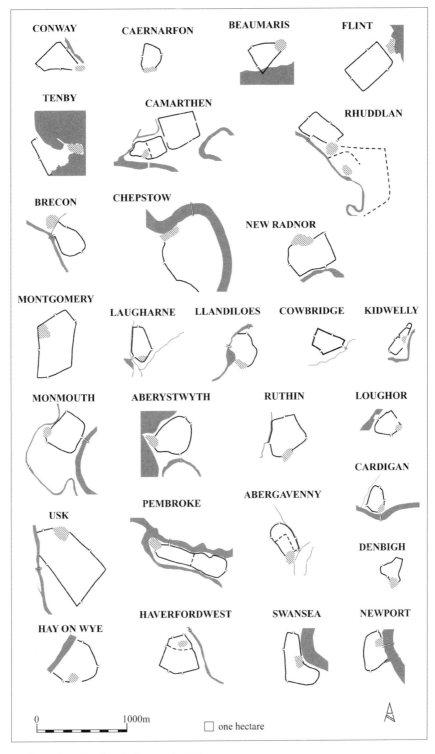

6 Plans of medieval walled towns in Wales

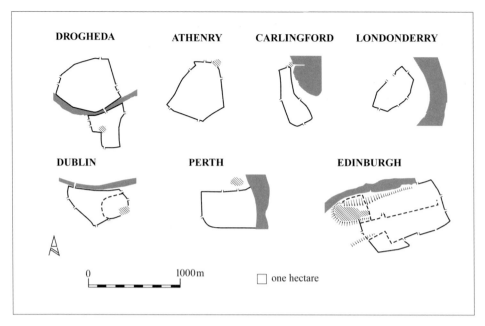

DROGHEDA   ATHENRY   CARLINGFORD   LONDONDERRY

DUBLIN   PERTH   EDINBURGH

0   1000m   □ one hectare

7 Plans of medieval walled towns in Ireland and Scotland

It is also vital to recognise that not all urban communities that possessed defences have remained flourishing settlements to the present day. For instance, while Lydford was in the late Saxon period a local and royal urban centre of commerce and power provided with defences and a mint, it has shrunk internally since the medieval period to the proportions of a village. An example of a later medieval defended plantation that has similarly withered away is Trelech, ranking in the fourteenth and fifteenth centuries as one of the foremost towns of Wales but now little more than a hamlet, lying within the earthworks of defences enclosing a far larger area. Elsewhere, settlements have shifted so that they now lie primarily outside the walled zone, as at Denbigh, where the town was progressively moved downslope from the confines of a walled hilltop position adjacent to the castle in the later medieval period. Equally, a surprising number of medieval planted boroughs once provided with defences are now, literally, greenfield sites, as at places such as Castle Carlton, Caus, Dolforwyn and Dryslwyn. In such cases, physical traces of defences, burgage plots and street networks may be preserved as earthworks and in the alignment of property boundaries or else have vanished entirely. Put simply, walls did not guarantee long-term success. It is only by examining failed, abortive, small and middle-ranking settlements such as these that a fuller understanding of the functions and meaning of town defences throughout the urban hierarchy can emerge, enabling comparisons and contrasts to be made through time and between different regions and countries.

If considerable variation is apparent in the success of medieval towns equipped with defences, then an enormous level of variation is also apparent in the extent to which the defences themselves have survived. The visitor to Chester or York can hardly fail to be impressed by the upstanding remains of town walls of monumental proportions that still embrace the historic cores of these towns (*colour plates 1-5*). Yet far more often, in countless other British historic towns and cities, from places such as Carmarthen in the west to Kings Lynn in the east, members of the general public generally remain unaware how many settlements were formerly enclosed with impressive and costly defences. Quite frequently, there is only fragmentary physical evidence to suggest that a town was formerly walled or enclosed, and often these remains make little sense on the ground. In particular, the vast majority of medieval town gates have been erased totally from the urban scene due to redevelopment and, in particular, a pressing need to ease the movement of road traffic, while others have been incorporated into later buildings and their original form obscured, as at Ludlow (*8*).

Only infrequently are medieval town walls preserved intact as continuous features girdling an urban area, and very rare indeed are those town walls with intact and accessible wall-walks, as at Denbigh (*9*). Many more survive as isolated lumps of masonry and discontinuous stretches of walling, as at King's Lynn (*10*). In the otherwise reasonably well preserved circuits such as those of

8 Ludlow: Broadgate, viewed from the south, showing later properties built into the flanking towers. *Authors' collection*

9 Left Denbigh: surviving wall-walk. *Authors' collection*

10 Below King's Lynn: fragment of town wall built into a public house. *Authors' collection*

Colchester and Tenby, stretches of walling have been dismantled, thus exposing sections through the masonry, giving an excellent impression of the dimensions of these features (*11*). Some fragments of town walls are incorporated into buildings and below-ground structures such as car parks, cellars and even subways, as is the case with parts of the London wall; others still are buried and amenable only to archaeological investigation. In areas of Exeter, the lines of vanished parts of the walled circuit are marked by distinctive paving; at Hull the only upstanding vestige of the town's medieval defences, the Beverley Gate, is preserved as a series of excavated remains in a modern pedestrianised development. At Cardiff and Beaumaris, the only visible traces of town walls are short lengths of masonry attached to the castles under whose shadows enclosed towns grew up. Elsewhere the lines of former ditches may be evident in the form of cracks in subsiding buildings, as apparent in several parts of the now vanished circuit of Barnstaple. The only tangible evidence of former defences in countless other towns is preserved in street patterns that grew up in and around them, fossilising the alignment of parts of the circuit, as for instance at Devizes (*colour plate 6*). In a physical sense, town walls and related structures have thus suffered considerably, and it was not generally until the late eighteenth and nineteenth centuries that a conservation ethic emerged prompting communities and municipal authorities to value town walls as part of their

11 Tenby: exposed section through the town wall. *Authors' collection*

urban heritage. These early efforts represent the forerunners of present-day conservation programmes that exploit the cultural value of town walls as a part of modern built environments.

THE CHARACTER OF TOWN DEFENCES

Town walls are not all they seem. Far more than simply features of 'military architecture', town walls, gates and related structures are strikingly multifunctional, representing a complex blend of military pragmatism and commercial logic, allied with the aspiration for communities to express their political identities and social status through conspicuous building projects. While the need for defence against various levels of violence, insecurity and military threat was undoubtedly a crucial motive in the construction and maintenance of many town walls, this was not by any means the sole reason for their existence. The casual amenity value of walled enceintes to communities should also not be underestimated; in the late medieval and early modern periods it is clear that many wall-walks were used by townsfolk to escape from fetid streets. Town walls also played a crucial role in bounding medieval urban space: they sometimes marked the limits of borough law, were also clearly emblems of civic pride and might symbolise the relative independence of a corporation. At Coventry, according to the Annals of the City, it was the mayor, Richard Stoke, who laid the first stone of the circuit in ceremonial fashion at New Gate in 1356.[3] An indication of the long-term determination needed to bring these projects to fruition, often in tortuous fashion over many lifetimes, is apparent in the fact that this wall, for which funds were raised as early as 1329, was not completed until the 1530s – a period of more than 200 years. Social rivalry between urban populations and emulation of the achievements of other communities was certainly an important motor behind the growth of urban defences, especially in the later medieval period. We should also recognise, however, that especially in the case of post-Conquest new towns, defences might symbolise lordly influence and status rather than communal identity and commercial success. The late thirteenth-century walled enceinte of Caernarfon, for instance, was, in addition to being a defensive work, an emblem of the town's political importance – being intended as the capital of the Principality – rather than any reflection of its commercial status, which was always limited. The notion that town walls were an important part of urban identity was, of course, not a new phenomenon in the medieval period, and it can be illuminating to consider the extent to which the urban traditions of antiquity inspired or influenced the design and construction of medieval town defences (12).

We should also recognise that town walls presented different images to different viewers. Of particular note is the fact that most town walls were more

12 The walls of
Constantinople, based
on a medieval
manuscript
illustration. *Parker
1882*

impressive externally than internally, and a vivid impression of this can still be
experienced in small walled towns such as Conwy (*13*). While a continuous
enceinte studded with towers and gates presented an icon of power and perma-
nence externally visible to all, within the urban zone a wall cluttered by
buildings and obscured from view would have been less impressive and at its
presence not particularly apparent in day-to-day life, apart perhaps from the
gates. This raises the related observation that, in terms of shaping perceptions
of the medieval world, town walls may have had more impact on outside populations and travellers than on urban populations themselves. Quite frequently,
features such as towers and gatehouses ostensibly identified as 'military architecture' might give a fierce outward appearance of martial strength, yet from
the urban interior appear less awesome and more commercial or domestic in
character (*colour plates 7-8*). This is the case with numerous gatehouses bristling
from the outside with militaristic architectural paraphernalia, yet inwardly
designed to provide accommodation and civic facilities (the Southampton
Bargate being a prime example), while the 'open backed' designs of many
medieval mural towers gave an essentially similar dual impression.

While we might tend to think of those town walls that survive in current
townscapes as linear features, we must remember that this is the product of
centuries of erosion and encroachment upon what was originally a more
extensive zone of defence and urban definition. From within a town, the
'mural zone' might start with an intramural street, path or open strip of land
giving access to the defences. The belt of defences would usually continue
beyond the wall or palisade (usually with an associated bank), extending to
include an external berm and ditch or ditches, and in some cases other features
such as bridges across adjacent rivers or wooden 'bars' set beyond the gates.
Thus in their contemporary built environments, walls were but one
component within a complex topography of defence, the removal of much of
which has left walls as apparently isolated fragments. But while it may be
tempting to think of town walls forming parts of defensive 'systems', we should
also recognise that most lacked any real uniformity or regularity. As products
of long sequences of building and rebuilding, the fabric of most medieval town

13 Conwy: mural towers on the north side of the circuit. *Authors' collection*

walls lacked standardisation. The plans of their circuits, meanwhile, reflected the topographies of urban growth rather than being designed for maximum military efficiency, as evident in the irregular circuits of places such as Coventry and Newcastle and the almost total absence of the most defensible form – the circular enceinte. Even those town walls built *de novo* in relatively short spaces of time, such as those of Caernarfon and Conwy constructed as a royal initiative in the late thirteenth century, show elements of inconsistency and even changes of plan within their circuits (see page 101).

Throughout the post-Conquest centuries, one thing above all distinguishes traditions of urban defence from those of the preceding period: little evidence can be found that town walls were built strategically or planned and funded centrally due to the needs of national defence. Rather, the town walls of the medieval period provide remarkable evidence for the initiatives of communities acting essentially in their own interests, though sometimes with royal help and occasionally direction in periods of perceived national threat. At towns such as Bristol and Southampton (*14*), in particular, where great walled circuits were not based on Roman or early medieval foundations, town defences reflected the growth and prosperity of mercantile centres. An important concept here is that of the 'oligarchy'. In the context of medieval towns, oligarchies eventually comprised small and highly organised sectors of the

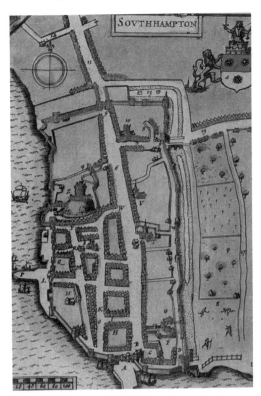

14 Southampton as depicted by John Speed
in the early seventeenth century

urban elite who monopolised power for the benefit of their own social and
economic interests, for instance through the regulation of trade and craft guilds
and implementation and supervision of tolls and taxes. Town walls were, of
course, not the only symbols of a community's pride and identity, however.
Perhaps the other most prominent symbols of urban authority were guildhalls,
many examples of which featured complex iconographic architecture evocative
of justice, control and identity.[4]

Besides reflecting the ambitions of urban communities and coteries within
them, the construction and maintenance of town walls could also benefit the
lords of smaller planted towns. The lords of walled medieval boroughs might
accrue additional income because of the more rigorous control over access into
urban space that a walled circuit allowed, facilitating the rigorous regulation of
tolls. Civic fiscal records sometimes shed light on such arrangements. For
instance, many town gates were certainly staffed by porters responsible for
collecting the market tolls that traders were liable for. In addition, a new town
provided with walls might be especially attractive to new settlers because of
security advantages and the inherent prestige of a walled urban establishment.
At a variety of levels, therefore, town walls and gates represented the architecture of power; we might seek to question, however, whether this was the
power of lords, kings and urban oligarchies, or the collective power of entire

communities. Indeed, the range of stakeholders involved in the construction of town walls reminds us that traditions of 'public' and 'private' defence in the middle ages were not entirely separate, but interrelated at a number of levels.

At a wider scale, the establishment and maintenance of walled towns were clearly seen by rulers to contribute to the stability and defence of regions and, in combination, to enhance national security. The clearest example of this in practice was the development of a defensive system of fortified centres, known as *burhs*, by the West Saxon kings in response to the Viking threat in the ninth and tenth centuries. Through these policies places such as Cricklade and Shaftesbury were effectively founded, and established places such as Bath and Winchester enjoyed continuing or renewed status; all functioned (to different degrees) as centres of royal power and points for the collection of rents, tolls and tribute as well as fortified installations. In later centuries too, the foundation or maintenance of fortified towns could be related to wider strategic goals pursued by kings and ruling elites. The Norman expansion into Wales, Scotland and Ireland, and the later establishment of English 'bastides' in Gascony, for instance, saw fortified boroughs used as instruments of colonial settlement.[5] Fortified royal port towns on the south and east coasts of England, such as Hull (1293) and Portsmouth (1194) similarly had military-strategic functions, while on the west coast the royal borough of Liverpool (1207), in a position less exposed to external attack, remained unenclosed in the medieval period. The foundations of these three places, like so many medieval 'new' towns, represented developments from and formalisations of existing settlements. In the fourteenth century, walled towns on the south and east coast of England such as Rye, Sandwich and Winchelsea formed centres of resistance and refuge in the face of French raiding and piracy, and ultimately contributed to national security, hence the interest taken by kings in their defences. The processes were not confined to the middle ages, however. English policy towards Ireland later employed fortified towns to secure and settle newly confiscated lands, starting in the second half of the sixteenth century and culminating from 1609 with the plantation of Ulster, that included the foundation of new walled towns such as Coleraine, [London]Derry and Strabane.[6]

The fabric of town defences

Town gates formed critical points on a town's walled circuit but not just because of their apparent strength; most featured the finest architectural detail in the circuit, and surviving accounts demonstrate that they were also usually the most expensive and best maintained parts. The architecture of town gatehouses was not simply functional, but often had symbolic undertones. Far from being purely utilitarian features, these frequently incorporated complex iconographic elements, proclaiming the apparent wealth, status, identity and independence of urban communities to travellers and traders. At Southampton, for instance, while the town wall was built in piecemeal fashion over many generations and was architecturally inconsistent and in some areas poorly built, the gates were municipal showpieces constructed to far higher levels of sophistication in shorter spaces of time, as manifested in the architecture of the Bargate. It is also far from coincidental that many medieval towns featured their most impressive gate spanning the main route from London. In a visual sense, gates marked the point of arrival and departure from the urban zone and might be thought to mark the effective interface between the town and the outside world. As will be seen however, the growth of extramural suburbs would tend to blur this distinction, while detailed examination of topographies often shows that the limit of a town's jurisdiction and its wall might not always be coterminous. For instance, many towns featured wooden bars that marked the suburban limits beyond their gates, while urban wards did not usually end at the wall but extended to encompass extramural areas.

Part of this symbolic importance was related to the topographical significance of gates as the points at which individuals would be permitted or denied access, where visiting dignitaries, occasionally including rulers, could ceremonially enter the urban zone, and others turned away. In short, a town's gates acted as a closely controllable filter system. They were also invariably important nodes in a town's religious geography, often supporting, containing or standing next to chapels and churches. As well as forming physical barriers, a town's defences thus constituted moral cordons around communities. It is this iconic significance of town gates that accounts, for instance, for the decorative brick-built exterior of Beverley's North Bar, the armorial decoration on the gates of York (15), and the appearance of King's Lynn's South Gate, the external face of which displays proud turrets that actually contain garderobe chutes and with an overall design reminiscent of a monastic gatehouse (colour plate 9). Overall, it is clear that while town gates were defensive features, they were not necessarily designed to be primarily defensible. Town gates clearly had important commercial functions, especially as places where tolls were collected, and it was not uncommon for them to incorporate domestic facilities for administrative officials. Town gates also had social significance in a multitude of other ways. They were, for instance, the points where the night curfew was imposed and enforced, and where undesirables such as beggars, criminals or plague victims refused right of entry. It is no accident that areas immediately inside and outside the town walls were often the places where prostitution took place and the location of stocks and pillories.

Many town gates were clearly at the 'sharp end' of contemporary architectural thinking and not simply derivative of castle architecture, as demonstrated for instance by the inclusion of early gunports in examples such as the West Gates of Canterbury and Winchester (16). The significance of town gates was such that many stone examples are known where the defences of most of the rest of the circuit were of earth and timber, as at Newport, Salisbury and Sandwich. In addition, Banbury, Beverley, Bewdley, Chesterfield, Glasgow,

15 Left York: engraving of Micklegate Bar. *Britton 1814*

16 Below Winchester: gunports and armorial decoration on West Gate. *Authors' collection*

Halesowen, Morpeth, Oakham and Tewkesbury were among the many places that seem to have possessed gates across streets but no surrounding defences. Other towns possessed not permanent gates but movable wooden bars built to control access into commercial districts or marking the limits of urban jurisdiction, while in other cases stone-built gatehouses were supplemented with bars set beyond them. No such structures survive, however, and their presence is only confirmed by documentary references and street names (see page 130).

If there was more to town defences than defence, then there was also far more to town walls than the walls themselves. Indeed, while in a British context it is customary to talk of the 'town walls' of a particular place, technically this is incorrect, for only exceptionally was there more than one circuit or an extension to it, and 'town wall' is normally a more appropriate label. In addition, we might note that although in the modern world, the word 'wall' has come to be associated with multi-purpose free-standing structures of masonry or brick, it originated as a Saxon or Anglo-Frisian adaptation of the Latin *vallum*, meaning a rampart or wall of earth, turf or stone built for the purpose of defence and/or demarcation. Likewise, we should be aware that in medieval documents the Latin word *fossatum* could be taken as meaning an embankment, a ditch or a combination of the two. In the medieval period, many towns were enclosed or defended without the need to build a surrounding wall of stone. Ditches in conjunction with ramparts mounted with timber palisades seem to have been deemed sufficient in places as diverse as Devizes, Framlingham, Pleshey and Taunton, which were never walled in stone. And nor were earth and timber town defences necessarily found only at earlier sites or those of lower status. In the late thirteenth century, for instance, grid-plan towns appended to two of Edward I's castles in North Wales, at Flint and Rhuddlan, were enclosed with massive double banks and ditches and not walled in masonry, the accounts relating to their construction showing the mass employment of carpenters and diggers rather than masons. Therefore, just as the traveller in the eleventh to thirteenth century would have seen landscapes dotted with timber castles (as well as those of stone), so he or she would have seen many towns, large and small, surrounded by earth and timber fortifications. And in the case of both timber and stone-built defences, these works would on a day-to-day basis have resembled building sites in varying states of decay and reconstruction, rather than the 'finished product' that we often assume in the context of archaeological study.

Thus, while the view of medieval town defences as comprising stone walls and gates is one that dominates both the popular imagination and a good deal of academic study, a more balanced view must also take into account the critical role played by timber and earth defences between the late Saxon period and the thirteenth century. The use of this technology is demonstrated not only by its archaeological discovery (for example at Hereford and Northampton), but also by the documentary evidence for its replacement with stone walls, as on parts of York's circuit in the thirteenth century. There is a broad parallel here with the world of castle studies, where the previously underestimated longevity and importance of earth and timber fortifications have been reassessed.[7] We should also not neglect those urban settlements whose enclosure depended primarily on town ditches rather than expensive multi-layered defences. Works of this nature are remembered for instance, in the names of the 'Bar Dyke' at Beverley; the 'King's Ditch' at Cambridge; the 'Pales Dyke' at Dunwich; the 'Burdike' at

Grimsby; the 'Battle Ditches' at Saffron Walden; and the 'Monk' or 'Tonman Ditch' at St Albans. Town ditches could also serve a variety of functions beyond the purely defensive. The casual use of ditches as municipal dumps was a commonplace expedient, while at Aberystwyth, Cardiff, Conwy, Hereford and Oxford, water from the town ditch drove mills. Stafford, York and Caernarfon all had a 'King's Pool' (i.e. royal fish ponds) linked to their moated town defences, the last featuring an elaborate swan's nest constructed for Edward I in 1304-5.[8]

Within many walled circuits were found other enclosed or fortified units, including private and royal castles and ecclesiastical palaces and precincts. Frequently, the town's circuit also defined the outer boundary of such an institution, which might be fortified, as at Rochester, where part of the castle's curtain wall was also the city wall, or not, as at Wallingford, where the north-west corner of the *burh* defences delimited the precinct of the Benedictine Priory of the Holy Trinity. At York, the area north-west of the early medieval city known as Earlsborough – representing the enclosed residence of the earls of Northumbria – was developed after the Conquest as St Mary's Abbey, defined by a fortified precinct projecting beyond the city wall. Such topographies ensured that one social group rarely had a monopoly on defence, with friction between competing interest groups surfacing not unusually. Often, town walls were thus contested spaces and arenas for internal social conflict at a variety of levels.

The fabric of town walls or gates was rarely the result of a single episode of construction only. Most town walls are complex palimpsests – or multi-layered documents – displaying physical evidence of multiple periods of building, rebuilding and restoration over long periods of time. With skill, the fabric of these walls can be deciphered and 'read' like text. The walls of Canterbury, Chester, Colchester, Exeter and York, for instance, comprise collections of material accumulated from the Roman period to the present day; the walls of Tenby and Newcastle are among the many displaying structural inconsistencies equating to breaks in construction in the medieval period. Only infrequently do standing vestiges survive of Roman town walls that were not modified in some way in later periods, a notable example being Caerwent (*17*). Mixed building technologies incorporating timber and stone elements also seem to have characterised many town walls, as was the case with castles. Timber elements could be used as the basis for floors and other structures within towers and gatehouses, as well as wall-walks and hourds (galleries that projected over the edge of the wall). Interval towers punctuated the walled circuits of many larger towns, while most featured points of access marked by gatehouses that might be accompanied by ancillary features such as barbicans (defended passages projecting beyond the gate) or other outworks. Incorporated within these might be found specific architectural features associated with defence (e.g. arrow loops and gunports), access (e.g. wall-walks and postern gates), residential or domestic functions (e.g. garderobes and chapels) or others that were primarily decorative and symbolic (e.g. coats of arms). In coastal towns or

17 Caerwent: remains of wall and rounded bastions of Roman date. *Authors' collection*

those on major navigable rivers another important component of many town defences by the later medieval period was a chain or boom covering harbours or waterways, as at Hartlepool, Norwich, Yarmouth and York, both for general security and to facilitate the collection of tolls from merchants.

Closely associated with a walled circuit might be found a variety of earthworks. Most common of these were the ramparts that stone walls were terraced into or built as revetments in front of, and the wet or dry ditches that lay outside them. Associated with many other town walls were contemporary earthen banks piled against the interior of the circuit to form massive strengthening buttresses that also provided ready access to the wall-walk for defence and repair. York's defences are very unusual in that the medieval wall sits directly on a massive rampart (*18-19*), perpetuating for much of its course the Roman wall piled over with a bank in the early medieval period; more often, pre-existing earthworks were cut back to receive masonry or levelled entirely. But earthworks were not obsolete in the later medieval period; indeed, the age of artillery signalled a renewed role for earth and timber in town defences. In the English Civil War new bastioned circuits of earth, topped by timber or wickerwork palisades or emplacements were hurriedly built around towns such as Newark and Oxford, while elsewhere semi-redundant masonry structures were bought back into military service. At Exeter, for instance, some of the hollow towers punctuating the wall were filled with earth during the English Civil War to form artillery bastions (*20*), while the rampart behind the wall of Great Yarmouth was a late addition completed in the face of military threats in the late sixteenth century.

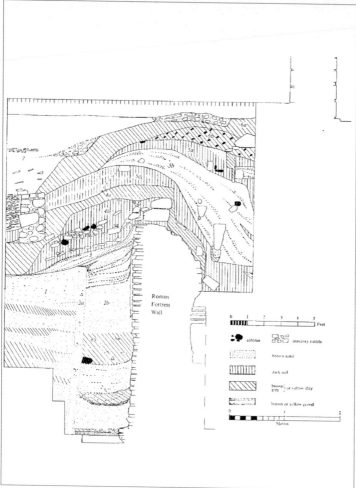

18 *Above* York: town bank and ditch on the north-west of the circuit. *Authors' collection*

19 *Left* Excavated section through York town defences. *Radley 1972*

20 Exeter: restored medieval bastion on the east side of the city wall, bounding the garden of the bishop's palace. The doorway and plaque are not original features. *Authors' collection*

Townscapes and defence

We must also not neglect the important relationship that often existed between the walled circuit and the evolution of other aspects of urban topography. In terms of urban growth, a town wall formed something of a morphological frame that conditioned planning and growth. An important distinction can also be made between those new post-Conquest towns where defences were planned from the start, such as Caernarfon and Conwy, and those where defensive provision was secondary, perhaps entailing the enclosure of organic growth as well as planned units, as at Alnwick and Coventry. In the case of the former, the street pattern would tend to be planned relative to the enceinte, while towns in the latter category are likely to display more irregular circuits reflecting the nature of previous urban growth.

Even as relict features, town walls often marked parish and other administrative boundaries long after they had ceased to have other meaningful functions. Modern streetscapes bear the imprint of town defences in many ways. At Canterbury, Hereford and Norwich, twentieth-century ring roads closely follow the outer lines of walled circuits. But original medieval roads intimately related to the walled circuit may be identified as well. An intramural street, following a line immediately within the walls in order to allow unrestricted access to them, was an integral part of many defensive schemes. Elements of some of these circuitous routes survive to the present day, as at Hereford and Winchester, while Exeter, unusually, had an intramural street surviving on one side only, along the length of the town wall facing the River Exe. Here, an open strip of land inside the wall and occupying the approximate width of the late Roman rampart still survived in places until the eighteenth century.[9] Thought to be a provision to maintain access to the walls for defence, this feature may be an original element of the Saxon *burh*.

If commerce was the lifeblood of a successful medieval town, then the road system linking a centre to its hinterland represented its veins and arteries. By dictating the principal points of access in and out of a town, the positions of town gates played a decisive role in influencing the growth of a street network and the development and differentiation of commercial zones. The positions of a town's principal gates also usually marked the points where suburban development grew up, creating the familiar pattern of 'ribbons' of properties flowing away from gates seen in many early modern town maps. Even where the internal street pattern altered markedly between the Roman and medieval periods, as at Winchester and other *burhs* based on Roman foundations, the medieval town gates often still perpetuated the sites of their Roman forerunners. Of the seven known gates of medieval London (none of which survive), no fewer than six lay on the sites of Roman gates, and only one (Moorgate) was entirely of medieval origin, being the site of a postern enlarged early in the fifteenth century. Yet while the long-term existence of walls and gates in a town plan might at one level symbolise continuity, it was not uncommon for the street plan itself to evolve and change markedly within its confines. At Canterbury, Exeter and Winchester for instance – three towns that retained walled circuits on essentially similar lines from the Roman to post-medieval periods – primary street plans were largely lost to be recast in the late Saxon period, when similar layouts were being formed within new *burhs* of non-Roman origin.

It is important to note that the social geography of medieval towns was, in a very broad sense, the reverse of modern urban settlements, with housing of the highest status tending to focus around the urban core, and suburban and extramural settlement usually reflecting a poorer quality of life. The defence of towns was, accordingly, part of the wider pattern of the 'zoning' of urban functions. Thus, while particular characteristics might be given to a specialist urban zone by a major church, castle or concentration of rich merchants' houses and associated shops, so also the line through which the defences ran would also have its own distinctive qualities. What then, were the wider social characteristics of this zone? A common characteristic of the economic geography of medieval walled towns was for the street frontages with the highest rental values to face directly onto one or more arterial routes connecting the town's gates. In contrast, 'dead end' side streets that terminated at the wall would tend to be less favoured and were not usually as fully developed. It is due to these factors that medieval town plans such as that of Winchester exhibit side streets with 'funnelled' plans, attributable to the gradual encroachment of buildings onto the street frontage nearer the central spinal street, and the widening out of the street closer to the line of the wall because of less pressure on land. Intramural streets, forming links between side streets and giving ready access to the backs of defences, had been a common feature of later Anglo-Saxon urban planning. Many of these, however, failed to develop, and were swallowed up by later medieval intramural expansion, although they might be fossilised in street alignments and even indicated by street names. A lane representing the original intramural road of Hereford (*colour plate 10*), for instance, was known as *Behindethewalles*, being referred to in the grant of a tenement in 1364.[10]

The locations of marketplaces were often influenced by the format of town defences. Lincoln's historic townscape displays a number of marketplaces both funnelling away from and lying immediately inside gates. Marketplaces may have existed outside the defences of some early medieval *burhs*, including Hereford, Northampton, Oxford and Stamford, some of which were later embraced in expansions to the walled areas. Others developed in the later or post-medieval periods, such as the commercial focus outside Leicester's east gate that grew up in the sixteenth century. Certain types of marketing, such as trade in cattle and horse, would tend to lend themselves to extramural locations, as reflected in the late Saxon street name *Rithercheape* at Canterbury. The importance of this facility is indicated by the fact that the city's only gate of Anglo-Saxon origin (Newingate, now St George's Gate) was built into the Roman circuit to provide access to this market. In contrast, the marketplaces of most post-Conquest walled medieval towns lay within the circuit and often near the centre of the town. Edward I's planted town of Caernarfon featured a rare case of an extramural medieval market, this apparently perpetuating the site of the bailey of an earlier Norman castle.

A paradox in the study of urban defences is that while, at a broad level, walls and gates represented status symbols for rich communities, at a local scale they could create restrictions for the inhabitants of adjacent properties. The physical obstacle presented by a wall and ditch would create a constraint on property development, while living adjacent to such features must sometimes have had its unpleasant side, given the use of ditches as dumps. Indeed, the filthy past appearance of town ditches is itself paradoxical given the connotations of status and pride associated with town walls. Internal colonisation of this intramural zone can be seen in the eventual encroachment of buildings and other features right up to walls, and the raising of internal levels with successive episodes of occupation, sometimes to the extent that, internally, the wall disappears. The zone immediately beyond the wall might witness the encroachment first of grazing animals, then gardens, then properties and streets developed up to the wall itself following the abandonment of ditch maintenance. Parallel encroachments might be found in other areas of urban topography, for instance over the outworks of urban castles, the perimeters of churchyards, and along bridges, which by the later medieval period might be lined with structures and partially obscured from view.

Defensive topography might also structure the growth of medieval industrial activity. Excavations in towns such as Hereford, New Radnor and Perth have shown that the strip of land immediately inside defences was sometimes utilised for small-scale industrial activities such as malting and corn-drying. The use of the intramural strip and indeed the town wall itself for stretching out and drying manufactured cloth is well documented in late medieval Exeter, and the place name 'Tenterbanks' immediately inside the defences of Stafford indicates the same sort of activity. Other industries, such as potting and the notoriously noxious tanning industry were typically extramural activities. The extramural Exe Island was Exeter's principal medieval industrial quarter, for instance, while Dublin's potters were clustered in a district outside the city's west gate.

The funnelling effect on road traffic caused by town gates – often resulting in approach roads to towns being wider outside walls than they were within – could also present opportunities for informal trading and commercial opportunity. At Winchester a survey of 1148, giving a detailed overview of the town's economic geography, indicates a strong association between the location of the town's gates and the distribution of blacksmiths' properties either immediately inside or outside the wall, suggesting that livings were made by shoeing the horses of travellers. A particular clustering of blacksmiths' properties can be detected on the west side of the town, for instance, where Robert the smith held two properties either side of the street immediately outside the West Gate.[11] Religious institutions, too, might be sited with reference to town walls. Most major post-Conquest towns had churches outside their gates that were founded to serve the suburbs that straggled away from the urban core, while other chapels and churches were incorporated into the gates themselves or lay immediately inside them (see page 175). Medieval Christian (as opposed to Jewish) cemeteries were both intra and extramural features, unlike those of the Roman period. Medieval hospitals tended to cluster at points of access into the enclosed area, while many friaries were founded on undeveloped land in the immediate extramural or intramural zone and leper hospitals were set well beyond the walled perimeter. It is also well attested that hermits occupied gates and towers, as at London, either as residents or in the service of the urban authority.

The sheer longevity of many of Britain's town walls also highlights their value to communities. Towns such as Exeter and Winchester still feature walled circuits ultimately of Roman origin that have been prominent features of urban topography for almost two thousand years; at places such as Chester and Rochester (21) medieval circuits partly coincided with Roman predecessors. For this reason, it is only natural that town walls have been adapted and reinvented by successive generations to fulfil diverse needs, highlighting the immensely strong attachment that could develop between communities and their defences over extremely long periods of time. During the twentieth century, town walls have become an increasingly valued part of modern built

21 Rochester: medieval mural tower on the north-east corner of a walled circuit of Roman origins. *Authors' collection*

environments – features to be cherished and managed sympathetically for educational, recreational and aesthetic reasons. The present fate of town walls varies from those that are maintained as showpieces of municipal pride, as at Chester, to others neglected as unofficial urban dumps, as is the case with parts of the Saxon *burh* defences of Wallingford. Ironically enough, however, these are both functions that characterised urban defences from the very beginning of their development.

Nevertheless town walls could still exert a profound influence on urban form. [12] Where defences were occasionally expanded, either through planned phases of expansion or the enclosure of suburbs that had grown up organically, the former perimeters of town walls might be fossilised by the lines of roads or areas of open space. The street plans of formerly walled towns often show discontinuity between areas previously enclosed within and those lying outside the defences, with 'dead ends' sometimes terminating near the line of the wall. The impact of town walls on urban topographies might be further marked where the defences also defined a sharp change in the level of streets to either side. Yet the impact of defences on townscapes was far more than physical: in many towns, town walls, whether still standing or now dismantled, invariably still define different social and economic zones. Particularly common is the tendency for the lines of walls to mark the boundaries of dedicated 'heritage' quarters, conservation areas, or pedestrianised zones.

Furthermore, if town walls shaped the settlements that they contained, then they also played an important practical and psychological role in marking the

point of interface between a medieval town, its suburbs and the rural hinterland beyond. Whereas in the late eleventh century, members of urban communities sometimes also worked adjacent field systems, by the thirteenth century
the distinction between rural and urban communities had usually become
more formalised, with the old relationship between the *burh* and shire for
defensive support gone, and urban guilds well established, although in many
cases 'town fields' remained. What is important in this context is that this
period witnessed the increasing definition of urban qualities, with walls playing
one part in this process. To any traveller visiting a major town in later medieval
Britain, the position of town walls and gates (and/or the 'bars' beyond them),
along with a range of characteristic suburban features such as leper hospitals,
left no doubt in the mind as to where the countryside ended and the town
began. To many, town walls must have seemed symbols of communal superi-
ority and even arrogance. Indeed, a great part of the value of town walls to
urban communities lay in their visibility and impact on the senses, providing a
deterrent to hostile action and sometimes demarcating in a conspicuous
manner the jurisdiction of the town. It is this important iconographic quality
of town walls that largely explains their vivid depiction on many medieval
town seals and on the miniature bird's-eye views of towns inset as vignettes into
the corners of John Speed's famous county maps of the early seventeenth
century. In other cases, however, urban jurisdiction extended well outside the
walls and included suburbs and extramural portions of wards (see page 188).

Perimeter walls and related structures were, of course, not the only defensive
features to be found associated with towns, nor were they the only installations
intended to contribute to the protection of urban communities. A number of
medieval towns, such as Chester and Monmouth, possessed fortified bridges
where towers were placed to overlook the river crossing – a tradition of
defence with parallels in Roman defences and the late Saxon period, when
'double *burhs*' such as Bedford are known to have been founded. Enclosed
ecclesiastical precincts can be identified in many medieval town plans in settlements such as Exeter, Lincoln and York that were walled; places such as
Lichfield, St Andrews and Wells that were not; and others, such as Plymouth,
where town defences were later additions. These intramural walled enclosures,
usually provided with their own elaborate gatehouses, point to one interesting
subdivision within medieval urban communities and reflect issues of both
security and jurisdiction. Also relevant in this context are the numerous extramural friaries allowed to encroach over town walls, as at Oxford Greyfriars.
Another feature providing excellent evidence of a different type of social
division within towns was, of course, medieval castles. These were imposing
structures within many urban communities and have had enduring legacies on
the development of townscapes to the present day. Castles might take many
forms, ranging from great royal fortresses superimposed within earlier settlements (e.g. Dublin Castle and the Tower of London), to the defended resi-

22 Carlingford: The Mint, a merchant's tower house in the medieval town. *Authors' collection*

dences and estate centres of major magnates around which fortified medieval towns developed (e.g. Arundel and Pembroke). In all these cases, the essential quality differentiating the castle from the town wall was that, while the former was private fortification, the latter represented part of a long-lived tradition of 'communal defence' that can be traced back to late prehistoric hillforts. In Irish and some Scottish towns, we often encounter a rather different type of site: the urban tower house. Largely absent from the English and Welsh urban scene, but commonplace in parts of southern Europe, these later medieval sites when found in Scotland and Ireland usually represented the defensible dwellings of wealthier members of the urban classes such as merchants (*22*), or the urban properties of the landed gentry. Also rather different from town walls are those military sites built to contribute to the protection of towns by providing 'point defence' rather than being integrated within a defensive perimeter. The clearest examples of such sites are those early artillery fortifications including the late fourteenth-century Cow Tower at Norwich and the late fifteenth-century artillery tower of Dartmouth Castle that formed self-contained gun platforms. In this context might also be included outlying artillery forts built beyond town defences in the English Civil War, as with the number of 'sconces' built around Newark in the seventeenth century. The twentieth-century descendants of these sites were the numerous Second World War pillboxes still found guarding militarily important features around towns, including river crossings and railway junctions.

ORIGINS

Study of the early medieval framework of defended urban places is not only interesting in its own right, but also illuminates some features critical to the development of urban defence in subsequent centuries that is the main focus of this book. Three particular issues are of significance. First, by *c.*1000, there existed a framework of defended towns whose distribution formed the foundation of the later medieval hierarchy of walled urban places. By this early date, two of the three major categories of defended town existed, namely those established in the Roman and in the late Saxon/Anglo-Scandinavian period; to them was added (especially from the twelfth century onwards) many seigneurial and royal 'new towns', a far smaller proportion of which were defended. Indeed, it should not escape attention that the immediate pre-Conquest period saw a far higher proportion of towns walled, among the whole urban spectrum, than in subsequent centuries. Second, by this time the essential technologies of urban defence were well established, namely masonry, earthworks and timber often in combination. This variety continued to exist down to the thirteenth century, after which masonry tended to predominate, although not to the overwhelming extent that is sometimes supposed. Third, the circumstances through which defended towns came into being in the early medieval period help to explain a major characteristic of later medieval urban society. In this early period, the crucial motor for the plantation of or renewal of walled towns was royal initiative. Although in subsequent centuries 'new towns' were founded by a variety of lords in large numbers, there nevertheless remained an immensely strong connection between kings and urban communities which, despite their growth and acquisition of liberties, never achieved levels of independence comparable to those found in some other parts of Europe.

The notion of the walled town in English context is easily represented by images from such places as Chester, York and Southampton, all of which preserve monumental remains of gates and walls of the later medieval period. Yet this impression is the culmination of a far longer-lived tradition whose roots can be traced to the later prehistoric period, whereby communities – or labour forces employed or coerced by them – enclosed their important settlements. While the defensive qualities of the 'causewayed enclosures' of the Neolithic remain a subject of debate, it is generally accepted that the major defended settlements of the Iron Age represent the earliest large-scale evidence of communal defence, with the overtones of pride and display that such works represented. In those areas of Britain subject to Roman rule, the urban phenomenon expanded both in quantity and diversity, so that a complex hierarchy of smaller and larger towns and cities – from walled *coloniae* such as Gloucester to enclosed small towns such as Great Casterton – spread across the provinces. Crucially, however, not every town in Roman Britain was defended, and this remained true of urban settlement into the late medieval period. This observation is of fundamental importance to understanding the whole subject under review in this book: urbanism and defence were not simply synonymous but had a complex relationship resting on a variety of military, social, economic, legal and demographic factors.

The Roman Legacy

Far more complex than simply a case of 'continuity or cataclysm?' as sometimes portrayed, the fate of urban society and settlements in the post-Roman period was subject to a diverse pattern of developments best under-stood on presently available evidence with reference to particular circumstances rather than general trends. The extent to which town defences survived in this period, either as relict features or active defensive installations subject to continuing investment and refurbishment, remains a very obscure subject indeed. In addition, it is unclear whether large hillforts reoccupied in the post-Roman centuries, such as South Cadbury (Somerset), possessed 'urban' qualities in any sense.

Any discussion of the uses of defended places in the immediately post-Roman centuries (i.e. *c*.AD 400-700) is made challenging by a number of gaps or difficulties in evidence. First, there is the overall problem of the extent to which Roman centres continued to be used following the collapse of the provincial administrations. This issue continues to perplex historians and archaeologists, and remains a contentious and ongoing subject for debate. Second, and related, is the sparse nature of specific evidence relating to the defences of such places: even where occupation of a former Roman town or fortress might be in evidence, can we also assume that its defences were being maintained? This problem is compounded by the fact that, where such places have a later flourishing history, the fabric of Roman defences has often been truncated by medieval building operations, thus removing potentially critical evidence. Third is a problem of definition. In studying the Roman period we have a well-developed sense of the functions of defended places, whether military fortresses or civil settlements. Yet in the following centuries, even where there is evidence of occupation within a Roman defended circuit, we cannot always be certain that the functions of the enclosed community can be defined as 'urban', either by the standards of the Roman period or the middle ages. It has therefore been suggested that a useful distinction can be made in our interpretation of this period by separating notions of 'life in towns' from 'town life'.[13] Thus, the study of defences in the early medieval period is inevitably bound up with a wider problem of defining what, if anything, constituted urbanism at this time.

During the fifth and sixth centuries AD, there developed a number of new kingdoms whose authority spread gradually northwards and westwards at the expense of indigenous 'Celtic' rulers. In all these areas Roman defended places were to be found, ranging from great centres such as *Londinium* (London) and *Eboracum* (York) to small towns such as Dorchester-on-Thames in Oxfordshire. The fates of these numerous places varied widely, from more or less continuous activity to total abandonment. The uses to which their defences were put are very difficult to identify, and interpretation can only be advanced on the basis of indirect evidence, either in the form of historical or archaeological material.

Five examples illuminate these issues. Writing in Northumbria in the early eighth century, the Venerable Bede described Canterbury at the time of the Augustinian mission (AD 597) as the centre (*metropolis* and *civitas*) of King Aethelbert's Kentish kingdom. Allowing for the time-lapse between these events and their written description, this provides a tantalising glimpse of the role of a former Roman defended town, but does not really assist with the problem of whether the early Anglo-Saxon kings of Kent maintained the fabric of the walls. Although no royal palace has been discovered, it has been suggested that the Roman stone-built theatre within the walls may have been the assembly place for the royal court of the Kentish kings, even though the town may have been thinly if at all populated at this time.[14] What we can reasonably surmise, however, is that the royal presence added to the prestige of the location, and the town and its outskirts were certainly considered the most suitable location for the foundation of new churches that followed Augustine's arrival. Clearly, Aethelbert controlled the interior of the city, as indicated by his extensive grant of land in its northern portion for the building of Augustine's church. The area around the precinct of what became the cathedral, bounded by Palace Street, The Borough, Burhstreet and Burgeat, that forms the north-east part of the walled area, has been suggested as a self-contained *burh* within the larger unit.[15] The existence of this early intramural unit has, however, been called into question as further archaeological and charter evidence has revealed more extensive early medieval occupation in the southern half of the Roman walled area.[16] As at other southern English towns such as Canterbury, Exeter and Winchester, the Roman street pattern was lost and a new one with burgage plots emerged in the late Anglo-Saxon period. Part of this new street pattern included a new intramural lane – comprising a continuous route following the internal face of the defences – that was an entirely new feature and not the successor of a Roman *pomerium*, and whose presence presumably indicates the more intensive use of the walls at this later point in time.

A geographically contrasting example comes from western Britain. The late ninth-century Anglo-Saxon Chronicle (incorporating written and oral traditions of earlier dates) related that in 577 the West Saxons defeated the British at a place called *Dyrham*. The outcome of this battle placed in English hands three cities (*ceastra*), Gloucester, Cirencester and Bath, formerly ruled by three British kings named, respectively, as Coinmail, Condidan and Farinmail. This English victory was of crucial importance to the future political geography of western Britain since it divided the 'West Welsh' of the south-west peninsula from the 'North Welsh' of the area now known as Wales. The equating of three defended Roman cities with three units of British government raises the distinct possibility that their defences had been maintained in conjunction with their political role, but, perhaps inevitably, the documentary source does not take us to this conclusion in a clear manner.

Another tantalising reference in the Chronicle occurs in 491, when the Saxons attacked the Roman coastal fort at Pevensey (*Andredesceaster*) and slew the British occupants who were defending it. Whether it had become a permanent settlement, whether its defence was opportunistic, or even whether the fort merely represented a landmark near the battle is not revealed. A similar problem relates to London itself. In 457 the English defeated the British at Crayford (Kent), and the fleeing Britons took refuge in London, again prompting questions over its defended status or lack of maintenance.

A comment from Bede illuminates a further dimension to this problem. In reference to the early seventh century (but more probably reflecting the situation of his own time in the early eighth), Bede referred to London as a market (*emporium*) to which men from many nations came by sea and land. On present archaeological evidence, this settlement seems to have lain to the west of the city of *Lundenwic*, in the Strand and Aldwych areas, and not within the Roman walled zone, where lay the separate ecclesiastical focus of St Paul's.

Finally, in a famous poem written by Alcuin (d. 804), York (*Eoforwic*) is described as a centre to which people travelled in search of wealth from all over the known world, apparently reflecting a level of urban trading activity comparable to eighth-century London. Again, as at London, the archaeological evidence places the focus of this activity outside the walled area of the Roman defences. Some parts of the north-west and north-east parts of the Roman fortress walls may have remained visible throughout the early medieval period, especially the 'multangular tower' on the south-west side of the former Roman fortress (*23*). The clearest physical evidence of pre-Viking addition to York's defences is the 'Anglian' tower located immediately north-east of this feature, comprising a rectangular structure with a barrel-vaulted lower level built into the Roman wall. The north-west and north-east sides remained as a defensive circuit in the Anglian and Viking periods and were not cut through by new streets. Excavation has shown that remains of the Roman walls were covered by new ramparts, presumably carrying timber palisades. On the south-west and

23 York: the Roman and later multangular tower on the western corner of the Legionary
Fortress. *Authors' collection*

south-east sides, however, the fortress walls were abandoned and cut through
by new streets. Access to the trading settlements along the rivers Ouse and Foss
was clearly crucial and the Roman walls regarded as an impediment.
Eventually, the north-west and north-east defences were extended down to the
rivers, though at what point this process began is unclear.[17]

Historians and archaeologists alike tend to the view that both York and
London had continuous sequences of occupation through the post-Roman
centuries, though this occupation was not always contained within the same
specific areas or the walled zones in particular. But this still leaves unanswered
the question of whether occupying communities, subject to Northumbrian
and mainly Mercian royal rule respectively, carried out any active maintenance
of Roman defences. Archaeological evidence, in fact, points to the commercial centres of activity in both places being outside the Roman walled areas,
taking better advantage of riverside settlement, towards the River Ouse in York
and along the Thames in the vicinity of The Strand and Aldwych in London.
In both cases, the convenience of a trading site seems to have outweighed the
advantages of protection provided by extant walled circuits.

Thus, while excavations in a number of places have revealed traces of immediately post-Roman occupation, the significance of these activities for the
nature of 'urban life' in general and the maintenance of old Roman defences,
in particular, remains problematic. The former Roman town of Winchester
(*Venta Belgarum*), had a subsequent history as an important centre for the West
Saxon kings, being the site for the foundation of a minster church in the
seventh century. Excavation has revealed early post-Roman occupation, but
the role which Winchester played in the early history of the West Saxon

kingdom remains somewhat controversial. Polarised arguments have either stressed the much later date for specific evidence of Winchester's importance, or postulated a much earlier importance based on a back-projection of its later history as the major royal centre of Wessex.[18] Such a variation of interpretation clearly has implications for any presumed maintenance of the Roman walls in the early post-Roman centuries. The only known alteration to the defensive circuit was the blocking of the Roman south gate with new masonry and accompanying ditch, probably in the seventh or eighth century, although this was later re-opened in the late ninth or tenth centuries during Winchester's large-scale redevelopment as a West Saxon *burh*. Whether the motivation for this alteration was to enhance defensibility, or whether it was a reflection of some unknown change in intramural property ownership is, however, unknown. One possibility is that these blockings were designed to filter traffic through the King's Gate on the south side of the circuit and thence into the precincts of the Old Minster (and, arguably, the precincts of a putative royal palace). A similar sequence may have also applied to the north gate, whereas access through the east and west gates remained continuous from the Roman period onwards. Overall, the evidence suggests that refurbishment of Winchester's defences took place only part-way through Alfred's reign: in 860 the Vikings sacked the city with apparent ease; and in 868 the perimeter of the city was referred to not as a wall but as the 'King's city hedge' in the boundary description of part of an estate given to Alfred's wife Ealhswith at the time of her marriage. As well as the Burghal Hidage listing for Winchester's defences reflecting arrangements in the Alfredian period, the walls are referred to (*portwealle*) in tenth-century charters and the east, south and west gates were also referred to in charters of this period. At Wroxeter (*Viroconium Cornoviorum*), excavation has revealed a massive reconstruction in several phases, from the late fifth to the mid-seventh century, of an area focused on the baths *basilica* and adjacent streets; a major question mark hangs over the fate of the defences, however, which were certainly not refurbished as a complete circuit.[19]

On present evidence, the conclusion to be drawn is that there was no obvious correlation between a successful trading centre and defence in the immediate post-Roman period. Other possible motivations for the maintenance of old Roman defences can be identified. To what extent, for instance, might the kings of the new Anglo-Saxon kingdoms who had inherited the fabric of Roman provincial authority have viewed the defences of former Roman cities and fortresses as symbols of prestige, loaded with imperial imagery? Even where the defences of former Roman centres may have lacked serious military qualities, they may have provided a level of *ad hoc* security and some deterrent quality. Finally, the pattern of earliest ecclesiastical foundation in walled centres in south-east England such as Canterbury, London and Rochester, and its subsequent extension to places such as Lincoln and York, provides us with additional clues about the attraction of old Roman sites. Might these places not only have provided opportunistic building sites with plentiful materials, but also have maintained a link with the urban pattern that had been crucial to the development of Christianity in the continental Roman provinces? For example, the selection of the former Roman walled centre of Rochester in 604 as the site of a second Kentish ecclesiastical foundation reflected its location in a former sub-kingdom of Kent. This correlation between new churches and old defended places also reveals the simple fact that Roman centres are likely to have been parts of Anglo-Saxon royal estates. Overall, however, the case for the ongoing importance of Roman walled places in the British provinces is a far less strong one than is the case across the Channel.

Town Defence in the Early Medieval Kingdoms

It was not until the middle Anglo-Saxon period (c.AD 700–900) that we see this pattern of old Roman defended centres added to, with the foundation of new ones. While places such as Hereford, Oxford, Tamworth and Wareham originated in this period and ultimately grew to become flourishing medieval towns, a question mark exists over whether all the new or refurbished places were originally envisaged as settlements with a full range of urban functions or were initially more specialist foundations and church centres.

Intriguingly, when Anglo-Saxon kings developed a new interest in urban affairs in the seventh and eighth centuries, this was not simply a question of revitalising old Roman centres provided with defences. At this time, we find evidence of new trading centres fostered by Anglo-Saxon kings, collectively known as *emporia* or *-wic* settlements (derived from the Latin *vicus*) normally outside rather than within former Roman walled settlements, and without their own defences. Thus in the eighth-century the commercial heart of London (*Lundenwic*) lay along the Thames west of the Roman city, while in the north, the corresponding settlement of York (*Eorforwic*) lay on the banks of the Ouse outside both the fortress and *colonia* settlements. The most extensively excavated of such sites is *Hamwic*, located on the west bank of the river Itchen and now lying under the St Mary's area of Southampton. Far from being a spontaneous nucleation, *Hamwic* was a deliberate and planned creation and, as at York and London, lay close to a former Roman site (possibly *Clausentum*: modern Bitterne Manor, on the opposite side of the estuary). Part of the gridded settlement's western boundary was marked by a ditch, with a V-shaped profile width of some 3m and depth of 1.5m, although it is uncertain whether this was accompanied by a bank.[20] This feature may have been discontinuous and was filled in by the mid-eighth century having been excavated c.700, and seems not to have been seriously defensive in nature, rather serving as a symbolic demarcation of the settlement's limits. Other comparable settlements, though less well known archaeologically, are revealed by place name evidence, as at Dunwich, Harwich, Fordwich, Sandwich and, more doubtfully, Swanage (*Swanawic*). Notable in this revival of trading activity was the willingness of sponsoring rulers to eschew the security of old Roman walled areas in favour of the convenience and commercial potential of more estuarine and riverine locations. This phenomenon was but one manifestation of a wider revival of trade occurring across the north-west seaboards of Europe that included settlements such as Rouen in Normandy, Quentovic in Northern France, Dorestadt in Holland, Lübeck in Germany, Wolin in Poland, Hedeby in Denmark and Birka in Sweden, some of which did, however, eventually possess their own defences, though most did not.[21]

The confidence of the eighth century, during which trading activity was largely undefended, gave way to a more cautious attitude. The various Viking incursions and invasions that afflicted northern and eastern England in the ninth century and then threatened the south, motivated the foundation of military installations that also created secure locations encouraging commercial growth. The most prominent manifestation of this was the development of a network of defended *burhs* famously described in the document of *c.*900 known as the Burghal Hidage, highlighting a reinforcement of links between royal power and urbanism that was to be such a critical feature of English urban history. This document lists 30 fortified centres in Wessex and three (Buckingham, Warwick and Worcester) beyond its borders, along with details of land allocation by which manpower for the maintenance and defence of these places was drawn from the shires.[22] The list was thus an administrative source describing a particular mechanism of defensive organisation, and should not be taken (as it so often is) as a definitive guide to the numbers of defended places at this time. Dorchester, for instance, an Anglo-Saxon shire town of Roman origin (and with Roman defence) is not included but is generally reckoned to have had equivalent status to the Burghal Hidage sites.[23] The distribution of these *burhs* is also not a product of chance. Along the northern edge of Wessex, sites such as Bath, Cricklade and Wallingford have the appearance of border fortifications guarding the approaches from Danish Mercia. Exeter, Portchester, Wareham and Watchet all provided defence against seaborne Viking attack, and overall the distribution ensured that few *burhs* were further than 20 miles from one another. The scale and origins of the defences of these sites vary broadly along one of three lines. The largest and most elaborate defences (although the smallest group) were associated with former Roman centres; examples include Bath, Chichester, Exeter and Winchester. At sites such as Cricklade, Oxford, Wallingford and Wareham, defences were built *de novo*, on approximately sub-rectangular plans perhaps of ultimately Roman inspiration and in association with regularly planned street networks. A miscellany of smaller defended sites, often referred to as burghal 'forts', comprised irregularly shaped enclosures with more limited street planning. Within this category fall places such as Lewes, Lydford, Lyng and Shaftesbury. Ironically, the first category, where the defences were most substantial, provides us with the least opportunity to study whatever was built through archaeology. Characteristically, such places preserve Roman material low down and a variety of much later medieval phases above. As with many aspects of town wall archaeology, it is the least long-lived sites that preserve the best opportunities for archaeological enquiry, while at the most permanently occupied, whose walls received much later rebuilding, earlier fabric is less available for study (although Exeter is a notable exception: see page 123).

It is easy to assume, quite possibly wrongly, that places listed in the Burghal Hidage had been fortified for the first time only in the later ninth century. There was, in fact, a much longer history of '*burh* work', which is referred to in Kentish charters by *c*.800, Mercian charters (discussed below) by the mid-eighth century and West Saxon charters by the mid-ninth century. It is highly likely that the smaller *burhs* that did not develop urban characteristics had never even been intended for urban growth, lying firmly in the tradition of immediate military need. In contrast, the evidence for street plans, mints and markets which emerged at the old Roman *burhs* and the larger new Anglo-Saxon centres probably indicates that these were envisaged with urban growth in mind from the outset. At Worcester, whose foundation is uniquely described in a charter of the 890s, this urban quality is clearly evident, with an emphasis on legal, commercial and ecclesiastical interests bound up with defensive provision; tenth-century written evidence here reveals that rural thegns who were episcopal tenants kept urban properties within the *burh*, perhaps connected with their defensive duties.[24]

A prominent example is London, whose Roman walled area was reoccupied by King Alfred of Wessex in 886; from the late ninth century, the intramural zone evolved as a secure political and commercial centre, while the earlier extramural settlement declined. Despite its pre-eminence, London was not listed in the Burghal Hidage, almost certainly because the origin of this West Saxon list pre-dated Alfred's reoccupation, in contrast to Southwark on the south side of the Thames, which was included. This development altered the focus from London*wic* to London*burh,* and, as elsewhere, a new street pattern developed obscuring the Roman plan beneath. Although the excavated evidence is not wholly clear, the fourth-century Roman defensive ditches were subsequently recut on several occasions and this process had almost certainly started in the late Anglo-Saxon period. Excavation near the Old Bailey and elsewhere has revealed a sort of 'pit-free' zone, just inside the Roman walls in the late Anglo-Saxon period, as though the area was deliberately kept free of occupation to make it more accessible for defence. No unambiguously Anglo-Saxon masonry, however, has been identified in the surviving fabric of London's walls.[25]

Two royal centres from the Mercian kingdom have produced concrete archaeological evidence of defences without Roman antecedent that pre-dated those of the Wessex *burhs*. At the Staffordshire town of Tamworth, excavations in the 1960s demonstrated parts of an earth and timber circuit that may have originally enclosed a Mercian royal residence, although the degree of defensibility remains unknown, as does the precise date of these works.[26] At Hereford, a place of presumed military importance (the place name means 'army ford', with reference to the River Wye) located on the Mercian border with Wales, an antecedent to the Alfredian *burh* is suspected. A primary enclosure bank again underlay the more substantial late ninth-century defensive enclosure, at least on the west side of the town, as revealed by excavation in the 1960s and early 1970s.[27] These examples highlight a recurring methodological issue in the study of town defences through archaeological excavation. Given the likelihood of rebuilding along a defensive perimeter, the origins of a town's earliest defences can be extremely obscure, as the levelling of old defences to build new ones can effectively remove or seriously truncate earlier works. In many ways this is a parallel issue to the thorny archaeological problem of castle origins. It has also been suggested that King Offa built a number of *burhs* in the later eighth century, designed to resist Viking river-borne raids; these had in common riverine positions and included old Roman centres such as Godmanchester and Leicester, as well as new foundations such as Tamworth and Winchcombe.[28] Thin though this evidence of early Mercian town defences may be, of equal interest is the corresponding emergence into the documentary record of royal fortifications. Mercian charters of the period recording alienation of royal land commonly reserved for the king certain fundamental obligations, notably service in the army and provision of labour on bridges and fortifications. Another Mercian system of raising fortifications of a different sort is visible archaeologically in the form of Offa's Dyke – an enormous undertaking indicating a sophisticated means of royal control over labour and resources, even if the revisionist interpretation of the monument (occupying only the central Welsh border) is adopted.[29] It may well be, therefore, that the actual pattern of Mercian fortification was far wider than archaeology can reveal. Notwithstanding these arguments, we cannot say with confidence that the settlements to which such fortification applied were significantly urban and may rather have served as specialised nodal points within settlement patterns. Their growth did, however, belong to an embedded tradition of royal control over fortification, which was soon to play an indisputably major role in urban history. We should also remember that the tradition of urban development around minster churches in this period – including places such as Gillingham and Bampton – usually took place without defensive provision.[30]

The Danelaw, including East Anglia, eastern Mercia and Northumbria, contained numerous places which by the tenth century had some urban characteristics and many of these places had some defences. Apart from York, the most famous historically, were the 'Five Boroughs' of the eastern Midlands, thought to have had their origin in the military organisation of the Danelaw following its Viking occupation in 877. Although defence was undoubtedly an important function of these places (Derby, Leicester, Lincoln, Nottingham and Stamford), virtually nothing is known about the physical character of these defences or their organisation.[31] At Derby, the situation is completely obscure. At Lincoln, while the Roman defences of the upper and lower cities remained massive and substantially intact barriers in the early medieval period, there is no evidence that the circuit was reconstructed, and investment may have focused rather on the gates, though archaeological information is lacking.[32] The same may have been true of Leicester. At Nottingham, excavated ditch-works of pre-Norman date may represent the perimeter of the Danish enclosure on the north side of the River Trent. Edward the Elder subsequently built a second *burh* on the south side of the river (its location is still controversial), and connected them with a bridge. The overall topography of a similar two-element plan, with Danish *burh* and English counter-*burh* on opposite banks of the River Welland has also been established at Stamford. Apart from the defences, however, the growth of these places in the Anglo-Danish period has also been illuminated by the study of street plans and the distribution of datable archaeological evidence. It has been established, for example, that occupation had extended outside the Roman walls of Lincoln during the first half of the tenth century. In addition to these famous five, archaeological and historical sources point to the existence of a small number of other centres which probably possessed earth and timber defences, including Doncaster, Ipswich, Newark, Norwich and Tadcaster.

Defended towns on the eve of the Conquest

The network that existed by the time of the Norman Conquest thus comprised a variety of centres with different origins. Some, for example Bath, Chester, Chichester and Exeter, were ultimately of Roman origin, whose defences were refurbished. Others, such as Wallingford, Wareham, Warwick and Worcester were planted *burhs* with new defended perimeters and street plans. In addition, places such as Shaftesbury and Lydford were both smaller and less formally planned. Further north, in the areas of Scandinavian influence, similar developments occurred. Centres such as Nottingham, Stamford and Derby were developed as new fortified centres by Viking authorities, and older towns such as Leicester, Lincoln and York, all of Roman origin, saw further development under Scandinavian rule. Further complexity was added to this pattern in the wake of the English reconquest in the tenth century when, in places such as Bedford, Stamford and Nottingham, *burhs* were built in opposition to Scandinavian centres, subsequently brought under English control, resulting in the plans with double foci. The creation of such an additional defensive focus could have an enduring effect on urban form. For instance, when John Speed mapped the town plan of Bedford in the early seventeenth century, the settlement still comprised two distinct elements linked by a bridge over the Ouse, each focused on a separate church and market.

In addition to these many and varied defended towns, other settlements with apparently urban characteristics had developed by the time of the Norman Conquest. We should not neglect, for instance, those centres of political or economic importance possessing defences that were essentially relict features by the middle of the eleventh century, such as the former Viking centre of Thetford and the old Roman town of Dorchester, by this time effectively the shire town of Dorset. Domesday Book also hints at other places whose urban character had been developing, though unrecorded in either history or archaeology and whose defences or otherwise are obscure. One example is Bodmin, which by 1086 seems to have been a locally important commercial centre with a substantial population and a market under the control of St Petroc's church; another is Melton Mowbray, which also possessed a Domesday market.

By this time, a crucial defining feature of walled towns in England was being established: their 'royal' allegiance. This character arose not simply from their military origins and the fact that kings clearly regarded old Roman towns as part of their royal inheritance, but also from the way their populations and institutions developed in the early burghal period. Their inhabitants can only have been drawn from the countryside, and originally had loyalties to a variety of landlords (royal and other) with urban properties. But, the developing royal administration, exercised through sheriffs and others and controlling mints, courts, markets and trade, created an atmosphere in which the heterogeneous loyalties of the population gave way to a particular form of communality where allegiance was owed to a single lord who was the king.

FURTHER READING

For an introduction to the historical geography of English towns see D.W. Lloyd, *The Making of English Towns: 2000 Years of Evolution* (Victor Gollancz/Peter Crawley, 1992); for topography and social history see K.D. Lilley, *Urban Life in the Middle Ages, 1000-1450* (Palgrave, 2002). For an introduction to town plans see B.P. Hindle, *Medieval Town Plans* (Shire, 1990). For excellent guides to the archaeology of medieval towns in Britain and beyond see M.W. Barley (ed.), *European Towns: Their Archaeology and Early History* (Academic Press, 1977) and J. Schofield and A. Vince, *Medieval Towns: The Archaeology of British Towns in their European Setting* (Continuum, 2003).

For discussion of early medieval urbanism in its wider European context see N. Christie and S.T. Loseby (eds), *Towns in Transition: Urban Evolution in Late Antiquity and the Early Middle Ages* (Ashgate, 1996) and G.P. Brogiolo,

N. Gauthier and N. Christie (eds), *Towns and their Territories between Late Antiquity and the Early Middle Ages* (Brill, 2000). For studies of the *burhs* of Wessex see D. Hill and A. Rumble (eds), *The Defence of Wessex: The Burghal Hidage and Anglo-Saxon Fortifications* (Manchester University Press, 1996) and for early medieval Wessex towns in general J. Haslam (ed.), *Anglo-Saxon Towns in Southern England* (Phillimore, 1984). For towns of the Viking age see H. Clarke and B. Ambrosiani (eds), *Towns in the Viking Age* (Leicester University Press, 1991). For a recent synthesis of knowledge on the towns of the Danelaw see R.A. Hall, 'The Five Boroughs of the Danelaw: a review of present knowledge', *Anglo-Saxon England* 18 (1989) pp.149-206. Examples of accessible studies of individual towns include R.A. Hall, *English Heritage Book of Viking Age York* (Batsford/English Heritage, 1994) and T.B. James, *English Heritage Book of Winchester* (Batsford/English Heritage, 1997). For the geography of this period see D. Hill, *An Atlas of Anglo-Saxon England* (Basil Blackwell, 1981).

For an account of the study of town walls in an English and Welsh context mainly through documentary evidence see H.L. Turner, *Town Defences in England and Wales* (John Baker, 1970). An introduction to the Irish material is provided in J. Bradley, *Walled Towns in Ireland* (Country House, 1995) and a more detailed account in A. Thomas, *The Walled Towns of Ireland* (Irish Academic Press, 1992). For a European perspective on the topic see G. Perbellini (ed.), *The Town Walls in the Middle Ages: Les Enceintes Urbaines Au Moyen Âge* (Europa Nostra Bulletin, 2000), and a global view J.D. Tracy (ed.), *City Walls: The Urban Enceinte in Global Perspective* (Cambridge University Press, 2000).

2

EXPANSIONS: POPULATIONS, ELITES AND MURAGE IN THE LATER MEDIEVAL PERIOD

The period from the eleventh to the sixteenth century that is the subject of this chapter saw an enormous growth in urbanism. The proportion of the British population living in towns – defined in a broad sense – is estimated to have doubled to perhaps as much as twenty per cent through different types of urban growth. A large proportion of the urban settlements established in earlier centuries, especially those that had emerged as centres of regional significance continued to flourish and expand, particularly from the eleventh to the thirteenth centuries. But perhaps more significant was the multiplication of urban settlements through the plantation of new boroughs and the transformation and growth of certain rural settlements into towns, which reached a peak in the thirteenth century. The roles of smaller towns within the medieval economy and landscape, long-recognised but still underestimated, have recently been the subject of detailed scholarship.[1] The crucial motor behind this second type of urban expansion was the patronage of the wealthier and more powerful people in medieval society – kings, secular lords and churchmen – who founded and promoted towns as sources of income and as a means of enhancing their authority. Also of great importance in this regard, but easily overlooked, were those medieval rural communities that were granted rights to hold markets and fairs in settlements that never grew to become fully-fledged towns. Far from a peculiarly British phenomenon, this growth in urbanisation was part and parcel of a far wider pan-European trend. The outcome of these processes was the emergence of a complex urban hierarchy comprising towns of national, provincial, regional and local significance that, through their marketing and other functions, were intimately bound not only together, but also integrated with the economy of the medieval countryside.

Yet despite this boom-time for urban settlements in general, we should recognise that town defences were not a universal requirement. While it is commonplace to see the possession of town defences as an important part of urban identity, in fact it was the minority of boroughs that were enclosed. Well over 600 boroughs existed in medieval England and Wales (although the precise number is debatable and not all coexisted at any single time), yet only a minority possessed urban defences of any description (see page 218), and a high proportion of these were provided with earth and timber circuits rather than masonry walled enceintes. In addition, while the hierarchy of towns grew in complexity from the eleventh to fourteenth century, this process of urban-isation was not evenly distributed in all areas. Accordingly, great variations in the proportion of towns that were enclosed can be noted not only between different regions, but also between groups of towns with different circum-stances of foundation and lordship (see page 217). Ireland witnessed a further stage in the urbanising process during the seventeenth century when the plan-tation of English and Scottish settlers involved the establishment of towns such as [London]derry, equipped with up to date defences in the angled bastion style.[2] Given the overtly political and military context of their foundation, it is not surprising that such places were enclosed.

While the majority of medieval towns flourished, a significant minority withered away or did not witness continued growth. In the context of a study of town defences, two distinct groups of such settlement are important. First, a small but significant proportion of the *burhs* of the late Saxon period (some of which never started out as towns and in particular many of the smaller examples) declined in importance in the post-Conquest centuries. Thus places such as Cricklade, Langport, Lydford and Lyng declined in significance or withered away entirely, while Bedford, Hertford and Huntingdon continued as shire towns but did not see serious investment in defences after the Norman Conquest, and at Burpham a *burh* was eclipsed and effectively replaced by a nearby castle-town (Arundel). Second are those abortive or ultimately failed defended towns planted after the Norman Conquest, a relatively large number of which lay adjacent to castles, including a particular concentration in Wales and the Marches such as Caus, Dolforwyn, Dryslwyn, Kenfig, Kilpeck and Richard's Castle. Far from representing anomalies, these settlements represent part of the kaleidoscopic pattern of long-term rural and urban settlement growth and decline, of which the numerous deserted villages are the most familiar medieval rural remains. The abandoned or shrunken status of such settlements ensures that they represent extraordinarily valuable resources for the study of medieval urbanism as their topographies and below-ground remains have often escaped the ravages of later development.[3]

1 *Above* Conwy: aerial view showing the Edwardian castle and attached walled town. *RCAHM Wales*

2 *Below* Chichester: Roman and later flint-built town wall, with rounded bastion. *Authors' collection*

3 Opposite Canterbury: medieval mural tower with 'keyhole' type gunports. *Authors' collection*

4 Right Caernarfon: town wall north of the castle, showing surviving 'gap-backed' towers and wall walk. *Authors' collection*

5 Below Chester: city wall, north side, showing Roman and medieval work above the cut for the Chester Canal. *Authors' collection*

6 Devizes: aerial view showing the street pattern fossilising the line of the former town defences attached to the castle (tree-covered, on the right). *English Heritage*

7 Kidwelly: exterior of the town gate, which contained a town hall and prison. *Authors' collection*

8 Kidwelly: interior of town gate, showing complex internal planning over three storeys. *Authors' collection*

9 King's Lynn: South Gate, of late medieval date, showing affinities with contemporary ecclesiastical gatehouse architecture. *Authors' collection*

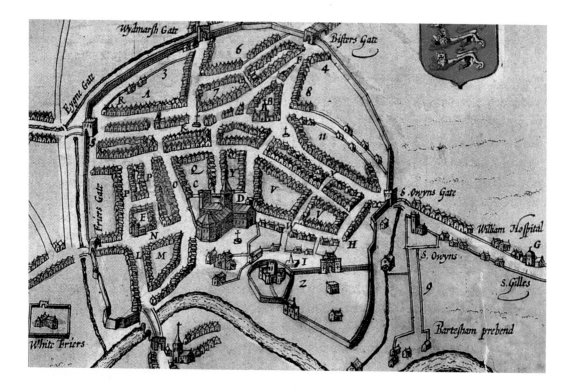

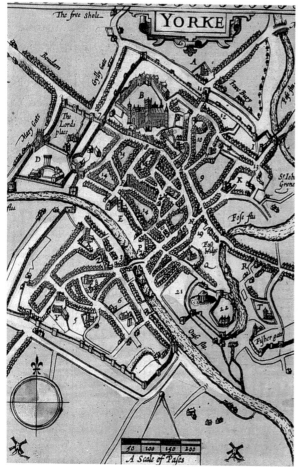

10 *Above* Hereford as depicted by John Speed in the early seventeenth century

11 *Left* York as depicted by John Speed in the early seventeenth century

12 Rye: Ypres tower, an unusual example of a
'town castle'. *Authors' collection*

13 Salisbury: crenellated wall of the cathedral precinct. *Authors' collection*

14 London: medieval bastion near the Museum of London, with later brick additions. *Authors' collection*

A Prehistoric and middle Saxon ground surfaces.
B Late Saxon bank with slot for post and plank timber revetment.
C New revetment constructed in limestone and gateway inserted.
D 12th - century ironstone wall of the medieval town defences.
E The recutting of defensive ditches during the Civil War.
F 18th - century levelling of the medieval town wall.
G Industrial buildings conceal and disturb the remains of the defences.

15 Isometric projection of excavation on a multi-period town wall and associated features, based on evidence from Northampton. *Realise Designs*

16 Exeter: crenellations of probable late Saxon date (infilled in the Norman period), in Northernhay Gardens. *Authors' collection*

17 King's Lynn: ship's ballast incorporated into the town wall, including material from the Baltic region. *Authors' collection*

18 Above, left London: late medieval brick diaper work on the city wall in the area of The Barbican. *Authors' collection*

19 Below Tenby: 'Five Arches' medieval town gate. *Authors' collection*

20 Left Bristol: St John's Gate, showing statuettes of Brennus and Belinus, the legendary founders of the city. *Authors' collection*

21 *Above left* Monmouth: Monnow Bridge, viewed from the south showing the medieval bridge gate with machicolated front. *Authors' collection*

22 *Above right* York: 'Anglian' Tower, showing excavated remains of the tower on the north side of the Legionary Fortress. *Authors' collection*

23 Denbigh: the Goblin Tower on the west side of the circuit, containing a well. *Authors' collection*

24 Oxford: reconstruction of the city walls, showing the concentric lines of defence at the north-east corner of the circuit. *Realise Designs*

25 Conwy: medieval garderobes on the town wall, part of a group of twelve similar features. *Authors' collection*

26 Newcastle: the Heber Tower, showing architectural details including a garderobe, arrow loop and corbels, perhaps to support a timber superstructure. *Authors' collection*

27 Langport: 'Hanging Chapel' over the medieval gate. *Authors' collection*

28 *Left* Oxford: St Michael-at-the-Northgate, showing the late Saxon church tower on the former line of the city defences. *Authors' collection*

29 *Below* Shrewsbury: aerial view showing the position of the medieval walled town within a loop of the River Severn. *English Heritage*

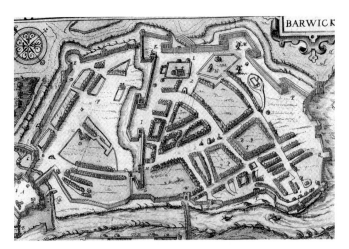

30 *Above right* Berwick-upon-Tweed as depicted by John Speed in the early seventeenth century

31 *Right* Carlisle: The Citadel, the early nineteenth-century re-built structure of a Tudor artillery fortress on the south side of the city. *Authors' collection*

32 *Below* Exeter: city wall in the East Gate area, as depicted by John Hooker. *Reproduced by permission of the Dean and Chapter of Exeter Cathedral*

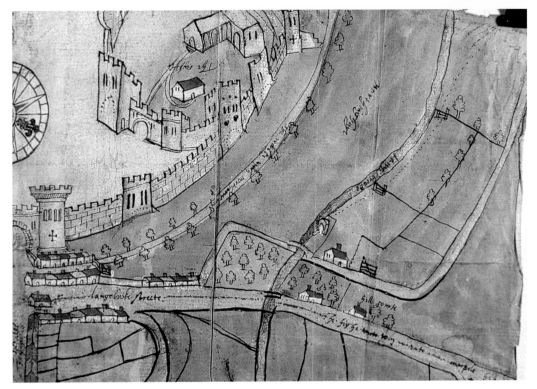

33 Chester: North Gate, as rebuilt in the mid eighteenth century to a design that preserved the continuity of the wall walk. *Authors' collection*

34 Caernarfon: St Mary's church, showing recently conserved wall fabric near the north-west corner of the circuit. *Authors' collection*

NORMAN TOWN DEFENCES

The Norman Conquests and colonisation had an enduring impact, both directly and indirectly, on English townscapes. From one perspective, the construction of great royal castles within important pre-Conquest centres had an immediate destructive impact on many urban areas, but from another, the new northern French elite and their descendants were also energetic founders of numerous new towns that were integral to economic growth and prosperity. But our understanding of the defence of Norman townscapes is seriously hampered by a lack of detailed documentation, a limited volume of excavation and minimal surviving above-ground evidence. Within the documentary evidence, we are largely limited to charters and chronicles, which are patchy in their coverage, and royal Pipe Rolls. For instance, Matthew Paris recorded that in 1174, Leicester's defences were levelled in revenge for the city's role in Prince Henry's revolt of 1173-4, while Carlisle, Chester, Canterbury, Hereford and Rochester all appear in Pipe Rolls where allowance for expenditure on wall maintenance was recorded at various dates from late in Henry I's reign to Richard I's reign.[4]

Domesday Book is a problematic source of information for the reconstruction of eleventh-century townscapes: inconsistencies in coverage, along with the challenges of penetrating legal and fiscal jargon, mean that its evidence must be treated with the utmost caution by the researcher. Concerned principally with taxable assets rather than sources of expenditure, let alone details of buildings and topography, the Domesday survey did not record manyphysical details, including town walls, consistently. It is only in a mere handful of the total of 112 Domesday boroughs, therefore, that an allusion is made to the presence of urban defences, and the terminology used to describe such places (including *villa*, *burgus* and *civitas*, sometimes for the same place) is loose.[5] Most commonly, the location of taxable property is mentioned relative to the line of extant defences. At Stafford, for instance, Earl Roger had 31 dwellings within the wall (*intra murum*). In other instances, Domesday Book suggests that settlements had grown beyond the confines of defensive perimeters: at Colchester, one of the five houses in the hands of Ranulf Peverel lay outside the wall (*extra murum*), and Hereford was recorded as having 103 men dwelling 'inside and outside the wall' before 1066. At Canterbury eleven houses lay in the city ditch (*fossatum civitatis*), and 'seventeen houses and another six houses' are recorded in a similar position at Nottingham, seemingly implying pressure on urban space. Little or no information is provided, however, about the appearance of these defences or the arrangements for their garrisoning or upkeep. One rare exception is the reference within the entry for the Bishop of Durham's Essex manor of Waltham Holy Cross, which included properties in London including one of the city gates, assessed at 20s. Another is the entry for Oxford, which intriguingly records a number of 'wall-dwellings' (*mansiones murales*), some of whose occupants were responsible for repair of the city wall (see page 179), while at Chester the relationship between upkeep of the walls and rural hidation was mentioned (see below).

In terms of investment in urban defence, it has been customary to speak of the eleventh and twelfth centuries as a period in which disproportionate attention was given to the fortification of castles as opposed to towns. While it is certainly the case that castle-building was a very high priority for the ruling classes, it is perhaps easy to underestimate the degree to which contemporary town defences may also have been maintained or revitalised. This traditional interpretation is heavily influenced by the changing nature of the written source material. Whereas up to the Norman Conquest written narratives of war are largely concerned with the use of defended towns by the English and Vikings, such sources in the late eleventh and twelfth centuries are more concerned with the roles of castles. Although the enormous importance of the castle in warfare and politics cannot be denied, it may be that the contemporary role of the defended town has been underestimated. For instance, we should be aware that in the Latin vocabulary available to writers a common word such as *castellum* might be applied not only to a castle, as commonly understood, but also to a defended town. Far from being completely silent on town defences, documentary sources in fact provide tantalising glimpses of urban defensive activity. In 1092, for instance, the Anglo-Saxon Chronicle records that William I went north to Carlisle, and as well as erecting the castle 'restored' the city. Particularly enticing is the following reference in the Domesday account of Chester, seemingly implying the continuation, certainly up to 1066, of a system whereby labour for the city wall was drawn from the surrounding hinterland, in a manner echoing that described in the Burghal Hidage for Wessex:

> For the repair of the city wall and bridge, the reeve used to call out one man to come from each hide in the County. The lord of any man who did not come paid a fine of 40s to the king and earl.

This snippet of evidence from Domesday Book provides a tentative hint of an expansion of a Burghal Hidage-style system northwards in the wake of the conquest of the Danelaw. In addition, a similar system of labour recruitment and organisation may have been transferred and adapted in some cases to the building of royal castles. A revealing reference to such arrangements is found in the entry within the Anglo-Saxon Chronicle for 1097 which demonstrates that labour drawn from the surrounding shires was applied to work on a fortification surrounding William the Conqueror's famous fortress-palace of the White Tower.

These references are, however, little more than glimpses into how labour was organised, and on the whole we remain remarkably ignorant of this crucial aspect of the practice of urban fortification in the Norman period. The twelfth century, in particular, represents something of a Dark Age for our under-standing of town defences, reminding us that documentary sources do not steadily 'improve' in terms of their availability and scope through the medieval period. Occasionally, archaeology has shed light, although the experience of towns seems to have been extremely variable. At Norwich, for instance, exca-vations have shown parts of the ditch of the Anglo-Scandinavian *burh* to have been neglected and backfilled by *c*.1100, and no pressing evidence exists to suggest that the enlarged city defences were established any earlier than the thirteenth century.[6] The neglect of Canterbury's ancient enceinte in the post-Conquest period was such that in at least one place its refurbishment in the early fourteenth century entailed the removal of over 1ft (*c*.0.3m) of debris to reach the masonry, while in another place a building on the Roman bank was removed.[7] At Leicester and elsewhere, new Norman castles obliterated parts of earlier circuits rather than strengthening urban defences for the communal good (see page 69). At Northampton, however, excavation on the site of Green Street in the mid-1990s provided an exceptionally clear sequence indicating the progressive upgrading of the former *burh* defences through the Norman period. A tenth-century clay bank with stone revetment (replacing a timber predecessor) was strengthened in the twelfth century with a town wall *c*.1.85m wide.[8]

In contrast to our rather patchy knowledge of the extent to which urban societies refurbished extant town defences in the Norman period, relatively plentiful information does exist for the growth of settlement units appended to Norman castles. Many such communities grew into fully-fledged market towns provided with planned street networks and embraced within gated defences; illustrative examples from England include Devizes, Launceston and Ludlow; in Wales, Brecon, Laugharne and Pembroke.[9] But interesting questions remain concerning the original forms of these settlements and the motives of the lords responsible for their growth. Was the original intention necessarily to found a settlement with a full range of urban functions, or were these initially specialist communities either forced to nucleate by lords, or that grew up spontaneously to support castles in their functions as estate centres, garrisons and natural marketing points? Particularly instructive in providing some sort of answer are those settlements appended to castles that did not grow into later towns (see page 80).

The Pipe Rolls, which illuminate so much financial detail of royal govern-ment from 1154 onwards, including an almost continuous record of royal castle expenditure, also shed occasional light on investment in town defences. From the reign of John, early in the thirteenth century, the upsurge of record keeping by royal government illuminates the daily workings of government as never before, including some direct grants of royal funds or building material to help towns build or maintain walls. By the 1220s these records include 'murage grants' giving details of the financing of town walls, sustaining a more detailed analysis of urban defence than is possible up to this point. Thus the apparently low level of activity focused on town walls in the twelfth century may be more a product of the changing nature of the source material than an actual reflection of historical reality. According to the evidence of chronicles, for instance, the town of Stamford was subjected to three separate sieges in the civil war of Stephen's reign. The fact that it withstood the first two and only fell to the third provides circumstantial evidence that it was defended well before the first receipt of murage in 1261, though in the absence of hard archaeological data this is of course otherwise difficult to prove.[10] Far from always indicating the construction *de novo* of masonry defences, frequently we may suspect that murage taxes represented 'top-up' grants, whereby existing fortifications were repaired, strengthened or extended, or where earlier works of earth and timber were rebuilt in stone.

Urban castles and tower houses

Domesday undoubtedly provides vivid evidence for the rapid arrival on the urban scene of an essentially new type of defensive site characteristic of the Norman period – the castle. Evidence from a number of rural excavations has challenged the notion that private defended seats of lordship were a phenomenon only imported by the Norman conquering classes. Excavations at sites such as Goltho and Sulgrave, for instance, have revealed that Saxon lords could enclose their halls with defensive ramparts. In the towns, however, there is little doubt that William I's whirlwind campaign of castle-building in the years immediately after 1066 signalled a radical departure from earlier defensive traditions, although these new tighter fortified nuclei were invariably set within extant perimeters.[11] In eleven towns, Domesday records that property and occasionally other taxable assets had been destroyed or disrupted to make way for new Norman castles: Cambridge; Canterbury; Gloucester; Huntingdon; Lincoln; Norwich; Shrewsbury; Stamford; Wallingford; Warwick; and York. Archaeological evidence from other towns reminds us that Domesday overlooks other instances where Norman castles intruded into urban settlements. At Winchester, for example, the royal castle was constructed over part of the late Saxon street plan [12], while excavations on surfaces sealed by the Norman motte at Oxford have revealed building debris and pits from occupation levels.[13] At Lincoln, the Norman castle-builders effectively converted the entire Roman Upper City into a castle. Examination of the former Roman town gates in this area shows that they may have been 're-edified' in the early Norman period (24), and from the 1070s the Upper City became a centre of ecclesiastical as well as secular power when the cathedral was built within it, in an appropriate pseudo-military style.[14] In another category are towns such as Exeter, where documentary sources record the construction of an urban castle prior to 1086, yet Domesday Book makes no

24 Lincoln: the Newport Arch, a Roman gateway marking the point of entry into the Upper City, rebuilt in the Norman period. *Authors' collection*

specific reference as to whether 'wasted' property was destroyed on account of the castle or for other reasons. Overall, approximately 3,500 properties were recorded as destroyed in 30 boroughs, though, in many cases not due to castle-building, as at Canterbury, where 27 properties were cleared to make way for the archbishop's residence. Such sites were thus not 'additions' to defended towns as much as 'impositions' upon and within them.

Of great significance here is that the vast majority of Norman castles founded within earlier towns (as opposed to those around which later urban settlements grew up) were located invariably inside existing defensive perimeters, typically using an angle of the pre-existing enceinte to form part of the defensive perimeter. This indicates an interesting type of long-term military continuity, with elements of communal defences being adapted to create new private fortified sites. Yet the defences of urban castles were not necessarily built to fortify towns themselves; at Leicester, for instance, excavation has shown that imposition of the castle disrupted the town defences, which were obliterated by the cutting of the bailey ditch and seemingly abandoned at this point on the circuit.[15]

While the outer defences of such castles were later integrated with the lines of town walls and served to strengthen the enceinte, it is important to remember that in the late eleventh century they were built to hold down populations, as well as to act as centres of political power, and were thus symbols of conquest rather than urban protection. The placement of castles in key urban centres was both systematic and strategic, so that by c.1100 most English shires featured a royal castle in their principal town. London was unique in the imposition here of three urban castles (Baynard's Castle and Montfichet Castle to the west and the site later known as the Tower of London to the east), all of which were located immediately within the Roman city walls, while two early castles were built to dominate the two foci of the city of York, one on either side of the River Ouse (*colour plate 11*).

Great variety can be detected in the plans of Norman urban castles and their topographical relationship with town defences. At Leicester, Norwich, Oxford and Wallingford immense mottes formed the dominant element, with associated baileys taking in large areas of urban space. By contrast, the plans of castles at Exeter, Rochester and Winchester were all based on large embanked and ditched enclosures sometimes referred to as 'ringworks'. Most of these sites were also visually impressive symbols of new Norman authority. The White Tower in London and the principal building at Colchester Castle were extraordinarily imposing buildings and obvious statements of royal power, the latter being built on the site of the Roman Temple of Claudius and conspicuously incorporating much Roman fabric. The motte at Thetford, almost 20m in height and approximately 100m wide at its base, is commonly cited as second only to Silbury Hill as the largest artificial earthwork in England. Given the immense topographical significance of this field monument, it comes as some surprise to note that the castle of Thetford was completely undocumented during its occupation, with a single reference dated to 1172-3 recording its demolition under the orders of Henry II.[16] Yet not all urban castles were dominant features of urban topography. The earliest castle at Gloucester, located typically in the angle of the former Roman wall, for instance, was replaced by another on a fresh site early in the twelfth century. Canterbury and Stafford also contained primary Norman urban castles abandoned at early dates and superseded by others nearby, while Derby's Norman castle was a similarly short-lived feature of urban topography and its site was eradicated from the townscape by the eighteenth century.

Only very rarely in England and Wales do we find evidence of defended urban residences built by townspeople, as opposed to castles inserted within towns or around which urban settlements developed. Towns such as Lincoln, Norwich, Southampton and York preserve evidence of twelfth- and thirteenth-century stone-built houses constructed for wealthy merchants or guilds and featuring halls at first-floor level.[17] Perhaps the most widely recognised example of such a building is the 'Jew's House', The Strait, Lincoln, dated largely on stylistic grounds to the late twelfth century. Yet while these structures indicate a concern with security and embodied the social status of their owners, they were certainly not seriously defensible in any real sense. We should also recognise that some fortified buildings built in and around English townscapes and often labelled as 'castles' were actually built or part-funded with communal effort to serve urban populations (or sectors within them) in a manner meaning that they fall outside the realm of 'private defence'. Much later in date but worthy of consideration in this context are the coastal fortifications of Plymouth and Dartmouth (in their earliest form built in the fourteenth century by the municipal authorities) and the Ypres Tower, Rye (built in the mid-thirteenth century by the overlord of the town, Peter of Savoy, and functioning as something of a 'town castle': *colour plate 12*), as well as the Caesar's Tower, Coventry (a tower of *c.*1300 adjoining the Guildhall of St Mary).

Tower-houses were, however, relatively common features in the later medieval townscapes of parts of northern and western Britain. Good Scottish examples of urban towers can be found in towns such as Alloa, Kirkcudbright, Mauchline and Stranraer, which were not provided with organised town defences in the medieval period.[18] In Ireland, urban towers are usually found within settlements that were themselves walled. Two particularly well-preserved examples (The Mint and Taafe's Castle) can be identified at Carlingford, while other settlements contained a proliferation of such features: late medieval Carrickfergus, for instance, featured ten or a dozen towers, as indicated by standing structures and historic map evidence.[19] We can make a broad distinction between urban towers in Ireland, which were predominantly the strong-houses of merchants (and sometimes stood adjacent to contemporary warehouses), and examples in Scotland, which were more often built by the rural gentry. Indeed, urban towers were also a familiar part of the wider European urban scene, especially in the Mediterranean zone, as exemplified by towns such as San Gimignano (Tuscany), where the medieval skyline featured more than 70 tower-houses, some up to 50m high, built by the patrician families as symbols of their wealth and status. In England and Wales castle-building initiated by members of the urban elite was rare indeed, and where it did occur was focused on rural locations; the prime example is at Stokesay Castle (Shropshire), which was adapted from an existing manorial site following receipt in 1291 of a licence to crenellate by the wealthy merchant and clothier, Lawrence de Ludlow. While the reasons for the marked absence of defended town houses from the townscapes of England and Wales are undoubtedly complex, perhaps the central factors are the relatively high level of centralised political control, in particular, the enduring link between kings and urban society, and the deep-rooted rural lifestyle of the nobility and gentry. The ambition of the wealthy seems generally to have been the building of castles rather than urban palaces, though the latter were sometimes built around London by prominent aristocrats wishing to achieve proximity to the royal court.[20]

New Town Foundation
Between the late eleventh and late thirteenth centuries, we are accustomed to think of an expansion in the range and quantity of urban settlement. The phenomenon of the 'new town' was of enormous importance in the

emergence of the fully developed map of urban places and coincided with a period of economic and demographic growth. Many of these new towns, however, were small and many lacked defences. In terms of medieval topographies, British walled new towns compare poorly to the bastides of south-west France, such as Aigues Mortes, Beaumont du Périgord, Sainte-Foy-la-Grande and Villeneuve-sur-Lot, and do not show the same regularity of planning, particularly in respect of the central marketplace. By c.1300, the phenomenon of new town foundation had reached and passed its peak. Three major types of foundation had occurred, each the product of a different type of patronage. Towns such as Flint (1277) and New Winchelsea (1288) were royal foundations, with Queenborough (1368) being the last of this group. Among the numerous towns established by ecclesiastical lords were Battle (1070), Hindon (1219-30) and North Shields (1225). However, secular landlords of various status were responsible for the majority of foundations, among them New Buckenham (1145-56), New Malton (1154-73), Okehampton (pre-1086) and Usk (pre-1131).

A substantial proportion of the new towns of the middle ages owed their existence to the ambitions of lords who also owned and built castles, and a great many of these settlements are physically associated with castles. So strong was the link between castle and town that in England it has been estimated that 75 per cent of towns founded before c.1150 were physically associated with castles, while the figure in Wales is closer to 80 per cent. Castle and borough foundation are even more closely linked in Scotland, where of the 33 royal towns founded before 1286, no fewer than 31 lay adjacent to castles. At places that were honorial *capita* or baronial centres, such as Arundel, Castle Acre, Launceston, Richmond and Tonbridge, a walled town was the symbol and substance of lordship every bit as much as the castle from which the defensive circuit emanated. In some of these cases, the walled area could be tiny: at Richmond, for instance, Leland commented that the town wall enclosed little more space than the castle, encompassing only the semi-circular marketplace in front of the seigneurial centre, the houses around it and the gardens behind them. A major factor to consider here is the role of seigneurial authority in enclosing settlements of small or middling size. Many of the smallest communities provided with defences are also those most closely associated with seigneurial sites. Those defended towns without castles (or else where castles were envisaged yet not completed or otherwise short-lived) tended to be larger and more commercially focused towns, such as Boston, Coventry, Ipswich and Kingston-upon-Hull.

We must also remember, however, that in certain cases, boroughs could be physically remote from the castles of their founding lords. This was the case at Okehampton, for instance, where the castle occupied a spur-end site and the borough was planted in a more sheltered and low-lying position approximately one kilometre distant, perhaps reflecting (as in other southwestern English examples such as Restormel castle and Lostwithiel borough) the dispersed character of the settlement pattern in general.[21] The 'detached' character of such seigneurial boroughs from castles usually meant that they were less likely to be fortified, largely because so often borough defences were integrated with those of the castle, which 'anchored' the entire enceinte. Also distant from one another can be the earliest borough charter and the actual date at which the physical town itself came into existence. Taken in isolation, borough charters may be imperfect guides to the foundation dates of new towns. At Plympton, for example, the borough charter granted in 1194 by William de Vernon, Earl of Devon, post-dated by some 50 years the earliest reliable documentary reference to the borough: charters granted in the 1140s referred to burgesses and the chapel of the borough, and since the castle here was in existence not later than 1130, it is quite likely that castle and borough were twinned foundations.[22] In this case, the borough never received independent fortifications through the building of town walls: it simply nestled in the lee of the castle's defences.

In England these developments increased several times over the number of urban settlements, but in Wales they marked the introduction of towns for the first time since the Roman period. In Ireland, the Anglo-Norman conquest from the late twelfth century included energetic castle-building related to the establishment of many associated new walled towns (25), the upgrading of extant rural centres to borough status, and the revitalisation of former Viking fortified seaports such as Dublin, Waterford and Wexford. In Wales, however, the sole example of a defended early medieval urban settlement was in the north, where the *burh* of *Cledemutha* (Clwyd-mouth) was founded in 921 by

25 Trim: great tower of the castle and the Sheep Gate into the medieval town. *Authors' collection*

Edward the Elder. This can probably be identified as the enclosure adjacent to which Edward I founded the new castle and bastide of Rhuddlan late in the thirteenth century, which itself lay immediately adjacent to an abandoned Norman castle-borough.[23] Yet the urban sequence at Rhuddlan was discontinuous, involving in effect the sequential foundation of three separate defended towns (and the 'failure' of two of them), highlighting in this particular context an inseparable relationship between militarism and urbanism.[24] There is also no evidence that settlements originating as Viking trading centres, such as Swansea, possessed defences before the post-Conquest period, nor that Celtic ecclesiastical or monastic foci that later developed as towns, such as Bangor and Llantwit Major, were enclosed. At both Caerleon and Carmarthen, Norman castles and towns were built close by the sites of Roman fortresses. While we know from the writings of Giraldus Cambrensis that impressive Roman masonry or 'brick' defences were visible in the twelfth century, these works were not remodelled or renovated.[25] The borough at Caerleon remained undefended, while the medieval town walls at Carmarthen were independent of the Roman enceinte. Likewise, at Loughor, where the Norman castle lay within an angle of the Roman fort of *Leucarum*, extensive excavation has shown no evidence for refurbishment of the defences to enclose the small borough that grew up here.[26] At these three places, as in much of Wales, the overwhelming majority of new Norman towns were founded in direct association with new Norman castles, as twinned elements securing the colonisation of hostile territory.[27] Consequently, new towns in Wales were generally enclosed, whereas those in England sometimes were and sometimes were not. Indeed, so closely entwined were the processes of castle foundation and the foundation of enclosed boroughs in Wales that only a single definite example of a walled town without a castle nucleus can be identified: Cowbridge, founded as a demesne borough by Earl Richard de Clare in 1254 (26). The town was located on the old Roman road known as the Portway, its east and west gates spanning the route and the plantation clearly geared for maximum commercial advantage.[28]

Another piece of evidence that emphasises in a different way the status of walled towns as colonial settlements in Wales is the far higher proportion of planted English boroughs provided with encircling defences relative to boroughs established by Welsh lords, and the total absence of masonry defences around native boroughs. Indeed, so sparse is the evidence for native foundations provided with defences that only one secure example can be identified: the settlement of Llanidloes, prompted by Owain de la Pole in the 1280s, which was encircled with a bank and ditch.[29] The Welsh town of Bangor was only enclosed as the result of an English initiative, when Edward I erected town defences in 1284, though their plan is unknown.[30] The only other possible candidate is Dolforwyn, where Llewellyn attempted to establish a market town *de novo* at his new hilltop castle in the Severn valley in 1273, although this was

26 Cowbridge: town gate, viewed from the south. *Authors' collection*

soon thwarted by English military action.[31] While the site of the abortive town cannot be identified positively, topographical arguments point to its positioning, like so many other castle-boroughs in Wales, within the outworks of the castle's bailey. In contrast, the nearby plantation of Newtown, which had emerged by the early fourteenth century, lay on a low-lying site and did not have defences.

Town defences in Scotland
In Scotland, the process of urbanisation was effectively initiated by the policies of King David I (1124-53), whose grants of burgh status bestowed upon communities social and commercial privileges and established the basis for a network of royal towns including places such as Aberdeen, Dunfermline, Haddington, Lanark and Montrose (it should be noted that the equivalent to the English and Welsh borough was the Scottish 'burgh'). The vast majority of Scottish early royal towns were associated with castles and had certain 'strategic' qualities, although subsequently ecclesiastical authorities were to play a greater role in town foundation, including the establishment of centres such as St Andrews and Glasgow. The combined result of these processes was the foundation of something in the region of 150 burghs by 1500, although most of them were small and little more than villages in physical terms.[32] Yet relative to England and Wales, Scotland had very few genuinely fortified towns and these formed only a small portion of the total range of urban settlements. Those that can be identified positively (most prominently Berwick, Edinburgh, Peebles, Perth, Stirling) were mainly royal centres, most of which received their defences relatively late in the medieval period and often in periods of English occupation or influence.

In many cases – probably most – the limits of Scottish burghs were defined not by expensive defences built by communal effort, but by the garden walls, fences, hedges and ditches at the backs of individual plots. A particularly characteristic plan-form of the Scottish medieval burgh was a single axial street linking focal points such a church, marketplace and castle, and flanked on either side by long thin strip-like 'rigs'. Such an arrangement ensured that many individual plots terminated at the town boundary. The custom of providing 'watch and ward' was certainly an important obligation of burgesses in Scottish towns, and the maintenance of ditches or 'back dykes' at the tails or 'heidrooms' of individual plots was a common way in which a town's limits were defined. Such measures were clearly non-military in character, rather serving to mark the limit of the urban zone for commercial and legal reasons, and as a measure against low-level threats and the spread of pestilence: at Glasgow, for instance, during visitations of the plague the burgh authorities closed the gates and specifically prohibited entry into the town via the 'tails' of individual plots.[33]

Another characteristic of Scottish medieval towns, seen less commonly in England and Wales, was the existence of town gates or 'ports' in the absence of integrated defensive circuits. St Andrews preserves the only intact medieval town gate in Scotland, the West Port, a twin-towered structure with gunports, built in 1589.[34] Yet this feature was not linked to organised town defences or walls, serving rather as one of four main ports blocking the principal routes into the town and controlling the movement of road traffic for largely commercial reasons. Excavation on the burgh boundaries of Aberdeen has suggested the absence of defining walls or defensive ditches, but the medieval town again had ports across the main thoroughfares, the last one being removed in 1769.[35] Dumfries and Glasgow are other clear examples of medieval Scottish towns provided with gates but not organised enclosing defences.

Yet we should take care not to overlook the genuinely defensive qualities of a small number of burghs: it seems certain, for instance, that Pedro de Ayala, Spanish ambassador to the court of James IV, exaggerated when he claimed in 1498 that 'there is not more than one fortified town in Scotland because the kings do not allow their subjects to fortify them'.[36] This source does, however, remind us that the urbanisation of Scotland reached a far lower level of intensity than in much of western Europe, with Edinburgh standing alone as a town equipped with integrated, multi-phase masonry defences that might in any way approach those of important centres on the wider British and European stage. Of the tiny handful of Scottish burghs where the existence of walls can be confirmed, only Edinburgh had a defensive perimeter that was substantially enlarged during the medieval period. The earliest known wall was King's Wall (built from 1427), which ran, apparently in irregular fashion, along the south side of the linear burgh that stretched away from the castle, the Nor' Loch providing natural defence on the north side. Later extensions to the south of this circuit comprised the Flodden Wall (1514-60), funded initially with a murage toll of £5 Scots per burgess, and Telfer's Wall (1628-36).[37]

The 'crag and tail' relationship – reflecting the arrangement of hilltop castle and settlement below – between the early castle and town defences of Edinburgh was essentially similar at Stirling, which still preserves traces of a wall complete with interval towers and gunports embracing part of the burgh (*27-28*). That this circuit perpetuated earlier earth and timber defences remains a distinct possibility – as it does at Edinburgh – but has not been confirmed by archaeological evidence. Several interest groups funded the building of the later medieval wall: work apparently commenced in 1547, when sums released by the town's council, in addition to contributions from a range of private individuals and the Queen Dowager, employed the master mason John Coutis; further work is also recorded in the 1570s.[38] The wall at Peebles was also relatively late in date, being erected from 1570, when the mason Thomas Lauder undertook to oversee a projected four-year building operation that would link up the town's existing ports.[39] Archaeological excavation has cast light on the town defences of Perth, which were upgraded from a primary bank and ditch through the addition of a stone revetment and then a wall, as demonstrated by

27 Aerial view of Stirling, showing the course of the medieval town wall. *RCAHM Scotland*

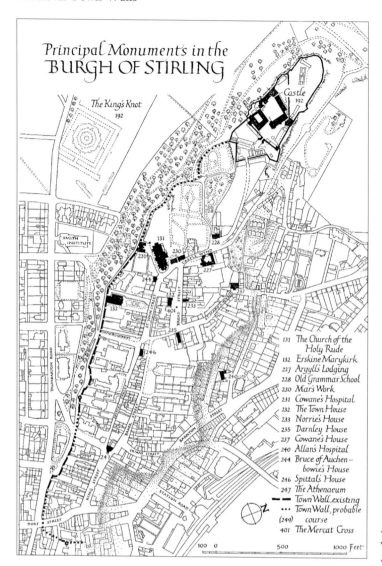

Principal Monuments in the
BURGH OF STIRLING

The King's Knot
192

Castle
192

SMITH
INSTITUTE

131 The Church of the
    Holy Rude
132 Erskine Marykirk
227 Argylls Lodging
228 Old Grammar School
230 Mar's Work
231 Cowane's Hospital
232 The Town House
233 Norrie's House
235 Darnley House
237 Cowane's House
240 Allan's Hospital
244 Bruce of Auchen-
    bowie's House
246 Spittal's House
247 The Athenaeum
━━ Town Wall, existing
··· Town Wall, probable
(249)   course
401 The Mercat Cross

100 0   500   1000 Feet

28 Stirling town
wall. *RCAHM*
Scotland

excavations on High Street and Mill Street.[40] Like the first organised town
defences of Berwick-upon-Tweed, started four days after the town's capture by
Edward I in 1296, there is a good possibility that Perth's town wall was an
English royal initiative, although how complete it was remains difficult to
assess. In 1304, for instance, it is recorded that Master Walter of Hereford (who
is known to have been involved in building operations at Caernarfon) was
employed in building the town wall, the sub-rectangular circuit of which
clearly defined the limits of urban growth by this time.[41] In addition to these
walled communities can be identified a small number of towns furnished with
surrounding banks and ditches of substantial and genuinely defensive character,
including Inverness and Selkirk.[42]

Defended villages and 'failed' towns

It is frequently overlooked that some medieval villages possessed defences. Provided with ramparts and ditches and usually appended to the more substantial defences of a castle, the manner in which such settlements were enclosed was clearly different from the numerous deserted medieval villages in Midland England, encompassed by hedged banks separating communities from open fields. Clear examples of the many medieval villages embraced within village enclosures attached to early castles are: Anstey and Therfield (Hertfordshire); Ascot d'Oilly (Oxfordshire); Boteler's Castle (Warwickshire); Castle Camps (Cambridgeshire); Castle Bytham (Lincolnshire); and More (Shropshire).[43] The identification of such sites is not straightforward given the difficulties of differentiating enclosed rural settlements from failed or abortive boroughs (see page 84). In addition, the earthworks of such settlements can easily be confused with those of garden features, or where earth and timber castles were adapted as manorial sites.[44] At Stafford, for instance, the interpretation of earthworks in and around an outer bailey of the castle as the remains of a fortified settlement has been called into question, a detailed re-survey suggesting that much of the field evidence instead relates to garden features.[45]

Rather larger in scale than these sites was the rectangular settlement enclosure attached to the important castle of the de Warenne family at Castle Acre. Elevated almost twelve metres above an outer ditch, this substantial earthwork embraced a planned settlement west of the castle, but which was never recorded as a borough.[46] The status of such settlements remains unclear. Were they, on the one hand, rural communities emulating urban traditions of defence for reasons of status, or is it rather that we have failed to identify what were effectively small towns or failed boroughs because of a lack of documentary material? The fact that the overwhelming majority of such sites are closely associated with Norman castles suggests, however, a more likely explanation: that these were nucleations whose establishment was closely tied to the seigneurial unit, and that their enclosures were effectively enormous outer baileys of the castle rather than genuinely communal defences.[47] This likelihood also, of course, throws interesting light on the assumed 'private' nature of medieval castles as fortified institutions, as in the eleventh and twelfth centuries the outer defences of many castles clearly embraced settlements. An intriguing example of a defended medieval rural settlement without an associated castle is, however, the Nottinghamshire village of Wellow. Enclosed on two sides by a substantial rampart and ditch known as 'Gorge Dyke' and flanked on the remaining side by a stream, this unusual settlement, planned in regular form around a central green, was created to accommodate peasants evicted due to Cistercian land clearance associated with Rufford Abbey in the mid-twelfth century.[48]

While the numerous deserted medieval villages in British landscapes have attracted enormous amounts of attention from archaeologists and historians from the 1950s onwards, the phenomenon of failed towns – many of which were enclosed and preserve excellent physical remains – has remained rather more obscure. We must be careful, however, in using the labels 'failed' or 'deserted' to describe such sites, as in many cases these settlements may have been abortive or stillborn nucleations, planned yet never realised or populated to their potential. In his masterful *New Towns of the Middle Ages*, Maurice Beresford counted 41 examples of planted medieval towns in England and Wales that failed in one way or another.[49] To this list can be added several more cases of deserted settlements of probable urban character or potential but which have no surviving documentary evidence of borough charters. An instructive example of the latter is the site of Castle Carlton. While the earthworks of a settlement adjacent to the motte and bailey castle have traditionally been interpreted as the vestiges of the deserted Domesday 'village' of Carlton, references in the fifteenth-century source known as the Wigston Manuscript suggest rather the existence of a borough established by the castle lord *c.*1157-8. Further proof of the settlement's origins as a plantation of the castle lords is provided by parochial topography: the alignment of parish boundaries suggesting that Castle Carlton was carved out of the earlier entities of Great Carlton and South Reston. Detailed examination of the site shows this settlement to have been embraced within a rectangular earthwork measuring *c.*500m x 140m attached to the castle, seeming to represent the vestiges of earth and timber defences.[50] Those medieval towns that, for one reason or another, have severely contracted rather than undergone total desertion, also preserve outstanding evidence of town defences and related street patterns. An exceptionally well preserved Welsh example is New Radnor, which exhibits the skeleton of a substantially shrunken medieval grid-plan town embraced by the earthworks of a town wall and ditch, probably indicating a twelfth- or thirteenth-century defended expansion from a castle-church core.[51] The irregular line of these defences on the south side of the town, now comprising a bank up to *c.*2.7m high and an external ditch, has a topographical explanation, as here the medieval builders closely followed the steep scarp of the river terrace.

In the absence of significant post-medieval alterations, the buried deposits of such sites hold immense archaeological potential and provide some of the clearest topographical evidence for the planning of defended boroughs. At Almondbury and Caus, castle-dependent boroughs were inserted into late prehistoric hillforts, with the geographical settings of these sites creating an obvious impediment to economic sustainability following the abandonment of the castle focus. At neither place, however, is it absolutely clear whether the massive earthwork ramparts and ditches were recut or reconditioned for the purposes of defending the medieval plantations. A more widely recognised example is Old Sarum where a medieval borough, focused on a large Iron Age hillfort also embracing a castle and cathedral, was gradually deserted from 1219 in favour of the newly planted town of Salisbury. The immense disadvantages of the original hilltop position are expressed vividly by Henry d'Avranches, a court poet of the time of Henry III in a poem justifying the move to New Salisbury:

> A fortress stood upon the hill, exposed only to the winds, which were strong enough to shake its summit. Little water was to be found; but chalk in abundance. The winds howled, but no nightingale ever sang. The chalk soil was bad enough, but the shortage of water worse. The former dazzled the eyes, and the latter provoked thirst. The silence of birds was a loss still worse than the violence of the wind. The one deprived us of pleasure, and the other destroyed our very dwellings.[52]

Rather different in character are the earthworks enclosing the failed castle-dependent settlement of Kilpeck, which appears to be a *de novo* creation of a castle lord. The earthworks at Kilpeck are especially clear. A rectangular enclosure east of the castle embraces the earthworks of tenement plots arranged either side of an axial street, traces of a marketplace, and the architecturally famous parish church. The right to hold a weekly market and fair at Kilpeck was granted in 1259, although there is no specific documentary evidence that it was a borough. Along with a Norman castle and Benedictine priory, Kilpeck represents a remarkably integrated unit of Norman settlement, and excavation in the vicinity of the church and castle has produced a range of finds of the late eleventh to twelfth century and later.[53] Perhaps the clearest surviving field evidence of such a settlement, however, is to be found at Pleshey. Here, attached to a large motte and bailey castle survives the earthwork of an almost circular embanked and ditched settlement enclosure, comprising a substantial bank and an external ditch up to c.13.5m wide and c.3.5m deep. The present village lying within this unit is disposed around a curving road, running concentric with the embanked and ditched defences, which seem to represent the vestiges of an original medieval street pattern. The place name is of Norman-French derivation, meaning a fenced enclosure of interwoven trees, and seems to reflect well the status of its earliest settlement as a community embraced within an earth and timber precinct appended to a seigneurial site. While, like Kilpeck, the settlement has no surviving borough charter, burgesses are mentioned in a document of 1336, and markets, shops and stalls are recorded in the fourteenth and fifteenth centuries.[54]

Among the modest number of deserted castle-boroughs that have been exposed to systematic open-area excavation is Dryslwyn, where castle and town are squeezed tightly together on the summit of a prominent hill in the Towy valley (*29*). Embraced by a wall and flat-bottomed ditch, against which can be identified the walls and terraces of properties, the town had a transient existence from the thirteenth to the fifteenth century and had no significant life independent of the castle[55]; other important examples, in England, are

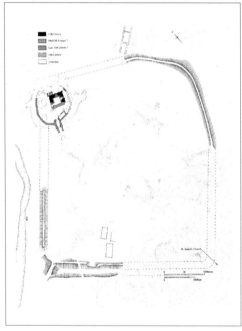

29 Above Dryslwyn: deserted castle-borough, with the grassed-over remains of the town wall and an intra-mural building. *Authors' collection*

30 Left Kenfig: deserted castle-borough, now obscured by sand dunes. *Spurgeon 2001*

Richard's Castle and Boteler's Castle (see page 84). In Wales in particular, however, many deserted boroughs appear to have lain partly or entirely within the baileys or outer defences of castles, including Dinefwr, Dolforwyn, Cefnllys and Knucklas; less certain cases include Castell y Bere, Deganwy and Painscastle. The desertion of most of these boroughs (with the prominent exception of Kenfig: see below) can be attributed ultimately to economic factors.[56] In particular, the late thirteenth-century conquests of North Wales, in reducing the military roles of other castles, must in turn have also removed some of the sustenance of their boroughs.

Quite different reasons accounted for the abandonment of Kenfig (*30*). A remarkable site now overlooked by steelworks and the M4 motorway, and cut into by a railway track, this site was deserted due to the progressive encroachment of the adjacent dunefield. The loss of property to the sands is recorded from early in the fourteenth century, and by the time John Leland visited the site, the town was 'almost choked and devoured with the sands that the Severn sea there casteth up'. Sufficient traces can be discerned within the dunes to confirm that here too a borough was an embanked and ditched dependency of the castle. Other enclosed settlements appended to castle foci may, of course, have left no visible traces in the present landscape. At the timber castle of Hen Domen, the site of Old Montgomery, documentary evidence suggests that the de Boulers family attempted to found a borough at the end of the twelfth century, yet even a very extensive programme of excavation and field survey did not detect any signs of a resultant settlement. It is just possible that a fragmentary earthwork outside the bailey represents the abandoned start of an enclosure that was the first step in founding a borough, soon brought to an end by the fading family fortunes of the castle lords.[57]

Careful scrutiny of the plans of some more fully developed medieval market towns provides glimpses that many such settlements may have originated as enclosed appendages to Norman castles. Aspects of the town plan of Richmond, for instance, suggest that this is another settlement that, along with Devizes, clearly seems to have been nucleated within an oval or D-shaped enclosure or outer bailey; other probable examples in England include Bridgnorth, Launceston, Oswestry, Tickhill, Tonbridge and Trowbridge. While by the later middle ages castles were contained within towns, integrated within their circuits and contributing to their defence, in the Norman period towns (or the nuclei from which they formed) could, in effect, be contained within castles, so that the phrase 'castle-town' is appropriate.

The lordships of south Wales had something of a proliferation of medieval towns that grew from initial enclosed nuclei attached to castles. This reflects the periodic status of much of this region as a frontier zone from the eleventh to the thirteenth century, as well as motives of ambitious Norman landlords keen to make their mark on local landscapes. The topographies of medieval boroughs at Laugharne, New Moat, Pembroke, St Clears and Wiston all show signs of early defensive circuits enclosing initially small dependent communities attached to Norman castles.[58] At Kidwelly, the twelfth-century borough adjoining the castle grew up within a triangular earthwork enclosure of just over 3ha; only part of this was walled, however, suggesting a shift of location that left part of the settlement a deserted site.[59] In contrast, Welsh lords appear to have founded very few fortified towns (see page 74). The impression that castle baileys could act as defended nuclei for urban growth is strengthened where the triumvirate of Norman castle, borough and priory initially lay within what was in effect a single enceinte. At Brecon, for instance, the foundation charter for Bernard Newmarch's priory specified that the church of St John and five burgages granted to the priory lay within the bounds of the castle, although the town later migrated to the opposite bank of the River Honddu.[60]

Many of these sites raise a question of definition: did these embanked and ditched enclosures represent early town defences or large baileys? In reality, to make such a rigid distinction would be rather misleading, as a continuum existed between the two types of fortification. The distinction between 'communal' and 'private' medieval defensive traditions may thus be rather more blurred than is often acknowledged. It is virtually impossible and actually rather meaningless to distinguish the point at which a defended unit attached to a castle and embracing habitations and other features could be viewed as a means of communal defence as opposed to an extension of a private fortification. An instructive case in point in this regard is the site of Boteler's Castle, near Alcester. Excavations in the immediate vicinity of this Norman earth and timber castle in 1992 and 1993 revealed the existence of an attached ditched enclosure, hitherto unrecognised.[61] This feature was approximately 5ha in area and contained evidence of a small gridded settlement apparently created as an appendage to the seigneurial site some time in the twelfth century yet abandoned after a century or so of occupation. That the assemblage of finds (including evidence of small-scale industry) and environmental evidence (indicating a 'consumer' rather than a 'provider' economy) pointed towards this being more than an agricultural community is highly significant. While there is a total absence of documentary material relating to this short-lived settlement, what seems likely is that the enclosed site represented the type of defended nucleus that could, in different circumstances, have emerged as a market centre and town.

TOWN DEFENCE IN THE LATER MEDIEVAL PERIOD

From the 1220s, a new type of documentary source is available to us for the study of town walls: the murage grant (31-32). The meaning of murage grants is often misunderstood, however. Rather than recording any type of financial transaction, a murage grant recorded a grant of permission from the king to an urban community, empowering it to levy tolls on goods imported for sale into the town, with the resulting income being used to fund the construction or maintenance of walls. Most such grants had a specified expiry date; many of the earliest examples ran for a year, although a common time limit for later murage grants was either three, five or ten years, and many were renewed many times so as to create, in effect, a continuous rolling programme. What is crucial about the date of the first murage grants of 1220, to towns such as Bridgnorth and Shrewsbury, is that they are clearly not simply the first surviving examples, but represent a radical new initiative for the funding of town walls. In essence

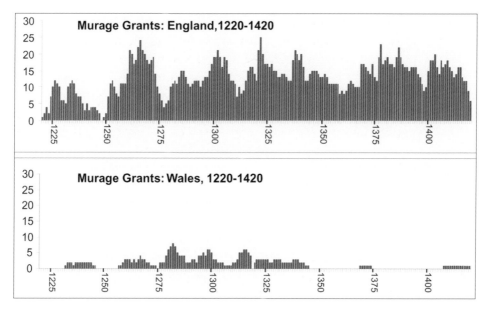

31 Distribution of murage grants through time in England and Wales. *Compiled from Turner 1970 and other sources*

this removed the burden of providing defences from the king or the resources of the surrounding hinterland and placed it squarely on the shoulders of the urban authority. The finance itself came from trade.

The list of goods to be taxed in this way at Coventry, following a grant of Edward III in 1329 to the Prior, Convent and good men of Coventry provides a snapshot of the towns's economy as well as something of a hint of the logistical difficulties in imposing murage tax:

> Corn; horses; oxen and their skins, fresh, salted or tanned; cart-loads of salt-meat; bacon, hams, salmon, lampreys; sheep and goats and their skins; deer; the skins of lams, kids, hares, rabbits, foxes, cats and squirrels; salt, cloth, linen and canvas, cloths of Ireland, Galloway and Wosted, and, entering the luxury trade, cloth of silk with gold, of Samite, Diaper, and Baudekyn [the richest dress stuff of the middle ages, with gold warp, silk woof, and super-added embroidery]; sea fish, casks of wine; horse; loads of ashes [used in washing raw wool], honey, oil, sacks of wool; iron, lead, tallow, grase; and materials used by the dyers – woad, alum, and copperas; for every thousand onions for sale, one farthing; for every horse-load of garlick for sale, one half-penny; herrings and meal; cordwain [a soft leather], boards, laths, mill-stones, faggots; cheeses; butter, coal, wood, lime, nails, horse-shoes; brewing-cauldrons, and finally an omnibus clause covering every truss of whatsoever merchandise coming into the town for sale, exceeding the value of two shillings one farthing.[62]

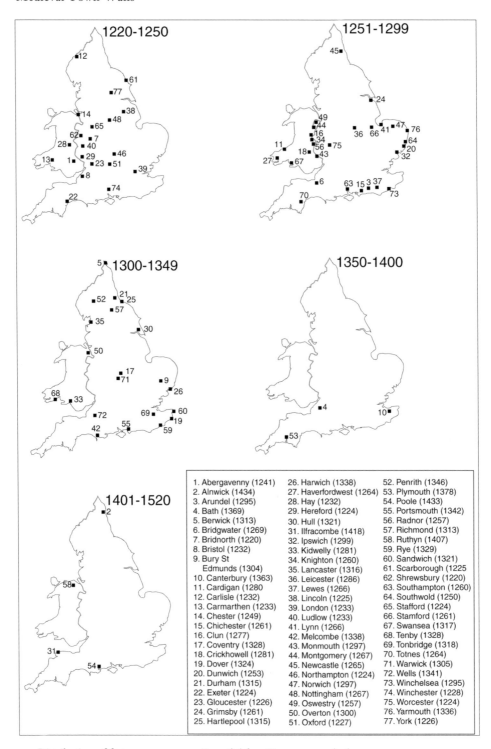

1220-1250

1251-1299

1300-1349

1350-1400

1401-1520

1. Abergavenny (1241)
2. Alnwick (1434)
3. Arundel (1295)
4. Bath (1369)
5. Berwick (1313)
6. Bridgwater (1269)
7. Bridnorth (1220)
8. Bristol (1232)
9. Bury St
   Edmunds (1304)
10. Canterbury (1363)
11. Cardigan (1280)
12. Carlisle (1232)
13. Carmarthen (1233)
14. Chester (1249)
15. Chichester (1261)
16. Clun (1277)
17. Coventry (1328)
18. Crickhowell (1281)
19. Dover (1324)
20. Dunwich (1253)
21. Durham (1315)
22. Exeter (1224)
23. Gloucester (1226)
24. Grimsby (1261)
25. Hartlepool (1315)

26. Harwich (1338)
27. Haverfordwest (1264)
28. Hay (1232)
29. Hereford (1224)
30. Hull (1321)
31. Ilfracombe (1418)
32. Ipswich (1299)
33. Kidwelly (1281)
34. Knighton (1260)
35. Lancaster (1316)
36. Leicester (1286)
37. Lewes (1266)
38. Lincoln (1225)
39. London (1233)
40. Ludlow (1233)
41. Lynn (1266)
42. Melcombe (1338)
43. Monmouth (1297)
44. Montgomery (1267)
45. Newcastle (1265)
46. Northampton (1224)
47. Norwich (1297)
48. Nottingham (1267)
49. Oswestry (1257)
50. Overton (1300)
51. Oxford (1227)

52. Penrith (1346)
53. Plymouth (1378)
54. Poole (1433)
55. Portsmouth (1342)
56. Radnor (1257)
57. Richmond (1313)
58. Ruthyn (1407)
59. Rye (1329)
60. Sandwich (1321)
61. Scarborough (1225
62. Shrewsbury (1220)
63. Southampton (1260)
64. Southwold (1250)
65. Stafford (1224)
66. Stamford (1261)
67. Swansea (1317)
68. Tenby (1328)
69. Tonbridge (1318)
70. Totnes (1264)
71. Warwick (1305)
72. Wells (1341)
73. Winchelsea (1295)
74. Winchester (1228)
75. Worcester (1224)
76. Yarmouth (1336)
77. York (1226)

32 Distribution of first murage grants. *Compiled from Turner 1970 and other sources*

It should also not be overlooked that murage did not stand alone; rather it was one element within a system of taxation increasing in complexity and diversity through the thirteenth century. This included *pontagium* (dues on crossing bridges), *passagium* (dues on passing through a town), *rivagium* (tolls imposed on river traffic), *levagium* (tolls on landing wares), *lestagium* (a toll on selling by measures), and others where funds could be directed towards public utilities, as with *pavagium* (for paving streets).[63] In London, a document of 1376 makes it clear that additional taxes were levied on goods transported through Aldgate – then the residence of the poet Geoffrey Chaucer – in order to maintain the heavily used road outside the gate. The levy comprised: a tax of two pence per week on every iron-bound cart bringing victuals into the city, and carts or cars transporting animal blood or entrails; a penny on non iron-bound carts or cars carrying dung; and a halfpenny on horses laden with grain.[64]

While it is tempting to see the thirteenth and fourteenth centuries as something of a 'golden age' for medieval town defences, it should also be borne in mind that a great number of urban settlements were not walled in this period. Despite the advantages that walls might give a newly planted community, the majority of medieval new towns were not planned with, or did not gain, walls (see page 218). Where towns were walled through murage, this would seem to have been in response to three basic sets of circumstances. In the first category were those towns, like Alnwick in the north and Portsmouth in the south that were vulnerable to different types of external threat. Second, many walled towns in the west of Britain were part and parcel of wider colonial expansions into Celtic-speaking areas and the consolidation of new lordships. Third, and perhaps most difficult to explain of all were those towns in central England not directly exposed to any obvious military threat, and where the enthusiasm for urban defence can be explained only by social and economic stimuli. It is principally these factors that would seem to explain, for instance, the walling of Coventry, in piecemeal and protracted fashion and on a highly irregular plan, during the fourteenth and fifteenth centuries.

In attempting to relate the documentary evidence of murage grants to evidence on the ground, it is important to remember that a grant of murage does not necessarily represent the date at which work on town walls commenced. Some grants were never acted upon, while embezzlement of resulting income and other financial irregularities reduced the effectiveness of others. Indeed, it was partly the abuse of murage grants by urban authorities, as evident in records of litigation, that prompted the gradual emergence of a new system of financing town defences, from the fourteenth century onwards, through the taxable assessment of urban property. Independent collaboratory evidence is usually necessary to confirm that the date of a murage grant correlates with the date at which work was carried out; such evidence may come in the form of other documentary sources relating to expenditure, or result from archaeological excavation or from architectural study. While murage grants were made to towns, the benefits that this might bring to the lord of a seigneurial borough should not be overlooked, as enhanced control of access to urban space and market facilities would naturally tighten the regulation of other tolls as well, and make the borough more attractive to tenants.

Far from being a simple index of insecurity, the distribution of murage grants, both in time and space, reflects a complex interaction of social and economic factors within a framework of defensive necessity. An additional reason why a murage grant might not necessarily lead directly to the construction or maintenance of a defensive wall applies to towns of coastal character, where funds might be used to build defences against the sea. This seems likely to have been the case at Dunwich, for instance, which received a grant of murage on 13 May 1222 as the sea had flooded the town and there was a need rapidly to build a sea wall.[65] Intriguingly, the defences of the rest of the town (now largely inundated by the sea), seem rather to have been of earth and timber, excavation revealing the profile of the large 'Pales Dyke' (*c.*40ft wide and 15ft deep) with an accompanying rampart.[66] One corner of Beaumaris's town wall, built early in the fifteenth century following the town's sacking by Owain Glyn Dwr, was broken by the sea by 1460, and had to be rebuilt on a new line, perhaps as late as 1536-40 when new works are recorded.[67]

As with castle-building, urban defences from the eleventh century onwards exhibit no smooth transition from the use of earth and timber to masonry technologies. In many cases, medieval towns featured defences incorporating masonry elements alongside earth and timber, often because of the protracted, piecemeal and labour-intensive nature of building in stone, or from the fourteenth century onwards, sometimes in brick. In this respect, later medieval town defences continued a tradition well established in the pre-Conquest centuries, where towns were similarly provided with defences incorporating mixed technologies. It should also not escape notice that direct royal grants of materials for use in town defences frequently involved the donation of timber, either for use in palisades or for wooden components in masonry structures. At Oxford, for instance, the king made a grant of joists and timbers for use in the town's turrets and bastions in 1233.[68] At Stamford, a royal grant of timber was received in 1218, 43 years before the town received its first murage grant, and similar grants are recorded for Stafford (1215) and Bridgnorth (1220).[69] It may be relevant that such grants represented a relatively simple and inexpensive form of donation, since timbers could be drawn direct from royal forests or, indeed, recycled from redundant structures, there being a considerable element of prefabrication in the timber-building industry.

At King's Lynn, a section of the later medieval town defences in the south-east part of the circuit, just north of the South Gate, was of earth and timber construction and not built or rebuilt in stone, like most of the rest of the town wall. The earthwork was traditionally known as the 'Clay Walls', and the outer ditch as 'Cockle Dyke'. From 1337 the Chamberlain's Accounts contain references to work on these features, including payment for clay and spades, and for the wages of ditchers; in 1374-5, it was specified that small sums were paid for 'mending the earthen wall at the end of the stone wall near the South Close'. Of particular significance in this context is that the word 'wall' was used interchangeably for constructions of earth or masonry.[70] A similar situation existed in Scarborough, where in the sixteenth century Leland noted that the town was walled 'with a little stone, but mostly with ditches and walls of earth'. Dating to the late fourteenth century the first town defences at Portsmouth also comprised earthworks, and by Leland's time a length of the eastern defences were seen to comprise 'a mudde waulle armid with tymbre', on which cannon were mounted.[71] At Stafford, timber defences were apparently used to plug gaps in the circuit: in 1233 the king granted the burgesses 60 oaks from Cannock Forest to repair three such breaks, and by 1600 at least two portions of the enceinte still comprised lengths of palisading.[72] The town defences of Sandwich were stone-built only on the side facing the River Stour, the remaining sides being closed by massive ramparts, while expansions to the defended areas of town such as Lincoln and Winchester comprised ditched and embanked works rather than walls. Where a circuit of earth and timber was replaced by one of brick or stone, the time taken to realise the new enceinte in full would mean that the defences would feature different building technologies. Other evidence for combinations of timber and stonework within circuits is provided by joist-holes indicating the presence of hoards or bretaches (see page 149). At Southampton, the mixed technologies employed in the town defences are highlighted in a report of c.1460:

> First please your lordships to understand that the third part and more of the walls of the said town by the land side, where most doubt and fear is, be feeble that they may not resist any gun shot, and so thin that no man may stand upon them to make any resistance or defence, but as we have yearly made scaffolds of timber for men to stand upon and countermured it with earth, to us an importable cost and charge which timber and countermuring yearly wastes and is consumed by force of weathering under such a form that it can never have end without the gracious aid and comfort of the King our Sovereign Lord.[73]

By way of contrast, in important medieval cities such as Exeter and Winchester, where the walled circuits, ultimately of Roman origin, were adapted in the late Anglo-Saxon and post-Conquest centuries, town defences always had a masonry component. Nonetheless, the eleventh and twelfth centuries saw very few new schemes of town defence realised in stone, and earthen and timber defences were deemed adequate for many important plantations. The new cathedral city of Salisbury, developed in the low-lying meadows by the River Avon, for instance, was never provided with a surrounding wall, the charter of 1227 granting the bishop the right to enclose the new plantation with a ditch. Rather than having a principally defensive function, this work seems to have been intended primarily to segregate the area under burgage tenure from the surrounding estate. It was built primarily on the north and east sides of the town, which were not defined by the river, and punctuated by two stone gateways.[74] The authorisation of the burgesses to build a stone wall in the late fourteenth century did not lead to the construction of a masonry enceinte, and the borough remained surrounded by an enlarged earthwork and its stone gates into the later medieval period, while the cathedral precinct was defined with a (partly) crenellated wall from the 1320s, built in part from demolished stone from the site of Old Sarum (*colour plate 13*).[75] Cambridge was another major town enclosed with a ditch rather than a wall, the curving water-filled King's Ditch forming an enormous D-shaped enclosure against the River Cam. While this work was strengthened in the thirteenth century, and moves to build a wall were initiated by the king at a time of threat from the late 1260s, a walled enceinte was never completed.[76]

Another medieval town provided with gates and a surrounding ditch but never walled in stone was Beverley, in the East Riding of Yorkshire. Here, documentary evidence in the form of the town keepers' account rolls reminds us that the use of timber in medieval town defences was not limited to the construction of palisades, but could also be used for the construction of wooden 'bars'.[77] Notable is a reference in 1445-6 to the construction or maintenance of a wooden 'bar' on the outer town bank at North Bar (i.e. beyond one of the town's brick-built gates). This intriguingly demonstrates the existence of a multiple barrier at this point of the town's defences, presumably not for military reasons, but as a further measure to facilitate the efficient collection of tolls and regulate the movement of traffic. Other entries in the mid-fifteenth century indicate the construction or renovation of numerous additional wooden bars, made of oak and set in foundations, as well as turnstile-type structures at choke points on the street plan, and fees due to the keepers of individual bars are also recorded. It is clear from documentary sources that Coventry had bars across major roads in the thirteenth century, at a time before the town was walled, and instead enclosed with a ditch.[78] Wooden bars built on the roads approaching the town gates were also certainly in existence at Hereford by the end of the thirteenth century, effectively marking the limits of the suburbs.[79] In London there were bars on all major roads into the city including on the west side Temple Bar and Holborn Bar.[80] The major roads to Canterbury had bars on the city's approaches, and there are references as early as the twelfth century to: Saint Sepulchre's Bar beyond Ridingate; Wincheap Bar beyond Worthgate; and Coldharbour Lane Bar beyond Northgate.[81] Overall, the occurrence of bars in documents almost certainly under-represents their true number. While it seems clear that in the case of developed towns it was the bars rather than the gates and walls that marked the extent of the city's property and jurisdiction, what is rather less certain is exactly what manner of control over traffic they actually facilitated.

Rather less substantial and far more impermanent than town gates, these features seem to have been manned, movable barriers erected across roads, perhaps where some tolls could be collected. Other features used to regulate access into medieval urban environments were chains that could be drawn across streets (33), and wooden turnstiles, the former existence of which is suggested in the Oxford street names Cheney Lane and Turl Street (34). The latter is derived from the word 'tirl' (meaning a wheel-like structure) and indicating the position of a turnstile in the medieval city wall, a reference of c.1590 mentioning 'the hole in the wall called The Turle'.[82] The former existence of a turnstile through a defensive perimeter is also indicated by the street name Whirligig Lane at Taunton, in existence by 1588 when described as 'Hurle Goge'.[83] At Caernarfon, traffic approaching the east gate was controlled by a

33 Fanciful illustration of a chain across a medieval street. *Grose 1801*

34 Oxford: Turl Street. *Authors' collection*

toll booth situated on the outer side of the bridge over the River Cadnant.[84]
At Beverley in 1391, a series of chains was handed over to the Town Keepers:
one in Flemingate of 50 links, one at the Beck with 52 links, one at the North
bar with 44 links, and two at the Guildhall with 36 and 26 links respectively.[85]

Expansions and contractions

The majority of British towns provided with urban defences show no evidence
of expansions or contractions in their defensive circuits. Major centres such as
Chichester, Colchester, Exeter and Winchester preserved town walls along
essentially the same lines from the Roman into the post-medieval period,
while the burgesses of smaller planted towns such as Brecon, Dungarvan,
Ludlow and Stirling did not enlarge their walled enceintes.

Particularly instructive are the circumstances of alterations made to the city
wall of London. The area enclosed by the former Roman enceinte remained
static until the late thirteenth century (with the exception of reclaimed waterfront property). Yet despite a certain level of independence that the city had
gained by this time, subsequent alterations to the circuit were in no way
intended to enhance the security of the population at large, including growing
suburban areas.[86] Rather, the extension of the circuit south of Ludgate, on the
west side of the city, enclosed the site of the Dominican Blackfriars (founded
*c.*1275). The precinct was defined with a new wall equipped with rectangular
towers, in contrast to the rounded bastions on the remainder of the circuit
(*colour plate 14*), the new defensive line blocking off at least two pre-existing
routes in and out of the city.[87] This period also saw Montfichet and Baynard's

Castle (also inside the west side of the city), disused and their sites subsequently swallowed up by inward colonisation. Yet any notion of a changing balance of power in favour of the citizens is dispelled by the massive expansion by Edward I, on the opposite side of London, of the Tower into a concentric fortress facing into the city, swallowing up land both within and without the walled circuit. The extensive suburbs, however, were never included in the type of walled expansion that occurred at so many major European cities, and the centre of royal government at Westminster remained a separate and unde-fended focus, designated a city in its own right in the sixteenth century.

There were, however, two main scenarios that could sometimes lead to the enlargement of a town's walled circuit: first, internal pressure on urban space might prompt the planning of new walled extensions; and second, suburban development beyond the original defended area might be enclosed secondarily. Considerable variations are apparent in the topographies of those towns where walled circuits were expanded. The defences of towns such as Bridgnorth, Christchurch, Norwich, Northampton, Shrewsbury, Stamford and Warwick were extensions to, or expansions of early medieval *burh* type settlements, while at places such as Bolsover, Carmarthen and Haverfordwest, the suburbs of post-Conquest planted towns were enclosed. Only a very small proportion of walled new towns witnessed expansions to their defended areas, due partly to their generally smaller size, but perhaps also to the restricting influence of certain types of lordship (see page 217). More complex sequences are apparent at the major centres of Bristol, Edinburgh, Norwich and York, involving multiple episodes of defensive enlargement in a number of separate directions. Yet overall, few towns and cities of medieval Britain show the successive rings of defences built around great European centres such as Bruges, Cologne, Florence, Nuremberg and Paris.[88]

One of the clearest examples of town defences displaying evidence of enlargement from an early medieval enclosed core is Nottingham. Here, William the Conqueror raised a castle in 1068 on a rocky eminence *c.*500m west of the Anglian borough. By the end of the eleventh century the focus of the town had shifted to a new settlement that sprang up between the castle and the *burh*. Known as the 'French borough', in contrast to the earlier 'English borough', this new unit originated as an immigrant community attracted to a new commercial centre established at the castle gates, and preserved its separate legal identity through the provision of its own bailiff and sheriff.[89] When the town defences were extended to integrate the French borough with the defences of the castle and those of the earlier *burh*, the walls enclosed an area of almost 50ha, more than quadruple that of the pre-Conquest defended area of approximately 12ha. The extension of Chester's walls was similarly closely related to the new Norman castle, built in 1070 beyond the south-west corner of the rectangular Roman circuit, next to the River Dee. Transformation of the defences, to produce an enlarged enceinte of approximately two kilometres, was rapid.[90] Shipgate, on the new riverine southern wall, was in existence by the 1120s, and the strip of land on the west side of the city embraced within the new circuit was colonised by the new foundations of Greyfriars, Blackfriars and a Benedictine nunnery.

It was the walling of suburbs to the north and south of Bristol from the thirteenth century onwards that transformed the settlement from a modestly sized *burh* to one of Britain's largest walled cities, encompassing a total area of over 55ha.[91] Defensive necessity was clearly only one factor here. The walling of Bristol's suburbs was one component in a massive scheme of civic engineering involving, from the 1240s onwards, the temporary diversion of the Avon and construction of a magnificent new stone bridge, and the cutting of a new channel between the Avon and Frome and associated reclamation of land.[92] Despite such investment, large areas of Bristol's riverside and quayside remained unprotected, demonstrating the tensions that might exist between the needs of defence and the viability of port towns.

In certain instances, communities clearly extended beyond their town walls at early dates. At Winchester, the survey of 1110 captured the medieval town at its zenith and provides a very detailed insight into the balance of population both within and without the ancient enceinte. In addition to the total walled zone of *c*.58ha (much of it comprising high-status precincts: see page 109), a substantial extramural settlement of *c*.49ha had grown up to the south, and further suburbs of *c*.20ha each to the north, east and west.[93] The settlement beyond the west wall, recorded from the late twelfth century as *Erdberi*, was enclosed within the corner of a pre-existing Iron Age earthwork that was now refurbished.[94] Yet these works may not have been entirely finished, and the entire extramural settlement was not fully enclosed. And notably, when major funds were injected into an upgrading of the city's defences in the early thirteenth century, it was the former Roman circuit that was modernised through expensive refacing, rather than an improvement or formalisation of the outer perimeter.

At Lincoln too the urban core remained encompassed within Roman walls, despite the enclosure of suburbs on all sides. It was only on the south side of the city that the Roman circuit was extended, so that it ran up to the Brayford Pool. The fabric of the rest of the wall embracing the Upper and Lower Cities remained substantially Roman in origin throughout the medieval period, work taking the form of cosmetic repairs rather than wholesale rebuilding. By the later medieval period, the progressive enclosure of four suburbs, in addition to the construction of Close Wall, which partly projected beyond the Upper City, ensured that Lincoln's defensive topography was complex and fragmented.[95] To the north, the suburb of Newport was encompassed by an earthwork enclosure. To the east, Butwerk was at least partly walled, and one of the roads into it was marked by a stone-built bar. To the south, the straggling settlement of Wigford was embraced within the line of a diverted watercourse (the King's

Dyke) supplemented with two stone bars (Great and Little Bargate) linked by a short length of wall at its southern extremity. To the west, Newland was encompassed by a gated earthwork. The overall impression is of a 'polyfocal' defended town representing piecemeal initiatives rather than a single walled entity (see page 213).

Suburban growth was early at Canterbury. Domesday Book shows that extramural settlement was well established by the Conquest, and rentals from the twelfth century provide snapshots of how space outside the walls was used. For instance, a rental compiled in 1163-7 describes settlement in *Baggeberi*, an extramural suburb that may have been encompassed by an earthwork. Of particular note in this context are the four *mansure* and a smithy that lay outside and next to one of the town gates, while dwellings were packed up tight against the wall in the place where effluent from prior Wibert's new sewer discharged through the wall.[96] The extent of Gloucester's city boundary was marked by at least two gates positioned beyond the Roman north wall: Alvin Gate (a rare example of a gate reflecting a personal name, Saxon *Aelfwyn*); the outer north gate; and a third may have also existed.[97] The lack of any serious defensive function is apparent in the fact that these were free-standing structures, not linked by a wall or bank. At least one of Chester's bars ('The Bar' on the Boughton side of the city) was a stone-built structure, through which a small arch for foot traffic was pierced in 1608.[98]

Those Welsh medieval towns that exhibit evidence of extensions to defended perimeters were mainly centres of regional significance; in contrast, the vast majority retained simple circuits emanating from a castle nucleus. The first Norman settlement at Haverfordwest was known as the 'Castleton', a small enclosed unit nestling around a marketplace adjacent to the castle, subsequently dwarfed by the expansion of the defended zone in the thirteenth century.[99] Enlarged circuits can be recognised at Cardiff and Carmarthen, where early enclosed towns in the shadows of castles were eclipsed by walled extensions in the fourteenth and fifteenth centuries respectively; other possible expansions occurred at Abergavenny, Pembroke and Monmouth.[100] We may speculate as to whether towns with secondary enlargements to their circuits maintained the defences and gates of the inner defensive ring. At Carmarthen, for instance, John Speed's map of *c.*1610 clearly depicts the Dark Gate, which had marked an original entrance to the Norman castle-town but which, following the construction of the town's walled extension, stood as a central feature in the late medieval townscape.

We should also be careful not to make a simple correlation between the area encompassed by the defences of a town and the size of its population, as vast spaces could be taken up with high-status precincts of various sorts, as well as gardens, while numerous towns contracted within the lines of their circuits. For instance, late medieval Norwich – whose defences included four kilometres of walling – was physically the same size as London but contained less than one quarter of the population due to the open spaces within the enceinte.[101] It is a mistake to envisage a simplified process by which the walled interiors of medieval towns gradually filled up and overspilled beyond their walls, with suburban development always a secondary process. Often, in fact, the walled area included open spaces of various types, and suburban growth is known historically and archaeologically from the twelfth century onwards, as at Exeter and Winchester, as well as Canterbury. This distinction, between intramural and extramural growth, was based not so much on available space, but more on variations in wealth and economic activity, as well as on the high-status precincts within the walls which took up much space (see page 104). The original twelfth-century walled circuit at Durham, for instance, was completely dominated by the cathedral precinct and castle (35). The commercial focus of the city represented by the Market Square remained unenclosed until at least 1315, after which a walled extension was built following a petition for murage by the burgesses, the suburbs having being ravaged during a Scottish raid in 1312 (see also page 213).[102] We should also

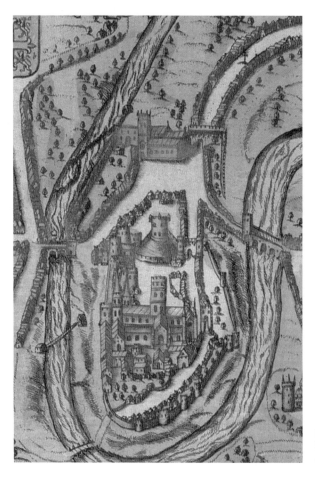

35 Durham as depicted by John Speed in the early seventeenth century

allow for the possibility that the lines of walls might be heavily influenced by natural topography, which might ensure that a far larger area was enclosed, than was actually developed.

In a great many Welsh towns, the extent of the walled perimeter seems to have marked a medieval high-water mark of development, to be followed by depopulation, retrenchment and the abandonment of intramural plots. Descriptions and depictions of Welsh towns in the early modern period frequently show that walls defined the maximum extent of urban growth far more often than was the case in England. No building beyond the wall of the Edwardian planned town of Aberystwyth was permitted until 1797, for instance.[103] John Speed's early seventeenth-century map of Cardiff depicts large areas in the southern part of the walled area taken up with gardens and other enclosures, and the pattern is repeated at places such as Cardigan and Flint, where open spaces are also shown. The sixteenth-century itinerary of John Leland provides further evidence: at Chepstow, for example, he noted that the southern part of the enclosed town was 'converted into little medowes and gardens' (here, the long perimeter of the town's defences was a product of its setting in the loop of a river, and it enclosed a far greater area than ever intended for built-up settlement), and similar observations were made about at Hay-on-Wye. Even successful cities such as Bristol, which extended its enceinte on several occasions, and London, whose population level far outstripped that of any other British town, nevertheless contained within their walled areas numerous open spaces, as depicted in early modern maps. For such places the term 'garden city' is not entirely inappropriate in a medieval context. Thus, while it is tempting to conceptualise medieval town walls as products of flourishing economies and self-confident communities, in other ways they might provide physical evidence of the limitations of communal effort, or of grand ambition never realised. The town walls of King's Lynn were built at the zenith of the town's development in the late thirteenth to early fourteenth centuries. Yet the intramural green-belt depicted in early modern maps demonstrates a subsequent urban contraction, while the mixture of walled and embanked defences and occasionally haphazard nature of the masonry show that this was a defensive scheme that, due to urban impoverishment, was never completed as planned.[104] A marked change in the quality of masonry has also been observed in portions of the thirteenth- to fourteenth-century town wall of Newcastle, where excavations highlighted a marked break between regular lower courses and the apparently hastily built irregular upperwork.[105]

Only in the most exceptional circumstances can evidence be identified for a reduction in the walled area. Perhaps the clearest example is Berwick upon Tweed (Northumberland), where major upgrading of the town defences of c.1300 according to the principles of Renaissance-inspired artillery fortification in the sixteenth century, resulted in a reduction of the enclosed zone to approximately two-thirds of its original area. A contraction of the circuit of

Beaumaris, in contrast, was due to a sixteenth-century rebuilding that cut off one of the corners of the enceinte lost to the sea (see page 99). A rather different sequence is apparent at New Winchelsea, where the decline of the settlement in the later medieval period meant that the original scheme to enclose the remarkable grid-plan town established by Edward I was never fully completed, although its gates survive (*36*). When fresh attempts were made to enclose the town in the early fifteenth century, part of the west side of the original town-plan lay outside the new town walls, which were themselves never finished.[106]

But abandonment of a walled zone might not always signify urban decline. At Denbigh the population of the hilltop walled borough of *c*.3.8ha planned in the thirteenth century as an appendage to the castle was smaller than the suburbs stretching down the northern slopes of the hill by the early fourteenth century. By 1305 there were 183 extramural burgages compared to only 52 within the walls, while in 1334 both a 'borough within the walls' and a 'market without' are distinguished in records.[107] Here, the modern town is the successor to the extramural settlement and not the walled nucleus.

36 Winchelsea: New Gate, a now isolated feature of the town's original perimeter, with an adjacent stretch of ditch. *Authors' collection*

Bastides

Although the late thirteenth-century programme of castle-building by Edward I in Wales has often been viewed as representing the zenith of castle design in England and Wales, less attention has been paid to the fact that most of Edward's castles were associated with new defended towns. Nor was this ambitious programme, in which the king displayed an unusually personal level of involvement, restricted to Wales; in England, the coastal towns of Berwick-upon-Tweed, Kingston-upon-Hull and New Winchelsea, all of which were provided with defences, were plantations of Edward I. At Berwick, the royal initiative behind the town's new defences erected from 1296 was symbolised by the fact that Edward personally wheeled the first barrow of earth.[108] Both Hull and New Winchelsea were unusual among Edward I's bastides in that in neither case were the town defences linked to those of a castle, although at the latter land was retained for this purpose in the 1280s but the fortification was left incomplete, or perhaps never started. In Wales, the royal castles of Aberystwyth, Caernarfon, Conwy, Flint and Rhuddlan were twinned with new towns fortified through direct royal financing. Yet such measures might not always provide security; an anecdotal snippet of evidence, from the report of Bogo de Knovil, justiciar of west Wales in 1280, highlights that while Aberystwyth had walls and gates (as authorised in the royal chater of 1277), these had no locks, bolts and bars and apparently swung open day and night.[109] But not all the Edwardian boroughs in Wales were intended to be defended. Settlements associated with the castles at Criccieth and Harlech were never enclosed, while the towns of Beaumaris and Ruthin were only provided with defences in the early fifteenth century, in the wake of sackings by Owain Glyn Dwr.

Probably influenced or inspired by planned towns in France and Gascony and often known as 'bastides', the topographies of most of these towns were characterised by arrangements of straight streets intersecting at right angles to form rectangular *insulae*, while the plans of their defences show that these were usually integrated with, and built broadly contemporary with, those of the castles. Despite high levels of regularity, however, none of these towns were geometrically perfect in the formats of their defences and street plans. In some cases natural topography proved an impediment, while at Caernarfon the plan and location of the castle were influenced by the fact that it reoccupied the site of a motte and bailey built by a follower of the Norman Earl of Chester in the late eleventh century.

These plantations also have in common their coastal or estuarine locations, and most incorporated harbour facilities, ensuring that they could be supplied from the sea. At Caernarfon (*37*), for instance, the two gates are positioned at opposite ends of an axial street, with one of them opening directly onto the quay.[110] At Conwy, (*37*) a projecting spur-work ending in a now vanished tower flanked the harbour, forming a breakwater as well as a defensive feature. At Rhuddlan, a massive engineering operation, involving the canalisation of the

River Clwyd, was carried out in the late 1270s and early 1280s to make the site accessible to shipping. Several kilometres in length, this new tidal canal (*fossa maris*) was constructed with the employment of many hundred specialist ditchers transported from the Lincolnshire fens.

While these sites were founded during the English conquest and suppression of North Wales in late thirteenth century, we must appreciate that the association of castle and planned borough had more than a simple military rationale.

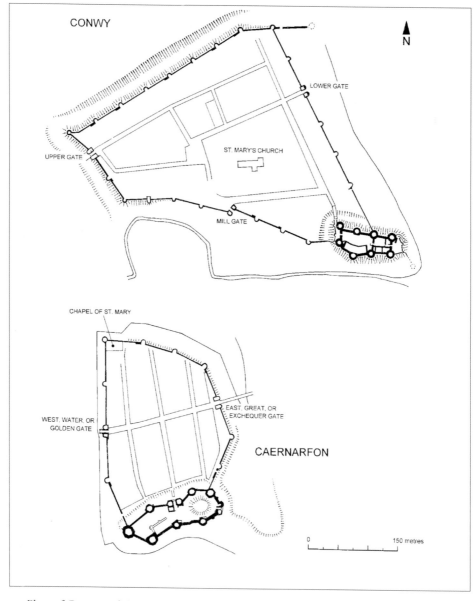

37 Plans of Conwy and Caernarfon

As well as functioning as fortified strongholds within conquered territory, the association of castle and town represented a partnership of military and economic interests. These defended towns were not built solely to accommodate garrisons and personnel associated with the administrative functions of castles (though this was important), but were intended as viable commercial centres and magnets to settlers encouraged by favourable rents. We should also not overlook the symbolism inherent in these new fortified complexes, which were unambiguous icons of an English colonial settlement. This was particularly evident at Caernarfon, where the castle's conspicuous banded masonry and polygonal towers were built in emulation of Constantinople, with echoes of Roman imperial authority; notably, one of the town gates (Golden Gate) was named after one of the Roman gates there.[111] The foundation of the town and castle (itself the successor to an earlier Norman fortification) also meant the clearance of a Welsh settlement on the site. Building operations commenced on both castle and town in June 1283, and in the middle of July of that year a force of 20 men were employed for five days to take away the timbers of houses dismantled to make way for primary earth and timber defences around the town. Construction work on the town walls commenced in the week beginning 9 October 1284, it being highly significant that this occasion appears to have coincided with the king travelling to Caernarfon in order to formally present the borough charter.

At Conwy, the Edwardian town lay on the site of the Cistercian abbey of St Mary, an important Welsh foundation and the burial place of Llywelyn the Great, which was moved elsewhere, as well as the hall of the Welsh princes, which was retained in the town defences.[112] In perpetuating a site imbued with such high-status connotations, the castle and town signified the powerful presence of a new order and the displacement of the old. Moreover, and crucially, the inhabitants of these new bastides remained, for several generations, exclusively English, further emphasising the repressive and colonial character of their foundation. The military character of these castle-town foundations is reflected not only in their visible form and English exclusivity, but also in an important detail of their social organisation. Unusually, within the overall framework of town–castle relationships in Britain, the constables of the royal castles of Flint, Rhuddlan, Conwy and Caernarfon were also the *ex officio* mayors of the boroughs.[113] Although liberties were extended to burgesses to attract them as settlers (with customs based on those of Hereford), and while they were permitted to elect two bailiffs annually in their borough court, there was no sense here of any independence on the part of the town community.

Far from representing *de novo* foundations, many of Edward I's towns and castles were thus raised on sites that had been occupied previously, and in effect symbolised reconquest. The plantation of Beaumaris entailed the depopulation of the Welsh centre of Llanvaes and the removal of its population to the new foundation of Newborough.[114] The construction of Rhuddlan town and castle in fact effectively involved a transfer from one site to another. A motte and bailey castle raised in 1073 and an accompanying borough in existence by 1086 were replaced by a new foundation, chartered in 1278, at a little distance to the north-west along the banks of the Clwyd. As at Flint the town, characterised by a symmetrical grid-plan, was not walled but fortified with earth and timber. A bank and ditch surrounded the town on three sides, with the steep river cliff defining the remaining side.

Documentary evidence also makes it clear that the fortifications of towns were built at an early stage, and not as successors to the castles. At Caernarfon, Conwy and Flint it is clear that the areas later to be occupied by towns and castles were enclosed with ditches and palisades very early in building campaigns in order to provide secure bases for building operations, and labour forces were evidently used interchangeably on both castles and town defences. The sheer volume and variety of the labour forces used emphasises the gargantuan nature of these building projects, which included the employment not only of quarrymen and masons, but specialist ditchers (*fossatores*), woodcutters (*coupiatores*), smiths, plumbers, carpenters, watchmen, and a miscellany of administrative personnel.

Surviving financial accounts and other sources provide a uniquely detailed view of how these sites were built, emphasising both the enormous drain on royal resources that they represented, and the speed with which they were accomplished.[115] Compared to the often tortuous and piecemeal manner in which many medieval towns were walled, Edward I's programme in North Wales represented a whirlwind of activity, emphasising what could be achieved when royal resources and political will were mobilised simultaneously. Yet even with such backing, the progress of building operations was not always smooth. Accounts for Caernarfon demonstrate extremely uneven expenditure during the period of construction from 1283-1330, with work severely reversed during the Welsh revolt in the spring of 1284, and operations ceasing almost entirely in a five year period from 1299 when royal attention and resources were diverted to the Scottish war. In total, expenditure on the town walls of Caernarfon was approximately £3500 of a total expenditure of more than £12,000. At Conwy, where the entire building project cost in excess of £14,000 in five intense seasons of building work in 1283-7, work on the town walls was not completed through direct royal finance, but pursued subsequently by the burgesses them-selves, who received a grant of seven years' murage in 1305. What all these walled boroughs had in common was that the ostentation and expense of their defences was completely out of balance with their commercial functions. Even the burgesses of the largest of the Edwardian towns in North Wales, Beaumaris, had agricultural lands[116] and, despite its political importance, Caernarfon's 'urban' economy remained undeveloped in the middle ages.[117]

Those parts of south-west France that were subject to English control and influence in various ways from the twelfth to the fourteenth century, have a partic-ular concentration of bastides. The 'English' bastides of Gascony fall into two basic groups: those French foundations subsequently taken into English control; and those founded by English kings or their agents.[118] Crucially, in this context, however, a bastide was not necessarily a fortified town; while they were colonial establishments linked to the control of territory, only a little more than one third of all bastides were fortified and in many cases this was clearly a secondary measure.[119]

While the bastides of England and Wales and those of Gascony were parts of a single town planning 'movement', the relationship between town plan and town defence displayed in south-west France shows some distinctive features. Despite the metric regularity of the gridded street plans that was one of the hallmarks of Gascon bastides, relatively few defended circuits display similar levels of regularity. Often, the enceinte followed natural topographical features, as for instance at Monségur, Gironde (founded 1263) and Puymirol, Lot et Garonne (1246), where vestiges of walled enclosures surmount and follow rocky ledges; elsewhere, circuits were built at different orientations to the street grid, as at Sauveterre de Guyenne, Gironde (1281). Where circuits were planned on the same alignment as the grid, these were relatively simple affairs, their gatehouses notably devoid of trappings of architectural symbolism or elaboration. Illustrative examples include the somewhat austere rectangular gatehouses of Damazan (bastide founded c.1269) and Vianne, Lot et Garonne (1284), and Monpazier, Dordogne (1285); the circuit of Cadillac, Gironde (1280) is unusual in the complexity of its military architecture (38). Fortified Gascon bastides are also generally very small and few show evidence of extensions to the enclosed area, and some, such as St Pastour, Lot et Garonne (c.1259) exhibit shrinkage. In terms of defensive topography, perhaps the most distinctive feature of these bastides is the fact that so few contained castles. The enceintes of these towns were thus self-contained systems, neither linked to nor complementing the defences of royal or private fortified nuclei, as was almost invariably the case in England and Wales. Yet exceptions can of course be identified, including: Domme, Dordogne (c.1280) where the castle lies at one end of an irregular circuit whose perimeter defined a naturally defensible hilltop site; Durance, Lot et Garonne (1320) where the chateau in the north-west corner of the tiny rectangular circuit is a later addition that was probably a hunting lodge; and Molières, Dordogne (c.1278-84) where the seneschal's adjoining castle was left unfinished. This marked absence of private or royal defended residences within bastides was counterbalanced, however, by the frequent presence of fortified churches. In some senses, the status of castles as the anchor of town plans and walled circuits in Britain was paralleled in Gascony by these fortified churches that so frequently dominated walled bastides. Particularly clear surviving examples can be identified in Monflanquin, Lot et Garonne (1256) and Beaumont du Périgord, Dordogne (1272), where large churches formed part of the defensive perimeter and display arrow slits, and Villeréal, Lot et Garonne (1265) where the main west door of the church facing on to the central *place* was protected with a drawbridge.

38 Cadillac: medieval gate on the south side of the walled circuit of an English bastide in Gironde, south-west France; the gatehouse is of an unusually high level of sophistication for a Gascon bastide, featuring projecting machicolations and arrow loops facing into the gate passage. *Authors' collection*

Urban Precincts

The ecclesiastical precinct was an especially important topographical influence on many medieval towns. Especially notable from the fourteenth century was the appearance, in many of the larger British towns, of walled enclosures with defensive qualities (or else the appearance of defensive strength) built in association with monastic houses, bishops' palaces, cathedrals, or a combination of these institutions, sometimes as the result of a licence to crenellate.[120] In certain cases the ecclesiastical precinct might dominate the entire town plan: at Dunfermline the ecclesiastical precinct took up a larger total area than the adjoining burgh until the sixteenth century.

The architectural focus of such an ecclesiastical precinct was invariably the gatehouse, and many examples exhibit iconographic as well as defensive qualities, in the manner of town gates. The scale and architectural qualities of monumental precinct gates such as those at St Albans and Bury St Edmunds (*39-40*) might rival or even overshadow the gates of the towns. An instructive example is the great gate of St Augustine's, Canterbury, rebuilt in monumental form in the first decade of the fourteenth century for Abbot Thomas Fyndon (*41*). Located outside the walled city, this structure faced Burgate, one of the

39 Above, left Bury St Edmunds: the Great Gate, a late medieval gate into the monastic precinct. *Authors' collection*

40 Above, right Bury St Edmunds: the Norman gate into the monastic precinct, featuring fine Romanesque detailing. *Authors' collection*

medieval city's gates, at the opposite end of Church Street (St Pauls). When the town gate was completely rebuilt in the early sixteenth century, depictions of the (now demolished) structure show that its design emulated that of St Augustine's, its front also proudly displaying three windows and three plaques featuring the arms of citizens who contributed to the rebuilding.[121] Elsewhere, gated monastic precincts lay in unenclosed towns, as for instance at Battle. More commonly, in cases such as Exeter and Winchester, cathedral closes were fully walled and gated and occupied independently protected intramural enclaves. The loss of precinct gates sometimes ran in parallel to the loss of the walls and gates of the cities themselves; Exeter's Broadgate (*42*), representing the entrance to the cathedral precinct from High Street was itself demolished in 1825, soon after the main gates were taken down.

Among the many examples of walled cathedral precincts are Lichfield (1289) and Salisbury (1327), where in both cases the towns themselves were never enclosed with masonry defences. As well as surrounding the cathedral itself, such walled precincts usually enclosed the residences of the bishop, dean, canons and vicars choral, which were typically set around a large rectangular or square open space. At Wells, the ambitious building project carried out for

41 Left Canterbury: precinct gate of St Augustine's Priory. *Authors' collection*

42 Opposite Exeter: engraving of Broadgate, one of the gates into the cathedral precinct, demolished in 1825

Bishop Ralph from *c.*1340 involved not only the construction of a gatehouse featuring flanking polygonal towers, but also a crenellated wall complete with interval towers that encompassed the churchyard, his own moated, walled and gated palace, and those of the canons; the cathedral precinct also preserves another magnificent gate (*43-44*). These precincts were far more than mere architectural showpieces, however. The psychological deterrent value of imposing gates, in particular, must have been high in a period characterised by violent outbursts of civil strife sometimes directed at ecclesiastical buildings, their muriments and estates as well as personnel. The medieval townscape of St Andrew's provides an illuminating example of how a walled ecclesiastical enclosure could dominate yet also divide a community. We have a particularly clear idea of the town's appearance in the late medieval period given the survival of a remarkably detailed panoramic bird's-eye view of the late sixteenth century, probably created by John Geddy.[122] While the enormous cathedral precinct was enclosed with an imposing wall, complete with architectural trappings such as a walkway, gunports and bastions constructed by Prior Hepburn in the 1520s, these defences did not extend to encompass the adjoining planned burgh. Instead, the four major and two minor points of access into the town were marked with gates (or 'ports') comprising simple

arched or lintelled openings through otherwise featureless walls, the remainder of the town boundary being defined by the backs of individual burgage plots.

The outer walls of these enclosures often formed a component part of the total walled perimeter, either where ecclesiastical properties lay inside an original enceinte, as at Exeter and Winchester, or where precincts projected beyond earlier walled lines, as with Blackfriars, London and St Mary's, York. At the latter, the respective importance of the walls of the town and abbey were reflected in the conditions laid down in the licence to crenellate in 1318, this specifying that part of the abbey wall should not be crenellated in such a way that it could be used, in other circumstances, to attack the city.[123] While framed in military terms, we might wonder whether this provision rather reflects the relative status of the urban and ecclesiastical communities. At Lincoln, the design of the close wall, which defined an irregular circuit taking in a large area of space both within and beyond the walled Upper City, was governed by a series of royal licences. The close wall is recorded from the 1280s, and a grant of 1318 permitted that its height could exceed twelve feet and allowed turrets to be built.[124] At Leicester, the only expansion of the ancient walled enceinte laid out in the Roman period was the Newarke ('new work') developed to the south of the castle in the first half of the fourteenth century (45). While the

43 Above Wells: gate into the bishop's palace. *Authors' collection*

44 Left Wells: gate into the cathedral precinct. *Authors' collection*

town wall was apparently re-routed to encompass the new work, the defensive enlargement accommodated a high-status religious complex centred on a collegiate church rather than representing an enclosure of a suburb.[125] An analogous example, but on a far larger scale, was the late thirteenth-century expansion of London's wall to encompass Blackfriars (see page 92), while at towns such as Newcastle and Chester, by the close of the thirteenth century large strips of land lying immediately within town walls were taken up with the precincts of friaries of several different orders.[126]

Such topographies frequently gave rise to disputes and negotiations concerning whether the burgesses or ecclesiastical authorities were responsible for defences. Three contrasting examples of arrangements made to accommodate the sites of other new friaries on sites adjacent to town walls in the thirteenth century highlight the range of ways in which the needs of ecclesiastical lords might conflict with different interest groups. In 1244 the Grey Friars of Oxford were granted permission to demolish part of the walled circuit to accommodate an expansion of their precinct. While this was conditional upon a new wall being built around the enlarged precinct, this was not immediately carried out, and instead the friar's new church was built in the gap created in the original circuit.[127] This contrasts interestingly with the arrangement made when New College was established in the north-east corner of the city wall

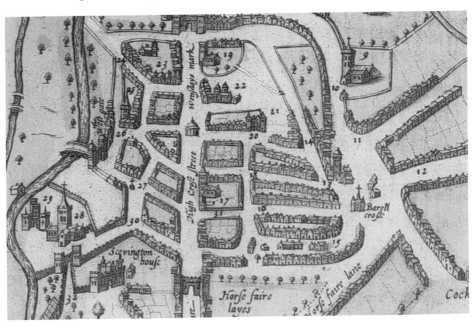

45 Leicester as depicted by John Speed in the early seventeenth century. The Newarke can be identified in the bottom left-hand corner of the map

from 1379, the new institution being obliged to maintain the wall where it formed the boundary to the collegiate precinct (see page 223). At Winchester too, conditions were attached to the establishment of the Greyfriars, here immediately inside the town wall, in 1258. Royal permission for the new intra-mural enclosure was conditional on access to walls being allowed for repair and assembly in wartime, the strip of land immediately within the wall being royal property.[128] At Northampton, the Carmelites applied to Edward I in 1278 for permission to enclose part of the city wall and block its crenellations in order to build their precinct.[129] A fascinating glimpse of the varied ways in which the townsmen valued their walled circuit is provided by the report of the jury in the ensuing enquiry. Not only, was it reported, would these alterations hinder the town watch in detecting approaching malefactors, but they would also deprive the population of a cherished amenity, as in summer the sick used the airy wall-walk as a perambulation, and in the winter it allowed escape from the muddy streets.

On the east side of the city of Exeter, the cathedral and episcopal properties eventually had boundaries and walls that ran to the inside of the city wall, thus blocking the continuous access to it necessary for the mayor's annual peram-bulation as well as access for defence. This led to a period of friction eventu-ally resolved in an agreement of 1327 by which these boundary walls were pierced with a series of small posterns to which both the church authorities and the mayor of the city held keys.[130] These little posterns were still clearly visible in the sixteenth century, when the area was depicted on a map.[131] An extreme, though nevertheless instructive example of the considerable challenges in apportioning responsibility for wall maintenance is Winchester.[132] Here, some money from murage was spent through the secular body of the citizens. Yet money spent on the walls near Wolvesey palace was disbursed through the bishops, and money spent on walls near the cathedral close was disbursed through the cathedral prior. The east gate of the city was maintained by St Mary's abbey with monies from murage it collected there. The south-west of the city wall was maintained in conjunction with the royal castle. Thus in the later middle ages more than one third of the walled circuit was maintained through bodies other than the citizens themselves. This fragmentation sometimes led to friction, notably in the mid-thirteenth century when the citizens argued with the cathedral priors over the maintenance of adjacent walls and their gates, the conflict coming to a head during the attack on the city during the Barons' Wars, after which a new agreement was made between the parties in 1266.

By the later medieval period the defensive topographies of larger medieval towns could thus be extremely complex. Defensive structures might include not only town walls of different phases, but also a royal or baronial castle (and occasionally more than one, as at London and York), in addition to one or more ecclesiastical precincts. Together, these features represented the sometimes complementary and sometimes competing interests of a range of social groups and elites. For this reason, walled areas within towns, as well as stretches of the walls themselves, might actually be quite fragmented, both physically and socially.

Town walls and gunpowder artillery

The introduction of firearms did not, as is sometimes assumed, immediately render obsolete existing traditions of medieval military architecture. While the first evidence for the use of gunpowder artillery in a British context dates to the second quarter of the fourteenth century, the new technology was not immediately applied to batter down buildings. It was not generally until the third quarter of that century that fortifications were adapted to accommodate firearms, and later still before fortress design was significantly adapted to provide defence against this new technology.[133] We should also remember that cannon were not the first type of artillery to be mounted on town defences; at Southampton, for instance, an inquisition of 1353 shows that the walls carried springalds and mangonels, and limestone balls presumably for use in such machines have been excavated from fourteenth-century contexts near Westgate.[134]

The most obvious structural evidence of artillery provision within medieval town walls takes the form of gunports. The earliest of these comprised a circular port beneath a vertical observation slot, giving the appearance of an inverted keyhole from the outside, while the interior featured a splayed embrasure to maximise the field of fire, and a low cill upon which the firearm rested (*46*).

While the earliest dated gunports in Britain are generally believed to be those built in the precinct wall of Quarr Abbey on the Isle of Wight in the 1360s,[135] those in the blocked openings of the Southampton Arcade appeared only a little later and were technologically more developed. This stretch of walling, on the west side of the town, comprises a row of arches in front of earlier walling (47-48). Openings in the earlier walling were blocked, but the blocking masonry pierced with 'keyhole' type loops with high cills and wide splays suited to handguns, the most likely dating being c.1378-9 after French attacks on the Isle of Wight.[136] That the 'keyhole' form of gunport might indicate multi-purpose provision for guns and bows is suggested by the fact that these slots are absent in later gunports on town gates, which tended to be built as simple circular apertures, as seen at Kings Lynn's south gate of the fifteenth and sixteenth centuries. Among the additions to Southampton's circuit made in the fifteenth century was the Catchcold Tower (49), projecting further from the wall face than other mural towers and incorporating keyhole gunports, a boldly projecting parapet with machicolations beneath, and constructed in a vaulted form that suggests the upper levels were also designed to support cannon.[137] Simple splayed rectangular gunports of the mid-sixteenth century – resembling closely those of Henrician artillery forts – were added to the earlier (fourteenth-century) structure of the Southampton West Gate, which led to the quays (50).

What is crucial to note in this context is that urban defences actually show some of the earliest evidence for early specialist artillery; most importantly, it

46 Canterbury: 'keyhole' type gun port in West Gate; the circular opening is 25cm across.
Authors' collection

47 Southampton: blocked arcades on the south-west side of the medieval circuit. *Authors' collection*

48 Southampton: detail of blocked arcade, showing a 'keyhole' type gun port; the circular opening is 15cm across. *Authors' collection*

49 Southampton: Catchcold Tower, a late medieval addition to the circuit for the provision of gunpowder artillery. Note the keyhole type gunport. *Authors' collection*

was in town walls and gates, rather than private castles, that the provision of gunpowder artillery in purpose-built structures can first be identified. By the end of the fourteenth century, at some town gates (including the West Gate, Winchester, and West Gate, Canterbury), as well as some castle gatehouses (including Carisbrooke, Cooling, and Bodiam), simple gunports formed part of the wider panoply of architectural features, partly functional and partly for show. We should not overlook the symbolic significance of urban gunports, which in many cases added to the impressive external appearance of a town gate. While the provision of gunports in Southampton's arcade was designed so that the fields of fire from individual apertures overlapped to ensure minimum 'dead ground', in certain cases they were certainly not placed for maximum military efficiency. At Walmgate Bar, York, for instance, the effectiveness of two second-floor gunports was limited by the fact that the portcullis winding gear behind them would have rendered the use of firearms difficult, while their fields of fire were obstructed by the bartizans that added to the gate's impressive appearance.[138] A gate such as this had great military style but far less defensive substance. At Tenby, one of the mural towers near the southern end of the town wall displays 'keyhole' gunports at first-floor level, added in the fourteenth or fifteenth century (51).[139] The fact that these features have no associated cills, meaning that guns could not actually be accommodated, seems to suggest that these features were more for external impression than having real military value, and they may well have been adapted from arrow slits.

The concentration of gunports in the West Gate, Canterbury (built from 1380), constituted a far more powerful battery, comprising three tiers of loops designed for small, short, manoeuvrable firearms. Yet even in a structure such as this, raised at a time of intense threat from French raids and lacking the fine non-functional external architectural detailing visible in many other gatehouses, domestic trappings were not lacking. Fireplaces were installed in the base of each drum tower, their flues emerging at the level of the parapet yet hidden behind merlons, thus preserving the integrity of the design.[140] An often overlooked and unusual structure demonstrating provision for gunpowder artillery in an innovative design is the Tile Tower, Carlisle, a rectangular mural tower of likely twelfth-century origin rebuilt in its upper portion in brick from 1483.[141] Provision for handguns is apparent in the three gunports accommodated in the brick-vaulted basement, the embrasures provided with cills and flanking recesses for ammunition. Yet an apparently functional artillery bastion such as this was not free of architectural symbolism, the rebuilt structure prominently displaying Richard III's white boar badge. Even the use of brick may have been a sign of extravagance as well as having practical benefits in that the partially brick-built structure would have been more resistant to the concussion of artillery discharge.

Two other urban buildings of this period merit special attention because they were specifically built for gunpowder artillery: these were the Cow Tower,

50 Above, left Southampton: West Gate, showing rectangular gunports. *Authors' collection*

51 Above, *right* late medieval gun loops in a mural tower at Tenby. *Authors' collection*

Norwich, and the God's House Tower, Southampton. Located on the bend of the River Wensum on the north-east side of the city, and connected by timber palisades to the city defences and the fortified Bishop Bridge, the Cow Tower was a free-standing artillery fortification added to Norwich's defensive circuit in the late fourteenth century (*52*).[142] The city walls themselves preserve other important, but often overlooked evidence of early artillery fortification. In the vaulted mural tower near the site of St Stephen's gate are set simple gun loops which, if contemporary with the rest of this structure (dated by documentation securely to the 1340s), are among the very earliest in Britain and perhaps earlier than Quarr.[143]

Often described as a brick-built structure, architectural survey has shown the Cow Tower to have been largely built of flint and only faced with a thin layer of brick; in terms of overall design it is a one-off with no obvious British parallels.[144] Our knowledge of this building is especially good given the survival of the City Treasurer's Accounts for this period, containing a full reference to the building works of 1398-99, as follows:

The Dungeon. Paid to Robert Perkyns for 1,000 bricks (*tegul*) 5s 6d. To Godfrey Coupere for 12 hoops of 2 barrels, 8d. To the same for 6 hoops and 2 *barrelleshedes settyngin*, 4d. For the carriage of 20,000 bricks, 2s 1d. For the carriage of hirdeles and piles from the Stathe, 4d. For the carriage of 3,000 bricks from the Common Stathe as far as the Dungeon by water, 4d. To Richard Wilbegh for 3,500 bricks, 17s 6d. To Robert Snape, mason for 12 shotholes at the Dungeon, price 9d a piece, 9s. To the same for 30 *nowels* price 3d a piece, 7s 6d. For making the *wyndes* and *rote*, 2s. To William Blakehommore for 5,350 bricks, price per 1000 5s, 27s 3d. To Thomas Fyncham for 3,000 bricks at the Dungeon, 12s. To William Chaudeler for 1,000 bricks, 5s. For a barrel bought at the Dungeon for tubs, 6d. For making 4 tubs of the said barrel, 6d.[145]

Within the three-storey tower, provision for artillery was made in two ways: twelve openings in two tiers were equipped with cross-shaped gunports for handguns, and the flat roof with its massive parapet and nine splayed embrasures presumably accommodated larger artillery pieces. Internal arrangements indicate a probable mess room, sleeping quarters and storage space and the structure was equipped with windows, fireplaces and garderobes. Yet the tower's residential character was more garrison block rather than private dwelling, and anticipates, in an urban context, the arrangements that became common in the sixteenth century in royal coastal forts such as Deal and Camber. Also notable is the Cow Tower's relatively isolated location, which was not linked by stone walls to the town's circuit. In this sense too, it anticipates later traditions of 'point' defence, of which seventeenth-century batteries and twentieth-century pillboxes are later manifestations.

The slightly later structure of God's House Tower, Southampton, (53) is different in that it forms an extension of *c.*1417 to an earlier gatehouse on the south-eastern side of Southampton town wall.[146] It comprises a corridor-like block of two storeys, with a further tower of three storeys. This structure also accommodated two types of artillery: smaller pieces provided with gunports (here of 'keyhole' design); and larger pieces on the roof platform. It too featured accommodation for gunners and represents, like the Cow Tower at Norwich, urban adaptation to the challenges of an evolving form of warfare, and in some ways anticipated future developments in military engineering.

The defences of coastal towns also indicate that as well as enclosing populations, medieval defence works were often designed to guard seaward approaches and protect maritime assets. At Portsmouth, for instance, the town's first fortifications of the early thirteenth century were apparently focused on the royal docks, a royal order specifying that these should be enclosed with a wall to protect the king's ships, although how much was completed is unclear.[147] It was common by the later medieval period for the approaches to vulnerable harbours

52 Norwich: Cow Tower. *Authors' collection*

to be protected with booms or chains. At Plymouth, the town's first defence against attack by ships on the harbour at Sutton Pool took the form of a retractable chain in a tower, operated by windlass and in operation by 1400.[148] At Hartlepool and Yarmouth, chains across harbours were integrated within defensive circuits, while at Dartmouth, Fowey and Hedon boom towers were freestanding structures, not linked to town walls. The system at Dartmouth is particularly well understood: built from 1491 on the site of an earlier fortification, Dartmouth Castle comprised a double tower, featuring a semi-circular platform taking the chain and a rectangular artillery tower. Spanning the mouth of the haven and permanently fixed to a structure on the Kingswear side (54), the chain was operated by a pulley and capstan system.[149] Another type of response is evident at Chester, where the medieval Water Tower projected on a spur from the city circuit to protect the quays, although silting of the river means that it now stands some way back from the river bank; similar spur-works projected from the walls of Conwy and Lincoln. At Norwich two surviving boom towers, either side of the River Wensum, were used to support a chain that could be lowered and raised to facilitate the collection of tolls. York had two such systems by the fourteenth century: on the upsteam side a chain was stored in Lendal Tower (55), and on the downstream side in Davy Tower, enabling the waterways to be blocked at night for the regulation of tolls.

53 Southampton: God's House Tower. *Authors' collection*

54 Kingswear: artillery tower opposite Dartmouth Castle. *Authors' collection*

FURTHER READING

For a chronological overview of medieval European urbanism see D. Nicholas, *The Growth of the Medieval City from Late Antiquity to the Early Fourteenth Century* (Longman, 1997) and *The Later Medieval City* (Longman, 1997). For a more thematic approach see K.D. Lilley, *Urban Life in the Middle Ages, 1000-1450* (Palgrave, 2002). For medieval town plans in general see M. Aston and C.J. Bond, *The Landscape of Towns* (Sutton, 2000), and for an overview of medieval economic urban history see R. Britnell, *The Commercialisation of English Society 1000-1500* (Manchester University Press, 1996).

For discussion of the wider place of castles in medieval society and community see N.J.G. Pounds, *The Medieval Castle: A Social and Political History* (Cambridge University Press, 1990), and O.H. Creighton and R.A. Higham, *Medieval Castles* (Shire, 2003). Relationships between castles and town defences are examined in O.H. Creighton, *Castles and Landscapes* (Continuum, 2002).

For the classic account of medieval town plantation in England, Wales and Gascony see M.W. Beresford, *New Towns of the Middle Ages* (Lutterworth Press, 1967). For detailed documentary and topographical accounts of Welsh boroughs see R.A. Griffiths, *Boroughs of Medieval Wales* (University of Wales

55 York: Lendal Tower, located
on the bank of the River Ouse
opposite the North Street Postern
Tower, to which it was connected
with a chain. *Authors' collection*

Press, 1978) and I. Soulsby, *The Towns of Medieval Wales: A Study of their History,
Archaeology and Early Topography* (Phillimore, 1983).

The most comprehensive treatment of murage tax is to be found in H.L.
Turner's *Town Defences in England and Wales* (John Baker 1970). Early artillery fortification is covered in B.H. St J. O'Neil, *Castles and Cannon: A Study of Early Artillery
Fortifications in England* (Clarendon, 1960) and A.D. Saunders, *Fortress Britain:
Artillery Forts in the British Isles and Ireland* (Beaufort, 1989). Town defences during
the Hundred Years War are particularly well dealt with in A. Curry and M. Hughes
(eds), *Arms, Armies and Fortifications in the Hundred Years War* (Boydell, 1994).

3

INTERPRETATIONS: TOPOGRAPHY, ARCHITECTURE AND ARCHAEOLOGY

Because walled towns still form part of our present built environments, and because surviving walls and gates are treasured components of our managed heritage, it is tempting to make assumptions about the character of town walls in the medieval period that are based on present-day preconceptions about their importance. On the one hand, a central argument of this book is the continuing status of town walls as significant elements in townscapes at a number of different levels, being rebuilt and reinvented by communities up to the present. On the other hand, however, we must recognise that in our attempts to understand the medieval world we should take great care also to allow for traditional modes of inference from primary data sources, while keeping our minds open to a range of interpretations. This principle – of the need to consider primary data and critical methodology – is the subject of this chapter. In basic terms, the primary data relating to town walls are amenable to levels of inference of different sorts. Three major approaches to the physical remains of town walls are addressed here: topographical study; architectural analysis; and archaeological inquiry.

Topographical evidence for town walls comprises defensive perimeters and their physical relationship with other aspects of townscapes. We can study these data both from scrutiny of present-day urban environments and, very importantly, from analysis of depictions on antique maps and other pictorial sources that pre-date changes that have obscured the phenomena we seek to illuminate (56). Cartographic sources with high levels of resolution, including large-scale Ordnance Survey maps and others produced for commercial and administrative purposes, can also reveal topographical information including details of property boundaries, minor streets and open spaces, all of which might relate

56 Part of the London
wall at St Giles,
Cripplegate, from an
etching published in 1812.
Besant 1902

in some way to town defences. These observations can also be usefully
amplified and sometimes illustrated dramatically by aerial photography.
Topographical study can also be pursued on the ground through observational
fieldwork, as well as non-intrusive archaeological methods, such as geophysical
and metrological survey (measuring boundaries). From methods such as these
we can deduce something about the survival or non-survival of defensive
circuits, reconstruct the course of such circuits and make inferences about the
relationship between defences and other features of the townscape. Such topographical information also provides valuable insight into the comparative sizes
and plans of walled circuits and their relationship with natural topographies.
Thorough topographical study can illuminate the extent to which the lines of
(now demolished) walls preserved the distinction between intramural cores and
extramural suburbs and influenced the development of open spaces such as
gardens and specialist secular and ecclesiastical precincts.

The architecture of town walls and gates can be studied at a number of
different levels of detail, ranging from informed observation through to the
meticulous recording of masonry fabric through drawing and photography.
Particularly high-resolution recording can be achieved through photogram-
metric methods, whereby stone-by-stone plots of masonry remains are created
with a high level of precision from photographic records (57-59). Such data can

57 Recording of Exeter's city wall. *Exeter Archaeology*

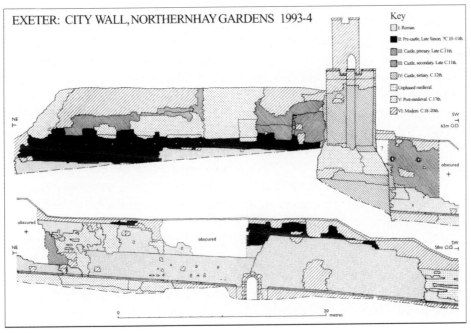

58 An elevation of Exeter's city wall, with interpretative phasing. The elevation depicts the stretch of walling shown in fig. 57. Buried crenellations of Anglo–Saxon date can be seen clearly. *Exeter Archaeology*

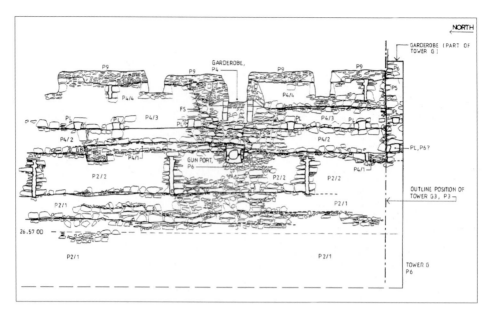

59 Detailed recording of an elevation of the town wall of Tenby, with annotations. *Acanthus Architects*

highlight phases of construction and indicate the use of different types of building material, whose sources will reflect the workings of local building industries and longer-distance contact. The sourcing of building materials can also provide a key to unravelling building sequences. While some structures associated with town defences are clearly utilitarian, other features exhibit details of quality and finesse that place them firmly in the world of architecture (*60-62*). This type of qualitative information, particularly found in gatehouses, means that town walls have a role to play in more general debates concerning the evolution, diffusion and emulation of architectural forms. Particularly pertinent in the medieval context is the continuing debate concerning the relative importance through time of security and symbolism in the 'military' architecture not only of castles but also of town walls. To this debate, intensive structural analysis can make a significant contribution.

Archaeology – in this context interpreted as the study of below-ground structures and deposits – recovers quite different forms of data (*63; colour plate 15*). In broad terms, it has transformed our understanding of medieval urbanism, as exemplified by major excavations in London, Norwich, Winchester, York and elsewhere. In relation to town defences, the impact of excavation has been rather less profound, although specific interventions have occasionally cast new light on aspects of the subject. Excavation has revealed structural evidence relating to wall and gate foundations and associated deposits, which, when suitably dated and analysed, can shed light on the everyday lives of adjacent communities, as at Hull, Oxford and Shrewsbury.

60 Conwy: detail of crenellations and arrow loops on the west side of the circuit, showing the levelled masonry courses on the wall and the inclined masonry courses of the parapet. *Authors' collection*

Among the many contributions of excavation to the study of town defences are its value in defining lost lines of wall-building and exposing details and different phases of construction, identifying chronologies of ditch filling and other encroachment, and revealing the (often major) changes in ground level that have influenced our present perception of town walls and their environ-ments. Where excavations have sectioned associated ditches, we are reminded that town defences comprised belts of interrelated features rather than simply the vertical barriers of gates and walls. Since deposits excavated from ditches may well be waterlogged and well stratified, they have much potential for the preservation of datable environmental and artefactual evidence reflecting contemporary social and economic life in towns and their hinterlands. Finally, archaeological evidence can show how the development of town defences fitted into longer-term sequences of occupation that may well have started before wall construction and invariably continued after their disuse.

While it is useful to separate these three methodological approaches, in practice explanation of the phenomenon of town defences demands judicious synthesis that recognises and evaluates their relative strengths and weaknesses. For instance, an historic town map may contain rich topographical detail but is specific not only to the place but also to the point in time at which it was compiled. In contrast, an archaeological excavation against a wall or through its ditch will reveal a sequence of events, which while equally place-specific, is spread through time. Similarly, while many maps depict towns in their totality, an archaeological or architectural inquiry will usually be targeted more closely

61 Conwy: Upper Gate, showing features of military architecture including traces of
a barbican and a drawbridge recess. *Authors' collection*

62 Rye: Landgate, viewed from within the town. *Authors' collection*

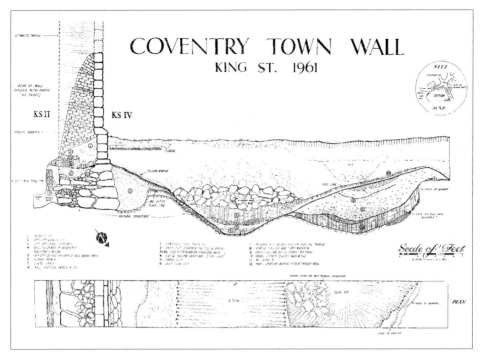

63 Excavated section through Coventry town wall. *Gooder* et al. *1966*

at a specific feature or set of features and afford a far smaller 'window' into the past. Different methods also hold different levels of potential for relative and absolute dating, depending for instance on whether a recorded stratigraphical sequence contains independently datable features, such as artefacts from below ground or architectural features above ground. Historic maps provide a very different type of dating: a *terminus ante quem*, i.e. the date by which the features illustrated must have existed, but with no separation of their origins.

These different sources and methodologies also contain different types of bias. In an urban context, building developments rather than research strategies have generally determined where excavations have taken place. Architectural analysis is, by its very nature, restricted by the limited (and non-representative) sample of extant remains, but can be pursued in circumstances not dictated by threat. Even within towns well known for their surviving walled heritage, there is considerable differential in the survival and integrity of above-ground remains. For instance, while York preserves its four major medieval gates, the fabric of the walled circuit is discontinuous and was extensively rebuilt in the Victorian period, while at Chester the enceinte survives uninterrupted, but has lost its medieval gates. Finally, whereas the physical remains of town walls are the real medieval vestiges of the past, all maps – even historic ones of some antiquity – are in themselves documents compiled with a purpose, and in the early post-medieval period this purpose was not 'historical' in the modern sense of the word. Thus, when using such maps, we must always examine the aims and sources of their compilers.

Although this discussion has centred on physical evidence, the study of town walls is also heavily dependent on the contemporary documentary record, the key sources of which are chronicles and legal and financial records. It is not simply these specific sources that illuminate town walls, however, but also the wider documented nature of medieval society, in which urban communities and their activities were embedded. In essence, the uses to which these data are put are twofold: first, understanding the chronology and geographical distribution of wall building and repair and; second, revealing the character and aspirations of urban communities, against which we can seek to evaluate their motivations for the construction and maintenance of defences. The most pressing and demanding challenge of all is, as more generally in medieval archaeology and study, to harmonise physical and documentary approaches to the past, without letting one dominate or prejudice the other.

TOPOGRAPHICAL EVIDENCE

In some cases, the natural setting of a town provided a ready-made defensive perimeter. Nowhere is this more evident than Durham, where a contemporary commentator remarked of Bishop Flambard (who initiated construction of the city's wall in the early twelfth century): 'Though nature had made a fortress of the city, he made it stronger and more imposing with a wall'.[1] The Northumbrian town of Warkworth similarly grew up in the tight loop of a river, the town defences focusing on a single gate that guarded access to the bridgehead (64). The defensive qualities of Malmesbury, a former Saxon *burh* located on a promontory between the River Avon and two of its tributaries, were recognised by Leland, who noted that in addition to its walled circuit 'nature hath dikid the toun strongly'. Walled towns on naturally defensible eminences are particularly common in Wales, as indicated by places such as Denbigh and Dryslwyn, while fortified towns such as Newcastle Emlyn, St Clears and Pembroke nestled along promontories or ridges that provided a level of natural security. Rather more exceptionally, at Knighton, part of the line of the town's defences seems to have been formed by the relict earthwork of Offa's Dyke. At Dorchester and Ilchester, Roman ditches were recut, the defensive perimeter remaining otherwise unchanged.[2]

In most instances where town walls follow closely the lines of Roman banks, the earthwork was cut back to accommodate the masonry structure, as at Exeter, Chichester, Colchester and Lincoln; York is somewhat unusual in this respect in that the wall was built on the summit of the subsequent rampart. The Anglian and Viking policy of mantling the remains of the Roman

64 Warkworth: medieval bridge-gate over the River Coquet. *Authors' collection*

defences with a massive bank provided the foundation for later work. Instead of cutting back this bank and facing it with a tall medieval wall, the builders constructed their masonry on top of the bank, thus giving the wall, when viewed in isolation, a relatively low appearance.

At Hartlepool and Tenby, the positioning of towns on coastal promontories meant that walls were necessary on the landward side only; at Rye steep cliffs again rendered a full circuit unnecessary, while at places such as Bridport, Hereford, King's Lynn, Newcastle, Salisbury and Yarmouth partial circuits were built against rivers, marshes or estuaries. Hastings was unusual in that here a single stretch of wall, containing three gates and with a tower at each end, blocked the southern (seaward) end of the steep-sided valley containing the Old Town, which was otherwise not enclosed. At Kingston-upon-Hull, a royal plantation of the late thirteenth century, the town occupied an approximately triangular site flanked on two sides by the rivers Hull and Humber. The construction in the fourteenth century of a great moat across the gap of almost 1.5km effectively converted the town into an island, and it was not until the 1930s and the filling-in of the Queen's Dock that the 'Old Town' was reunited with the mainland. The walled defences of Chepstow were similarly discontinuous: the medieval Portwall (65) flanked the town on the peninsula side only, the bend of the River Wye in which the town lay forming a natural perimeter on the other sides and defining a far larger area than was ever built

65 Chepstow: medieval Portwall, viewed from the landward side, showing a rounded mural tower. *Authors' collection*

up. At Norwich too, the medieval walls were planned in sweeping curves, here against the line of the River Wensum. By avoiding awkward changes of angle in the enceinte, the city defences incorporated open spaces that remained undeveloped into the post-medieval period, as described by Defoe, writing in the early eighteenth century that the city walls were '....three miles in circum-ference taking in more ground than the city of London; but much of that ground lying open pasture, fields and gardens.'

Another way in which town walls and gates left an enduring mark on urban topography is the way in which their presence or former existence is indicated in place names and street names. At Exeter, for instance, North Street and South Street were known in the middle ages as Northgate Street and Southgate Street.[3] Confusion can sometimes arise concerning the origins of the -gate element in street names, which can derive either from the Old Norse *gata* (street), or the Old English *geat* (opening). The location of the street within the overall context of the townscape can, however, often indicate which is the more likely origin.[4] The name of Lincoln's Stonebow unusually displays a name of Old Scandinavian origin (*stein*-bogi: stone arch).[5] The element -bar can derive from the Old French *barre* (gate or fastening), and is occasionally found in association with stone gates, such as the Southampton Bargate, and one of the lesser gates of medieval Dublin was known as Crocker's Bar. Occasionally, however, a -bar street name indicates the former presence of outer gates or wooden bars across streets designed for the collection of tolls or to mark the limits of suburbs. This is certainly the case with The Bars, Chester, which refers to the presence of the medieval Foregate (demolished 1770) that stood in front of the East Gate; other likely examples include Tollbar Street at Stockport and West Bars at Chesterfield.[6]

The many ways in which aspects of town defences could be reflected in street name evidence are represented well in the topography of the city of London.[7] In at least six cases, streets were named after the town gates with which they were associated: Aldersgate Street; Aldgate Street; Bishopsgate Street; Newgate Street; Ludgate Street; and Hog Street. The last two of these were associated with relatively minor gates: 'Ludgate' means 'back door or postern', while Hog Street (now Royal Mint Street) derives from the Old English *haecc* ('small gate or wicket'). Those few gates reflecting personal names (and therefore, perhaps, an original association with individuals) notably display pre-Norman nomenclature. The obvious examples are: Alvin's (*Aelfwyn's*) Gate and Aylesgate (*Aegel's Gate*), Gloucester; and Aldersgate, London, which was *Aldred's Gate* in the late Anglo-Saxon period.[8] Could this naming process reflect private qualities of residence, the patronage of building operations, or responsibilities for defence and maintenance? The notion put forward more than a century ago, that the *burhgeat* of a famous late Saxon document outlining the qualities of social ranks related not to the rural residences of the thegnly class but to their responsibility for the gateways of their local royal *burhs* or their residences in associated streets, might therefore deserve re-examination.[9]

In London, the street name Houndsditch reflects the position of the city ditch (and presumably something of its character: see page 162), and the street named London Wall intersects the line of the city wall. A tantalising reference in 1385-6 to the street name *Babeloyne* (Babylon) that ran along part of the city wall may well reflect a contemporary observation about the qualities of this feature, which was possibly compared to the Tower of Babel. Other street names indicating the former presence of defences may be more mundane, but still indicate something of the experience of living in the shadow of the town wall. In Wales or the marches we see examples such as Frog Street (Clun and Tenby) indicating a certain faunal presence in the town ditch; Darkgate Street (Aberystwyth and Carmarthen) and Dark Lane (Pembroke), showing the gloomy character of the intramural zone; and Hole-in-the-Wall Street (Caernarfon), indicating the position of a small postern.[10] A street name containing a rather different type of reference to a defensive circuit is Warser Gate, Nottingham, a compound of the Old English elements *weall* (wall) and *setu* (buildings), meaning 'buildings by the wall'.[11] At Bristol, the undeniable military properties of the town wall were reflected in the name Defence Street given to a route that hugged part of the line of the circuit, as recorded by William of Worcestre in the late fifteenth century.[12]

In other cases, and perhaps rather less commonly, gates were named after streets; Micklegate Bar and Walmgate Bar, York, are both examples of this. In the vast majority of cases, the name of a town gate described its location relative to the town (most commonly North, South, East and West Gates). In the thirteenth-century new town of Montgomery, the now vanished gate facing northwards was known in the post-medieval period as the 'Arthur Gate'. This apparently Celtic-associated name was actually a corruption of the Welsh word *Gorddwr*,[13] the name of the territory north of the lordship of Montgomery, towards which the gate faced. Many other gates were named after major topographical features, either in a general sense (e.g. Bridge Gate, Castle Gate, Water Gate), or more specifically (for example, Wye Gate and Monnow Gate, Monmouth, after the rivers of the same names).

Details of gates are also provided in written antiquarian accounts. Of these, few surpass the detail of William Worcestre, whose intricate account of the city of Bristol, written in August and September 1480, contains a wealth of detail about the town defences and their relationship with urban topography.[14] Of particular value was his metrological attention to defences, providing, for instance, the estimate that the 'Key and Marsh Wall' was 40ft high and 8ft wide, representing an invaluable source of information given the virtually total erosion of this feature from the townscape. The remarkable account includes references to no fewer than fifteen separate named gates: Aylward; Blind; Fromegate; Marsh; Marsh Street; Lawford's; Newgate; Oldgate; Pithay; Redcliffe; St Giles's; St John's; St Leonard's; St Nicholas's and Temple Street.

ARCHITECTURAL EVIDENCE

While examination of stylistic aspects of the architecture of town walls and related structures has an important role to play, so too has the systematic recording of surviving above-ground physical fabric in the form of drawings, photographs and digital records. Such records can provide the basis for strati-graphical analysis of standing fabric, whereby complex structures can be subdi-vided into periodic divisions and sub-phases. Related examination of other data, most notably documents and comparable architectural fabric from other buildings, can allow a framework for dating the construction and reconstruc-tion of town walls to be pieced together.

Quite how much impact such analytical techniques can have on our under-standing of a town wall's chronology is demonstrated clearly by the example of Exeter (*colour plate 16*). Here, painstaking recording of elevations of the city wall shed new light on the monument's complex phasing. During a total survey of the city walls carried out by Exeter Archaeology in 1993-4 a new interpreta-tion emerged for a puzzling component within a stretch of masonry whose complexity had already received attention from earlier commentators (*57* and *58*).[15] Near the northern corner of the walled circuit, where the Norman castle was inserted into the existing defences, a length of distinctive white Triassic sandstone work lies sandwiched between the grey-purple volcanic masonry of the Roman wall below and rougher rubble stonework above that resembles closely masonry on the Norman castle gatehouse (c.1068), and is therefore assumed to be broadly Norman.[16] Possible historical contexts for this work include Exeter's refurbishment as a *burh* in Alfred's reign, or its subsequent renovation in the tenth century, although an undocumented origin is of course far from impossible. Within the masonry in question are apparent the crenellations of a former wall top subsequently filled in and built up by the Norman work. The current ground surface lies at a height of 5-6m above the original surface, having been built up when the adjacent Norman castle was added, demonstrating the former crenellated parapet to have stood at an effectively defensible elevation above its contemporary ground surface. This masonry represents one of the exceptionally few fragments of recognisably late Saxon work visible in any town walls, and very probably the earliest surviving crenellations in Britain.

Wall-top crenellations 'fossilised' by later wall heightening are also visible in a small number of other cases, all of later medieval date. At York, a stretch of walling on the north-east of the city defences south of Monks Bar displays four blocked embrasures, demonstrating the wall-walk to have been raised over two metres.[17] A series of crenellations marking an earlier wall-top can also be noted in the town wall of Tenby, probably dating to the mid-thirteenth century and blocked during alterations of the fourteenth.[18] A rather different scenario is apparent at Canterbury, where a great chunk of the former Roman wall surviving to a height of c.6m was incorporated into the nave of St Mary Northgate church.[19] The crenellations, constructed primarily of knapped flint and rough sandstone and limestone blocks, appear likely to represent Norman renovation of a decaying but still monumental structure; while difficult to date, the subsequent raising of the wall level may be twelfth- or thirteenth-century. The stretch of wall on the site of Balkerne Gate (*66*), on the west side of Colchester's circuit is another where possible early medieval fabric may be recognised. At this point of the enceinte, a substantial wall of distinctive roughly coursed masonry blocks a Roman gateway of at least two phases. During excavations in the early part of the twentieth century, Wheeler assumed the blocking wall which, lacking peg tiles was most unlike the Roman masonry apparent in much of the rest of the circuit, to be Saxon. This rebuild could feasibly date to the reconditioning of the town's defences by Edward the Elder, although in the absence of independent dating evidence a late Roman or Norman date cannot be ruled out.[20] The Balkerne Gate at Colchester represents an extremely rare instance where the fabric of a Roman gate has been incorporated into a later circuit; the two other obvious examples are the Newport Arch, Lincoln (*24*) and Queningate, Canterbury, which survived intact until the late medieval period when it was blocked up, leaving the evidence of part of its relieving arch in the city wall.

66 Colchester: Balkerne Gate, showing surviving Roman masonry. *Authors' collection*

Another valuable mode of architectural enquiry is identification of the sources of materials used in town walls. Something of the immense potential of this type of work is demonstrated by an innovative survey of reused medieval ship's ballast built into the town wall of King's Lynn.[21] Of the estimated *c.*55,000 separate constituents of the surviving town wall, ranging from ashlar blocks to fragments of furnace slag, the number of identifiable ballast cobbles is approximately *c.*3,000, including examples from many areas of Sweden and south-west Finland (*colour plate 17*). As well as indicating how materials were incorporated into the wall in an apparently *ad hoc* manner, this evidence also shows how study of town walls can open windows into the wider medieval world – in this case illuminating the medieval port's place within a commercial network extending to the Baltic. The choice of flint as the main building material at Norwich, and the large quantities of mortar consequently used in its construction, mean that here individual 'lifts' (short episodes of building necessary to allow the masonry to settle) are particularly visible, each being *c.*0.3–0.5m in height.[22] As in all forms of medieval masonry, the choice of raw material influenced substantially not only the nature of the immediate product, but also its longer-term legacy. Materials were susceptible to weathering and wear to different degrees and also varied in their visual appeal and usefulness to later communities who so frequently used relict or decaying town walls as quarries. Different types of raw materials also, of course, lend Britain's town walls much of their individual character, an individuality that also formed part of wider traditions of building within regions and sub-regions seen in secular and ecclesiastical building generally.

Construction of town walls and gates in brick required rather different arrangements. This phenomenon was restricted to eastern England, and demonstrated most notably at Beverley and Kingston-upon-Hull. The finest of Beverley's gates and the best surviving example in England of a brick-built town gate is the North Bar (67), totally rebuilt in 1409-10 at a cost of £90 0s 11½d.[23] Hull was established by Edward I in 1293 (the first charter dates to 1299); its walls, containing an estimated 4.7 million bricks were largely a creation of the fourteenth century, representing the largest brick-built structure since the Roman period (68). The speed with which the town's earlier timber palisade was replaced with this wall from the late 1330s was limited not only by the funds available, but the annual capacity of the Royal or Corporation brick-yards, which in the fourteenth and fifteenth centuries averaged c.100,000 bricks, meaning that the walls were not completed until c.1409.[24] A plan of the town by Wenceslaus Hollar, made c.1540, reveals that the walls incorporated a mixture of some 30 rectangular, square and half round towers as well as posterns. Lengths of internal brick arcading, as at London, Norwich, Yarmouth and King's Lynn (masonry equivalents survive internally at Tenby and York and externally at Southampton), can also be identified on the plan,

67 Beverley: North Bar. *Authors' collection*

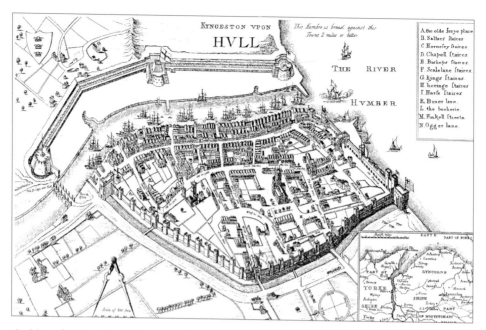

68 Map of Hull and its defences, as depicted by Wenceslaus Hollar in the seventeenth century

highlighting something of an eastern tradition, as can a brick-built 'alure' (a wall-walk immediately behind the parapet that surmounted the arcades).[25] When Henry VIII upgraded Hull's defences through the provision of an outer brick wall punctuated by three artillery forts, mixed building technologies seem to have been used, as building stone was recycled from monastic properties including Meaux Abbey.[26]

Brick was used fairly extensively in repairs to London's city wall from the fourteenth century onwards, with new work characterised by layers of brick and tile courses with Kentish ragstone.[27] The brick diaper work on portions of the London wall (*colour plate 18*) represent repairs attributable to the initiative of mayor Ralph Jocelin in the late 1470s; while a decorative quality to this work is undeniable, brick-built arches added in places to the back of the wall at this time may have been a measure designed to counter gunpowder artillery. On the north-west side of the city, Cripplegate, rebuilt from *c*.1490 following an earlier bequest from the mayor Edmund Shaa, may similarly have been a brick-built structure.[28] Financial accounts of building work at Conwy provide a tentative hint that parts of the walled circuit were not faced with bare masonry. Records for the 1285-6 building season, which focused on the southern section of the town walls, include references to the 'daubing' of the battlements of five towers for a cost of £1 5s 0d, six intervening lengths of walling at a cost of £3, and parts of the Mill Gate for 16s 0d.[29]

The survival rate of town gates presents a paradox. Although in the medieval period these structures represented the most prestigious and expensive elements of their circuits, in the post-medieval and modern periods their constricting effect on traffic led to them being swept away in large numbers (see page 236). This must represent one of the most significant losses of a major category of medieval monument, making the surviving handful of examples all the more important. To an extent, this great loss is offset by the wealth of pictorial sources, including engravings, maps and paintings, which so often depict town gates not only as structures but also in relation to urban topography. The volume of documentary and pictorial evidence that might exist for demolished town gates means that extremely detailed reconstructions are often possible; one example of such a thoroughly studied structure is the South Gate of Exeter (69-70) (see page 138).[30]

Allowing for the possible skewing of the data set by the small number of surviving examples, two fundamentally important observations may be made about the architecture of town gates. First, the plans and elevations of town gates are immensely varied, and cannot be organised neatly into a typology representing a clear chronological sequence, and 'one off' designs, such as the 'Five Arches' gate at Tenby can be recognised (*colour plate 19*). This individuality in design parallels the similar phenomenon in the sphere of medieval castle-building: just as the castle was the defining symbol of power and wealth for the landowning classes, so the city gate represented the power and wealth of the urban oligarchy. If the development of the plans of town gates is examined, the 'typology' is actually circular. Thus the sequence demonstrates the 'outmoding' of rectangular twelfth-century forms (e.g. Monk Bar and Bootham Bar, York), with structures incorporating rounded towers, at first as

69 Exeter: engraving of South Gate in the early nineteenth century

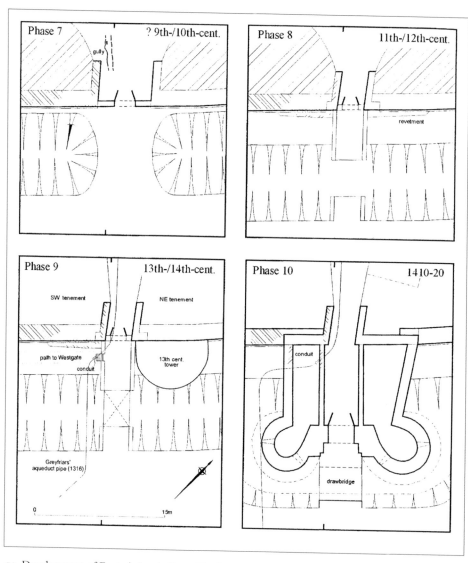

70 Development of Exeter's South Gate. *Henderson 2001*

curved projections (e.g. Caernarfon Westgate *c.*1283-6 and Conwy Upper Gate *c.*1283-6) then as fully-fledged circular towers (e.g. New Winchelsea Strandgate *c.*1350 and Canterbury West Gate *c.*1380), before reverting back to the rectangular plan, either in monumental form (e.g. Winchester West Gate *c.*1390-6 and King's Lynn South Gate *c.*1520), or less impressive structures (e.g. New Winchelsea Pipewell Gate *c.*1404 and Alnwick Bondgate *c.*1434-50). Analogous in a sense is the chronology of mural towers on the circuits of Canterbury and London, where rectangular forms were added to circuits otherwise featuring towers or bastions of rounded form. At London, three rectangular towers and one polygonal tower punctuated the extension of the city wall around Blackfriars in the 1270s, while at Canterbury square mural towers on the north side of the circuit were additions of Thomas Chillenden, prior of the neighbouring Christchurch Priory, in the period 1391-1411.[31] In the period of early experimentation with artillery fortification, rectangular or square forms could apparently have advantages; for instance, in the defences around Portsmouth harbour and town, the Round Tower (*c.*1415) was an earlier development than the Square Tower (*c.*1494).[32]

Second, most town gates are not single-phase monuments but demonstrate the addition and removal of fabric over long periods of time, as demonstrated, for instance, by the gates of Winchester. While the north and south gates, which had been blocked in the early medieval period and later reopened protruded from the defences, the others, with a continuous history from the Roman period, remained confined within the line of the wall itself. The Southampton Bargate is another complex multi-phase monument, originating as a simple tower-like structure in the late twelfth century, then unattached to any town wall (*71*). Later alterations saw the addition of two great flanking towers and a first-floor hall equipped for ceremonial occasions and used as a guildhall, and an elaborate crenellated and machicolated façade.[33] As this example so ably illustrates, town gates represent strikingly multifunctional features of medieval architecture, fulfilling a number of requirements, most notably those of defence and the control of traffic, and often others such as civic display, accommodation, and judicial and financial activity. While these varied functions are apparent in the documentary record, what is notable is that most can also be deduced from the physical fabric of the buildings themselves and from the architectural details within them when the buildings are, however infrequently, well-preserved.

Town gates frequently featured architectural elaboration not found on other features of the circuit; at Denbigh and Sandwich surviving gates display decorative chequer-work (*72-73*). On occasion, statuettes or other representations on gates featured prominent personalities associated with the city. Sometimes these figures might be religious icons or mythical figures, as on town gates at Bristol (Brennus and Belinus, St John's Gate: *colour plate 20*) and York (Ebraucus, Bootham Bar). Another type of association is demonstrated by the

71 Southampton: exterior view of Bargate, showing the (now free-standing) gate on the northern side of the medieval town, adorned with civic iconography and trappings of military architecture. *Authors' collection*

72 Denbigh: Burgess Gate, showing chequered masonry on the upper part of the western flanking tower. *Authors' collection*

73 Sandwich: The Barbican, a late medieval town gate with flint chequer-work in its flanking towers. *Authors' collection*

depiction of the emblem of the Cinque Ports on one of Rye's dismantled gates (74). At Alnwick, the surviving gate displays an eroded panel featuring the lion associated with the local Percy family – a relatively unusual display of seigneurial loyalty expressed in town gate iconography (75). Very often, the icons displayed on town gates displayed a partnership of interests, for instance by juxtaposing the royal coat of arms with that of the city. Royal coats of arms as well as those of the city are represented on all of York's four surviving gates; the stone figurines surmounting the parapets of three of them are known to have been in existence by at least the seventeenth century and represent part of a distinctly northern tradition better represented in castle architecture, as at Alnwick and Hylton. Three contrasting examples, from towns with gates now demolished, further illustrate this blending of iconographies on town gates. For example, the exterior of Exeter's massive South Gate, rebuilt in the early fifteenth century, displayed a niche containing a robed figure and angels, supporting both the royal arms and the city arms; when the East Gate was rebuilt on an equally massive scale in 1511-14, it was adorned with a statue of Henry VII over its archway.[34] The North and South Gates of Bath give another useful indication of the types of contrasting identity that might be reflected in town gate architecture. While both of these structures were dismantled entirely in 1755, their external appearances can be reconstructed in detail from a sketch

74 Rye: plaque from a
demolished town gate, depicting
the emblem of the Cinque Ports;
this is only remaining vestige of
the gate. *Authors' collection*

map of the city made by a Frenchman in *c.*1650.[35] The North Gate featured a
statue of the legendary King of Bath, Bladud, over the main gate passage, while
the South Gate displayed three niches, the central one featuring Edward III,
flanked by Ralph de Salopia (diocesan bishop) and John de Walcot (prior of
Bath). Replacement of the arms over town gates could also reflect changing
allegiances in changing political climates; at Leicester, for instance, the king's
arms were taken down in 1649-50 to be rapidly replaced by those of the
Commonwealth, which were themselves swapped with those of Charles II
following the Restoration in 1660.[36]

Documentary evidence also makes clear that the visual appearance of town
gates could be rapidly altered in order to welcome dignitaries processing into
the urban zone. Such actions often took the form of cleaning, repainting or
adding new heraldic symbols, or the addition of temporary features and decorations. At Exeter, visiting kings or their representatives were always met by
both the mayor and the aldermen at a town gate, where the iconography of
royal and civic coats of arms was particularly appropriate. Such visits included
Henry VI in 1451, Richard III in 1483, Henry VII in 1497, the Earl of Bedford
in 1558, and Charles I in 1664.[37] Some measure of the types of elaborate
ceremony that could accompany these events is provided by a detailed description of Henry VII's procession through Micklegate Bar, York, in 1484, high-

75 Alnwick: Bondgate; the weathered remains of a Percy lion can be distinguished on the panel between the flanking towers. *Authors' collection*

lighting the almost theatrical role of the town defences in a staged ceremony loaded with imagery and allusions. The gate was elaborately decorated with an artificial structure, including a representation of heaven, and trees and flowers bowing beneath the red and white roses; on entering a packed city, the king was welcomed with verse by Ebrauk, the legendary founder of the city and presented with a crown and keys.[38] Even in the Elizabethan era town gates could be given a makeover to welcome the monarch; at Leicester, for instance, when the queen was expected in 1602-03 the East Gate was painted and the West Gate washed and laid out in colours.[39]

Britain preserves only two intact examples of medieval bridge gates: Monmouth and Warkworth,[40] although comparable structures are known from documentary or cartographic sources but have no surviving physical traces, including examples at Bedford, Caernarfon, Holt, London, Newcastle, Norwich, Shrewsbury and Worcester. While none of the four main medieval gates of Monmouth survive, the Monnow bridge-gate was distinctive in that it rises directly from a bridge pier (*76; colour plate 21*). Located on the south side of the Monnow (on the opposite bank to the town) and dating from the late thirteenth or early fourteenth century, this compact structure incorporates fine architectural detailing including a corbelled garderobe and prominent machicolation, which may be a later medieval addition.[41] Notably, the gate was

143

76 Monmouth: architectural elevation of the Monnow Bridge gate. *Rowlands 1993*

not integrated within the original line of the town's defences, but was an outlying feature, located *c*.330m south-west of the town's West Gate. At Warkworth (*64*), the simple rectangular gatehouse, which incorporates a side guard chamber, lies on the town side of the river. At Chester the Outer Bridgegate lay at the far end of the Old Dee Bridge; while the gate was demolished in the late eighteenth century its former location is apparent in the substantial nature of the bridge's southernmost pier.

The Littlegate at Oxford and East Gate at Warwick were among the many medieval gates featuring two entrances to the town: a larger arch spanning the roadway and a separate, smaller arch for pedestrians. Very few gates preserve evidence of associated barbicans: Walmgate, York, is alone in preserving an intact example (*77*), though fragments can also be identified at Conwy (Upper Gate, with arrow loops) and Hull (the partially excavated Beverley Gate), while the West Gate at Caernarfon has something between a barbican and a porch.

Many clear links between the architecture of town gates and those of castles can be identified; crucially, however, the process of emulation was not 'one-way traffic', with the designers of town gates borrowing from castle architecture. Depictions of the (now demolished) Eastgate of Chester highlight a marked similarity between this structure and the king's gate of Caernarfon, particularly in its elaborate arrangement of decorative niches.[42] Far more than simply demonstrating a process of emulation, this town gate is but one manifestation of Chester's prosperity in the late thirteenth and early fourteenth centuries, when it became the key centre for the organisation of Edward I's campaigns in North Wales, which included the construction of Caernarfon

77 York: Walmgate, showing the surviving medieval barbican. *Authors' collection*

town and castle. As has been emphasised (see page 84), in many instances town defences were effectively extensions of the outer defences of a castle. In places such as Chepstow, Carlisle and Pembroke, the character of work in the town walls is paralleled closely in distinct episodes of building visible in the castle itself, which can provide valuable information relating to the dating of town circuits. At Pembroke, the mural tower known as Barnard's Tower may well have been the residence of an officer of the castle (*78*). It projected on a short spur-work from the furthest point on the circuit from the castle and, with its own portcullis, fireplace, latrine, windows and probable drawbridge has something of the character of a self-contained donjon.[43]

Mural towers take a great variety of forms, and like gates show no clear and explicable sequence of development, as demonstrated by the walls of York which feature a mixture of semi-circular, polygonal and rectangular structures. The only known mural tower with upstanding remains for which an early-medieval origin has been claimed is the 'Anglian Tower' at York, excavated in 1970 having been discovered in 1842 when the Recorder of York hit upon the structure during tunnelling operations designed to provide access to his stables in King's Manor (*colour plate 22*). Comprising a rectangular structure of oolitic limestone, measuring *c*.3.6 by 3.1m and surviving to a height of 4.7m, the tower was inserted into and projected above the Roman walls but was subsequently encased in the Viking-period bank. This feature was interpreted by its excavator, as a seventh-century addition to the defences, though reassessment based primarily on the nature of its building materials has suggested it may rather relate to an episode of refurbishment in the fourth

78 Pembroke: Barnard's Tower, on the eastern extremity of the circuit. *Authors' collection*

century AD.[44] Mural towers are markedly less common in seigneurial boroughs; as at Denbigh (colour plate 23) where the disposition of towers is far less ordered than in the royal boroughs of Conwy (79) and Caernarfon not far away, while at Oswestry, Leland noted that the circuit (now demolished) did not feature any towers.

Only Oxford had truly concentric masonry defences (colour plate 24; see also page 161), though on part of the circuit only. The distinctive double-lobed oillets in the arrow slits of the bastions in the surviving inner wall can, by analogy with Caernarfon Castle, be possibly dated to the 1280s, raising the likelihood that these features are later insertions or else demonstrating that the open-backed bastions (80) were themselves additions to the city wall.[45] Yet concentricity was not an innovation of the late thirteenth century, as often claimed. By the late 1220s, for instance, the southern side of Rochester's circuit was marked by two ditches (one (Deanery Garden Ditch) an earlier feature, and the other (King's Orchard Ditch), a later addition); another town with multiple ditches was Southampton.[46] Southampton also preserves one remarkable example of a mural tower adapted from an earlier feature, probably in the fourteenth century. A tower on that part of the circuit immediately north of God's House Tower started life as a dovecote (the chequered pattern of nesting boxes still being visible inside), and was incorporated into the circuit having been partially demolished in the second quarter of the fourteenth century to give it a 'gap-backed' appearance (81).[47]

A clear example of why the physical designs of town walls might not have been designed purely for communal interest is provided by the unique series of twelve privies corbelled out en echelon from the wall of Conwy (colour plate 25). Despite their superficial appearance of a public facility, this was not so. Rather, the accounts relating to their construction in 1286 make it clear that these facilities were built to serve the staff in an adjacent administrative complex comprising the hall of the king's wardrobe and the office of the master of the king's works in Wales.[48] The 'Garret' on the wall of Southampton was another non-public suite of latrines; later known as the 'longiles' or 'fryers jakes' they discharged into the town ditch and were accessible from the friary immediately inside the walls.[49] Single garderobes can be identified in mural towers at Denbigh and Newcastle (colour plate 26), and William of Worcestre's late fifteenth-century account of Bristol suggests that a public latrine lay inside the line of the town wall.[50] At Exeter the 'towne jakes' or public lavatories were situated inside the south-eastern angle of the city defences from the end of the sixteenth century, discharging their waste into the Exe via a stone-built outfall built into the wall.[51]

Usually, square holes on the internal or external faces of town walls can be identified as 'putlog' holes formerly supporting temporary timber scaffolding during the building operation. These are most commonly found in horizontal lines (e.g. Chepstow), although the Edwardian boroughs show examples of

79 Conwy: town walls around the Edwardian borough, as viewed from the south. *Authors' collection*

80 Oxford: mural tower in the grounds of New College, with a 'gap-backed' design and wall walk to either side. *Authors' collection*

81 Southampton: a medieval dovecote converted into a mural tower. *Authors' collection*

'helicoidal' arrangements of putlogs spiralling around towers (e.g. Conwy). In other cases, rows of holes could indicate the former presence of more permanent structures. In a stretch of the town wall of Norwich near the Black Tower, for instance, two rows of brick-lined holes indicate a platform allowing access to a series of arrow loops (*82*), which are set in the wall well above ground level and could not otherwise have been reached. At Tenby, improvements to the town wall in the fourteenth century clearly involved the addition of major timber components, including overhanging hourds, the former presence of which is indicated by groups of joist-holes suggesting structures of *c*.3-4m length (*83*).[52]

ARCHAEOLOGICAL EVIDENCE

An examination of the results of the numerous modern excavations on medieval town walls that have been carried out, especially from the 1950s, demonstrates many ways in which archaeology has thrown new light on the subject but also, it is tempting to argue, highlights many inherent 'limitations' in the method that arise because archaeological data are not always suited to answering the sorts of 'historical' questions that we might often wish to pose.[53] The excavation of a town wall is unlikely to be able to confirm or deny that the structure was built on or immediately after the first date at which a murage grant for a particular town is recorded. In contrast, excavation can prove especially illuminating where it produces data that contradict assumptions based on documentary evidence and prompts reassessment. At Bury St Edmunds, for instance, documentary evidence has been commonly thought to indicate the walling of the planned town under Abbot Anselm (1121-48), yet excavation has shown one portion of the projected wall to have been seventeenth century in date and the original circuit — in at least this one place — to comprise only a ditch and rampart.[54] It is also highly significant that while much debate about the functions of town defences has concentrated on the period from the thirteenth century onwards, much new archaeological information has illuminated the importance of defence in late Saxon and Norman townscapes, which is particularly important given the relative dearth of documentary evidence for these periods.

82 Norwich: a late medieval brick-built arrow loop on the east side of the circuit. *Authors' collection*

83 Tenby: holes for timber hourding in the town wall. *Authors' collection*

The spatial limitations of excavation, however, ensure that only rarely have sections through entire defensive zones been observed, while practical factors mean that excavation of town ditches to their full depth is very uncommon (*84*). A prominent case in point where the cumulative results of excavations and interventions made necessary by restoration have elucidated not only specific details at particular points on a circuit, but have revealed a broader picture of town defence evolution from Roman to modern times, was the work carried out at Chester in the 1980s. Here, a sequence has been established indicating how the original Roman defences decayed and were subsequently rebuilt in the medieval and later centuries prior to conservation in the modern period (*85*).[55] Where sections across the lines of buried walls have been excavated, it is not uncommon for actual physical fabric of masonry to be absent due to stone robbing, leaving 'robber trenches' containing only the vestiges of discarded masonry cores. The date of such activity may be surprisingly early. At Barnstaple, for example, parts of the wall had been robbed entirely by the end of the thirteenth century, reflecting a decline in defensive considerations at a time when the castle lords were non-resident and the castle in disrepair.[56] The sequential nature of many excavated town defences sometimes demonstrates that it is unclear at which stage a town became enclosed in a military as opposed to a purely jurisdictional sense. Construction of Hartlepool's town wall in the fourteenth century, for instance, followed a bank and ditch of two

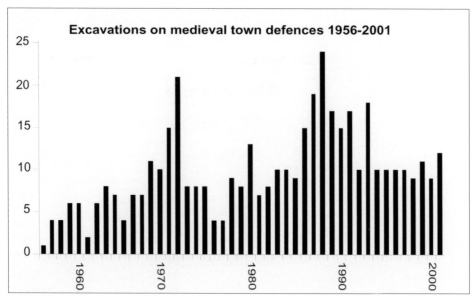

Excavations on medieval town defences 1956-2001

84 Excavations on medieval town defences in England and Wales, 1957-2001, as recorded in the journal *Medieval Archaeology*; structural surveys are excluded, as are excavations that revealed negative evidence

phases, the first a slight earthwork apparently marking out a perimeter and the second a more imposing work comprising a bank *c*.2m high and *c*.8.5m wide and an accompanying ditch.[57] The excavated town ditch of Farnham further illustrates this problem of defining exactly what constitutes archaeological evidence of defence. In existence by the early thirteenth century but largely infilled by the middle of that century, the ditch was *c*.8.5m wide and 2.5m deep, without positive evidence of an associated bank.[58] Defining a rectangular planned borough adjacent to a bishop's castle, it is likely that this work defined the status and exclusivity of the settlement, although it is possible that the ecclesiastical nature of the lordship also limited the ability of the community to develop town defences to any level of sophistication (see page 218). In many such places, which lack murage grants or where other documentation is thinner, archaeology has more potential to make an independent contribution to understanding the origins and development of town defence.

At its crudest, excavation has been used as a means of 'wall-chasing', simply removing overburden to define the lines of lost portions of circuits or test for evidence of masonry beneath earthworks, as carried out at Montgomery in the first half of the twentieth century.[59] An especially seminal excavation in the development of town wall studies was that carried out at Roushill, Shrewsbury in the late 1950s.[60] Here, the application of rigorous excavation and recording techniques highlighted one way in which archaeology could cast new light on an aspect of town defences not fully recorded in documentary sources: the

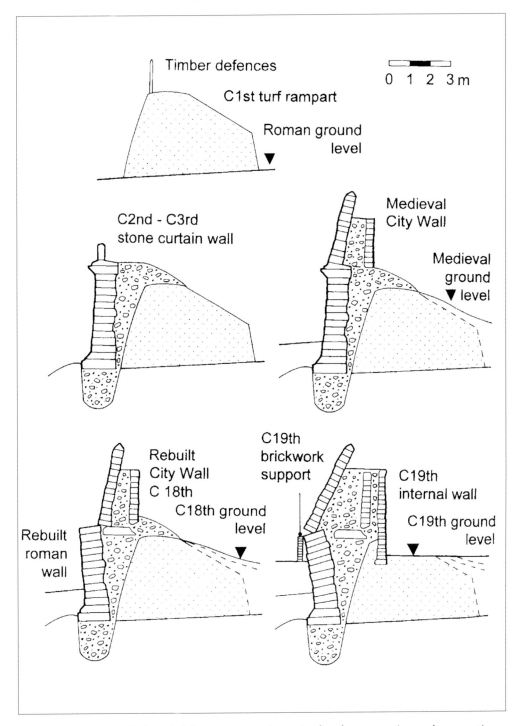

Timber defences

C1st turf rampart

Roman ground level

0 1 2 3 m

C2nd - C3rd stone curtain wall

Medieval City Wall

Medieval ground level

Rebuilt City Wall C 18th

C18th ground level

C19th brickwork support

C19th internal wall

C19th ground level

Rebuilt roman wall

85 The development of Chester's defences: a composite section based on excavations and conservation work. *LeQuesne 1999*

details of their construction processes (*86*). Erection of the town wall in the thirteenth century was preceded by systematic stripping of the ground surface down to natural clay and the creation of a substantial bank *c.*7ft (2.1m) high and at least *c.*30ft (9.1m) wide that was to back the masonry. The lower courses were carefully laid, comprising facing stones that had a parallelogram shape in section (so they would bed down naturally against the rubble core), above a plinth stepped to reflect the slope on which the wall was built. The zone immediately in front of the wall was consolidated with pebbles rammed into the clay surface to form an access path; other evidence of construction techniques included a large lime-slaking pit immediately behind the wall and a slotted and sharpened oak beam forming part of a scaffold structure. Other excavations have illuminated different aspects of the wall-building sequence. A section through part of the defences of Great Yarmouth has shown the thirteenth-century town wall to have been built as a revetment to a large flat-bottomed ditch lined with flagstones that provided a level foundation.[61] At

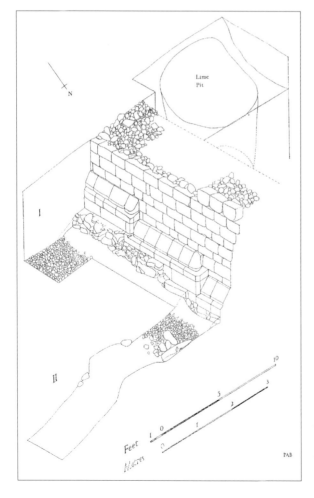

86 Three-dimensional reconstruction of the foundations of Shrewsbury's medieval town defences, based on excavated evidence. *Barker 1961*

Lincoln, excavation of the Lucy Tower, built *c.*1250 as the terminus to a spur of the town defences built to overlook Brayfood Pool, showed that the marshy site for the tower was painstakingly consolidated (*87*), including the construction of a platform comprising vertical timber piles wedged between limestone slabs, a framework of horizontal beams, and a thick matting of grass, twigs and reeds to create a stable construction surface.[62]

Another important contribution of archaeology is where excavated evidence challenges or contradicts broad historical assumptions that town walls were necessarily monumental and impressive both militarily and visually. At Southampton, for instance, excavations across part of the eastern defences revealed a rather feeble wall. Founded on three courses of unmortared masonry and with an unmortared core, the wall was in its lower levels only 0.76m thick.[63] Later alterations to the wall, as observed through excavations, seem to have been designed to compensate for its initial weakness: in the fourteenth century parts of the rampart were raised to strengthen the stonework, while in the fifteenth century a trench was dug behind it and filled with masonry.[64] There can have been few town walls, however, that were as flimsy as that surrounding Pembroke. Trial excavations on the north side of the defences near the castle showed the wall in this sector to have foundations on a shallow subsoil terrace merely 0.65m thick, this to support a wall 0.54m in its upper

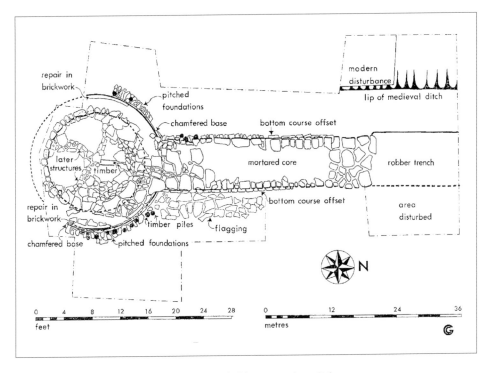

87 Plan of the Lucy Tower, Lincoln, as revealed by excavation. *Colyer 1975*

parts.[65] In both these cases we should remember that the wall was but one element in the town's defences; at Southampton, the wall would have relied also on its associated bank for strength, while at Pembroke the wall was largely a revetment of a natural slope rather than a free-standing structure.

Other excavated examples add to the impression of a sometimes lackadaisical approach to town wall building. The thirteenth-century rebuilding of Winchester's city wall has been shown to have involved the refacing of the outer edge of the surviving Roman core-work, meaning that the medieval defences were far thinner and weaker than their Roman counterparts.[66] At Boston, excavation on the line of the Bar Dyke, the line of the town's defensive perimeter from the early thirteenth century, revealed a brick wall on the ditch's inner lip only 0.6m in thickness, which seemed to be an addition of the four-teenth century, while the surviving sixteenth-century parapet wall at Hastings is similarly 0.65-0.7m thick.[67] Poor building practice has also been observed in the study of standing fabric at a number of other towns, further underlining the importance of not necessarily assuming wall construction to have been sophisticated (as at Kings Lynn: see page 134).

Edinburgh is another town where archaeology has shown that medieval town walls could be almost ramshackle constructions. Excavation of sections of the King's Wall has shown this part of the circuit to have comprised an uneven structure following a wandering zigzag line that suggests it was built, at least in part, by 'back-dyking', whereby individual burgesses were respon-sible for separate sections of the defensive line along their plots.[68] The wall is first recorded in 1427 and was strengthened in 1450 by a royal warrant obliging the burgesses to look to the defences of the town; it seems to have been built expediently by linking together extant walls at the point of development furthest from the street frontage. The construction of town walls by gang-building also frequently shows up clearly in the archaeological record. At Nottingham, excavations on Park Row showed the patchy and different quality of work in immediately adjacent areas of the wall, suggesting that one gang had economised on masonry and skimped alarmingly on foundations.[69] In other cases the sites for town walls could be prepared but the defences left incomplete: excavation on the Shire Hall yard site, Ipswich, for example, shows that at this place on the projected circuit a foundation trench was dug but the wall was not actually built.[70]

When conducted at sufficient scale, excavation can also explore the rela-tionship between defensive features and changing patterns of settlement both within and beyond the perimeter. At Shrewsbury, two medieval merchant's houses on the north-west side of the town have been shown to have been built directly over the wall, which was adapted to form undercrofts (88), little more than a century after its construction in the first half of the thirteenth century.[71] Multiple episodes of settlement encroachment and clearance were demon-strated through excavation near the town wall of Norwich in the Barn Road

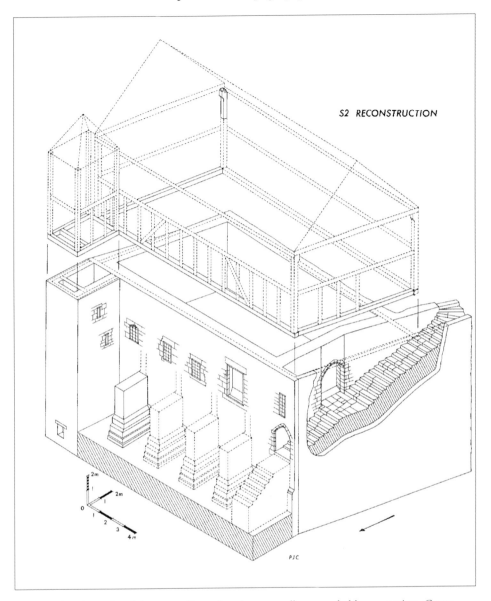

S2 RECONSTRUCTION

88 A medieval merchant's house on Shrewsbury's town wall, as revealed by excavation. *Carver 1977-78*

area.[72] Construction of the city bank and wall in the thirteenth century was preceded by the clearance of a pre-existing settlement; shortly after an informal squatter settlement encroached on the intramural lane behind the wall, prior to its eventual clearance to make way for a metalled road *c.*1500. At Wallingford, the north gate of the town was partly levelled and buried as part of a massive extension of the castle's defences in the period *c.*1275-1300, having been built only *c.*1250.[73] In this particular townscape there was no doubt where the power lay, the removal of the gate coinciding with a re-routing of the road from the north, providing a staged and carefully composed view of the castle with its elaborate remodelled defences and the neighbouring Benedictine priory.

Particularly telling has been the contribution of archaeology to understanding the plans of circuits built in earth and timber. In numerous cases, excavation has highlighted the existence of ramparted and ditched perimeters where previous evidence for defences was entirely lacking, or where fortifications underlying masonry defences were unsuspected. Many informative excavations on circuits never rebuilt in stone have taken place. At Tonbridge, the U-shaped town ditch was c.3.6m deep and 12.5m wide and the bank was c.2.1m high.[74] At Devizes, the ditch was V-shaped, c.5m deep and 9m across, but with no surviving bank.[75] At Taunton, the defences of the early thirteenth century represented the upgrading of an earlier earthwork of little more than jurisdictional function; the recut ditch was c.10m wide and 4m deep, and accompanied by a rampart 11–12m wide and 3m high.[76] The ditched and ramparted settlement enclosure attached to Boteler's Castle, Warwickshire, was unknown prior to rescue excavations in the early 1990s, which provided a far more detailed insight not only into defences, but the social and economic life of the short-lived community within them (see page 84). Representing far more than an outwork of the castle, these defences comprised a ditch in places over 7m wide and 3m deep, and while no associated bank survived, the line of a gully formerly running along its tail suggested that the rampart would have been over eight metres wide.[77]

Excavations in the vicinity of the London wall in the Cripplegate area have also afforded rare insight into the appearance of urban fortifications in the later Saxon period. Much evidence recovered in the wake of the Blitz has been re-evaluated and bought to publication;[78] of particular significance here is the evidence that the town ditch was cut in the late Saxon period, perhaps around 950, before substantial enlargement in the later medieval period. That the ditch, estimated to have been c.15m across, was constructed so as to leave a berm of c.15m between it and the former Roman wall may be highly significant. This may well indicate that the intervening space was taken up with a bank built against the wall in order to strengthen it, thus giving a possible indication of the wall's incomplete or semi-ruinous state at this time.

Another scenario is where archaeology has identified earlier unknown defensive circuits lying entirely within later walled perimeters. At Abergavenny, for instance, excavations in 2001 on the hillslope beneath the ridge-top castle revealed a substantial V-shaped ditch that seemed to define the perimeter of a Norman enclosed town whose rectangular defences defined a far smaller area than the later medieval oval *enceinte*.[79] This seems to have been a short-term fortification only, however, with clear evidence that it was infilled in the twelfth century, perhaps due to pressure on land, and seemingly leaving the growing town unenclosed in the interval before the redefinition of its defences in stone in the later medieval period.

In most cases, we may assume that banks carried timber palisades. While in certain cases evidence of former masonry remains or the vestiges of timber defences will have proved elusive owing to robbing and episodes of reuse and disturbance, we should bear in mind that in certain contexts towns may have been surrounded by bare earthworks alone. This may have been the case at Richard's Castle, where an embankment enclosing a small (and now largely deserted) settlement was added to the earthworks of a motte and bailey castle. Excavation of a section through this earthwork revealed the profile of a ditch 16ft (5.9m) wide x 12ft (3.7m) deep and a bank 8ft (2.4m) high and 37ft (11.3m) wide, yet with no indications of an associated wall or palisade.[80]

Yet an enormous question mark still remains over the appearance of the timber structures that must have crowned most earthworks. Traces of extant timbers have been almost totally lacking and evidence in the form of post-holes and slots for beams intangible, due to poor conditions of preservation and, in particular, the simple fact that many such circuits were rebuilt in stone, as well as the nature and extent of many of the excavations. Overall, the total data set compares very poorly indeed with the state of knowledge concerning earth and timber castles. On this analogous subject the documentary, pictorial and archaeological evidence sustain a thorough analysis,[81] and it is to such sites that we must turn for indications of contemporary technologies. But excavations on the city defences of Hereford have revealed a rare glimpse of the type of timber superstructure that might surmount an earthen circuit (*89*).[82] In one corner of the newly extended early thirteenth-century circuit, an arrangement of post-holes indicated a timber watchtower with accompanying cess pit, this having a short existence, however, being swept way when the defensive line was strengthened with a bastioned wall. Another scrap of direct archaeological evidence for the appearance of timber town defences has come from Warwick. Here, excavations on the northern defences of the Norman town, which had expanded beyond the perimeter of the *burh* to enclose suburban growth, revealed a series of post pits (*c.*0.3m diameter) on the rampart, suggesting a post-and-rail palisade structure.[83]

The fortifications built to enclose boroughs attached to the first two of Edward I's great castles in North Wales – Flint and Rhuddlan – demand particular attention on account of their apparently unique designs, begun more or less simultaneously in 1278 and illuminated by excavation in the early 1970s. The format of the defences, both comprising sub-rectangular circuits appended to castles, was so similar as to indicate a common design comprising a broad flat-bottomed ditch between two massive banks. At Rhuddlan, two sections near the north corner demonstrated the ditch to be 14m wide and 2.75m deep, the inner bank to be 13.40-18m wide, and the outer bank to be between 12.20-13.70m across (*90*).[84] At Flint, a section through the south-east

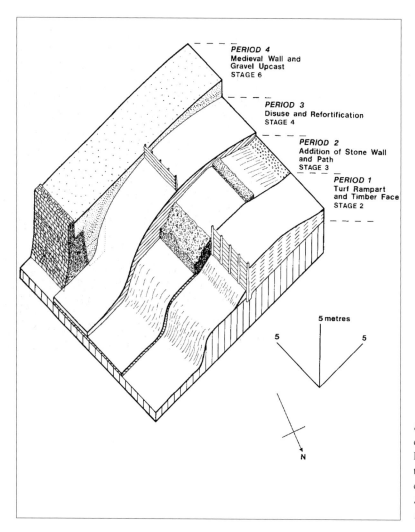

PERIOD 4
Medieval Wall and
Gravel Upcast
STAGE 6

PERIOD 3
Disuse and Refortification
STAGE 4

PERIOD 2
Addition of Stone Wall
and Path
STAGE 3

PERIOD 1
Turf Rampart
and Timber Face
STAGE 2

5 metres

5   5

N

89 Phased diagram of Hereford's town defences. *Shoesmith 1982*

defences in the early 1970s revealed the ditch to be 16m wide and 3m deep, and the inner bank to be 17m wide, although traces of the outer bank did not survive (91).[85] The carefully planned character was further indicated by small 'marking-out' trenches in front of the inner bank and to the rear of the outer banks. In their original form, these features thus defined a belt approximately 50m across. Given the perimeters of these sites (Rhuddlan, built against a bank of the Clywd, *c.*900m, and Flint *c.*1550m), the entire areas taken up with defences must have been in the region of five and eight hectares respectively. What is clear is both that these two works represent the design of town defences to a common plan, and also reflect a level of experimentation that characterises the designs of the castles themselves. Given the total absence of evidence for timber superstructures, somewhat less certain is precisely what these massive labour-intensive works were designed to achieve or whether the

90 An excavated
section through the
Edwardian borough
defences of Rhuddlan.
Henrietta Quinnell

designs were actually realised. Indeed, documentary sources suggest that the
vast stock of timber transported from Delaware Forest to Rhuddlan in the
spring and autumn of 1282 for the town palisade was transferred to Caernarfon,
following a writ from the king in June 1283.[86]

While some of Edward I's castles in north Wales are often labelled as
'concentric' fortifications, it should not escape notice that at Flint and
Rhuddlan it was the defences of the towns rather than the castles that were
actually concentric in form. Oxford's city defences were unique in a British
context in the use of concentric masonry walls (see also page 147). The reasons
why remain obscure. The outer city wall, *c.*1m thick and built *c.*10m in advance
of the inner wall and incorporating rounded bastions mirroring those of the
inner curtain was discontinuous surrounding only the north-east part of the
city.[87] Although a late thirteenth-century date for this work has been conjec-

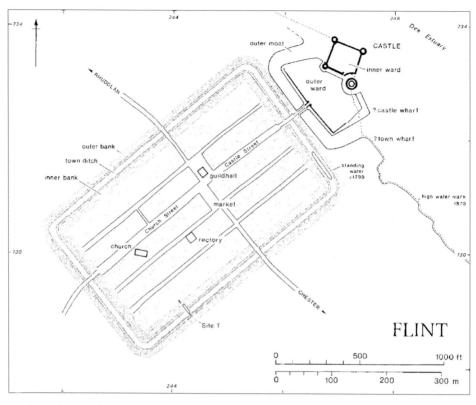

91 Plan of medieval Flint, showing the Edwardian borough encompassed by a massive double bank. *Miles 1996*

tured, excavation has done little to confirm or deny this; what is certain is that the line was well established by the late fourteenth century, a rental of 1387 describing the tenement of John de Windsor that lay 'between the walls of the town'.[88]

Occasionally, excavation has highlighted less formal activities in the vicinity of town walls. The name given to one medieval street running along part of the London wall was not inappropriate; excavation at 58-60 Houndsditch in 1989 revealed the ditch to be 18m wide and its fill to include several dog skeletons![89] At Perth, excavations on the Mill Street site have revealed a rough series of worn steps across the thirteenth-century stone revetment that marked the burgh's defensive perimeter, suggesting an informal passageway avoiding the tolls imposed at the town's main gates.[90]

We should also not neglect the value of excavation as a means of presenting the physical remains of town defences to the public. The excavation of Beverley Gate, Hull, was carried out in 1986 as a component of a scheme of urban improvement, its partially uncovered and consolidated remains representing a feature of interest in a pedestrianized zone (*92*). The brick-built structure, encasing an earlier timber framework, survived to a maximum of 34 courses, and was shown to be of superior construction to the adjacent town wall, to which it was not fully bonded and projected forward of. This was merely 1.03m thick and constructed using a different type of brick, showing the defences to have been built in modular fashion in replacement of the pre-existing palisade.[91] In contrast, the orange brick-built front of the twin drum-towered Sandown Gate at Sandwich (constructed in the mid-fifteenth century) was obscured beneath a plastered finish.[92] The East Gate of Rochester was demonstrated through excavation to have been a massive twin drum-towered structure constructed after *c.*1300, its design representing part of a south-eastern group of fortifications with similarly planned gates, including the West Gate of Canterbury and Cooling Castle.[93] Excavations of Exeter's East Gate (now vanished) have revealed details of the provision of artillery resulting from works in 1511-13, which included construction of a primitive 'caponier' equipped with a gunport positioned to rake the town ditch with fire.[94] Excavation of masonry structures other than walls can reveal architectural detail previously lost to view. Examples include the bastion at St Nicholas's Almshouses, Bristol, which was shown to have been provided with three recesses or 'stand-ins' for archers, each stepped and furnished with a single arrow loop.[95]

92 Excavated remains of the medieval brick-built Beverley Gate, Hull *Authors' collection*

FURTHER READING

For the archaeology of medieval towns in general see C. Platt, *The English Medieval Town* (Secker and Warburg, 1976), M.O.H. Carver, *Underneath English Towns: Interpreting Urban Archaeology* (Batsford, 1987), P. Ottaway, *Archaeology in British Towns: From the Emperor Claudius to the Black Death* (Routledge, 1992), and J. Schofield and A. Vince, *Medieval Towns: The Archaeology of British Towns in their European Setting* (Continuum, 2003). The only authoritative survey of the archaeological evidence of medieval town defences in England and Wales is provided in Chapter 10 of J.R. Kenyon, *Medieval Fortifications* (Leicester University Press, 1990).

The most comprehensive account of the standing remains of any town's defences is RCHME, *An Inventory of the Historical Monuments in the City of York, Volume II, The Defences* (HMSO, 1972). For a particularly illuminating study of how later medieval documentary sources can illuminate the defences of a particular town, see M.J. Stoyle, *Circled with Stone: Exeter's City Walls, 1485-1660* (University of Exeter Press, 2003).

Summary histories and descriptions of existing town defences are provided in A. Pettifer, *English Castles: A Guide by Counties* (Boydell, 1995) and much documentary evidence relating to individual walled circuits is provided in H.L. Turner, *Town Defences in England and Wales* (John Baker, 1970).

4

EXPLANATIONS:
URBAN IDENTITY, STATUS
AND DEFENCE

In the medieval period, town walls were but one manifestation of a far wider defensive tradition that also included castles, fortified manor houses, palaces, some church towers and ecclesiastical precincts, moated homesteads and tower-houses. The precise academic meaning of each of these categories can be open to interpretation, and even the usefulness of applying such labels can be questioned, as while some arise from medieval terminology, others are modern inventions. It is clear, however, that the individuals and authorities who built, owned and maintained these sites did so for a variety of motives that went some way beyond the simple need for security and defence, and included, to different extents, the desire to display prestige, wealth and social status. In seeking to account for the flourishing of fortified sites in the medieval period, what is crucial is that we do not create an artificial distinction between fortifications built for utilitarian reasons and others built to impress. There was, in reality, a continuous spectrum of emphasis from one extreme to the other, commonly with both qualities existing side by side in one place.

Arguing from architectural, archaeological and historical evidence, however, commentators have debated the extent to which the real motivation for medieval town wall building lay in military necessity or social and economic advantage. A parallel debate has been flowing through the field of castle studies.[1] Expressed in this way, however, this debate centres on a false dichotomy. Put simply, in the medieval period military and social needs cannot be as easily distinguished as they can in the modern era of centralised governments and standing armies. Rather, richer individuals and urban communities defended themselves in an essentially self-sufficient manner, simultaneously contributing to the wider strength of the realm to which they belonged, but at the same time displaying their own wealth through impressive building.

Governing rulers exercised political and military power which, while in one sense 'public' was in another sense personal. In this sense, the distinction commonly made between 'royal' and 'private' castles, and 'public' and 'private' defence can be misleading. Similarly, in the urban sphere, while walls contributed to the defence of the specific community, they also contributed to the defence of the country as a whole.

In addition, we must remember that changing circumstances could mean that town defences were constructed or refurbished to meet particular threats or to fulfil very specific functions, yet be continuously maintained for other more general reasons. Moreover, all medieval urban communities had their own identities and needs, and it is simply impossible to generalise about their circumstances. Unlike the Roman period on the one hand and the Renaissance on the other, when there were strong centralised authorities with virtual monopolies on military power, the medieval period saw a high level of interplay between many elements in society that possessed fortified places.

SYMBOLISM AND URBAN DEFENCE

The city wall features prominently in urban iconography to such an extent that the image of wall and city were often impossible to sever. The ancient Egyptian hieroglyph meaning 'city' took the form of a cross within a circle – an image representing a crossroads within a wall, with the implications of organisation, enclosure and cohesion that encapsulate the essence of the urban phenomenon, and in the classical world the city was the foundation stone of 'civilised' life.[2]

While rivalry between different urban communities was a key driving force behind the walling of British medieval towns, somewhat less tangible is the extent to which emulation of past urban models may have played a role in shaping town defences. Pictorial sources make it clear that familiarity with the antique urban heritage went some way towards shaping a notion of the 'ideal' medieval city; in this context it is notable that representations of Jerusalem and Rome consistently show that walls structured and lent cohesion to the urban image.[3] Such representations frequently imbued the physical attributes of the city with religious and moral significance. The illustration of New Jerusalem, derived from the Spanish Monk Beatus de Liébana's work of the late eighth century, *Commentary on the Apocalypse*, is a case in point. Thirteenth-century English copies show the city in stylised form as a walled quadrilateral dominated by detailed over-size depictions of the twelve gates, one for each of the twelve tribes of Israel.[4] It might well not be coincidental that when Cologne received its new wall early in the thirteenth century this, too, was planned with twelve gates.[5] The inspiration of this model is the Revelation of John, Book 21, verses 15-27: a description of the holy city of New Jerusalem, coming down from heaven. The city was square in plan, with sides 12,000 furlongs in length. Its walls were 140 cubits high. The city's interior was of gold, its walls were of jasper and their foundations adorned with jewels. There were twelve gates, each fashioned from a single pearl. They would never be shut by day (and there would be no night). While this image was of some general influence in the medieval period, a crucial difference lay in its lack of a temple, whereas medieval towns and cities commonly had many churches.

In important early cartographic representations of Britain such as Matthew Paris's famous mid-thirteenth century map and the Gough map of c.1360, towns are depicted as stylised icons rather than in a visually accurate manner, though often with representations of walls and defences. Very occasionally more detailed observations are apparent, as in the Gough map's depiction of Coventry's walls, on which work had only very recently started.[6] While medieval town maps may not contain details of town walls that can be relied on as evidence of their exact topographies and architectural qualities, they provide unique opportunities to illuminate how walled circuits were perceived in contemporary minds. One of the earliest detailed picture maps of a British medieval walled city is that of Bristol produced c.1480;[7] the portrayal of the city's defences is of great interest. Far from reflecting the complexity of Bristol's multi-layered defences, the map-maker manipulated the mural topography to create a simplified design comprising a walled ring around a central crossroads where four routes leading from four gates converged, the walls lending harmony, order and symmetry to the idealised urban image. A similar distortion of urban topography to create an impression of regularity is apparent in the monk Lucian's famous description of Chester, c.1195, *De Laude Cestrie* ('Of the Praise of Chester'). The intramural street pattern is again portrayed as a crossroads of routes running from the four gates, which faced respectively towards India (east), Wales (south), Ireland (west) and Norway (north); the impression that each cardinal direction was marked by a church is, however, created by moving the church of St Peter (which is centrally located) to the west.[8]

Medieval town seals are another important type of evidence providing some indication of how medieval urban communities conceptualised town defences, suggesting a strong link between growing urban organisation and identity with the walled image (*93*). Significantly, the earliest known municipal seal in Britain, that associated with an Oxford charter of 1191 (though used until the seventeenth century as Oxford's common seal), depicts a stylised bird's-eye view of the entire crenellated walled circuit, with an ox superimposed.[9] While the value of this source for understanding the architecture of Oxford's town walls at this date might be open to question, its use of imagery does underline the central importance of town walls to the identity of urban societies. Another illuminating seal in this respect is the second common seal of the City of London (1324), which shows the walls again playing a structuring role in a

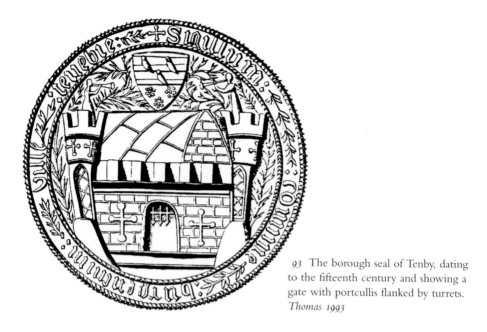

93 The borough seal of Tenby, dating to the fifteenth century and showing a gate with portcullis flanked by turrets. *Thomas 1993*

composition presenting an urban community's self image. Here the walls form the foreground to a skyline of towering church steeples, with the entire ensemble nestling beneath a dome representing London Bridge; other seals prominently depicting walls include those of Rochester, Shrewsbury and Winchester.[10]

The social and judicial functions of gates

The structures of town gates could house a wide range of activities. While some of these might be official in character, it is also clear from the thirteenth century onwards that urban authorities increasingly saw gates and attached properties and plots as potential sources of revenue, in particular as properties to be leased. But accommodation in or above town gates was by no means always of low status. At the pinnacle of his public career, Geoffrey Chaucer lived above Aldgate, London. In 1374 he was granted a rent-free lifelong lease on the dwelling, which comprised two storeys of rooms above the gate and a cellar below, although he only occupied it for twelve years. The agreement, made with the mayor and aldermen of London, specified that it should be kept in good repair, was not to be sub-let, and could be occupied in times of military need.[11] This residence was clearly fitting for Chaucer's appointment, shortly after the grant of the lease, as the controller of the customs of the port of London, and there is evidence that other gates housed influential individuals who received their dwellings as gifts and symbols of favour and status. Chaucer's friend Ralph Stode, an eminent lawyer and common sergeant of the city of London, lived over Aldersgate in the period 1375-82 and Aldgate itself was occupied by the royal esquire Richard Forester, in 1386, after Chaucer's residency.[12] Mural towers too could be rented out or granted to privileged individuals. At Coventry, a tower on the wall and the gatehouse at Bishop Gate, were let in 1518 to one Richard Marler, for a period of 40 years, on the condition that he paid two pounds of almonds annually and kept the stretch of walling in good order.[13] Particular clear evidence comes from Oxford, where medieval rentals show that most bastions on the city wall were let out at some stage; examples from the thirteenth and fourteenth centuries suggest that staff and students of the university frequently rented mural towers as dwellings.[14] The turret north of Ludgate, London, was used in the thirteenth century as part of a private residence, being granted for life to Alexander Swereford, Treasurer of St Paul's, by Henry III in 1235.[15]

The meeting of medieval municipal authorities in chambers above town gates is also recorded at the East Gate of Gloucester, and a room above the heavily restored gate known at the Stonebow at Lincoln (94) is still the venue for the city's council chamber.[16] The Stonebow had marked the site of one of the city's gates from the Roman period, was rebuilt in 1520, more as a processional way than a military feature, and equipped as the seat of the city government.[17] At Caernarfon one of the gatehouses housed the Exchequer in an upper storey, and at Southampton the first floor of the Bargate contained the Guildhall and the town's common chest was housed in the westernmost of its drum towers (95). A snapshot of the types of civic event that could be held in such a structure is provided in the Southampton

94 Lincoln: The Stonebow, a rebuilt town gate still housing the city council chamber in its upper parts. *Authors' collection*

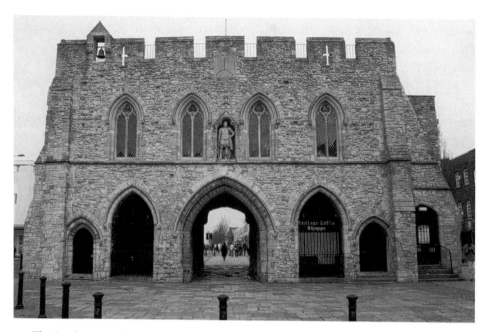

95 The Southampton Bargate, as viewed from within the town. *Authors' collection*

steward's accounts for 13 January 1434, when a banquet was held in the hall above the Bargate.[18] For this particularly lavish occasion, cooks and serving men were employed; rushes, fuel and 20 wooden cups supplied, and an immense variety of foodstuffs provided, including beef, pork, suckling pig, capons, rabbits, wine, beer, bread, flour, cheese, eggs, lard, salt, and vinegar, as well as more exotic items such as pepper, mace, saffron, currants, raisins and dates.

Quite how the residential, civic and defensive functions of walls, towers and gatehouses coexisted can pose problems of interpretation. Further architectural analysis and documentary research could, for example, reveal how citizens performing watch and ward (see page 184) on a wall-walk managed to fully perform their duties when their perambulation encountered mural towers or chambers in gatehouses that had been leased out as private residences. Particularly promising in this regard are the techniques of 'access analysis' applied to medieval buildings, which remain to be applied to surviving town gates.

The performance of different civic facilities at separate levels was noted by John Leland at Kidwelly, where the (surviving) town gate housed a town hall in the upper levels and a prison below. In a single town, different gates might also, of course, serve very different purposes. While the east and west gates of Cowbridge, for instance, spanned a major through route, with the borough situated to maximise commercial potential, the north gate, in contrast, provided access to grazing resources.[19]

Town gates were particularly common venues for gaols;[20] examples include Stafford's north gate (Gaol Gate); the north gate of Gloucester (for which an adjoining jailer's lodging was built in the late sixteenth century); Bristol's Newgate; Canterbury's West Gate; Chester's North Gate; Exeter's South Gate; Lincoln's Clasketgate; Southampton's God's House Gate; and York's Monk Bar and Fishergate Bar. It is at London, however, that we have most insight into such arrangements. The great gate of Newgate, ultimately of Roman origin, was converted into a gaol by 1219, while Ludgate was officially recognised as a prison from 1378. Notably, the two prisons accommodated different categories of felon: Newgate was effectively a national prison for serious offenders, while Ludgate was designated for the free men and women of the city.[21]

Gates clearly also had wider significance as judicial symbols. As designated 'public' places, the spaces immediately inside and outside the gates provided not only the focus for processions and pageants, but also for conspicuous warnings about the consequences of wrongdoing. Not uncommonly were stocks and other types of punishment or execution paraphernalia located immediately outside the gates, and the custom of displaying the heads of traitors on gates is well known. Among the more famous heads known to have perched on top of Mickelgate, York, for instance, were those of Sir Henry Percy (1403), Sir William Plumpton (1405), Lord Scrope (1415), the Duke of York (1460), the Earl of Devon (1461) and the Earl of Northumberland (1571).[22] The importance of the gates as the points on the circuit where the curfew was imposed is illustrated by the events at Exeter in Christmas 1285, when Edward I and his queen spent time in the city with the bishop to investigate the murder of Walter de Lichelade, the cathedral's precentor. The outcome of their investigation was the hanging of the city's mayor and the keeper of the South Gate for their negligence in leaving the gate open, thus allowing the murderers to leave the city.[23]

An important but often underestimated dimension to the social history of medieval town walls is the manner in which aspects of the ownership and maintenance of defences were contested between different interest groups. Frequently, town walls acted as arenas where power plays between different sectors of the urban community were acted out. One way in which the privileged status of certain parts of urban society might be reflected in the physical topography of town walls was through petitioning to create small gates providing private access to the extramural zone in a manner not available to the population at large. Such evidence is particularly plentiful for the thirteenth century, often relating to friaries or other monastic institutions set immediately within or beyond the wall. At Chester, the postern near the abbey known as Kaleyard Gate was built by the monks in 1275 so that they could reach their vegetable garden beyond the wall.[24] At Newcastle, the town wall through which the Black Friars were given licence to pierce a postern in 1280 was still described as 'new'; in 1312 their access was further improved through the construction of a bridge over the 'new dyke'.[25] Other circuits such as those of Chichester and Exeter also preserve gates created through town walls in order to link internal ecclesiastical precincts with other properties and numerous others are known from documentary sources, such as the Ham Gate at Bath. In these ways, particular types of social need might outweigh the importance of maintaining the integrity of walled circuits for reasons of communal security and prestige. Yet friction over the responsibility for different sections of a town wall could occasionally erupt into violence. In 1264, the citizens of Winchester directed their anger against the King's and Prior's Gates, following a protracted dispute concerning the custody of this stretch of wall, and an allegation six years previously that the priors had blocked the gates, thus preventing access to market.[26]

Less widely recognised are those minor gates or posterns built to provide relevant sectors of urban communities with access to harbours, waterways or fisheries. The late medieval Sandwell Gate at Hartlepool (96) was a secondary insertion into the town wall on the seaward side, probably dating to the fifteenth century. The gate's construction was primarily for convenience rather than to enhance defensibility, providing direct access to the sea for fishermen via a route that avoided the main medieval harbour, which was flanked by twin towers and closed with a boom chain.[27] A postern excavated in the north-east corner of Oxford's outer city wall was apparently an original feature but oddly positioned in that it led directly into the city ditch. Its function may be indicated by the lease of the moat in this area to one Adam de la Ryver 1378 mentioning fishing rights, possibly indicating that the postern was positioned to allow the leaseholder access to fish ponds managed within the moat.[28] Another indication of the value placed on fish — which were managed as a

96 Hartlepool: the Sandwell Gate, a medieval water gate. *Authors' collection*

symbol of social prestige as well as a dietary resource – is provided by evidence that the intended line of Coventry's city wall was altered to embrace a series of fish stews and St Osburg's Pool. Upon the request of Prior Shoteswell in 1462, the Corporation agreed to the diversion, despite the fact that it was projected to cost the City in excess of 500 marks extra on account of the dog-leg in the circuit, clearly discernible on Speed's map.[29]

Other medieval water gates through town walls opening on to riversides, harbours or anchorages are known from documentary sources, such as those at Hastings and London, but far more detail about the operation of these features has emerged where they have been excavated. At Worcester an excavated water gate of the late fourteenth century was associated with a rubble slipway into the tidal River Severn and featured mooring rings.[30] Two other especially important examples are known from Bristol.[31] A double-arched gate at Broad Quay, on the north side of the city, provided access from nearby tenements to a slipway into the River Frome, the openings comprising simple tunnels through the wall. In contrast, a water gate through the Portwall, on the south side of Bristol's extended defensive perimeter, was a high-status structure rather than a civic amenity. It served to link the intramural property of the Knights Templar (Temple Fee) to their extramural agricultural lands (Temple Meads) on the opposite bank of the massive tidal ditch, and its appearance reflected accordingly the complex military architecture and symbolism of this part of the wall (see page 213).

While we might think of town gates as symbolising the differences between communities within and beyond the walls, it should also not escape attention that actions directed at them could also arise from internal dispute or uprising. Occasionally citizens might vent their anger by collecting in the public spaces inside gates or even physically attacking and them, as occurred at Exeter in 1659 in reaction to the Commonwealth, or the town gates (as well as turnpike gates) attacked during the Rebecca Riots in Wales. In Coventry, citizens rioting in reaction to the ploughing up of some of the city's common lands in 1524-5 took the defiant step of shutting one of the city gates (Newgate) against the chamberlain's procession.[32]

TOWN DEFENCES AND RELIGIOUS INSTITUTIONS

Modern studies of the evolution of urban morphology have been heavily influenced by the work of the historical geographer Conzen, whose seminal analysis of Alnwick established important methodologies for the dissection of town plans.[33] An especially important construct of 'Conzenian' analysis was that of the fringe-belt – essentially the notion that in periods of urban stagnation and slow outwards growth, certain types of institutions not requiring direct access to the urban core would tend to occupy a distinct zone.[34] In the medieval period a classic example of this phenomenon was the location of hospitals and related religious institutions in the immediately extra- or intra-mural zone. While it is tempting to see urban growth as following such models, we should not forget that the placement of such institutions resulted from individual decision making spread through time, and that until the modern period there was no equivalent of 'planning policy'.

In marked contrast to other urban monastic houses, nunneries and friaries very often lay on the urban fringes. But, while it is commonly thought that friaries were sited on the urban limits, this was not always so. The availability of building sites was clearly an important factor in their siting, but so too was the character of the institution in question. At Gloucester, for instance, both the Franciscan and Dominican friaries established in the 1230s lay in intramural sites, only the more eremitic (and later) Carmelites (their friary established c.1270) building outside the walls.[35] Nonetheless, the precincts of a great many friaries were built against or even across town walls, a type of site that might require prior negotiation to ensure the continuing integrity of a walled enceinte (see page 108). Medieval hospitals commonly lay immediately outside the walled zone, not in secluded positions, but located prominently on roads outside gates where they might attract charity and pity. Typical examples of this are the hospitals of St John the Baptist at Banbury, Bristol and Nottingham, all of which lay immediately outside gates. *Leprosaria*, in particular, were sited in conspicuous extramural positions. The Yorkshire town of Beverley, for instance, had two leper houses: one directly outside the North Bar and the other external to Keldgate on the south; other examples outside gates can be identified at Bury St Edmunds, Nottingham and Worcester. In major urban centres such as York and London, multiple leper hospitals lay in a ring around the city limits. At Norwich five of the city's six specialist houses for lepers lay directly outside the gates, forming unmistakable landmarks for travellers entering the city from the north, west and south.[36] A range of practical factors could account in part for this patterning, with the availability of land for building and medieval public health concerns tending to favour extramural sites. Yet we should not overlook how the locations of such sites on the urban threshold might reflect the liminal nature of certain social groups.[37]

Some indication of the potential conflict of interests that could arise is indicated by the case of Oxford, where in the late fourteenth century negotiations were necessary to ensure the upkeep of the city wall in that part of the circuit containing New College, the area having previously suffered a decline of occupation.[38] The founder of the College, William of Wykeham, agreed with the city that it would be responsible for the upkeep of that part of the city wall that embraced the complex: a royal charter stipulated that the College should rebuild its 'parcel of wall, towers and turrets' where necessary, and provide posterns to facilitate the mayor's triennial inspection of the circuit.[39] The bell-tower situated on this stretch of the city wall is a secondary feature, built in replacement of a mural tower during the construction of the New College.[40] Bell-towers may have been rather more common features of walled circuits than we realise. The link between gates and churches and chapels is important, but so too were mural bell-towers. The only surviving example of a true mural bell-tower is at Berwick-upon-Tweed, comprising an octagonal structure forming an integral element in the medieval town's northern defences. While the present structure is a late sixteenth-century rebuild, the circular base on which it stands may represent a predecessor, recorded in the fourteenth century as a 'watchtower' with windows and a bell.[41] The structural comparisons between bell-towers and timber military towers have been discussed elsewhere.[42]

In the later medieval period, hermits frequently occupied gatehouses and towers; Winchester, for instance, had a 'Hermit's Tower', first recorded in the fourteenth century.[43] In the thirteenth century as many as four of London's mural towers were occupied by hermits, the most celebrated being Simon the Ankar (the Anchorite), who occupied the bastion next to the church of All Hallows on the Wall.[44] Purpose-built hermitages were also often located adjacent to town walls. Squeezed into the north-west angle of the London wall and closely associated with the chapel of St James was a Cistercian hermitage cell of Garendon Abbey, Leicestershire.[45] The marginalised status of another group in medieval society, Jews, was indicated in the location of their cemeteries, like those of the Roman period, beyond town walls, as well as the more general clustering of Jewries around royal castles.[46] Unlike medieval Christian cemeteries, which were invariably associated with churches, Jewish burial grounds were usually remote from places of worship and when, in 1177, Jews were permitted to create cemeteries at towns other than London, it was stipulated that these should always be extramural.[47] Northampton, Oxford and Winchester are among the major towns where Jewish cemeteries lay directly outside the town gates, and at Bristol and London Jewries were located close to royal castles that occupied familiar positions on or near the edges of walled circuits.[48] Thus, while on the one hand, masonry enceintes could display the status and privilege of communities who lived and traded within their bounds, they could also serve to marginalise the activities of certain social groups beyond them. As well as structuring the physical development of townscapes, town walls were clearly a powerful influence on their social geographies.

Gate chapels and churches

A strong association between ecclesiastical sites and town gates is also apparent in the form of churches or chapels incorporated into the upper storeys of gate-houses, or where churches or chapel lay immediately adjacent to them.[49] In visual terms this association gave the impression that a town or city enjoyed a form of spiritual protection, but practical factors too may have lain behind this phenomenon, for the location of churches near gates must have served to encourage the donation of gifts from travellers. The tradition of gate chapels is especially well represented at Warwick, where the two surviving medieval gates both contain chapels set longitudinally along the gate passage. The chapel of St James is perched on top of the West Gate (97), with the tunnel-like passage running beneath it, while above the East Gate stands the medieval chapel of St Peter, this largely rebuilt in fanciful gothic style by Francis Hiorn in 1788, including the addition of decorative crenellations.

Elsewhere, the Hanging Chapel at Langport (*colour plate 27*) was built in the fourteenth century or earlier over a simple town gate perpetuating one of the main routes in and out of the former *burh*.[50] The symbolism of this structure is apparent in the fact that the later medieval town was not walled and may have been undefended. At Winchester, the King's Gate still supports the chapel of St Swithun (98), and the city had churches or chapels in direct association with four of the five main gates; the others were St Michael (over the East Gate), St Mary (over the North Gate), and St Mary (adjacent to the West Gate).[51] Notably, the association between St Michael's and the East Gate at least was pre-Conquest in origin, the gate's dedication being recorded by Wulfstan in 993-4. Furthermore, in the suburbs a number of other medieval churches lay very close to the limits of the enclosing ditches, including St James and St Anastasia, which were both incorporated within the extended perimeter.[52]

Canterbury similarly had churches or chapels over many of its gates from an early date: St Mary Northgate was constructed over the Roman north gate of

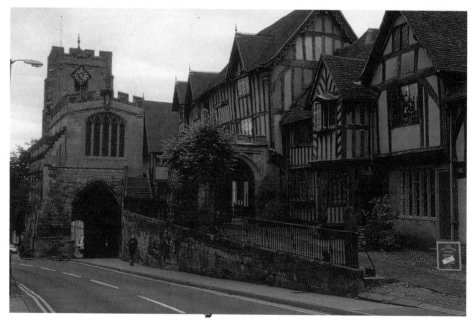

97 Warwick: West Gate, with a parish church above, and a medieval hospital immediately inside the town. *Authors' collection*

98 Winchester: King's Gate, with a chapel above. *Authors' collection*

the city in the later Saxon period; Holy Cross lay over the Roman West Gate; St Michael over the Roman Bargate; and, less certainly, St George's lay over Newingate and St Edmund's over the Riding Gate.[53] Bristol also had no fewer than four churches built directly over, or in very close association with the town gates of its inner defensive ring, walled *c.*1100. Only one of these structures (St John's Gate) survives, located directly beneath the late perpendicular tower of a parish church; the other churches associated with gates were St Lawrence, St Leonard and St Nicholas. Frequently, we have only incidental topographical references to chapels over gates. For instance John Leland noted that the single surviving town gate of Ilchester had a church or (more probably) a chapel over it, while at Chichester a reference of 1374 indicates the existence of a chapel of Our Lady over the North Gate. Among the many other walled towns featuring parish churches on or immediately inside town gates are: Bath (St Mary, North Gate and St James, South Gate); Cricklade (St Mary, North Gate); Exeter (Holy Trinity, South Gate and St Mary Steps, West Gate); Gloucester (St Kyneburgh, south-west gate); and Wareham (St Martin, North Gate). In London, it has been suggested that the positioning of St Mary Magdalen by Aldgate and St Peter ad Vincula by St Peter's Gate may reflect the subdivision of this part of the city into wards for the defence of the *burh*, with each ward being allotted a minster church.[54] How often such a pattern was repeated is yet to be established.

A structure more open to interpretation is the west tower of St Michael-at-the-Northgate, Oxford (*colour plate 28*), an impressive Anglo-Saxon structure of five stages featuring particularly fine belfry openings in its upper two storeys, to which the nave of the church was later added.[55] The tower stood immediately inside the line of the pre-Conquest town defences and seems very likely to have been part of a gateway structure. Whether this structure originated as a secular or ecclesiastical building remains unresolved. One intriguing possibility is that the tower, with a ground-floor door and second floor access onto a putative wall-walk, was an independently accessible unit used by the town watchmen and gatekeepers. It is also not entirely out of the question that it could have been the core of a late Saxon fortified aristocratic residence, feasibly that of a town official. What cannot be coincidental, however, is that an undeniably strong association exists between the positions of the gates of Anglo-Saxon *burhs* and the locations of medieval churches and chapels, many of which are demonstrably pre-Conquest in origin. Bath, Canterbury, Cricklade, Exeter, Gloucester, Lewes, London, Norwich, Oxford, Wallingford, Wareham and Winchester all contain examples suggesting that churches or chapels were closely juxtaposed with gates through pre-Conquest town defences. Crucially, virtually all these examples highlight the existence of gate-chapels and churches in towns of pre-Conquest origin, while they are virtually unknown in planted boroughs of the post-Conquest period. The chapel of St Mary at Caernarfon, inserted into the north-west angle of the town wall in the early fourteenth century, however, incorporated an angle tower used as a vestry. Patterns may be apparent in the dedication of these gate churches and chapels; particularly significant, for instance, may be the dedications to St Botolph (an ascetic frequently associated with bridges, boundaries, travel and trade), St Peter (the doorkeeper of heaven) and St Michael (guardian archangel), although this awaits systematic study.[56]

BUILDING, MAINTENANCE AND MANPOWER

The history of manning and maintenance of town walls proceeded through a succession of distinct phases. In the late Anglo-Saxon period the burden fell on the shires within which the royal *burhs* were situated. In Alfred's reign, a number of hides were attached to each *burh*, producing a man from each hide, and the distribution of the rural hidation around the *c.*30 *burhs* of Wessex was described in the famous document known as the Burghal Hidage. Vestiges of this system were still visible late in the eleventh century (see page 66), but for how long this system continued we do not know, and the obscurity of the situation is made worse by the low level of attention given to urban defensive matters in twelfth-century sources. What seems clear is that its origins lay in a period when urban populations alone were too low for the job of defending towns.

By the twelfth century, the populations of many of the old Anglo-Saxon *burhs* had expanded considerably. While it is a reasonable assumption that a Burghal Hidage type of arrangement would have been extended in the tenth century to those defended centres that became the principal defended towns of midland shires, such as Leicester and Lincoln, rather less certain is how places such as Newark and Doncaster — where archaeology has revealed pre-Conquest town defences — were maintained. In the intervening period we may expect a gradual shift of responsibility to have taken place from rural hinter-lands to the towns themselves. The clearest evidence for this process comes from Oxford.[57] During the tenth century the original *burh* was extended, which must have made the earlier arrangements at least partly obsolete. By 1086, some houses in the town, the mural mansions, were exempt from royal obligations (other than *fyrd* service) because their owners provided mainte-nance of the city walls, as recorded in Domesday Book. Most of these proper-ties (whose locations can be traced through later documents) were in the north-east ward of the city, corresponding with the tenth-century extension of the original *burh*, which suggests that the system may have originated then. The obligations of these mural mansions were still theoretically working in the 1220s, when the sheriff of Oxford attempted to apply it, but the direct labour system that it represented was soon eclipsed by the new system of murage grants (see page 180).

Long ago, Maitland argued that this Oxford evidence was a specific reflec-tion of something more generally revealed in Domesday Book, where the frequent reference to properties in towns belonging to rural estates and their lords was made.[58] This, he felt, was a result of original Burghal Hidage arrange-ments: rural lords, probably kept tenants in towns through whom they discharged their duties to the towns' defences. The Domesday Book entry for Chester (see page 66) reminds us that some shires still had this responsibility in the late eleventh century. But certainty on the interpretation of urban proper-ties with rural lords is impossible, since they may also have arisen during the period of urban growth of *burhs* after their initial military foundation. Alongside this, we may envisage growing defensive responsibilities of the townfolk themselves. There seems to have been a period in which different mechanisms existed side by side. Thus, in 1204, the ditch around Ipswich was dug by the men of Cambridgeshire, in the old tradition. But in 1189 occurred the first (known) example, at Hereford, of a king granting permission for a town to levy a toll on its inhabitants for expenditure on the defences.[59] Alongside such arrangements, kings from time to time provided direct contributions of materials or finance, as occurred in John's reign and early in Henry III's, partic-ularly for southern coastal towns (see page 202). The early thirteenth century was clearly a transitional period.

Although the general trend in defensive arrangements was from a shire-based system in the late Saxon period to an urban-based militia one from the late twelfth century, some reflections of town-country links are found at a later date, as highlighted by two exceptions to this general trend. At King's Lynn, a memorandum of 1325 describes an area stretching some ten miles south and south-east of the town, and whose population was responsible for upkeep of the south gate. This was, notably, at this date still a timber structure, like the town's others – including at least one that was apparently mobile and prefab-ricated.[60] When early in the fifteenth century, the gate was recorded as being in a dilapidated state, this was seen as a matter for concern not only for the urban population, but the surrounding territory. Reporting to a meeting of Lynn council on 14 April 1413 the mayor, Roger Galyon, warned that the 'South Gates, besides the bridge there, are broken and ruinous and all in decay to the detriment of the town of Lynn and the country in which it lies'.[61] At Malmesbury, a record of responsibility for the building and/or repair of the town wall in 1283 makes it clear that responsibility for a total of 26 designated stretches of the circuit was delegated to separate estates that lay outside it – an arrangement that seems likely to have perpetuated an established tradition.[62] In the late thirteenth century responsibility for the upkeep of the town wall of Lewes rested largely on the manors and tenants of the barony, who contributed £5 per knight's fee in 1275, even though a grant of murage had been issued in 1266.[63] An illuminating parallel is the medieval bridge over the Medway at Rochester, where in the twelfth century outlying manors were responsible for the maintenance of the structure. The document of this date known as the *Textus Roffensis* records that designated manors of the king, the archbishop of Canterbury and the bishop of Rochester were responsible for each of the nine piers of the bridge – an arrangement that seems likely to have had late Saxon ancestry.[64]

Murage tax

Around 1220, direct royal contributions were replaced by the murage 'grant': a system involving a duality of royal and local involvement. The king gave permission for a tax to be raised, thus underlining the overall royal control of taxation and defensive works, but the tax itself was levied and administered by the town's own officials and collected its at gates and/or bars. Grants of murage are studied primarily through the royal copy kept as a record of central govern-ment; accounts of monies raised and spent, however, are found recorded in local accounts maintained by civic officials. The murage grant relating to Shrewsbury (*colour plate 29*) for 1220 reads:

> The king to the sheriff of Shropshire and all the men of that shire, greetings. Know that we have granted to our burgesses of Shrewsbury, to aid in the enclosing of the town of Shrewsbury, for the security and safety of that town and of adjacent parts, that they may take, every week for four years from the Feast of St John the Baptist in the fourth year of our reign,

from every cart from Shropshire carrying goods for sale into the same town of Shrewsbury, one half-penny. And from every cart from another shire carrying goods for sale into the same town, one penny. And from every horse-load of goods carried for sale there in excess of a bushel, one farthing. And from every horse, mare, ox or cow led there for sale, one penny. And from 5 sheep or goats or pigs, one half-penny. And from each boat coming in the same town of Shrewsbury on the River Severn loaded with goods for sale, four pence. (And nothing shall be taken after the specified four years have elapsed).[65]

What is sometimes overlooked is that this particular murage grant was preceded, in October 1218, by a royal instruction to the burgesses, to 'strengthen and enclose' Shrewsbury, as a measure against the king's enemies, presumably in this context, the Welsh.[66] Clearly this was a time of experimentation in matters of funding and supporting urban defence.

As an example of a local type of record, the well preserved Receivers' Accounts of Exeter may be quoted, which survive as rolls from the early fourteenth century to the early eighteenth century. Murage occurs in the records kept by the Receiver, whose responsibilities included supervising the city's various incomes and expenditures and keeping appropriate records. Income from murage and consequent expenditure of the proceeds was recorded sometimes in the general accounts and sometimes in separate accounts called 'murage rolls', amongst which the roll for 1341-42 survives in particularly full form. It provides the names of those who collected murage as well as the names of the gates at which they operated and the sums then expended on labour, materials and carriage.[67]

Thus, the murage system involved no outlay on the king's behalf; moreover, although the administration of the tax fell to the townsfolk, it was paid by visiting merchants from the countryside and other towns. It is quite likely that the popularity of murage was also enhanced by the developing nature of defensive building. Whereas in earlier centuries the technology of fortification was frequently earth and timber, by this date serious new defensive structures were predominantly of stone. While in earlier times ordinary households may have been able to contribute to maintenance with their own skills, it was probably now more effective – indeed, necessary – to have cash with which to pay stonemasons and other craftsmen. Started in c.1220, this system peaked in the late thirteenth and early fourteenth centuries and gradually declined, though lingering on through the fifteenth century, sometimes with grants in perpetuity, as at York (1449; abolished 1483).[68]

Murage must also be seen against the wider economic and financial background. First, it was made possible by the buoyant economy that was sustaining the growth of towns. There is no widespread evidence that the exaction of murage was ever a disincentive to trading activity, which must have been sufficiently healthy to sustain it. Second, murage was only one element in an array of fiscal experiments which thirteenth-century kings implemented. Overall, it was a system that suited both king and locality. At Southampton, murage grants of 1282 and 1286 included mandates allowing resulting monies to be spent on improvements to the defences of the royal castle that lay against the north-west side of the town wall; an excavated lime kiln of sophisticated type, located during excavations on the Maddison Street site and dated to the late twelfth century, may reflect work on the castle at this time, when little other royal expenditure on the site is known.[69] Although petitions associated with murage were to a degree formulaic, they nevertheless probably reflected a genuine dualism in motive as when, in 1253, the burgesses of Norwich petitioned Henry III for the building of a wall 'to the benefit of the king and for the greater security of the town'. Thus, as a recent commentator has rightly observed 'a local tax it might be, but the effects which it produced were national, as had always been intended'.[70] An interesting and exceptional variation is the successful petition for murage made by the burgesses of Hull in 1321, arguing that the security which possession of a wall would give would guarantee an increase in domestic and international trade.[71] A diametrically opposed view was taken by the burgesses of Portsmouth about the murage grant received in 1342, which was argued to have been detrimental to trade, although unexpressed alterior motives may have been relevant (see page 214).

Two of the flexible features of the murage system were, paradoxically, to bring about its decline. First, since a grant of murage specified the list of goods on which tolls could be exacted, the lists themselves were by definition flexible in length, and during the thirteenth century there was a tendency for them to become longer, more complex and more onerous in their practical implementation. Second, because the system, while locally applied, had a royal driving force it was easily manipulated by kings who granted exemptions to those deemed worthy of favour. By the early fourteenth century, the accumulation of exemptions, to the burgesses of entire towns, to individual merchants and to religious institutions meant that much potential revenue was being lost and the system itself became less attractive to urban authorities. A classic example of exemption was Edward I's treatment of the burgesses of Chester and his new towns in north Wales, all of whom were exempt from paying murage anywhere in his kingdom.[72] Edward's boroughs in North Wales had, of course, been initially defended not through levies of murage but through direct royal expenditure in association with new castle building.

But murage grants must be interpreted with caution. Crucially, we should not assume that in all cases where murage was granted building operations ensued and circuits realised. At places such as Lancaster and Penrith, and perhaps Grimsby and Overton, there is no pressing evidence that murage grants were actually acted upon. Bridgwater received a single grant, in 1269, but the town never seems to have been fully walled. In the mid-sixteenth century, the antiquarian John Leland observed that the town was bereft of an enclosing wall, but that together, the stone-built properties of the burgesses formed a continuous perimeter obstacle of some sort.

> The towne of Bridgwater is not wallid, nor hath not beene by any lykely-hood that I saw. Yet there be 4 gates yn the towne namid as they be sette by est, west, north, and south. The waulles of the stone houses of the toune be yn steed of the towne waulles.[73]

Such expediency was matched at Edinburgh (see page 156), where separate lengths of the fifteenth-century town wall were built across the widths of individual burgage plots.

In other instances murage grants were revoked, for example where another town made an objection. In addition, the local implementation of the tax made it particularly open to embezzlement and unauthorised uses, leading to regular complaints. Famously, at Southampton Edward III pursued an enquiry in 1360 into whether works were actually being undertaken.[74] When Poole was elevated to the position of Port of the Staple (head port of Dorset, supplanting Melcombe) in 1433, the grant also included a licence to fortify. With the exception of the construction of one gate, and perhaps a ditch, this was apparently not acted upon, however, and the town probably remained essentially undefended until the 'invasion scare' of 1538-40.[75]

In the decade 1215-25, the numerous grants recorded in the form of refunds of royal taxes, or of direct contributions of materials such as timber, were to towns that already had walls, and the earliest murage grants in the 1220s were also directed at existing walled towns. Later in the 1220s, however, murage grants were used to enable walled circuits to be built *de novo*, and a high proportion of mid-thirteenth century grants related to places in Wales and the Marches. It appears that permission to raise murage was obtained by urban communities through petitions variously presented: to the king if he was nearby; through a supportive intermediary at the royal court; through the intervention of a royal administrator; or, later, through a petition in parliament.[76]

As the popularity and effectiveness of murage faltered in the fourteenth century, towns began to supplement it with other mechanisms for raising capital. These took three principal forms: first, requests for refund of part of the fee-farm due to kings; second, requests of permission to levy taxes on the urban community itself, on the basis of property held within the towns; and third, the apportionment of part of the income raised from judicial fines and customs duties to wall-building. Increasingly, such mechanisms became the norm for raising money for building operations. Where in local records receipts are recorded by gate, we may suspect an origin in murage tax, and where they are recorded by ward or street we may suspect property tax. As the murage system gradually fell away, towns in effect became solely responsible for the raising of monies, and the varied ways they met this challenge continued into the post-medieval period. An early example is Winchester, where in 1355-6, dues were being paid by landlords in accordance with the rental values of their properties and the money thus raised being apportioned for work on the walls; that deriving from the bishop, for instance, funded work on the walls adjacent to Wolvesey Palace in the 1370s.[77]

By the end of the middle ages, towns and cities were deploying a variety of means, supplementary to the property taxes, for the raising of necessary funds. At Exeter, for example, the miscellaneous sources exploited from the fifteenth to the seventeenth centuries were: building materials drawn directly from properties outside the city owned by the city chamber; making craftsmen 'freemen of the city' in return for free labour; making costs of repairs integral parts of lease agreements for rooms in gatehouses and towers; fining civic officials whenever they lapsed in their duties; deploying loans direct from the mayor and aldermen for immediate works in times of emergency; encouraging citizens to make gifts to the city or leave bequests; and organising voluntary contributions from citizens that might in time of emergency or its aftermath be encouraged with such authority that they were effectively taxes.[78]

Watch and ward

Closely related to the issue of finance was the issue of manpower. In the primary burghal period, labour for maintenance and defence was drawn from the shires. Gradually, however, this system gave way to a greater and eventually total dependence on the populations of the towns themselves. This transition was a slow one and probably proceeded at different rates at different places. Oxford, quoted above, was already at least partly dependent on urban manpower by the late eleventh century, but in most cases we cannot clearly observe the chronology of the changes involved. For example, early in 1068 Exeter withstood an eighteen-day siege by William the Conqueror's army: in what measures manpower from the countryside and from the city contributed to its defence, we do not know, though in his description of the event the chronicler Orderic Vitalis simply talked of 'the citizens'.

While the evolution of medieval urban parishes is a relatively well studied phenomenon, rather more obscure are the urban 'wards' that were far more closely connected to the defence of towns.[79] There is widespread evidence that sizeable towns and cities were divided into wards (99), but at what points in time they came into existence is a question that seems never to have been examined as a general phenomenon. The word 'ward' has an Old English origin, but was also related in meaning to Old French garde, in both languages having a meaning of 'protection'. As a verb, as opposed to a noun, 'ward' retained this sense down to modern times, as in the phrase 'ward off'. Although the documented functions of the wards of medieval towns and cities

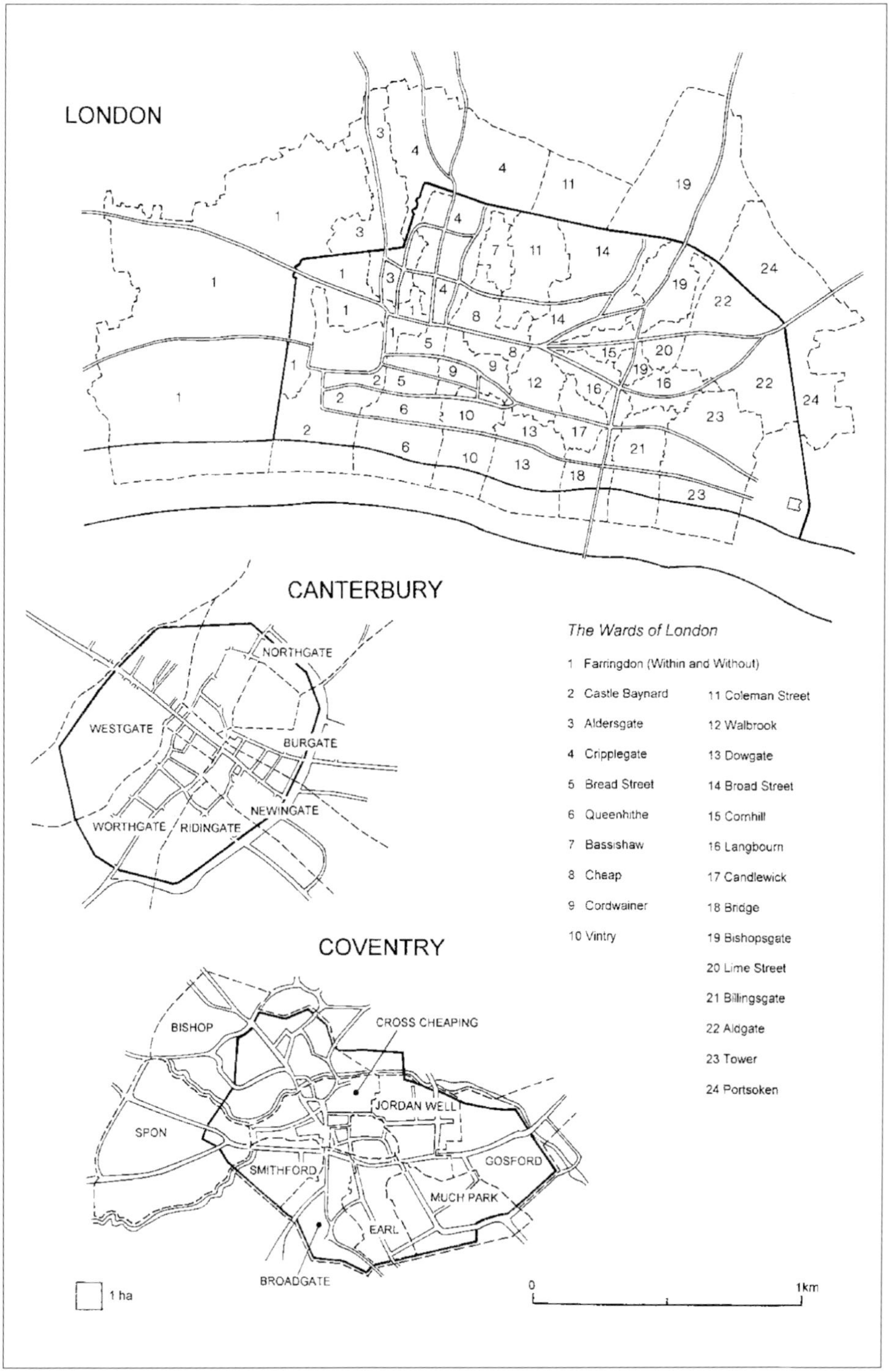
LONDON
1
1
1
1
1
1
1
2
2
2
3
3
3
4
4
4
4
5
6
6
7
8
8
9
9
10
10
11
11
12
13
13
14
14
15
16
16
17
18
19
19
19
20
21
22
22
23
23
24
24
24
CANTERBURY
NORTHGATE
WESTGATE
BURGATE
NEWINGATE
WORTHGATE
RIDINGATE
The Wards of London
1 Farringdon (Within and Without)
2 Castle Baynard
3 Aldersgate
4 Cripplegate
5 Bread Street
6 Queenhithe
7 Bassishaw
8 Cheap
9 Cordwainer
10 Vintry
11 Coleman Street
12 Walbrook
13 Dowgate
14 Broad Street
15 Cornhill
16 Langbourn
17 Candlewick
18 Bridge
19 Bishopsgate
20 Lime Street
21 Billingsgate
22 Aldgate
23 Tower
24 Portsoken
COVENTRY
BISHOP
CROSS CHEAPING
JORDAN WELL
SPON
SMITHFORD
GOSFORD
MUCH PARK
EARL
BROADGATE
1 ha
0
1km

99 Plans of medieval wards in London, Canterbury and Coventry

were varied, on etymological grounds it seems highly likely that their military function was either their primary one, or at least amongst their primary ones. Chester had a very fragmented pattern, with fifteen wards;[80] by the sixteenth century each was named after a gate, church or market. At Hereford the five wards were named after five of the city gates on the walled circuit extended in the post-Conquest period.[81] At Newcastle the 24 wards were organised so that each contained either a gate or a mural tower.[82] The system at Norwich was apparently unique in its two-tier arrangement of wards, comprising twelve 'small wards', which in groupings of three made up the four 'great wards'.[83] Examples of non-walled towns with wards include Cambridge (seven wards) and Reading (five), revealing that their non-defensive functions were in other places equally important.

A recent survey of later medieval provincial towns (i.e. excluding London) identified the 24 largest from the fourteenth century onwards. Of these, 19 provide evidence of wards of some sort, and all had been walled at some point in their evolution (including defences of both Roman and medieval origin). Yet the effectiveness of wards as units of administration must have varied greatly: there was no correlation between the area of towns and their number of wards, and variations underline the complexity of ward origin in specific places.[84] Disentangling the daily realities of urban life is also made difficult by what appears sometimes to be the virtual interchangeability in the local records of wards and parishes as units of organisation. For example, in 1522 Henry VIII's government conducted a national enquiry, disguised as a military survey of the ancient militias, but actually with a view towards the revision of taxation. Contrasting records of the results can be observed at Exeter and Coventry; in the former, the relevant population, their property value and arms, were listed by parish, but in the latter by ward.[85]

In general, urban wards were the subdivisions of the townscape in which eventually a mixture of judicial, financial and military functions were organised. Each ward, on this overall pattern, was supervised by an alderman, who was a member of the town's council or corporation, and beneath whom served one or more constables. The ward had a court and was the basic unit through which the ordering of a well-regulated urban society was achieved. The wards were also the units within which manpower was organised for manning the walls where necessary, and for providing watchmen for the daily and nightly rounds of their security. It has been pointed out that the title 'alderman' is a variation on the originally rural office of *ealdorman*, who in the late Saxon period was responsible to the king for military and other matters in the shire. Further, the urban application of this word, documented from the twelfth century onwards, follows the period when (in the final generations of the Anglo-Saxon kingdom) the title was replaced in its rural context by the Anglo-Scandinavian word *earl*. Moreover, since the shire framework over which the *ealdormen* had presided consisted of hundreds, it has been suggested

that the ward was in some ways analogous, an urban variation of a rural administrative unit, and on a smaller scale. To pursue the rural-urban comparison,
analogy has also been drawn between London's 'folk-moot' and the shire
court.[86]

There are nevertheless various problems in understanding urban wards and
on present evidence it appears difficult to suggest a universally applicable interpretation for their origin. Some occur in relation to late Saxon towns and a
reasonable case can be made for the wards also having late Saxon origins, as for
example at London, Canterbury and Exeter. On the other hand, wards are also
found in townscapes of later date, including Coventry. Other complications
occur as at York, where the eventual city covered a much bigger area than the
original nucleus and establishing at what point in this evolution the wards were
laid out is very difficult. At Oxford, the original *burh* was extended within the
late Saxon period, and part of this extension included the area later known as
the north-east ward of the city, in which the location of many of the mural
mansions of Domesday Book has been established.[87] Other complications arise
in the relationship between ward boundaries (where these are known in detail,
which is not always the case) and boundaries of other units of urban topography, notably intramural and partly extramural parishes and the boundaries of
various fees and liberties held wholly by civic authorities, or by ecclesiastical
institutions or some secular magnate. In addition, ward boundaries were still
being altered in the Municipal Corporation and Local Government Acts of
1835 and 1888. All in all, there is a fruitful field of further research in this
matter, but in the present context some salient points concerning some
published case studies may be helpful.

By *c*.900, London, which was not listed in the Burghal Hidage, presumably
drew its defensive manpower from Middlesex, which had no other *burh*. It has
been convincingly suggested that London's wards emerged during the tenth
and eleventh centuries as the city's own population grew. The first mention of
an alderman was in 1111, earlier than in any other city, and it may be that
London established a pattern emulated elsewhere. London's aldermen
organised manpower in the wards relative to the walls and gates and it has been
plausibly suggested that if, in the original arrangement, each ward theoretically
produced the same number of men, then the considerable difference in size
between the wards reflects considerable variations in population density in the
tenth century. If this was the case, then the central and riverside wards were
more densely populated than those on the northern, eastern and western sides
of the city. Whether all wards were created simultaneously is not known,
though it has been suggested that the Bridge Ward was a secondary creation of
c.1000 to provide for the maintenance of London's new bridge system of that
date, and its shape does seem to have been carved out of an earlier group of
primary wards.[88] The earliest documentary view of London's wards comes
from a property list of St Paul's cathedral dating to 1124, and from a perambu-

lation of 1246 the pattern emerges more clearly. The accompanying map shows the wards in their late fourteenth-century form, by which time they numbered 24. A peculiar feature of the London data is that the wards were originally named after the families of important aldermen, with the result that their names changed from time to time.

As elsewhere, many of the London wards were not wholly intramural; instead, their alignment shows striking non-conformity with the lines of walls and parishes.[89] Although the origin of this phenomenon is not fully understood, and the possibility of influence from pre-existing units of land tenure must be borne in mind, in the context of their medieval functions, wards of this shape would make sense since in time of crisis a defensive function might reasonably be expected from the town's inhabitants not simply in relation to the wall and its gates, but also in relation to a zone of approach some way in front of it. At London, as elsewhere, the wards were not simply the mechanism by which manpower could be raised in time of crisis; indeed, in an English context such occasions were rare. More common and therefore a regular and daily application of the ward system was provision of manpower for the daily and nightly function of 'watch and ward', that is provision of watchmen, patrols, keeping gates and other security functions, as well as the regular judicial and financial functions of the ward courts.[90] The document of 1205–06, known as the 'Customs of London' described many features of the city's life, including provision for watch and ward at this early date.[91]

At Canterbury, wards are clearly revealed in rental documents of the 1160s in the eastern and northern parts of the city and named after its gates: Burgate, Northgate and Newingate. Three further wards (Ridingate, Worthgate and Westgate) are documented by the end of the twelfth century, and in this same period aldermen appear in connection with them. Thus the overall pattern was of six wards relating to six gates, some of them with extramural portions. Their outlines are known from maps of the 1830s and their layout in relation to the walls and roads was simpler than in London, taking the form of segments with all wards incorporating a mural stretch.[92] In 1377 Edward III instructed the Mayor of Exeter to compel the city's citizens and clergy to contribute to the costs of maintaining the walls.[93] The surviving 'Murage Roll' of the same year was entitled 'First tax of Exeter levied for the repair of the gates, walls and ditch'. This internal property tax – a local tax for local people rather than a traditional raising of murage through tolls – was organised through four wards: East, South, West and North Quarters, which were separated intramurally by Exeter's four main streets. In the City Receivers' accounts we can see that the money raised amounted to £28, representing far more than had been obtained by murage in any single year previously. The wards extended beyond the city walls and included the extramural parishes of St Sidwell's in the east and St David's on the north, as well as St Edmund's parish and the extramural portion of St Mary Steps on the west and a suburb outside the south gate. The wards (often referred to as 'quarters' in Exeter's local records) were formally introduced as such in 1281, at the same time that 'alderman' was recognised as a title; they also served from the early fourteenth century as the units through which the mayor's 'tourn' (or court) organised its business.[94] There is however a remarkable general consistency with the intramural and extramural territories of the city that can be defined by comparison of the evidence of Domesday Book with the eighteenth-century mapping of the city's bounds carried out for the City Chamber.[95] There is, therefore, a strong likelihood that the wards had late Saxon origins, perhaps (as suggested above at London) reflecting the move away from dependence on the shire as the city's population grew. Interestingly, the defensive origin of Exeter's east, west, south and north wards, each overseen by an alderman, was attributed in one local tradition to the tenth-century king Aethelstan, to whom was also attributed the building of the city's walls in stone.[96] We must assume on the basis of other cities' experiences that the wards of Exeter had performed not only judicial but also military functions, and later evidence for this emerges from seventeenth-century muster rolls of the militia (known as the Exeter Trained Bands) that were also organised on a ward basis.[97]

In the meantime, documentation between the late fifteenth and early seventeenth centuries reveals in practice four sorts of contribution to the practical defence of Exeter.[98] First, through the wards could be raised a militia of all adult male citizens which were inspected in periodic 'musters', producing over 1000 men in this period. Second was a smaller group of watchmen and wardsmen who patrolled the streets and guarded the gates, the former at night and the latter by day. Third, and now lying outside the ward system, were specialist groups, especially in this period skilled gunners. The City Chamber, for example, purchased new artillery in 1545, and employed specific men for its maintenance and use. Fourth, the city employed porters, responsible for shutting and opening the gates at sunset and sunrise, and for closing them at any time if the 'hue and cry' was raised. Each of the four gates had a porter and when the new Water Gate was cut through the city wall in 1565, a fifth post was created.

At York, the emergence of the city's subdivisions must have been complicated by the expansion of its enclosed areas between the Roman and Anglo-Scandinavian period and the thirteenth century. But clear evidence emerges for an internal system of manning the walls from two documents, of 1315 and 1380, known on account of the arrangement described, as 'Custodies'. Here, the walled circuit was described in successive portions, the manning of each of which was allocated to a group of parishes (with occasional exceptions, notably the archbishop's responsibility for the area known as the Old Baile). In addition, the 1380 survey named those responsible for holding keys to the city gates as well as those responsible for chains drawn across the River Ouse. Though these surveys were based on parishes, these in turn were grouped into wards known from other sources. Comparison of the 1315 and 1380 Custodies reveals that the allocation of parishes was an evolving process, as the framework was not static between these two dates. The lengths of city wall specified in the 1380 Custody varied from 100 to 650 yards; comparison of the parish groupings with the Lay Subsidy data of 1381 suggests they were manned, at least in theory, by groups of adult population totalling *c.*250, of whom some 50 percent would be the men actually relevant to the manning of the walls. Thus, there are hints of a system sustained by groups of perhaps 125 men, each probably under the direction of a constable. Another key document of 1327 had specified a system of watchmen for gates, of custody of keys, of nightly patrols, and the nightly curfew from 9pm, all under the inspection of constables, and the administration of this system can be traced in the city records down to the seventeenth century. Up until *c.*1350, there were six wards, named after the main gates of the city; from the sixteenth century this number was reduced to four. Each ward had a warden who inspected the fabric for deficiencies and reported on repairs carried out. The parishes grouped in the two fourteenth-century sources comprised between them seventeen 'custodies' that were spread over the 35 intra and extramural parishes.[99] Thus the system was a complex layering of three elements: parishes, custodies and wards. How this complexity had developed in the period before the fourteenth century is not known in detail. But in 1086 York had seven 'shires', one of which had been occupied by the royal castles, so it is tempting to equate the remaining six with the later medieval wards. If this hypothesis is correct, York provides another example of a 'ward' system having pre-Norman origins.

York was one of only four towns mentioned in Domesday Book as having internal subdivisions; the others were Cambridge (ten *custodiae*), Stamford (six *custodiae*, one of which was 'across the bridge', presumably on the opposite (south side) of the River Welland and Huntingdon (four *ferlingi*).[100] But given Domesday's general lack of consistent treatment of urban matters, its silence on other places may not be meaningful. The other examples discussed here may show the phenomenon to have been more widespread at an early date, and wards may provide something of a missing link between arrangements of the burghal period and the better documented worlds of urban militia and murage in later centuries.

A series of maps has been published for Southampton, depicting the evolution of its wards between the late thirteenth and late sixteenth centuries.[101] In 1454, a very full survey of the four wards was drawn up, listing all properties within them together with their owners and tenants, and frequently with retrospective data about past owners. To each property was allocated responsibility for the maintenance of a piece of town wall, described in terms of units called a 'loupe' (i.e. an embrasure). In general, a standard house tenement maintained one embrasure; a large tenement might maintain two, three or four; and two cottage tenements would share the maintenance of one. This system probably originated in 1377, in the context of a scare of French attack, when Edward III instructed the mayor to survey the walls and properties and to make arrangements for all to contribute to the maintenance of defences according to their wealth. At the same time, the king pardoned the city from payment of the fee-farm for a specified period so that extra funds could be spent on the walls. The 1454 survey was also made in the context of a security scare, now a perceived French threat following the English loss of Normandy and Gascony. The late thirteenth-century wards, reconstructable from sources of the Guild Merchant of that date, were supervised by aldermen and had the traditional combination of judicial and military duties, including watch and ward.

Coventry (99) differs from the above case studies in developing its walled circuit relatively late in its history, from the fourteenth century onwards. It had ten wards embracing only two large ecclesiastical parishes, and extending well beyond its walls; its bounds have been reconstructed from an eighteenth-century map.[102] Each ward was supervised by an alderman, and beneath him six constables, and had the customary collection of functions, being the basis for collecting taxes, judicial matters, organising the use of the city's common lands outside the walls, and providing watchmen for the walls and gates (in which duty the wards acted in rotation).

While it is through the wards that duties of watch were executed, the duty itself was not the product of purely local initiative, but was part of royal provision, in both town and country, extending back many centuries. In the immediate pre-Conquest period, the rural population had been obliged to serve in the royal *fyrd*, and even when the defence of *burhs* was originally dependent on the surrounding countryside we must assume that their modest resident populations will always have contributed *de facto* to defence. And these general obligations of the population had a continuous history right down to the militias of the post-medieval period. In 1181, Henry II's creation of both rural and urban militias through the Assize of Arms had long-standing consequences; in this context it was specified that burgesses were to arm themselves with leather jerkin, iron cap and spear. This general militia provision occurs in Henry III's renewed assize of arms in conjunction with a statute of 1252 enforcing watch and ward in towns. This was also included in Edward I's Statute of Winchester (1285), obliging free men to keep weapons at home for use when required. This was not repealed until the reign of James I, after which militia service continued but with arms provided by the state. The specifically urban component in the acts of 1252 and 1285 required that town gates be shut from sunset to sunrise and that watch be mounted during these hours by sixteen man at every city gate, twelve men in every borough gate and six or four in every rural township.[103] Whether these numbers were always achieved in practice we do not know, but they indicate the seriousness with which urban defence was perceived by kings who were prepared to take the initiative centrally rather than leave security entirely in the hands of local organisation. But, as in the case of murage, while kings took initiatives, local people carried the responsibilities.

Civic records frequently shed additional light on the arrangements of watch and ward. At Chester, for instance, this duty had emerged by the end of the twelfth century, a charter of *c.*1178 granting land in the city to a tenant, including freedom from obligations including 'watch'.[104] Notably, Chester's four gates were held (along with toll collection rights) by serjeanty tenure of the earls, and these arrangements continued after the earldom was taken over by the Crown and in some cases into the eighteenth century.[105] A variety of townspeople would also have had different stakes in the day-to-day running of gates. The 1148 survey of Winchester afford some insight into such groups: one gatekeeper (*barrar*) is listed, who held property near the King's Gate, in addition to three watchmen (*vigil*), each at a different one of the town's gates.[106]

Builders and masons

Surviving documents that identify masons responsible for building operations, sometimes along with details such as materials, costs and other technical specifications, represent another dimension to the social history of medieval urban defence. That it might be possible to demonstrate with a high degree of certainty a link between a known mason and the physical fabric of a length of walling or a gate can undoubtedly lend a human dimension to otherwise somewhat anonymous remains. Yet making a correlation between a building account and a physical feature of town wall architecture can also be extremely hazardous. Overall we should remember that the builders and designers of most medieval town walls remain totally obscure, the documentary record affording the tiniest of windows into the personnel of building operations.

From the corpus of available data, it is clear that there was no universal practice for the commissioning of labour; rather, surviving accounts demonstrate a number of clear categories of work in which masons were involved.[107] At one end of the spectrum was work on individual architectural features, such as Matthew the Mason's payment of £1 10s 0d for carving a stone lion over the arch of Bondgate, Alnwick in 1450 and Robert Snape's creation of 'shotholes' in the Cow Tower, Norwich in 1398-9. Other work clearly involved repairs, such as those carried out by Robert Couper on Walmgate, York in 1453. Other masons were commissioned to build or rebuild gates apparently from scratch, as with Robert Glasham's work on a new gate in Chester in 1307-8. In a rather different category are payments to masons for work best described as consultancy. In London, Robert Beverley, the mason celebrated for his work on Westminster Abbey and the Tower of London, sat in 1277-8 on a commission making the decision to rebuild the wall between Ludgate and the Thames so as to include the new buildings of the Blackfriars. Other cities had dedicated individuals responsible for inspection. At York there was a 'city mason' from the late fifteenth century; Robert Davyson, for instance, was appointed in 1477-8 to a post involving inspection of the walls and reporting faults, and the city had four elected 'muremasters' responsible for overall supervision of building works.[108] Chester similarly had its 'murengers' who continued as civic officials down to the eighteenth century, the names of some of them occurring in an inscription of that date on one of Chester's mural towers.[109]

This last point reminds us that while town walls were, at one level, features of military architecture, they were not necessarily designed and built by people we should characterise as military architects. One of the foremost masons of late fourteenth-century England, Henry Yevele, was the designer of Canterbury's West Gate, one of the most monumental of all examples of town gate architecture (*100-101*). Yet this achievement reflects only one small part of his career's work, which included castles (for instance Cooling and Queenborough, Kent) and churches (notably Canterbury Cathedral).

100 Canterbury: West Gate, viewed from within the town. *Authors' collection*

101 Canterbury: West Gate, viewed from outside the town. *Authors' collection*

Not all masons were masters of their trade. For instance, the London mason Robert Hertanger was appointed *c*.1416 to rebuild the decaying structure of the South Gate at King's Lynn but failed to fulfil his contract having spent the entire sum of money before half the work was complete, leaving the Corporation to finish the work as best they could. The gate was not completed until 1520, when Nicholas and Thomas Hermer sealed an indenture with the mayor and burgesses for eleven months of work. Notably, restoration of the structure in the early 1980s highlighted that a projected rib-vault had been abandoned in favour of a barrel vault, and identified that immediately below this section can clearly be identified a deterioration in the quality of facing stone, prior to a change higher up in the structure from Ancaster to Barnack stone.[110]

While we occasionally glimpse the nationally or internationally famous mason at work on, or organising operations on specific town walls – most notably in North Wales, where the walls of Edward I's bastides were built as part of the same construction programme as the castles led by master James of St George – generally speaking, town defences were the product of local building traditions and of a myriad of workmen, some of whose names are known to us in civic records, but who remain overwhelmingly anonymous. In certain cases we may distinguish regional architectural qualities in the architecture of town defences. The decorative flint chequer work in the upper portions of the towers on the walled circuit of Yarmouth (*102*), for instance, is paralleled in parish church architecture in the surrounding district.

At some places we know specifically that necessary building works were identified during annual inspections. Exeter is a well documented example, whose 'murally walk' (a phrase probably deriving from the French *muraille*) is known from the 1320s and died out only in the 1830s. The circuit of the city was examined by the mayor, aldermen and other officials, but in practice this annual event would be supplemented by particular inspections in time of emergency as well as by *ad hoc* reports made by citizens to the City Chamber. Works resulting were carried out through one of two routes. First, the city receiver would authorise directly relatively minor repairs and disburse appropriate funds. Second, major works were authorised by the mayor and City Chamber. Works were then contracted out to a mason who organised all necessary tasks, or a committee of aldermen might be appointed as an organising body. In almost all cases, the workmen employed were from the city's own population, and in the very full records of the later medieval period numerous trades occur: masons, carpenters, blacksmiths, glaziers, roof-tilers, painters, pavers, plumbers, quarrymen, sawyers, thatchers, labourers and carriers. Most recruitment was on an *ad hoc* basis, with a smaller number of craftsmen retained semi-permanently; from 1591, the chamber appointed a civic mason on a permanent basis. Thus, as well as illuminating events in towns, the study of building works on their walls is also a reflection of the

102 Yarmouth: a mural tower with gunports. *Authors' collection*

wider building trade and its economy, with observable developments being the product of wider national economic conditions. As an example, in Exeter between the late fifteenth and seventeenth centuries the rates of wages paid to these categories of craftsmen tripled in scale. In the late medieval and early modern period, with the exception of roofing slates, all the building materials used in the walled circuit came from within ten miles of the city, further underlining the essentially local nature of the enterprise.[111]

WALLS AND WARFARE

Walled towns faced potential or actual threats of attack at various times throughout the centuries covered by this book. In the late pre-Norman period, English and Scandinavians attacked each others' *burhs*. The English rebellions against William the Conqueror led to his ravaging of numerous shire towns. Towns were attacked by internally competing forces in the twelfth century civil war, in the Barons' Wars of the thirteenth century, and in the Wars of the Roses in the fifteenth. Indeed, arguably the bloodiest encounters involving walled towns were internecine: the civil wars of the 1640s. Alongside these internal conflicts were ongoing problems generated beyond England's borders. Western English towns, as well as towns founded in Wales and the Marches, were vulnerable to attack in the drawn-out wars which lasted to the 1290s and in their revival in the first decade of the fifteenth century. Northern English and Scottish towns were vulnerable to the passage of armies in the numerous stages of late medieval conflict between the two kingdoms. A *coda* to this saga provided the final military involvement of any English walled town: Carlisle was attacked and occupied by the Jacobites in 1745, and York was sufficiently alarmed at the prospect of this advancing army that it undertook expenditure on its walls.[112]

In the Anglo-Danish and early Norman periods, it is evident that defended towns were frequently the object of attack. The English attacked centres in the Danelaw, just as Viking armies had earlier attacked English centres, and between 1066 and 1070 William the Conqueror's need to control the framework of English shire towns led to the rapid imposition of urban royal castles within the perimeters of newly conquered towns. Thereafter, for a period, the situation becomes slightly less clear because when warfare was conducted against a town that now contained a castle, the terminology used by contemporary chroniclers does not always allow us to distinguish clearly between them. When Wallingford was attacked several times during Stephen's reign, however, it is clear that both castle and town resisted in unison; in contrast, Anarchy-period attacks on Exeter and Oxford were directed at castles, which were held separately from the walled cities in which they lay.[113]

In the popular imagination, a crenellated wall punctuated by defended gates represents primarily a military phenomenon (*103-104*). We should, from the British perspective, remember that in comparison with many other European countries, the military experience of later medieval towns was for the most part relatively limited, and generally influenced by proximity to the land borders with the Celtic-speaking world and the coastline facing France. The impression given by general histories is that fighting over walled towns was especially important in the Anglo-Danish wars and the Norman Conquest of England, then fell away during the 'castle centuries' before resurfacing dramatically and violently in the 1640s. Although attacks on towns and cities were an important part of Western European warfare in the Viking period, in the later period major sieges of cities were rare before the thirteenth century, with some exceptions such as Barbarossa's campaigns in Italy *c.*1160.[114] Even from the thirteenth century, when city sieges in Europe became more common, it is notable

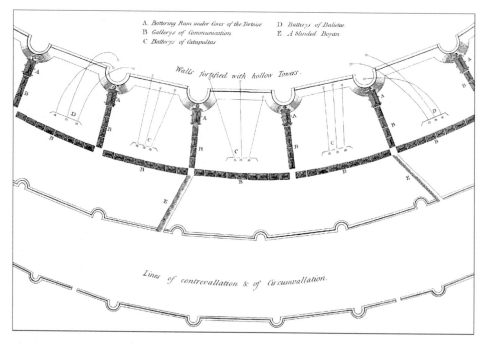

103 Schematic representation of siege theory as depicted in an antiquarian publication. *Grose, 1801*

how in Britain, even though towns were from time to time attacked and sacked, they tended not to be the subject of substantial siege operations of the sort sometimes still applied to castles. The scale of activity relating to towns in Britain was relatively modest in comparison with the experience of parts of continental Europe and the Middle East. Thus, general surveys of medieval siege warfare deal with castle sieges in Britain, but typically have little to say about towns.[115] In contrast, treatments of siege warfare in the early modern period include British urban events in the 1640s, many of which were conducted on a larger scale.[116] Accurate mapping of the occurrence of medieval sieges is, however, extremely hazardous, given the vagaries and inconsistency of historical sources. Yet it is undeniable that, of the total number of walled towns, a higher proportion were subjected to organised military assault than was the case with the total number of castles, simply because the numbers of the latter were so enormous.

An example of a siege of a walled town that we can reconstruct in particularly clear detail is the Scottish attack on Carlisle in July 1315 by the forces of Robert Bruce. The *Lanercost Chronicle* vividly describes the events of the ultimately unsuccessful ten day siege, which is also depicted in stylised form on a remarkable illustration based on the initial letter of a royal charter granted to Carlisle in 1316.[117] A great quantity and variety of siege machines and counter-siege devices were used. A stone-throwing device used against the wall and

104 A medieval siege, as depicted by Viollet-le-Duc

west gate by the besieging forces was outnumbered by seven or eight similar machines used by the defenders, who also employed javelin-throwing springalds. A timber-built belfry, said to be considerably higher than the city walls, was countered by a timber superstructure rapidly constructed by the city's carpenters and mounted on one of the mural towers, although the muddy conditions ensured that the attacker's device could not be effectively deployed. The Scots also employed siege ladders, a sow for mining the wall, faggots for filling ditches and wheel-mounted wooden bridges designed to span the moat. Yet despite the vicious and sophisticated nature of the attack, a mere two English deaths were reported: one a casualty of the stone-throwing device and the other slain by an arrow. The account also reminds us that as fortifications, town and castle were in this case practically indivisible, with both attacked simultaneously and cityfolk and garrison clearly united in defence.

In city sieges, damage to property was frequently inflicted as much by the defending forces as the aggressors, in attempts to clear defensive perimeters of encumbering housing. In Roger Mortimer's siege of Hereford in 1265, for instance, the citizens were said to have removed houses from around gates and burned others in the suburbs to enhance defensibility; widening of the city ditch, meanwhile, destroyed the prior of St Guthlac's mill and other properties of the bishop.[118] We must bear in mind, however, that direct physical traces of such dramatic events are of course elusive. Some indication of quite how ephemeral the archaeological traces of a major siege might be is provided by the case of Gloucester, the site of a well documented Royalist siege by over 30,000 men against a garrison estimated at 1,500, lasting a little under one month in 1643. Despite more than twenty excavations on the line of Gloucester's defences, nothing in the material culture would give the remotest indication of activity on such a scale.[119] Tangible physical evidence of martial activity from the period is restricted to a handful of cannon balls, musket balls, a ceramic grenade and odd items of personal equipment including a wooden priming flask, a fragment of a scabbard and a cartridge pouch. Despite the estimated loss of one third of the city, clear evidence of such destruction again proves elusive. This provides us with the salutary lessons that from earlier centuries we may well be entirely missing similar large-scale events that have remained undocumented, and that looking for physical correlations of historical battles and sieges within the archaeology may be fruitless and misleading, and only exceptionally possible (see page 231).

It is entirely correct to emphasise the social, economic, aesthetic and symbolic dimensions of town walls, themes that recur throughout this book. It is a mistake, however, to allow these emphases to detract from the protective qualities of walls, which were fundamental to the motivation of their building. In this context the careful and critical use of terminology is vital. In particular, it is helpful to make a distinction between 'security' and 'defence'. The word 'security' is useful as an indicator of the needs of urban communities for immediate protection. Here, the operation of the curfew and the control of animals, people and goods through gateways were essential mechanisms through which populations maintained orderly societies at minimum risk from more disorderly influences as well as from disease. This could also extend to the organisation of space within a town – hence the walling of internal ecclesiastical precincts whose gateways facilitated similar control over interaction between sometimes competing interest groups. At the other end of the scale, the word 'defence' allows us to consider more organised threats to which urban communities might sometimes be exposed. The experience of Exeter supplies us with examples of the types of threat that might be encountered. These ranged from a major attack of an organised military nature by a newly imposed authority (William the Conqueror's eighteen-day attack on the city in 1068) to a more local but also violent episode (the Prayer Book rebels' advance on Exeter in 1549), and finally major civil war, which in the 1640s led to massive attacks and sieges on the city's defences.

In addition to the role of urban defences as a protector of local interests, we must also acknowledge the importance of these interests in a wider collective sense in contributing to the defence of an existing kingdom or the conquest and colonisation of new territory. It is for this reason, perhaps more than the ostensible concern for communities, that in certain contexts kings made provision for an urban militia from an early date, and supported and sometimes initiated schemes of urban defence. For example, the interest shown by King John in promoting town defences in southern England must be seen against the background of a military threat from France following the loss of Normandy, while his port of Liverpool was founded in support of military action in Ireland. The Edwardian conquests of north Wales in the late thirteenth century saw the walled town used as an instrument of colonisation. In the fourteenth century it was again concern about the French threat that in the Hundred Years' War made kings sympathetic to the petitioning of communities for murage grants and other means of raising funds. Yet even if the initial construction of a town wall had a purely military rationale, the motivation for its subsequent upkeep generally came from wider social and economic stimuli.

Indeed, many factors actually hindered the military effectiveness of British town walls. The long and sometimes complex nature of their circuits, the often piecemeal and non-standardised nature of their construction, and the occasionally competing interests of the groups and individuals who had immediately adjacent properties and who might be responsible for their upkeep, might actually count against their defensive value. While sometimes able to hold off sporadic raids from external forces or resist violence and insurrection from the countryside, few town walls were designed or equipped to counter a full-scale military assault. Nevertheless, it has been argued they were strong enough to dissuade the competitors in the Wars of the Roses from focusing much attention on towns.[120]

If any sort of military rationale underlay the walling of British towns, it is important to bear in mind that ultimately they were being protected against wars fought largely by others, and in which they became entangled. Only when a king or lord founded a defended town as part of a campaign of conquest did the town have an 'offensive' quality of any sort, and for the most part in England town defences were precisely that: defences. Unlike the Italian city states, for example, no British urban community ever 'went to war' against another town. This holds an important lesson given that, were the distribution map of defended British towns to be examined from a hypothetical 'prehistoric' perspective – free of preconceptions based on documentary material – we would almost certainly assume that this map resulted from competition between communities as opposed to external stimuli and matters of status, though a coastal bias in some areas would also be observed.

CROSS-CHANNEL WARFARE

But however strong may be the memories of medieval competition between English, Welsh and Scots (and between factions amongst them), and however violent we know the reality of those conflicts sometimes to have been, it is the threat from across the Channel in the late medieval period which has perhaps more deeply affected English memory in such matters. This is, of course, partly

the result of an insular and maritime experience encompassing more than the
medieval period, and it may be that modern perceptions of a French threat in
the later middle ages are coloured by the later conflicts with France that lasted
into the nineteenth century. One suspects that there is also, from the perspective of a maritime country, something more 'romantic' and 'heroic' about both
the launching of, and resistance to, attacks from overseas – the failed Spanish
Armada of the late sixteenth century being the classic example in folk-history,
but the Dutch equivalent a century later less prominent in the popular memory
because it was less of a failure. It is important to grasp the *actualité* of the French
threat to England and its walled towns in the later medieval period. There were
two main periods, one very short and the other very protracted: in John's reign
and the early years of Henry III's reign on the one hand, and in the Hundred
Years' War of the fourteenth and fifteenth centuries on the other.[121]

The threat to southern coastal communities magnified following the loss of
Normandy in 1204, because English kings no longer controlled both sides of
the Channel, leading John to renew the charters of the Cinque Ports in 1205
in recognition of their important role in providing ships for royal service and
to invest in the naval facilities of Southampton and Portsmouth. Yet the importance of town walls appears to have been minimal: neither of these major
centres appears to have been provided with organised town defences at this
time, and when, in 1216-17 Philip pursued an English invasion with a view to
putting his son, Louis, on the English throne, the French army actually had the
support of London and did the traditional thing and attacked or threatened
royal castles, including Dover, Hertford, Berkhampsted, Colchester, Orford,
Norwich and Cambridge.[122]

The next major period of threat from across the Channel started with the
commencement of the Hundred Years' War.[123] An ongoing series of French
raids on southern English coastal towns started in 1338 with Portsmouth and
Southampton and in 1339 Dover and Folkestone. The well-chronicled devastating attack on Southampton in October 1338 by the French and their
Genoese allies highlights the potential limitations of urban defences against this
type of threat. Enquiries after the event highlighted the town's ineffective
seaward defences as a major factor contributing to the raid's success, leading
Edward III to command in March 1339 a stone wall to 'be built forthwith
towards the water', but this was not put into effect for a generation.[124] Prior to
this, the town had only been enclosed (with earthen defences and stone gates)
on two sides; the defences of the quays and waterfront had apparently
comprised ineffective timber structures, including a projecting barbican and
the gating of streets, demonstrating the conflicting interests that could occur
between the needs for defence and the commercial requirements of the town's
merchants. What is especially important about these events from an archaeological viewpoint is the clear evidence of early fourteenth-century destruction
horizons in numerous excavations.[125] While it is extremely hazardous in

medieval archaeology to seek archaeological correlations of such documented events, in this instance the widespread nature of this evidence and its relatively close dating means that such inferences can be made fairly confidently. Excavations in the 1960s on medieval tenements in West Street and High Street, for instance, revealed evidence of a massive fire in the form of burnt material on floor levels and thick charcoal horizons, while a number of pits filled with rubble and fire-damaged slate appear to indicate post-raid clearance. Properties on Cuckoo Lane, close to the medieval waterfront near the West Gate were not reoccupied following an episode of devastation. While physical damage resulting directly from the raid certainly contributed to the area's decline, then so too did the completion of the walled circuit in this area, with the wall's construction creating a market for reused stone and the area's property prices slashed because access to the waterfront was blocked. It is also not impossible that some of the 'destruction horizons' observed archaeologically in association with properties near the waterfront actually relate to the deliberate demolition of structures due to the construction of the new wall.[126] The fortunes of this area were thus reversed, converting in the course of the fourteenth century from a prosperous mercantile quarter to an economic backwater, the houses being cleared and the properties converted to gardens.

The significance of this raiding wasn't simply psychological alarm, or damage to trading places; rather it was a manifestation of the sporadic English-French struggle for control of the channel which was important in the pursuit of the wars, as well as the security of the places from which English armies embarked when kings led campaigns in France. The treaty of Bretigny (1360) brought several years of peace, open hostilities resumed with the burning of Portsmouth in 1369, plus raids on various places in the next few years, including in 1377 the burning of Hastings and Rye, a successful attack on Wight, and a failed attack on Winchelsea.[127] It was these events that motivated more royal initiative in coastal defence. 1360 saw an enquiry into Southampton's defensive weakness, and a review of Portsmouth's defences was carried out in 1386. Expenditure on southern towns concentrated not only on fabric (including, most prominently, the town gates of Canterbury and Winchester), but also on the provision of guns. Work also took place on royal castles including Carisbrooke, Corfe, Portchester, Pevensey and Southampton as well as private ones including Bodiam and Cooling.[128]

The threat of imminent military action during the reign of Richard II (1377–99) had a major influence not only on works carried out at towns and castles but an increasing incorporation of gunports in new fabric.[129] While it is the late fourteenth century that saw an intense period of raids, some did continue in the fifteenth century, although the focus shifted westwards, as demonstrated by raids on Plymouth, Dartmouth and Fowey.[130]

Overall, the attacks on these southern ports, and the responses made in the improvement of urban defences, were undoubtedly important in the evolving map of walled towns. The events which lie behind these episodes also provide a fascinating historical narrative reflecting England's long-term difficult relationship with its nearest continental neighbour. But two qualifying observations must be made, one relating to history, the other to the perception of history.

First, dramatic though some of these raids must have been, and carrying great psychological impact because they came from across the water, most of them did not constitute great military or naval events. Indeed, coastal raiding is by its nature fairly fleeting; these episodes did not generally lead to urban sieges, and Louis' campaign was conducted by an army that actually succeeded in staying in England for some considerable time. Defensive efforts occurred both in reaction to raids which had taken place and in anticipation of others, and involved early examples of 'point' defence as well as traditional walled circuits. These raids and their further potential, rapid though they often might be, were nevertheless crucial to the formation of English attitudes because in the fourteenth century the English could not be certain that raiding would not lead to more solid invasion efforts. Throughout the history of fortification, the possible and anticipated has been as influential as the actual. Henry VIII's massive scheme of coastal defence, pursued in the years either side of 1540, is an obvious example: he feared a combined threat from both Spain and France and was preparing for it (see page 221).

The second observation is that raiding on the south coastal towns, whatever impact it may have had on English attitudes, constituted no more violent activity than was perpetrated, in many other attacks on British towns, by the inhabitants against each other. The hatred and fear held for each other by the Scots and northern English was based on deeply felt ethnic and cultural differences as well as on a realistic knowledge of how cruel they could be towards each other in time of war. The relative lawlessness of the border territory added to the sense of insecurity. In Wales, the uprising of Owain Glyn Dwr involved a long sequence of violent events in urban settings (see page 99) whose character matched that of Anglo-Welsh warfare in earlier centuries. Overall, Wales shows something of a contrast with England in that many towns could be caught up in warfare, whether walled or not. Thus, the Welsh uprising of 1294–5 saw attacks on Trelech and Newport (in the south-east), Flint and Denbigh (in the north-east), and Caernarfon, Bere and Harlech (in the north-west); the revolt of 1400–4 saw attacks on Ruthin, Denbigh, Flint, Hawarden, Holt, Oswestry, Welshpool, Conwy, Caernarfon, Harlech, Kidwelly, Carmarthen, Haverfordwest, Caerleon and Usk.[131] In Ireland, the military campaigns of the sixteenth and seventeenth centuries still colour Anglo-Irish historical perception (the conflicts of the middle ages having, apparently, been relegated in popular imagination to a relatively amateur status in comparison). The two words, Cromwell and Drogheda (105), encapsulate a whole history of confrontation whose urban setting reflects so many tragic episodes in Irish history. The English dimension of the civil wars had itself involved violent sieges of defended towns on an unprecedented scale (see page 228). It has been rightly said that no conflict is as vicious as civil war.

Engaging though the 'French' narrative of the southern English defended towns may be, therefore, this external influence was but one part of a very complex story. From a French perspective, of course, it was pretty irrelevant in the long term: it led to no conquests and had little impact on lasting French perceptions. The latter were formed by quite different events: the experience of English armies marching around France, dealing with English attacks on towns and castles, engaging with them in massive field battles, and eventually expelling them. The French defeated the English, but in France rather than in England, and English defended towns ultimately played no part in the victory, though those which were also ports had been important as English bases for cross-channel efforts.

MOTIVATIONS FOR URBAN DEFENCE

Ever since the academic study of British town defences began towards the end of the nineteenth century, various contributions to the motivation of their building have been acknowledged. Explicit and implicit in all writings about urban defence have been comparisons between the relative importance of defensive issues, economic factors, and social symbolism. In illustration of this debate, which continues to play an important part in urban studies, may be quoted three discussions from the later twentieth century, in which a variety of interpretations have been pursued.

Terence Smith published a brief but forcibly argued statement in support of a traditional and militarily influenced interpretation, seeking to combat what was considered to be an unhelpful drift towards an overtly social and symbolic view of town wall-building in the post-*burh* period.[132] This argument rested on some simple observations. First, the well-documented attacks on southern coastal towns such as Rye, Winchelsea, Sandwich and Southampton in the Hundred Years' War, remind us that the need for urban defence in the face of military threat could be very real. Second, the role of kings in encouraging or even enforcing the building of defences reminds us that urban defence was not simply a local matter, but a national concern. Third, the flow of murage grants from kings to towns, while continuous from the thirteenth to the fifteenth centuries, also had peaks, reminding us that wall-building effort could be a barometer of insecurity. Fourth, town walls provide us with some of the earliest examples of gunports and up-to-date military paraphernalia, especially in the late fourteenth century. While slightly oversimplified, such considerations can support a view of town walls in which their protective value is paramount.

105 Drogheda: engraving of St Laurence's Gate. *Green 1893*

Charles Coulson extended his published arguments about late medieval castle-building based on licences to crenellate to urban studies, observing that some 29 towns received such licences (as well as individual properties within them).[133] This argument usefully reminds us that town walls were products of the rich urban classes, rather than the entirety of urban society. Urban elites sought licences for some wall-building projects for essentially the same reasons as castle-builders: the licence added to the social prestige of the enterprise and emphasised the link of loyalty between subject and ruler. According to such an interpretation, phrases within the licences relating to local and national security were formulaic expressions meeting the required formalities. In practice, however, only the enhancement of urban prestige can explain the overall level of effort, because as the author maintains, in military terms 'Town 'defences', with few exceptions, were too weak, too incomplete and too few to have provided an effective framework of national protection'.[134]

David Palliser, in contrast, took a multi-dimensional approach to the problem, allowing that in situations extending over many centuries motivations may have varied greatly with time, place and circumstance.[135] Rather than seeking an all-encompassing explanation, this approach emphasises the importance of the individual contexts of town wall-building. In addition, this view reminds us that explaining the motivations of wall-building should not be confined to examination only of walled towns. An holistic explanation lies in consideration of the occurrence of fortification in the wider urban tradition: walls were by no means an essential ingredient of town growth, and the historically significant question is really: why did *some* towns have walls? Most towns, taking an overall view of the British Isles, did not have walls (see page 218). Such a flexible approach allows also for important elements of non-conformity in situations where we might expect patterns to emerge. Thus, not all towns near borders were walled. Not all big towns were walled. Some towns tried to be walled but failed. Some towns were walled largely through local initiative, others as a result of royal policy. Finally, the contribution of two types of lordship – royal and seigneurial – was significant. Generally, kings were more supportive than other lords, and ecclesiastical lords in particular were very ungenerous in supporting defensive initiatives, as highlighted by examples of towns such as Beverley, Ely, Lichfield, St Albans, Salisbury and Wells, all of which were never walled despite their size, wealth and importance.

Illuminating though these approaches are, there can in fact be no single over-arching explanation for the phenomenon of town walls, whose building extended over many centuries and encompassed many circumstances. A militaristic emphasis within town wall study retains a legitimate place, as does the honorific interpretation of licences to crenellate, while examination of the spread of urban defence through settlement hierarchy links the debate to wider settlement studies. However, modern analysis of buildings allows for more flexible interpretation of their meanings, and we know that vast amounts of wall-building took place outside the context of military threat. Licences to crenellate, however illuminating in their own right, apply to only a tiny proportion of the total number of walled towns, and their specific circumstances make generalisation based on them hazardous. Most importantly, it is a serious mistake to create a false dichotomy between the 'military' and 'symbolic' importance of town walls that is over-simplistic in its implications. We hope the material presented in this book illustrates this crucial point clearly, underlining the exceptionally wide spectrum of functions fulfilled by town defences of all forms and dates.

Independence and division

It may be wrong to assume that the supposed attractiveness and status of walls around settlements was constant through time. In particular, in the late Anglo-Saxon period renewed occupation of old Roman walled towns and the building of new walled *burhs*, is too easily seen as a natural resumption of an earlier Roman practice, interrupted by an atypical period. In fact, the circumstances of the middle Anglo-Saxon period are very revealing. The English *wic* trading settlements deliberately eschewed the protection of nearby Roman defences, just as trading settlements at other places in the North Sea and Baltic regions were also not defended when first established.[136] Explaining the motivation for this condition remains problematical: did it reflect the wishes of merchants themselves or of the kings who were their patrons? Did it reflect independent mercantile spirit or an unwillingness of rulers to see trading communities established in separately defensible centres? The insecurities of the Viking period, however, led to renewed interest in defences and it can be argued that the policy of *burh* foundation led by Alfred had urban intent from the start, as revealed by new street plans and the establishment of mints. But Alfred's contemporary biographer, Asser, noted the reluctance of the king's subjects to work on *burh* building,[137] and the shire-dependent Burghal Hidage system suggests that the resident populations of *burhs* were initially very low (see page 58). Allowing for difficulties of dating and the differential survival of evidence, the impression gained from archaeology is that, while the occupation of *burhs* in the south picked up in the late ninth century, it was the later tenth century before activities were sufficiently wide-ranging to be described as 'urban life'.[138]

It may well be, therefore, that what from the later medieval perspective seems to have been a 'natural' development of defended towns was, in fact, something at which kings had to work hard in the later ninth and earlier tenth centuries. For them, the motivations were presumably partly military and partly governmental – these places providing not only defensive centres but also foci for their authority. But this enthusiasm may not have been matched in the early stages by their subjects, to whom 'urbanism' may not have had a natural appeal. And, if this was so, the civic quality of town walls cannot have been an original feature of burghal life, especially as they were maintained by the shires in the first instance. When William the Conqueror attacked English towns in 1068–70, their defences may have been a source of pride as well as having practical applications. But such a sentiment was likely to have been little more than a century old at the time of the Norman Conquest. In short, we may suggest that nucleation in its urban (and, to an extent, also its rural) forms, was actually seen as artificial by post-Roman populations whose instinct was for a more isolated lifestyle. And might the attitudes of the landowning classes regarding their own properties be revealing? Although, from the late Anglo-Saxon to the late medieval period the landowning elites maintained some urban properties, their preferences remained with rural life, which was not always the case in more intensively urbanised parts of Europe, especially southern areas.

In the later medieval period, it is easy to assume that walls and gates belonged to people living in towns in the same way that other urban properties did. On a day-to-day basis towns probably did feel they owned them, or at least their mayors, aldermen and corporations did. But, in another sense, urban defences belonged to those who had made their building possible. In the case of Welsh marcher defended boroughs, this might be a baronial family. But in England it was kings who had been either the enforcers or the enablers of urban defence, from their building of *burhs* in the ninth and tenth centuries (which depended on labour obligations due to kings from the shires), through their development of murage, their grants of licences to crenellate, and their eventual permitting of urban properties to raise property taxes in the towns themselves. Thus, to a certain extent, urban defences were always royal. The strong tradition of urban allegiance to English kings was part of the same picture. Sometimes, specific legal issues remind us of this. In the twelfth and thirteenth centuries, the strips of land immediately inside some walls were said to be specifically royal property when threatened with encroachment, as at Canterbury and Winchester, because they had been original features crucial to access to the defences.[139] When the city of Oxford obtained its fee-farm from the king in 1199, it also acquired some areas that had traditionally been royal property, including the city defences and moat and a strip of intramural space.[140] And such distinctions of ownership could persist into the post-medieval period. For example, in 1632–3 the Crown and City Chamber of Exeter were in conflict over the ownership of the immediately extramural strips of Southernhay and Northernhay, occupying the former city ditches, resulting in the city surveyor, Sherwood, creating a map to illustrate the properties in question.[141]

Particularly when viewed in the pan-European context, a central question to be addressed is how far the building of town walls in the British Isles represented the achievement of any level of independence by urban communities. The answer, in simple terms, is very little indeed, because British urbanism itself had no real political independence, but had a social independence limited to the creation and display of wealth, of communal identity, of limited self-government, and of a sense of separation from the countryside. Within these limited aspirations and achievements, town walls might play a part, since they were a visible symbol of these features. Nevertheless, as will be emphasised below (see page 218), walled towns were a relatively small proportion of the total number of urban places, as walls were not (as is commonly perceived) an absolutely essential symbol of medieval urban life.

During the twelfth and thirteenth centuries, English towns often achieved liberties, including rights to elect their own sheriffs, to have guilds, and to have the royal fee-farm (that is, to control the tax burden due to kings), and to possess seals that symbolised their 'corporate identities' (see page 167). Among provincial towns, Bristol received the exceptional right to be made a county in a charter of 1373.[142] More commonly, liberties were enshrined in charters granted by kings and others that have become a hallmark of urban status.[143] Nevertheless, kings and others remained undisputed lords of such towns, whose ambitions remained generally in the local rather than the political sphere. Although kings frequently granted privileges by charter, the independence of towns was effectively limited by the royal retention of jurisdiction over all but relatively petty offences. Lesser legal matters, together with a whole range of property, inheritance, finance and commercial issues, were dealt with by the courts presided over by mayors and councils that came to characterise many thirteenth-century towns.[144]

London's experience, however, was slightly different. It achieved its own sheriff and justiciar and controlled its own fee-farm as early as Henry I's reign. Twice, in Stephen's reign and John's reign, it achieved 'commune' status (itself a notion borrowed from French practice), with greater powers of self-governance and it was the first British town to have its own mayor, elected from amongst its aldermen, in 1190. Its leading citizens soon called themselves barons, by analogy with the landed gentry, and their ultimate ambition was probably to free London from the royal demesne and its liability to tallage.[145] Even in this period, however, the political ambition of the Londoners did not find expression in the extension of the walled enceinte. London was, in turn, troublesome to Stephen, John and Henry III, but Edward I brought it back firmly under royal control, his massive extension of the Tower of London a visible symbol of this reaffirmation of royal control. From then on, London was increasingly the royal capital rather than a place of independent political ambition. The Roman waterfront wall was a feature of later Saxon London's defences, though the inhabitants also developed the waterfront immediately outside as a trading place. But by c.1100 the demolition of the wall had begun. It is tempting to see this as a deliberate royal reduction of the city's defensibility to reduce its potential for resistance to the new Norman regime, although a less dramatic motive may have been the opening of the riverside for commercial use.[146] By the later medieval period, there were clearly no organised riverside defences, and the water gates were supplemented with timber bretasching in times of threat.[147] What is abundantly clear is that after the eleventh century London was, in terms of its walled enceinte, actually a less defensible place than before.

With the interesting exception of London's commune experience, the English experience was characterised by royal control over towns (and seigneurial authority in the case of many new towns), rather than by the independent urban ambition seen in so much of Europe. Although the details of lordship and allegiance varied – including towns and cities whose only lord was the king, seigneurial towns established in English shires, and seigneurial towns established in the quasi-independent marcher lordships – kings remained overlords of all. It was the late thirteenth century before we can speak of 'urban oligarchies' and the notion of 'patrician' urban government is barely applicable to the English middle ages.[148] These royal connections were rooted in the essentially royal character of late Anglo-Saxon urbanism and there was, throughout the middle ages a strong sense of loyalty between urban communities and kings; what was important to the inhabitants of so many towns was that their only lord was the king. The rebellions of the Anglo-Saxon shire towns against the new Norman regime between 1068-70 were a violent but perhaps atypical episode in urban history. On the whole, royal attitudes to towns were generous, and their extension of liberties engendered loyalty rather than independence. These circumstances, together with the generally low level of internal warfare, the generally small size of most towns, and the generally strong traditions of royal government, created a situation in which towns were integrated with the apparatus of royal power rather than in opposition to it. Anglo-Norman power in Wales and Ireland, and Scottish royal power in the northern kingdom had essentially the same experience. From another point of view, we might also ask whether the relative reluctance of seigneurial and ecclesiastical lords in England to support wall-building might be attributed not only to the fact that it would have given the burgesses ideas above their stations, but also that if murage grants were needed this would have effectively given the king more authority over their boroughs.

It is revealing that, while we are accustomed to think of borough charters as one of the main defining criteria of settlements with 'urban' status, their contents reveal a whole range of legal and mercantile matters, but rarely any emphasis on urban defences. This underlines the argument, made at various times in this book, that walls were not an essential quality of urbanism in medieval Britain. Oblique references to defensive matters do sometimes occur in borough charters, as at Inverness (1171x97), where the Scots king undertook to ditch the town while the burgesses should build a palisade on its bank; others include Bury St Edmunds (1121x38), Egremont (c.1202) and Corbridge (after 1212). But the incidence of such references in both the twelfth and thirteenth centuries is very sparse.[149]

While traditional narratives have seen town walls as symbolising rigid division between sophisticated townscapes and their rural hinterlands, we should bear in mind that the relationship between town and country was more dynamic and complex than this caricature suggests.[150] The walled enceinte provided a superficial display of unity for communities that could be remarkably fragmented and, as has been demonstrated, large sections of urban populations lived beyond the defences.

By embracing some portions of an urban population and excluding others, a town wall could make physical divisions of status within an urban population and might physically disrupt property, as at Southampton, where the fourteenth-century arcade truncated a series of merchants' houses (106), see also page 111). On occasion urban property could be destroyed or displaced due to the construction or redevelopment of defences, just as numerous Norman castles were imposed on inhabited urban areas in the late eleventh century. At Gloucester, for instance, the burgesses who were commanded by the king to enlarge part of the south town ditch in 1266-7 demolished a number of houses.[151] Whereas some urban centres had only ever comprised one focus of growth, in other cases the 'town' was the product of 'polyfocal' growth, in which a number of originally separate nuclei coalesced, with or without walls surrounding them. Several examples of this process have been encountered: a classic example is Norwich, whose walls, built in the later thirteenth and early fourteenth centuries, encompassed several originally distinct settlements. It is interesting to speculate how far identities and loyalties, belonging originally to separate places, may have survived the apparent 'unification' of the whole urban place. It has been pointed out that in some later medieval references to the wards of London, such territorial units were referred to as the *patriae* (homelands) of their residents.[152]

Where a new circuit was built around a sprawling town that had grown up organically, as at Coventry and Norwich, a new wall alignment would effectively amputate and 'suburbanise' elements of existing populations. Indeed, the sequence of wall-building at Coventry provides powerful evidence that the circuit was not built in a sequence dictated by defensive concerns alone. In a town historically divided into two parts – the northern sector belonging to the priory and the wealthier southern part a property of the earl – it was on the wall around the southern part that the earliest building operations from the 1350s onwards were focused. Notably, the walling seems to have begun very soon after the 'Tripartite Indenture' of Coventry in 1355, which afforded the town a new measure of unity.[153] Yet the royal confirmation of the Corporation's ownership of the wall in 1399 marked not the completion of a full enceinte, but indicated that the circuit had reached the boundary of the earl's property. Work on the remaining defences continued in tortuous fashion – at some stages involving notional construction of a small stretch of wall annually – into the sixteenth century.[154]

Another clear example of a town where the topography of defence represented social division is Nottingham. Here the communities of the 'English' borough (defined by the boundary of the former *burh*) and 'French' borough (representing from the late eleventh century the new commercial heart of the town, embraced within an extended enceinte linked to the castle) were originally ethnically distinct and still distinguished legally until the fifteenth century.[155] New Norman French boroughs planted adjacent to existing enclosed English settlements at Hereford and Norwich are also known; both were similarly later embraced within extended circuits. Issues of ethnic identity are also reflected in the settlement of the English bastides in North Wales. With the exception of Aberystwyth, all Edward I's castle-dependent bastides were intended as exclusively English settlements; at Caernarfon, for instance, two hundred years of English dominance was only brought to an end by royal charter in 1507, which allowed Welshmen to live within the walls.[156]

A particularly illuminating case where the physical properties of a town wall embodied the ambition and identity of a particular sector of the urban population is the Portwall on the south side of the city of Bristol, this representing a thirteenth-century expansion of the enceinte. Excavations on the northern

106 Southampton: a merchant's house, disrupted by the insertion of the town wall.
Authors' collection

part of the Portwall have identified a sophistication of military architecture lacking where this line of the city's defences has been sampled in other places.[157] The wall's internal face was pierced by some 22 'casemates' providing access to loops regularly placed at intervals of 5.75m, giving an appearance of immense defensive strength probably heightened by further loops in the 'spines' revealed by excavation of Tower Harratz that marked the terminus of this defensive line. A likely explanation for the unusual level of defence afforded to this sector is that in this part of the city, the wall embraced the area of Temple Fee occupied by the Knights Templar, being designed as the symbol and substance of their military authority and perhaps influenced by their Middle Eastern castles. That excavation showed the casemates to have been blocked in the fourteenth century may provide further, circumstantial evidence of this link, as the Templars were suppressed in 1319 and their lands confiscated.

Another way in which walls might represent division rather than inclusion is seen where urban growth took the form of several separate nuclei that coalesced into a compound settlement with one name (an illuminating analogy here is the 'polyfocal' model for the growth of villages between the eighth and twelfth centuries).[158] A particularly important case in point is Durham.[159] Here, the 'town' wall that had developed by the twelfth century enclosed only a very specialist focus, comprising military and ecclesiastical buildings and precincts, and was only extended northwards in the early fourteenth century around the marketplace of the Bishop's Borough (see page 95). Yet the bulk of the urban population, found in the four remaining boroughs (Old Elvet, New Elvet, St Giles and Old Borough), remained undefended. Moreover, although these boroughs had either the bishop or the prior as lord, they were not extramural suburbs that developed around an earlier nucleus, but represented semi-discrete settlements of equivalent antiquity, with their own street patterns and churches. The inhabitants of what later became known overall as 'Durham', for much of the medieval period identified themselves with the borough in which they lived. Arguably, however, the walled area would provide a refuge for these populations in the manner of nearby castles such as Bamburgh and Dunstanburgh, and there is some evidence that tenure of properties in the boroughs might involve contributing to maintenance of the walls. In this respect, there may be some limited analogy with the functioning of wards in other, larger, walled places (see page 184). What is important in this context is that the 'town' wall did not actually include the town, but represented the interests of specific, non-mercantile, high-status groups. Another analogy is the fragmented defensive topography of Lincoln (see page 94).

In other cases, the wall or ditch of a town might mark the boundary of a lord's park. At Coventry, for instance, the 'Hersum Ditch' defined the northern boundary of the twelfth-century park associated with an early castle, and the southern boundary of the town at this stage of its development. Something of the social function of this work may be indicated in the place name *Hersumdich*, probably deriving from the Old English root *hiran* ('to obey') and conveying the message to burgesses not to stray into what was effectively a seigneurial green-belt.[160] At Launceston, the topographical relationship between the town wall and adjoining deer park of the earls of Cornwall suggest a deliberately contrived approach highlighting that the entire ensemble represented a 'landscape of lordship'. Essentially similar planned relationships between castle and parks at places such as Castle Rising and Devizes may indicate other cases in point.[161]

While the overwhelming bulk of evidence points towards the security provided by walls being commercially advantageous, we should not overlook that wall-building could also be burdensome, and at least in one case, might actually prove to be detrimental to trade. At Portsmouth, the murage grant of 1342 (which had been received soon after a French attack on the town) was cancelled following petitioning from the burgesses on the grounds that trade was being lost, although we cannot of course be certain that this was their true motive.[162] Also of relevance here are those towns where murage grants are recorded but walling did not take place (see page 182), places where walls disrupted townscapes or condemned certain districts to decline (page 211), places where grand plans were left unfinished (page 98), and the many walled towns that failed (page 79). The simple message here is that defence did not necessarily guarantee success, though it might be an important ingredient in it.

Defence and the urban hierarchy

Since the late nineteenth century, debate has continued over the relative contributions to the growth of urbanisation in the medieval period, and the constitutional, legal, military, economic and social characteristics of towns have been variously emphasised; in this context, however, a useful guideline is that provided by Reynolds, who reminds us that, whatever variety of influences can be identified overall, at root two essential characteristics made an English town different from the countryside.[163] First, a large proportion of its population lived off a variety of non-agricultural activities (with marketing functions probably in consequence). Second, the elements of its population felt something in common with each other but something different from their rural neighbours, and probably something in common with the inhabitants of other towns. Within this basic framework, however, enormous differences existed between towns both walled and unwalled.

In the following discussion, analysis is offered relating to the quantities and types of town that were walled, together with their distribution through time and space. But it is useful to begin with the observation that, although the British Isles had many towns by the later middle ages (and, putting aside for the moment the issue of why so many of these were *not* enclosed), the scale of urbanism in individual British places did not approach that encountered in some other parts of Europe, particularly those influenced by the legacy of the former Roman provinces. Amongst British towns, though some such as Norwich and Bristol came to cover sizeable areas, it was only London where the size of population compared with the larger European cities. Of the walled towns of early fourteenth-century Europe north of the Alps and Pyrenees, only Paris and London were in the same league as the larger southern European centres with populations of 50,000 plus.[164] Thus, even the largest and architecturally finest British circuits pale into insignificance against Italian medieval cities such as Florence, where the sixth extension of the wall in the late thirteenth century increased the enclosed area to 650 hectares, and Siena, whose population lay within a monumental wall pierced by 36 gates.[165] The movements that saw many European towns achieve partial or complete independence from their lords hardly applied in the British Isles, where the defences of major towns, on account of their origins, were in a sense owned by the king – a notion that persisted into the nineteenth century at York. By the fourteenth century the expanded walled city of York just reached the size ranking of European towns such as Antwerp and Bremen, but represented a tier on the European urban hierarchy far below that reached in the Mediterranean zone. Very large numbers of British towns were very small indeed. As well as the difference in size between the walled towns of Britain and much of the rest of Europe, very few British towns had extramural jurisdictions (other than the extramural parts of parishes and wards), when compared to the rural areas sometimes attached to major continental towns.[166]

Thus the synonymity of walls and urban character and density of population was not as clear in Britain as it often was elsewhere, and consequently in a British context town walls characterised neither the notion of urban independent ambition nor the pursuit of warfare in the way that was true of much of Europe by the later middle ages.

One very simple indication of the status inherent in an urban community's possession of defences was where a walled shire town remained the only fortified community within that shire. Places such as Bedford, Chester, Launceston and Leicester enjoyed a monopoly on urban defence in this way. In the areas of England with the highest densities of later and new boroughs (and, consequently, where these tended to be small in size), it was generally only pre-Conquest towns, or those of exceptional size or importance, that were defended, as in Devon and Gloucestershire. In contrast, and one might almost argue paradoxically, in some contexts the custom of wall-building percolated down the hierarchy of British towns and reached a remarkably modest level of urban settlement, especially in Wales. Urban fortification was, therefore, certainly not spread evenly throughout the urban hierarchy, yet neither is there a 'cut off' point of population or size beneath which towns were never provided with defences. Nor was it simply boroughs with the most powerful patrons that had defences: the royal plantation adjacent to Windsor castle, after all, was never walled.

This last example provides an important reminder that royal association did not necessarily lead to urban achievements including the building of walls; indeed, it might actually retard growth and defensive developments. Up until 1110, the Norman kings used the Saxon palace at Old Windor alongside their new castle established at Windsor c.1070, but thereafter Windsor became a main residence and hunting centre. By the 1130s, a borough was developing here, but it remained securely controlled by the castle constable up to the late thirteenth century, and only in Edward I's reign did New Windsor have a borough charter and the right to appoint its own bailiffs. Even then, royal influence remained strong. Legal and financial records suggest the medieval town itself was never very prosperous. The royal household, its servants and the castle garrison always comprised a very large proportion of the total population of the settlement. Extensions of the castle site were sometimes to the detriment of urban tenements, as with Henry III's western extension of the Lower Ward.[167] An illuminating parallel is Ludgershall, where extensions to the royal castle and hunting lodge infringed on properties within the borough, the growth of which was restricted and indeed strangulated by the royal presence.[168] Other unenclosed boroughs adjacent to regularly used royal castles include Corfe and Orford; at Queenborough walls were intended but never built; at Odiham, and Portchester, associated settlements never attained borough status.[169] This observation – of royal influence limiting the achievement and defensive development of associated subordinate settlements –

contrasts markedly, of course, with the generosity that kings showed to the shire and other larger towns, in granting murage and other liberties, because such places were buttresses of royal power throughout the kingdom.

This in turn reminds us of two important distinctions to be made among the smaller walled towns. First, general statistics for the walling of towns reveal that seigneurial boroughs were less likely to have walls than the royal towns and cities, often because the latter were commonly early walled foundations and because wall-building by such communities was seen by kings not as an alarming display of independence but a demonstration of local security contributing to national security and thus a gesture of allegiance. Lesser lords, in contrast, may have been more suspicious of their burgesses' aspirations and this seems to have been particularly the case with ecclesiastical lords. Second, on the other hand, the numerous enclosed boroughs that developed alongside seigneurial castles from the eleventh to the thirteenth castles are manifestations not of the ambition of burgesses but of an extension of the social and economic influence of the lords of these castles. Such settlements approximated to outer baileys of economic character rather than representing socially independent units.

The proportion of failed boroughs that were enclosed is markedly higher in Wales than in England. In Wales, at least seven and probably twelve of the eighteen failed boroughs identified by Bereford possessed defences: Denbigh, Dolforwyn, Dryslwyn, Dynevor, Kenfig, Kidwelly, Rhuddlan and probably Bere, Cefnllys, Newtown (Dynevor) Skenfrith and Whitecastle. In England, only three and possibly five of the twenty three failures were defended: Caus, Skipsea, Richard's Castle and possibly Belvoir and Trematon. Given the overall proportions of boroughs that were walled in both countries, one thing is clear: in Wales (where a larger proportion of boroughs were walled), a defended town was more likely to fail than one that was un-enclosed; in England, the reverse was true. The principal reason for this trend is the fact that so many Welsh boroughs originated as castle-dependent nuclei, sometimes located in physical positions prejudicial to long-term commercial success, and always dependent on the viability of castles, which to some extent lessened after c.1300.

Any overall calculation of the proportion of towns that were defended is, of course, hazardous given the occasional impossibility of defining what consti-tuted a town (and how many existed, either cumulatively or at any given point in time), and what constituted defence. Different commentators have arrived at different figures for the number of defended towns in England and/or Wales and Scotland (see gazetteer). It is for these reasons that this book has not presented a definitive distribution map. Yet what is abundantly clear is that the number (and proportion) of towns that are known to have been defended has increased as new evidence – in particular derived from archaeological excava-tion – has come to light. With these caveats in mind, broad figures estimating the proportion of towns that was walled are useful. There existed some 640 boroughs in medieval England and about 90 in Wales, whereas the largest esti-mation of defended towns is 211 for England and just over 55 for Wales.[170] While not all these boroughs coexisted, and those that possessed defences did not necessarily do so at the same time, what is clear is that no more than perhaps one third of boroughs in England, and a little over half in Wales, were fortified in some way at some stage. This difference is thrown into sharper light when bearing in mind the non-urban nature of the Welsh landscape in the early eleventh century, whereas in England a higher proportion of the total number of towns were walled in the tenth century than at any subsequent stage. In short, defence and town plantation were far more closely linked in post-Conquest Wales relative to England.

An examination of the town defences of Scotland reminds us once more that the provision of walls was not necessarily the norm for urban settlement. Any comparison with the figures for England and Wales is hazardous given the high incidence of towns equipped with free-standing gates and/or town ditches in Scotland; perhaps more telling, however, is the fact that no more than five percent of the entire stock of Scottish burghs were walled before the fifteenth century. The phenomenon of walled towns is also not a simple index of violence and warfare. The taking and retaking of Scottish burghs was a char-acteristic feature of the Wars of Independence, yet a mere handful of towns here were enclosed in the medieval period, and where they were this was usually late (see page 75). The burgh of Peebles was burned by English forces on three separate occasions between the end of the fourteenth century and the middle of the sixteenth century, and it was only in 1570 that a decision was taken to wall the town. The low incidence of defended towns along the Anglo-Scottish border (including non-defended towns on the English side such as Hexham and Morpeth) is notable, and points towards town defences (which cluster far more thickly, for instance, along the Welsh Marches) being related to specific types of low-level threat and seigneurial policy. An illumi-nating parallel is the high density of early castles along the English-Welsh border relative to the Anglo-Scottish border.[171]

It is almost certainly not coincidental that a comparatively small proportion of towns founded by ecclesiastical lords possessed integrated defences. Many of the larger and more important examples, such as Beverley, Glasgow and St Andrew's, were provided with stone gates but no enclosing defences; at others, such as Bury St Edmunds, Salisbury and Wells, initiatives to build complete walled circuits were fizzled out or never started; and smaller ecclesiastical boroughs such as Farnham, were provided with surrounding earthworks that were jurisdictional rather than defensive.

FURTHER READING

The chronological and spatial character of medieval urbanisation is covered in D.M. Palliser (ed.), *The Cambridge Urban History of Britain, Vol. I* (Cambridge University Press, 2000). The development of the urban hierarchy in general, and urban–rural relationships in particular are the subject of D. Perring (ed.), *Town and Country in England: Frameworks for Archaeological Research* (Council for British Archaeology, 2002).

Medieval warfare in a European context is the subject of N. Hooper and M. Bennett, *Cambridge Illustrated Atlas of Warfare in the Middle Ages 768-1487* (Cambridge University Press, 1996).

5

LEGACIES:
THE FATE AND FUTURE OF
TOWN WALLS

If British town walls of the medieval period have received insufficient academic attention, then traditions of urban defence from the sixteenth century onwards have been even more seriously neglected. Indeed, for many places it was actually the English Civil Wars of the 1640s – representing something of a violent 'last hurrah' for town defences – that saw some of the most 'real' military use for circuits of Roman and medieval origin. Too often, the end of the fifteenth century has been seen as a cut-off point for the significant history of Britain's town defences, marking a downturn after a perceived heyday in the thirteenth and fourteenth centuries, with subsequent disinvestment in urban defence mirroring urban fortunes and pride.[1] It is tempting yet erroneous to see the Tudor period as heralding the death knell of British town defences. In many cases, walls and related features undoubtedly became derelict and progressively encroached upon by sprawling urban communities, while investment in royal military infrastructure was increasingly directed towards coastal artillery forts. The whirlwind programme of fort-building carried out by Henry VIII in response to the invasion crisis of 1538 resulted in numerous such installations being built in the vicinity of towns, including the 'castles' of Calshot (commanding an approach to Southampton Water), and Southsea (guarding Portsmouth Sound), and works at Melcombe Regis and Poole.[2] Yet these fortifications were components within a national scheme of defence, constructed to deny to an enemy military assets such as quays, anchorages and strategic harbours, rather than to afford immediate protection specifically to urban populations.

Continued activity in the arena of town defence can, however, be noted in two senses during the Tudor and early Stuart periods. First, we should not overlook that many towns, and in particular places with maritime connections such as Exeter, Harwich, King's Lynn, Rye and Yarmouth, did see continued investment in and maintenance of existing walls and gates, although their circuits were not radically reorganised. Second, a significant handful of towns with particular strategic value saw large-scale investment in new works that complemented and/or transformed existing medieval circuits, as at Berwick-upon-Tweed (*colour plate 30*), Carlisle, Hull, Portsmouth and Plymouth. In many of these cases, however, it was effectively naval facilities that were being protected rather than urban populations as a whole.

These Tudor improvements to existing town defences, usually initiated and funded by the Crown, took a great variety of forms. At Rye, for instance, massive investment during the late fifteenth and first half of the sixteenth century saw not only the scouring of the ditch and rebuilding of the medieval wall, but additional measures to face seaborne threats, such as the construction of stone-filled timber groynes to strengthen the northern part of the town ditch, the artificial scarping and steepening of surrounding cliffs and the addition of artillery bulwarks.[3] The massive destruction and sale of urban monastic buildings and properties resulting from the Dissolution could, on occasion, even have a positive spin-off effect for town defences. At Exeter, for instance, the church of St John's hospital found a new use as the city's artillery store, while stone from the priory of St Nicholas was used to patch up part of the ancient enceinte.[4]

Nor should we assume that town walls were not needed militarily in the post-medieval period. For instance, four of the five occasions on which the city walls of Exeter (as distinct from the castle) were attacked after the Norman Conquest, took place during or after the Tudor period (the full list being: William the Conqueror's siege in 1068; assault by the supporters of Perkin Warbeck in 1497; attack during the Prayer Book Rebellion of 1549; Royalist assault in 1643; and the Parliamentarian siege of 1646).[5] An analogous case is that of York. While the city was threatened militarily in 1216 and 1264 (rebel barons), 1319 and 1327 (Scots), 1469 and 1489 (local rebels), 1487 (Lambert Simnel's supporters), 1536 (Pilgrims of Grace) and 1569 (northern earls) the only serious military action it actually faced in the later medieval or early modern periods was during the eleven-week siege of 1644.[6]

Yet while in terms of overall levels of investment in *old* circuits and a near total halt in the creation of *new* circuits, an overall pattern of decline is evident in town defences by the sixteenth century, few generalisations are possible about the fate of town walls in England and Wales. The experiences of individual towns differed markedly, depending on factors such as pressure on urban space and the type of physical obstacle provided by defences, as well as physical location and the presence or absence of a strategic role, now from a government point of view, in changing military circumstances. Yet even a town in an unexposed inland position such as Coventry might maintain its defences into the seventeenth century: here as late as 1636, the burgesses rebuilt a crumbling part of their wall near Whitefriars to maintain the integrity of the enceinte.[7] An intramural route might also be useful for maintaining internal security: at Southampton, in 1633, for instance, a footpath behind the walls was built to allow the officers of the town to 'pursue Vagrant idle people and all sorts of other trespassers'.[8]

One trend that can be observed, however, is that many of the better preserved urban defences are found in towns that did not expand greatly in the post-medieval period. The survival of the town walls of Conwy and Caernarfon provides good evidence for this fact, as do the defences of Wallingford, which are arguably the most impressive urban fortifications of the late Saxon period anywhere in England, preserved largely because of the town's contraction from its medieval heyday (*107-108*). Another observation is that sometimes those parts of a town wall that bordered a high-status precinct were maintained and refurbished long after the citizens had neglected and robbed other parts of the circuit. At Winchester, for instance, the surviving stretch of city wall on the east part of the circuit was preserved because it also formed the precinct wall of Wolvesey Palace (*109*), while the walls of Oxford only survive where the circuit runs through the grounds of New College (*110*).

Mapping early-modern town defences

The development of artillery fortification in the Tudor period was closely – indeed inextricably – linked to the increasingly scientific art of map-making,

107 Wallingford: the bank and ditch of the *burh* defences on the west side of the circuit. *Authors' collection*

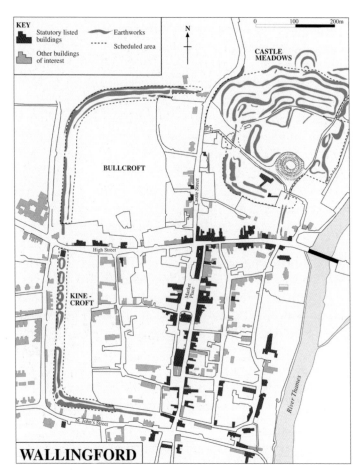

KEY

Statutory listed buildings

Other buildings of interest

Earthworks

Scheduled area

CASTLE MEADOWS

BULLCROFT

KINE - CROFT

High Street

Castle Street

Market Place

River Thames

St. John's Street

WALLINGFORD

108 Left Wallingford: plan of the burh, showing key archaeological features

109 Opposite, above Winchester: crenellated stretch of the city wall, in the vicinity of Wolvesey Palace. *Authors' collection*

110 Opposite, below Oxford: plan of New College, showing the surviving city wall in its grounds (the wall can be seen running from left to right approximately one third of the way down the illustration). *VCH 1954*

with the ability of maps to portray lines of fire from artillery installations becoming an essential part of fortification design. Of the first generation of scale maps drawn by military engineers in the sixteenth century, a high proportion depicted fortifications that in some way related to towns and ports, including good examples of Carlisle, Dover, Harwich and Hull.[9] The link between the emerging science of artillery fortification and the art of map-making is particularly well illustrated by the sequence of maps depicting the transformation of Carlisle in the 1540s by the Hungarian land-surveyor and military engineer Stefan von Haschenperg. The maps show that rather than renewing the medieval enceinte, Carlisle was re-fortified with two artillery forts at either end of the crumbling circuit, one a transformation of the medieval castle and the other a new work known as the Citadel (*colour plate 31*).[10] As was often the case with this type of source, however, this was a map of intent rather than a depiction of a completed project, the ambitious scheme being never realised in full. And it is also far from coincidental that the first surviving example of a town map drawn in plan form to an accurate scale (one

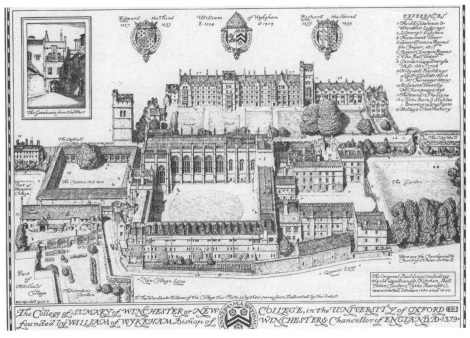

inch: 100ft) was of the strategically vital port town of Portsmouth in 1545. This showed a planned circuit complete with angled bastions, depicted along with the street plan in plain mechanical fashion, representing the art of the military engineer in a style far removed from the medieval picture-map.[11]

From the sixteenth century onwards, town walls and gates were prime sources of interest for antiquarians. Lively and detailed descriptions by figures such as Brome, Camden, Defoe, Leland and Stukeley demonstrate that such defences often remained highly visible features of urban topography, closely associated with the character of a given town. A particularly crucial source in understanding the fate of walls in the immediate post-medieval period is the *Itinerary* of John Leland compiled during the reign of Henry VIII.[12] At Teignmouth, Leland's *Itinerary* provides the main source of evidence that the settlement may have been walled, the physical fabric of these putative defence works having apparently vanished. Leland provides many scores of descriptions of town defences, usually commenting on their strength and repair and estimating the length of the fortified perimeter, frequently naming surviving town gates, and occasionally providing other details such as the presence of posterns, interval towers and ditches as well as subjective judgements about the character of defences. The walls of Newcastle were said by Leland to surpass all the walled cities of England and erroneously most of those in Europe in terms of their strength and magnificence. In other cases, the pressures of urban development had already resulted in the dismantling of town gates and the swamping of walls with development; at Nottingham, for instance, Leland noted that only three of the original six or seven town gates were still standing.

Cartographic and pictorial sources are especially valuable in understanding chronologies of destruction, as well as informing about the physical appearance of walls in the post-medieval period. The earliest surviving printed maps of towns, by cartographers such as William Cuningham, William Smith and John Norden and dating to the mid and late sixteenth century, are oblique views that frequently show communities still packed tightly within walls. The fore-shortened perspectives often used in these early town plans often make town walls appear visually more striking than they really were. Of even greater value are the slightly later town-plans of John Speed that are inset into the county maps of his *Theatre of the Empire of Great Britaine* (1612) (see *colour plates 10 and 11*). Over 70 such bird's-eye views of towns are known, approximately 50 of them apparently derived from original paced surveys, forming the first printed collection of town plans in Britain. Speed's maps are crucial sources in that they reliably signify the presence or absence of town defences, the positions of their gates, and depict whether a given town had expanded beyond the confines of its walls by the early seventeenth century.

Yet Speed's representations of defensive topography should not always be taken at face value; the map of Gloucester, for instance, depicts the defences in their sixteenth-century form, prior to adjustments known to have taken place by Speed's day.[13] The fact that most of these plans depicted features such as castles and town walls and gates in perspective means that they also provide a limited source of evidence concerning architectural detail, and many such structures are clearly stylised. A clear case in point is Speed's depiction of the Exchequer Gate at Denbigh. While the map clearly depicts a single tower adjacent to a simple gateway through the wall, excavation of the feature in 1982–3 showed it to be a far more monumental structure comprising flanking towers with a passage between, closely resembling the town's other main gate, the Burgess Gate.[14] Also of major value are the individual efforts of pre-Ordnance Survey local map-makers, such as John Hooker and his successors in Exeter (*colour plate 32*), whose local knowledge often meant that defensive topographies were depicted or described in particularly vivid detail.[15] From the 1720s onwards, the famous 'Town Prospects' by Samuel and Nathaniel Buck give a rather different impression.[16] Comprising detailed panoramic views of towns from a distance of one or two miles, these give excellent views of towns in their rural settings (*111*). While many show that defences had been dismantled, a small number depict surviving town walls in fine detail with surprisingly high levels of accuracy, including Lynn-Regis (King's Lynn, 1741), and Carlisle (1745).

The seventeenth century

The civil wars of the 1640s saw a renewed role for town defences, with the erection of new enceintes, outworks and siegeworks, and re-fortification of

111 The walled town of King's Lynn, as depicted by Samuel and Nathaniel Buck in an engraving published in 1741

urban castles known in a great many towns.[17] While it is easy to think of this period as representing something of a 'last cheer' for town defences, we should not overlook the immense effort that was injected into bringing town walls up to date. At Exeter there is no doubt that the civil war defences were the most expensive project that the city's inhabitants undertook in the early modern period.[18] Despite the fact that these works radically upgraded the defensive strength of the town, they also in a sense reinforced the city's essentially conservative view of its fortifications as the symbol of a loyal city of the Crown adding to the security and prestige of the monarchy.

In this relatively short burst of activity, many of the principles of the 'military revolution' – involving radically new methods of warfare based on artillery fortification – that had occurred a little earlier on Continental Europe were rapidly translated into a British context.[19] Technological advances in the art of artillery warfare ensured that the character of newly built (as opposed to reused) defensive works was quite distinctive from later medieval town walls. Most notably, the plans of Civil War town defences adopted the principle of the artillery bastion, whereby defensive earthwork enceintes incorporated multiple angled projections from which external ditches could be raked with flanking artillery fire, with the relative positions of bastions being carefully calculated to ensure mutual support. Projections from the main circuit could take a wide variety of forms, including arrowhead-shaped, triangular or half-moon (semi-circular) bastions, projecting 'hornworks' in front of gates, star-shaped redoubts, and simple rectangular batteries. Initially, the superior resources and engineering expertise of the Royalist commanders ensured that their works were more integrated designs, while those of the Parliamentarians – including Bristol and London – at least in their early stages, were less sophisticated, comprising banks and ditches linking separate forts.[20] As the war progressed, this position was evened out, as demonstrated by the integrated Parliamentarian siegeworks laid out at Newark.

These radically new designs were largely of French and, in particular, Dutch inspiration (although the concept of the angled bastion was itself an earlier Italian development) (112). The early seventeenth century saw the translation into English of important technical works on artillery fortification, and during the Civil War some new circuits were designed by foreign engineers, the most famous of whom was Bernard de Gomme, responsible for the elaborate defences around Royalist strongholds including Plymouth and Oxford. Another departure in the art of town defence was in the creation of satellite outworks or 'sconces', which operated as self-contained artillery platforms commanding important communications routes. The best surviving example of such a feature is the 'Queen's Sconce' at Newark, a symmetrical four-angled artillery fort built by the Royalists in 1645 to cover the south-west approaches to the town. Newark was defended with a new perimeter covering a far larger area than the walled medieval town, while the besieging Parliamentarians

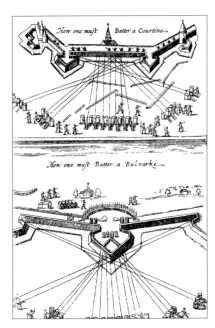

112 An attack on a walled enceinte equipped with angled bastions, as depicted by T. Venn in the military manual *Military and Maritime Discipline* (1672)

erected in 1645-46 a multi-layered system of siegeworks comprising village defences for headquarters units, sconces, and two lines of circumvallation, studded with redoubts, to blockade the town.[21] Another interesting example is located at Over, near Gloucester, constructed by modifying a medieval moated site through the recutting of its ditch and the addition of artillery bastions; other surviving sconces include 'Fort Royal' outside Worcester and 'The Bulwark' at Earith built to guard an approach to Ely.

Where Civil War defences were added to existing medieval town walls, as at Exeter, Oxford and elsewhere, this usually created a defensive system with multiple layers: the inner formed by the original medieval curtain and ditch; a new outer ring provided with artillery bastions and related entrenchments; and additional outlying satellite works guarding routes of approach and other assets. The cognate result of these developments was the construction of defence works taking up far greater areas than medieval town walls and requiring enormous resources of labour, giving rise to methods of siege warfare that were costly, protracted and immensely destructive for urban environments and economies. Despite these many innovations, however, in one important respect the town defences of the Civil War were something of a reversion to earlier traditions. In the large-scale excavation of ditches and the construction of enormous earthen bastions topped with wickerwork emplacements for cannon, Civil War defences represent something of a renaissance for earth and timber defence – a technology rooted in prehistory. Unlike elevated masonry structures built in the medieval tradition, the lower profile of earthworks, allied to their capacity to absorb and dampen the impact of cannon fire, made them eminently suitable for the age of improved artillery. In one sense it can be tempting to regard the town defences of the Civil War as something of a footnote to the subject, representing a 'final flourish' for urban defence. In another sense, however, this short period saw a greater intensity of military activity directed against many towns and more investment in their defence than ever before, even though this has left little enduring evidence in terms of surviving earthworks and long-term impact on urban form.

Historic map evidence is particularly valuable in reconstructing the layout of town defences from this period. The elaborate Royalist defences around Oxford, for instance, are depicted in detail on a well-known map of 1644 produced for Bernard de Gomme, showing the Civil War defences – though never completed as originally envisaged – to lie outside the line of the medieval walls, which were left as an inner defensive ring.[22] Referred to by Parliamentarian commanders as the strongest in the land and constructed at vast expense with the use of forced labour, these works provided deterrence and defence against attack throughout the Civil War, yet were rapidly abandoned, eroded and overwhelmed by the dark forces of urban expansion. At London, too, the enormous Civil War circuit (here of Parliamentarian design), incorporating a complex arrangement of outworks and star-forts, ignored the line of the medieval walls. Among the other major defensive systems of this period built around medieval walled towns were those at Bristol, Leicester, Malmesbury, Reading and Worcester, while at places such as Liverpool ambitious plans were made yet never bought to fruition. At Nottingham, in contrast, there is no evidence that the town's (as distinct from the castle's) defences were refurbished when the town was held by Parliamentary forces in 1642-6, perhaps due to their particularly advanced state of dilapidation. Another scenario is represented at the Dorset port of Lyme, where powerful new fortifications were built to defend a town that had not been enclosed in the medieval period. In the same category were the works at Plymouth, which in the late fourteenth century had received a small 'castle' on its harbour side built by the citizens but which did not have a traditional town wall of medieval date. But in 1642 it was given an encircling earthwork circuit and in 1643 this was cut back and fronted with a masonry wall. No longer extant above-ground features, they have nevertheless been located in excavations and were also depicted, together with an outlying circuit of batteries on the landward side, in an engraving of 1644 by Wenceslaus Hollar.[23] While we are accustomed to think of Plymouth (and other strategically important ports) having been defended primarily against external, seaborne threats, in this case major investment in defence arose from an internal, landward one. Defence works might also be built in opposition to towns: the outskirts of Colchester and Carlisle both featured substantial works built by besieging Parliamentarian forces in efforts to isolate these towns and contain their garrisons. In several places extant but outmoded medieval defences were upgraded during the Civil

War and integrated into new schemes of fortification. At Exeter, for instance, some of the medieval mural towers were converted into artillery bastions by demolishing their upper parts and filling the lower levels with spoil, and the town walls still exhibit new seventeenth-century crenellations in the area immediately north of the former South Gate and musket loops near the castle. At King's Lynn and Yarmouth, new angled bastions were added in front of medieval circuits whose alignments remained essentially unchanged.[24]

Surviving physical evidence of town defences from this period is, however, minimal. Medieval walls generally took up far less space and were more easily integrated within urban development than the huge outworks and angular bastions of the seventeenth century. The obstructive nature of these earthworks has ensured their almost wholesale clearance from British townscapes in the face of urban growth, while as purely martial works, lacking the status or symbolism of medieval walls, urban communities also had less reason to preserve them. Where newly built Civil War defences survive, it is usually only in incomplete form, as at Carmarthen. Here, the grassed-over earthworks of a single angled bastion and length of ditch known as the 'Bulwarks' are still well preserved, flanking the west side of the town. Other fragmentary earthworks of Civil War town defences, either newly built or added to medieval circuits, are preserved at King's Lynn, Newark, Oxford and Yarmouth, although in no single case does anything approaching a continuous enceinte survive. At Leicester, the walled medieval precinct on the south-west side of the town known as the Newarke was pierced with musket loops, many of which survive as crude circular embrasures.[25] Vivid evidence of Civil War reuse of the medieval defences of Chester is preserved not only in the form of battlements converted for the provision of cannon, but also where the walls were damaged during the siege of 1644-6. This is most apparent in the section of the city wall running through the 'Roman Gardens' just south of the Newgate on the east side of the town, where the repaired breach made by the Parliamentarian forces in September 1645 can be clearly identified (113).[26] Outside the walls, an array of earthwork bastions and other features were built at various points at this time,[27] though no longer surviving.

Archaeological excavation has in many instances revealed new evidence of seventeenth-century defences otherwise lost to view. A spectacular example is Exeter, where rescue excavations in advance of development revealed a massive collection of banks, ditches and underground tunnels relating to the Civil War sieges, built outside the south and east gates of the city.[28] At Leicester too, excavations on the Mill Lane site in 2001 revealed evidence of a ditch and rampart forming part of the city's southern defences in the seventeenth century. The original earthwork was estimated to have measured approximately 6.5m from the base of the ditch to the crest of the bank, although archaeological dating evidence was not sufficient to demonstrate whether the feature was built by the Parliamentarians or Royalists, the city having been taken and recaptured in

113 Chester: a stretch of the city wall, showing the repaired breach made during the siege of the 1640s. *Authors' collection*

1645. Gloucester is another town where archaeology has shed light on the format of Civil War defences, here constructed immediately prior to the unsuccessful Royalist siege of 10 August to 5 September 1643 and modified further until 1651.[29] Excavations in the 1980s on an earthen bastion outside the South Gate revealed a steep-sided ditch *c.*10m wide and 4m deep, with evidence of a *chevaux de frise* (an obstacle of sharpened stakes) in the base of the ditch. Yet while archaeology can provide information on the physical appearance of defences, here, as at Exeter and elsewhere, it can be hazardous to correlate such works with specific documented events. Thus while it might be tempting to link this particular defence work to the dramatic siege of 1643, the artefacts found in association do not confirm or deny this, and it is quite possible that it could have originated in a later context, such as 1646, when the defences were reorganised. Other measures taken to re-fortify Gloucester are known from documentary sources alone, such as the policy of piling earth behind stretches of the medieval wall, the construction of breastworks across certain streets within the circuit, and filling gates and towers with spoil.

In assessing the significance of Civil War additions to medieval urban defences, we must re-visit the crucial issue of what exactly was being defended. A major theme in this book has been the relationship between defence and community. In this context it is highly significant that, while in the Civil War it was undoubtedly in the interests of a community to protect itself from military assault, it was not of course the urban populations themselves that were primarily waging war. Although urban communities could be pressed into constructing large earthwork defences, and propaganda might sometimes portray populations as willing participants, the stimulus to this work was largely provided by the commanders of opposing armies who were competing for the control of towns, their resources, their territories, and the regions in which they stood. Correspondingly, urban property was far from immune to destruction in the face of these new military needs. Indeed, the erection of Civil War circuits and related sieges were usually characterised by scorched earth policies whereby properties were burned and pulled down to open up fields of fire and deny cover to opposition forces, with a devastating long-term impact on communities and in particular suburban settlements. At Exeter, destruction was particularly severe on the city's more vulnerable eastern side. In 1643 the devastation wrought by the Parliamentarian forces holding the city included the demolition of St Sidwell's Guildhall, almshouses, inns and private dwellings, including property of the Dean and Chapter said to be worth £110 per annum.[30] Likewise, the levelling of property to create a *cordon sanitaire* around Gloucester, for instance, resulted in the destruction of an estimated one third of the entire town, while in the region of 25–30 percent of the populations of Bristol and Newark are estimated to have perished in siege-related circumstances.[31] Not since 1066–70, with William I's building of castles in Anglo-Saxon towns, had such destruction been caused by war-related events. And the only subsequent parallel was from aerial bombardment in World War II.

Destruction and adaptation of walls and gates

In a recent review of British and European urban archaeology, medieval town walls have been described as 'an endangered species'.[32] In one sense, this is entirely true given the massive losses of walls and gatehouses through neglect, development and vandalism that took place in the later and post-medieval periods, with examples of continuing investment the exception rather than the rule. Yet this statement might also be modified in two senses. First, as will be explored below, the ongoing role of walls as recreational facilities and continuing symbols of civic pride was being recognised in some places as early as the eighteenth century. Second, in recent years heightened awareness of the values of built environments and the heritage industry now make it unlikely that major losses of town walls will be tolerated. Nonetheless, it cannot be denied that those walls and gates that survive in modern British townscapes represent but the tiniest fragment of the once extensive collection of urban defences in existence by the end of the middle ages.

It is commonly assumed that the greater the antiquity of a given archaeological site or feature, the less likely it is to survive in the present landscape. In the case of town defences, however, this is manifestly not true. The rate of survival relates not simply to date of origin, but more particularly to such issues as continuity of use, the extent to which features presented barriers to urban development, and their ongoing value as a social amenity. Thus, to take

114 Portchester: East Gate, showing the pre-Norman or early Norman arch in the former Saxon Shore fort. *Authors' collection*

contrasting examples, we can still see Roman masonry in the lower courses of town walls at Chester, Exeter, Winchester and York, and we can also see well-preserved Anglo-Saxon earthworks at Cricklade, Lydford, Wallingford and Wareham. On the other hand, the survivability rate of Anglo-Saxon masonry additions to Roman walls is incredibly low, the two widely acknowledged possible examples being Exeter's north wall and Portchester's Watergate, although in the latter case a very early Norman date is not out of the question (*114*).[33] Also showing extremely low levels of resilience are the massive Civil War earthworks discussed above, while medieval town gates, despite being the focal points of urban defences, have also survived extremely poorly, principally because by the eighteenth century their carriageways had become an unacceptable restriction to the growing flow of urban traffic. It is thus a paradox that while at many walled towns great quantities of more or less featureless masonry still survive in walled perimeters, the gateways, which in a medieval context were the most important features of all, are generally hidden from us with the exception of a few often spectacular examples. The peak period for the destruction of town walls and gates was the later eighteenth century, when in the face of intense pressure on urban land and growing volumes of vehicular traffic, a huge amount of fabric was dismantled by urban authorities as well as through piecemeal pillaging by individuals. Fortunately however, in many cases visual sources have provided us with a vivid record of their appearance, as with those published recently for Chester.[34]

In the face of pressure on urban land, town ditches represented a resource that could be exploited. Their use as dumping grounds in the middle ages was pretty much ubiquitous. Some measure of the volume of rubbish that might accumulate in a city's ditch is provided by the various disputes between the city of London and the king over the maintenance of that part of the city ditch adjacent to the Tower in the late fourteenth and early fifteenth centuries. The Letter Books of 1353-54, for example, record a complaint from the king that the accumulated filth from the city ditch had leaked into and filled the moat around the royal castle, which the city was then forced to clean out at its own expense.[35] In the later medieval period, civic records indicate conflict between townsfolk and urban corporations over the progressive encroachment of gardens and the intrusion of grazing animals into ditches, leading to (generally ineffective) bye-laws. At Stafford, for instance a borough ordinance of 1473-4 prohibited any digging or planting within six feet of the town wall.[36] At Taunton, in 1572 the mayor Richard Sprete ordered that the townsfolk should not 'cast any of his bloude of beastes or any fylthe upon Hurlediche'.[37] By the middle of the sixteenth century suburban development had crept up to and into stretches of London's city ditch and parts of it were used by clothmakers to dry their products on wooden frames; even so, the urban authorities still struggled to keep it clear where possible, for instance through leases specifying that spoil should be deposited in gardens rather than in the ditch, and attempts to clear the muck from the stretch between Cripplegate and Moorgate with a special boat acquired for the purpose.[38] Archaeological insight into the environments of town ditches can be attained with relatively small interventions; at Bath, for instance, deposits in the medieval city ditch near the appropriately-named 'Frogmere' area revealed the ditch to have been a stinking morass of stagnant water and filth.[39] And informal tipping of waste was not limited purely to the extramural zone: at Newcastle, excavations in the area of St Andrew's Street have revealed great quantities of industrial, domestic and building debris dumped against and inside the wall to form a layer more than 0.5m thick in the fourteenth and fifteenth centuries.[40]

While in the aftermath of the 1640s the earthen defences associated with Civil War sieges were rapidly absorbed in urban development, more surprising to note is that in certain instances communities continued to build and rebuild town gates into the seventeenth and eighteenth centuries. The main gate at the head of Edinburgh's High Street, Netherbow Port, was rebuilt in huge and magnificent form in 1603, its design emulating Porte St Honore in Paris.[41] At Bristol an entirely new gate was built in 1658 to guard the approaches to the town opened up by the demolition of the castle, and in the 1730s Redcliffe Gate and Temple Gate were both rebuilt in enlarged form with their porters retained.[42] Such activities provide good evidence that communities saw town gates and walls as active components within functioning early-modern townscapes.

Several of London's town gates were rebuilt in monumental form in the post-medieval period, many to have very short lifetimes prior to demolition in the late eighteenth century. Ludgate was rebuilt in Elizabeth's reign, and a statue of the Queen in full regalia, dated 1586, was later removed to the church of St Dunstan on the north side of Fleet Street when the gate was demolished c.1760. Other gates were rebuilt in the seventeenth century: Aldersgate (1617); Aldgate (1606); Moorgate (1622); and Newgate (1672), the last of these having a shelf-life of under a century, being pulled down in 1767. Something of the monumental appearance of these structures can be gauged from pictorial material. Like Ludgate, most incorporated statues of monarchs, 'twinned' with appropriate images to create compositions with powerful messages. The rebuilt Aldersgate, for instance, featured James I flanked by the prophets Jeremiah and Samuel, while Aldgate also featured a statue of James on the outer face, with a large figure of Fortune and gilded representations of Peace and Charity facing into the city.[43] A significant parallel is the statue of George III in imitation Roman style that still forms the centrepiece of the side of Southampton's Bargate facing into the town. Far from marking a departure in town gate architecture, these iconographies perpetuated a long tradition.

Orders for the sale and demolition of Leicester's gates were issued in 1773; an item in the *Leicester Journal* of 9 April 1774 demonstrates what an encumbrance they represented, claiming them to have been:

> ... so narrow that a foot passenger meeting a carriage went in danger of his life and so low that a high loaded waggon, or load of hay, etc., could not pass under them into the marketplace or other inner parts of the town. And what is more extraordinary, we had no other passage, but upon sufferance (through one yard only) by which such loaded carriage could pass.

> ... unaccountable as it may appear to a stranger, in this improved age, yet it is a fact that Leicester, a flourishing town of trade, situated in the middle of England, had her antique gates – those monuments of Gothic barbarism – remaining till this very period.[44]

In many cases town gates were swept away in very short periods of time. The gates of Chester were dismantled and replaced with large Classical style arches more friendly to road traffic in the space of little over 40 years: Eastgate (1766-9); Watergate (1778); Bridgegate (1782); and Northgate (1810) (*colour plate 33*) which was the last to go on account of its use as the city gaol. The great antiquity of the Eastgate was recognised during its demolition, when workmen discovered that the medieval structure encased the arches of its Roman predecessor, with a carved figure of Mars (or perhaps a centurion) between them, as a contemporary lithograph illustrates.[45] Whereas other places knocked down their gates to leave adjacent stretches of wall exposed to erosion and potential demolition, the building of new arches with walkways maintained the completeness of the enceinte and thus helped preserve Chester's walls in general from destruction. Elsewhere, Hereford's five gates vanished in the period from 1783–99; all eight of Norwich's from 1791–1810; Yarmouth's ten from 1785–1837; and Exeter's four from 1769–1819. Glasgow's last town gate went in 1755; Nottingham's in 1743; Oxford's in 1772; Salisbury's in 1781; Hull's c.1800; Cardiff's in 1802; Banbury's in 1817; Stafford's in 1820; Newcastle's in 1823; and Scarborough's in 1843. The overall outcome was that only a handful of medieval towns preserve anything like their full complement of gates in their medieval form, with Conwy and York standing virtually alone in this respect (see gazetteer). The Southampton Bargate presents a reversal of the usual situation where gates were removed to ease traffic flow, leaving formerly adjoining sections of walling largely unaffected. Following various plans to demolish or redesign the Bargate in order to alleviate the traffic jams that it caused in the late nineteenth and early twentieth centuries – including a scheme to transplant it to another location in 1914 and another in 1928 to create a monumental 'Bargate Circus' – the decision was taken in the 1930s to instead remove the walls to either side, leaving it as a traffic island.[46]

In some other cases, stretches of wall were demolished due to the pressing demands of transport. A long stretch of Exeter's west wall was demolished in association with the building of a new Exe Bridge and the creation of New Bridge Street to serve it in 1778.[47] At Conwy, the engineers responsible for the Chester and Holyhead railway, built in 1847, showed remarkable historical sensitivity in building a mock medieval arch – complete with walkway and crenellations – so that the line could pass through the south side of the town without breaking the integrity of the enceinte.[48] This was perhaps in reflection of Chester's own tradition of bridging over the gaps created in its walls. Yet again, individual towns could treat the legacy of their medieval defences very differently; the town wall of Newcastle-upon-Tyne, for instance, was repaired in the Napoleonic Wars to bring it to a state of defensibility, including the building up of embrasures and alterations to the parapet wall.[49] Unusually, town defences could even be prepared for military action in the twentieth century: lengths of the ditch around Sandwich were dredged in the Second World War to form an anti-tank ditch,[50] while various bastions on Southampton's circuits were used as emplacements for searchlights in this period.

While gates were usually the first features of the walled circuit to go, largely because they constricted a growth in vehicular traffic, at Coventry this order was unusually reversed. In 1662 King Charles II commissioned the earl of Northampton to destroy the defences at royal expense on account of their strength, and similar orders were issued with regard to the town walls of Gloucester and Northampton.[51] This reminds us that while in the medieval period royal authorisation to build walls could be a sign of favour to an urban corporation, the king's mistrust of a community's loyalty might be expressed in the seventeenth century through the concerted destruction of their walled heritage. At Coventry the order was rapidly carried out yet with the gates left

115 *Left, above* Coventry: Cook Street Gate. *Authors' collection*

116 *Left* Launceston: South Gate. *Authors' collection*

intact until the second half of the eighteenth century, when most were levelled. Mill Lane (Bastille) Gate was the last to go in 1849, leaving only the relatively minor structures of Cook Street Gate (*115*) and the blocked Swanswell Gate surviving. In other cases, the continued functions of town gates as gaols seems to have been a factor that contributed to their preservation to the present day, as with the South Gate of Launceston (*116*) and the West Gate of Canterbury. (*101*)

The matter of royal allegiance was still very much alive at a later date. At York, a military scare occurred in 1745 because of the perceived threat of the Jacobite army, and work on the city's defences ensued. But not long after, the city authorities were discussing the demolition of the gates and parts of the walls because, as in other cities, they were proving restrictive to the town's growing vehicular traffic. In 1753 and 1771 new passages were cut through Micklegate Bar and Bootham Bar respectively, though here to ease pedestrian traffic. By the 1790s the future of the walls had become controversial, and in 1800 the Corporation applied for an Act of Parliament to demolish the whole circuit on the grounds of its decay, inconvenience, expense of upkeep, and the limiting effects of its gates on traffic. It is notable that this process was explored,

117 Chester: part of the wall-walk on the north side of the circuit. *Authors' collection*

because the city's lawyers felt that, given the royal patronage that had sustained the medieval growth of the walled circuit, royal permission might be required for its demolition. George III's government proved reluctant to become much involved in the issue, and piecemeal demolitions began. Soon, however, pressure groups arose committed to the preservation of the walls (*117*), and extensive restorations were carried out from *c.*1830-90.[52] This narrative illuminates not only the origins of modern conservation in this particular place, but also the issue of exactly who owned, or who was thought to own, town walls (see page 208).

Far from always being redundant features of post-medieval townscapes, structures such as towers and gates could be reused and adapted for a remarkable variety of reasons, ranging from the general (such as tenements to be leased by corporations), to the more specific. At Newcastle eleven towers were used by guilds in the post-medieval period, and at Chester several, including the King Charles Tower, functioned as meeting places for these organisations.[53] The immense Black Tower at Norwich (*118*) was used as a snuff mill in the eighteenth century. In the eighteenth century, the Lendal Tower, York, had a steam engine installed within it to pump the city's water supply, while the drum towers of St George's Gate, Canterbury similarly held reservoirs from which water was piped to taps in the town hall and the city's markets. Towers could be converted into gates: at Oxford, one of the rounded bastions on the north side of the city wall was broken through and remodelled in the eighteenth century to form an imposing gateway into New College.[54] Today, by no means all towers and gates are relict features. Many mural towers and gates are adapted as residences and commercial premises (for instance, at Canterbury, Colchester, Launceston, Ludlow and Pembroke) (*119*), used as churches and chapels (Caernarfon, Canterbury and Winchester), and museums (Canterbury, Southampton and York). A unique instance of reuse is the adaptation of the Stonebow at Lincoln as a council chamber, although this harks back to the structure's medieval civic status. A particularly instructive case in point is the north-west tower on the town wall of Great Yarmouth. Since its construction in the middle of the fourteenth century, the tower has seen continued use for domestic, commercial and civic as well as military purposes. Following alteration in the seventeenth century to accommodate cannon, the tower had a history as chequered as its decorative exterior. Thereafter used as a hayloft, stable, pigeon-house, photographic studio, and as the place where the town's Christmas decorations were sometimes stored, it was not until 1991 that the tower again received serious municipal investment, when it was restored and opened as a Broads Information Centre. This monument's somewhat cyclical biography – from a symbol of medieval urban ambition and identity through phases of casual usage followed by eventual recognition of its value as a cultural asset – is not unusual, however and serves as a microcosm of the whole subject.

118 Norwich: the Black Tower, on the south-east side of the medieval circuit. *Authors' collection*

Walled heritage

While town walls always had something of an amenity value to communities, their value as a leisure resource saw particular recognition during the 'urban renaissance' of the eighteenth and nineteenth centuries. Where walls remained substantially intact, as at Canterbury, Chester, Chichester, Exeter and York, their circuits became promenades and arenas for fashionable social activities, where the townsfolk could 'take the air'. The adaptation of Chester's city walls in this way during the reign of Queen Anne (1702-14) was particularly early, representing the precursor to an ongoing sequence of conservation through the eighteenth and nineteenth centuries.[55] Led by the Corporation, these works included restoration of the parapet walk (*120*) and repair of the damage sustained in the Civil War, demonstrating a very conscious change of approach

119 Pembroke: mural tower with inserted gazebo on the south side of the circuit. *Authors' collection*

to the treatment of the city's defences little more than half a century after their most violent episode of military use. Unlike the later treatment of York's walls, however, no attempt was made to replace 'lost' medieval details such as crenellations, emphasising that this was 'conservation for the present' rather than 'restoration of the past' – a point which has resonances in the modern treatment of the fabric of town walls. The Northernhay Gardens of Exeter, landscaped from a stretch of the city ditch and counterscarp, were started in the early seventeenth century and among the very earliest public gardens in the country. At Canterbury, the Dane John Gardens, incorporating the south-east portion of the city wall and the earthwork remains of the first Norman castle, were designed by Alderman James Simmons in 1790-93, while the tree-lined promenade known as the 'Sally Walk' around the battered walls of Hereford was another development of the eighteenth century.

The attitude of nineteenth-century municipal authorities to their medieval heritage contains interesting paradoxes. In an era of increasing appreciation of the medieval past, as epitomised by the work of gothic revivalists and art and architectural historians in general, it is noticeable that other aspects of medieval topography were regarded as encumbrances. These could include narrow streets and bridges, as well as the physical fabric of town walls. In York, for instance, the Board of Health Committee recommended in 1855 demolition of the wall in the Walmgate area on the grounds that it was prejudicial to health by restricting the free circulation of air; similar arguments were put forward in favour of the destruction of walls at Hull in 1764 and Norwich in 1792.[56] Retention of the city walls of York was a particularly hard struggle fought by the Corporation through much of the nineteenth century, in the latter stages seeking the advice of the pioneering expert on military architecture, G.T. Clark. Their official opening in June 1889 was a proud and lavish civic affair, with the Lord Mayor commenting in his speech that the Minster, which could be admired from the renovated wall-walks, was 'like a gem re-set'.[57] The West Gate of Canterbury only escaped demolition in 1859 due to the casting vote of the mayor, after Mr Wombwell, owner of the famous circus, requested that the Corporation demolish it so that his parade of elephant-driven cars could process into the city, unencumbered by the narrow medieval gateway.[58] Such conflicts of interests often resulted in heated debates over the fates of town walls. In this period, although large numbers of medieval gates in particular were sacrificed on the altar of the transport industry, in other places local opinion was galvanised to the extent that a more conservationist approach resulted.

Nowhere in Britain, however, did town wall restoration approach the scale of Viollet-le-Duc's Carcassonne (2) or the gates of other French towns, such as the gothicised surviving gate of Libourne.[59] While the nineteenth century saw the erection of 'new' medieval castles such as Castell Coch, in an era of huge investment in civic building projects no urban authority dreamt of erecting a 'new' town wall. In general, and with the exception of York, restorations of British medieval town defences in the nineteenth and early twentieth centuries were of limited extent and focused on discrete structures, as seen in the more or less complete reconstruction of town gates at places such as Bridgnorth (North Gate, 1910), Cardiff (West Gate, 1921) and Lincoln (Stonebow, 1887). At a greater scale of magnitude was the rebuilding of that part of Canterbury's wall running outside the city bus station in the 1950s during the redevelopment of the St George's district, which included the wholesale reconstruction of two gap-backed towers. As well as enhancing urban environments for residents and tourists, such schemes of urban renewal might have some symbolic status, as was the case with the renovation of Exeter's eastern wall and its associated pedestrian way started in 1977 for the celebration of Elizabeth II's Silver Jubilee.

In most cases the interested visitor to a discrete historic urban site such as a castle, church or mansion, will appreciate the qualities of the monument in relative isolation. The visit to the town wall, on the other hand, by necessity involves a tour in which the relationship between the defended circuit and other features of urban topography ought to be very obvious. In this sense, town walls have added value for the historically minded visitor, because they encourage an holistic appreciation of historic urban environments rather than a narrow one. Thus an enjoyable tour of a town wall may also lead the interested visitor into a better appreciation of a whole range of features that the town contains.

In the twentieth and twenty-first centuries, the marketing of town walls within the heritage industry has seen them once more become a significant part of urban identity and a supplementary source of revenue. From the point of view of those organisations charged with the promotion of town walls, enhancement projects can have a variety of indirect effects, most notably the overall enrichment of a town's historic character, which might prove beneficial in a commercial and sustainable sense.[60] Founded in 1989 at Tenby, South Wales, the *Walled Towns Friendship Circle* is a confederation of over one hundred walled towns from many parts of Europe that share a common concern for their preservation and conservation in a modern heritage culture. Also on the wider European front may be noted the meetings of the Scientific Council of *Europa Nostra*, several of whose colloquia either side of 2000 have been devoted to issues of conservation and preservation in walled towns.[61]

From the 1950s onwards, urban planning has sometimes made efforts to maximise the visual impact of surviving portions of town walls, for instance by creating public open space around them and opening up attractive views of surviving masonry, as apparent at Chester and Norwich for instance.[62] With due caution, this point can be extended. In the last 60 years, British towns have faced numerous challenges including aerial bombardment in the Second World War, post-war reconstruction, the decline of urban industries, the growth of 'out of town' economic and retail centres, massive traffic congestion problems, and assaults on the powers of local government. Perhaps, in a limited way, the revival of the fortunes of town walls in the post-war period has elevated to the public eye an historic symbol of civic pride and identity that has been a welcome gesture and counterbalance to so many other difficulties.

Considerable variation can be noted in the attitudes shown by urban authorities to their walled heritage, however. At York and Southampton, large-scale restoration and conservation projects have been carried out, motivated partly by a need to maximise the potential of walls as a resource to attract visitors and invigorate the tourism sector of urban economies. Such projects have opened town walls up to an enormous audience. An estimated 2.5 million people per year are estimated to walk all or part of the walled circuit around York, for instance, now marketed as the 'longest' in Britain, while Chester's is marketed as the 'most complete'. But conservation has been limited not only to larger towns. The sympathetic conservation of town walls can also involve different decisions about which features to prioritise. In certain cases, the display of walls

120 York: a semi-circular mural tower on the west side of the circuit; most such features were heavily restored in the nineteenth century. *Authors' collection*

may be best served by dismantling later properties built against them. At many smaller towns too, the historic fabric of walls has been valued and conserved, notably at Caernarfon (*colour plate 34*), Conwy and Denbigh, where post-medieval domestic and industrial structures were selectively purchased and demolished by the (then) Ministry of Works in the late 1950s to enable full conservation and display of medieval fabric, as well as enhancing its accessibility for academic study.

Perhaps the best surviving example of a medieval wall around a small town relatively unaffected by post-medieval change, Conwy is now in the context of Europe's urban heritage, a place of international importance.[63] Other examples of clearance include Yarmouth, where parts of the wall interior bear the scars of demolished industrial buildings and housing; and Winchester, where the West Gate was stripped of encumbering structures in 1940. Yet there is, of course, a thin line between the removal of supposedly 'worthless' structures to reveal earlier work and the imposition of the will of heritage agencies to the detriment of communities and the history of other urban features. Such policies might be controversial: at Conwy, for instance, the treatment of the fabric of the town walls could, from one perspective, stand accused of erasing 'Welsh' heritage to produce a sanitised version of an intrusive 'English' medieval monument. Effective management of town walls clearly requires a partnership of interests between local communities and heritage organisations. Other factors can also account for the removal of structures built up against and obscuring the fabric of town walls. While aerial bombardment in 1942 destroyed the last standing vestige of Norwich's surviving town gate (Benedict's Gate, in 1942), elsewhere fabric of town walls hidden from view for centuries was revealed, as in Cripplegate (London), Bath and Swansea, by bombing and the subsequent clearance of damaged areas.

Of course we must also remember that a great deal of medieval expenditure on town walls had been, effectively, geared towards conservation, as at Canterbury where part of the repair work on the walls in the 1430s involved stripping ivy from that part of the circuit between the West Gate and Roser Tower.[64] At Exeter, by the middle of the seventeenth century the safety of children playing on and around the walls was a factor in maintaining the city defences, for in 1654 the Receivers' Accounts include a payment of 16s 11d to three labourers for removing the earthwork gun battery at Snayle Tower for convenience of passage and 'for prevention of danger of children from falling over the walles of the Cittie there'.[65] Another reflection on the modern treatment of the fabric of town walls is that the opportunism of civic authorities that characterised the nineteenth and twentieth century was nothing new. Thus, in the eighteenth century we find contrasting views expressed in debates conducted, for example at Chester (where a conservationist approach developed very early), in Leicester (where the medieval fabric was vilified and seen as an encumbrance), and York (where heated debate took place regarding the legality of demolishing the town's defences). Nor, indeed, was an opportunistic attitude confined to the post-medieval centuries. As the text of this book demonstrates, the medieval period itself witnessed an ongoing struggle between the needs of defence, civic display, and practical living.

For the purposes of managing and monitoring the rich archaeological resource beneath Britain's towns and cities, the lines of walls (whether or not physical fabric survives) are crucial in defining core zones of archaeological significance, notwithstanding the increased attention now also paid to historic suburbs.[66] The physical and topographical characteristics of town walls themselves present challenges to those authorities charged with their conservation and promotion that are often more complex than is the case with other major categories of ancient monument. Unlike other familiar features of our medieval heritage, such as castles and abbeys, it is not always possible to charge admissions fees to walk or inspect town defences, other than to gatehouses or towers containing exhibitions, displays or museums, such as Monk Bar, York. Health and safety issues are also relevant where visitors are permitted access to wall-walks, and it is for these reasons that parts of the surviving parapet walks at places including Caernarfon, Conwy and Southampton are not freely accessible. Equally, comprehensive access to view, let alone to perambulate, walled circuits cannot always be guaranteed given that surviving remains usually occupy or incorporate a complex range of properties. At Exeter, for instance, while the city council maintains the fabric of the city wall, this passes through some private properties, the grounds of the bishop's palace and a cemetery, as well as through more open areas of 'public' urban space. At Oxford, the principal surviving remains are in New College, originally founded within an angle of the city wall (*110*). At Exeter, Chester and elsewhere, pedestrian bridges spanning new inner ring roads help preserve the continuity of the walled circuit.

For the purposes of modern heritage conservation, it is also crucial that town walls are not severed from the context of their urban settings. The designation, in 1986, of the 'Castles and Town Walls of King Edward in Gwynedd' as a World Heritage Site testifies to the importance of treating town walls not in isolation, but as part and parcel of the fabric of historic townscapes. Another major challenge is to manage monuments that, while historically contiguous, are frequently dismembered into isolated fragments within modern built environments. Particularly welcome are initiatives that promote the treatment of these remains as unified entities. In London, for instance, the city wall was historically scheduled as 24 discrete monuments, yet an initiative at the beginning of the twenty-first century is moving towards rescheduling and the production of a unified Conservation Management Plan. In this context, effective presentation of surviving remains requires delicate negotiation and collaboration with private developers; the fine stretch of the wall at 8-10 Cooper's Row, for instance, has been displayed in an accessible open space as a component of a hotel development.[67] A good guidebook, as at London, can also help reduce the 'fragmented' effect created by the destruction of large parts of a circuit.

This boom in heritage conservation has brought with it a proliferation of literature aimed specifically at the tourist market. Information about town walls written at a popular level is often available in the form of pictorial guides to perambulations around circuits. Yet only infrequently are purchasable guidebooks available of a comparable level to those available at other major monuments such as castles. Indeed, in guidebooks produced by English Heritage, Historic Scotland and Cadw, town walls are invariably treated as footnotes to more detailed descriptions of castles. Only very rarely have town defences warranted their own dedicated 'official' publications, as with Berwick-upon-Tweed.[68] Restored town gates, or depictions of them prior to modern development or views pre-dating demolition, are prime subject matter for picture postcards and are sometimes used in public information panels, and can be found throughout ephemera of the heritage marketing industry. Yet relatively few guides to the defensive circuits of individual towns have been published that are both scholarly and accessible.[69]

In many ways the town walls of medieval Britain have a legacy that is more than physical. The custom of ringing the curfew is still observed in towns such as Kirkcudbright, where the curfew bell is rung from the seventeenth-century 'Tolbooth' that served as the headquarters of the provost and magistrates. Exeter cathedral's oldest bell, the Peter bell, is rung each evening to tell the world that the building is shut, representing the modern legacy of the earlier practice of the evening signal announcing that the precinct gate of Broadgate into High Street was being closed, and a similar practice is observed at Winchester. Events such as these were not invented for the heritage industry, but highlight the ongoing influence of town walls and intramural precincts on social practices. It is worth noting also that some of the features encountered in this book had enduring qualities linking the medieval and modern urban worlds. Wards (as well as parishes) link us administratively (allowing for boundary changes) to the eleventh-century in many cases. The offices of constables and aldermen extended down from the twelfth to the nineteenth century. The receivers and other financial officials were the direct precursors of city treasurers. The city masons were likewise the precursors of borough surveyors. Enclosed communities are, of course, not absent in the modern world. The phenomenon of neighbourhoods surrounded by barriers, to which access is restricted to residents and their guests through manned or computer-controlled gates, can be noted in townscapes as far apart as Saudi Arabia and South Africa. More striking still has been the emergence of the 'gated community' in modern North American town planning.[70] At the turn of the twenty-first century some eight million Americans are estimated to live in physically enclosed neighbourhoods, representing a means of defining and excluding different interest groups for reasons of perceived security, status and identity in a not wholly dissimilar vein to medieval town walls and their intra-mural precincts.

FURTHER READING

Specific studies of British town defences in the post-medieval period are extremely lacking with most relevant material to be found in publications tackling the topic indirectly. The influence of new technologies of artillery fortification on town defences is considered in A.D. Saunders, *Fortress Britain: Artillery Forts in the British Isles and Ireland* (Beaufort, 1989). Town defences of the Civil War period are covered by J. Kenyon and J. Ohlmeyer (eds), *The Civil Wars: A Military History of England, Scotland and Ireland 1638-1660* (Oxford University Press, 1998) and P. Harrington, *English Civil War Archaeology* (Batsford, 2004). Brief syntheses are provided in general works on post-medieval archaeology, including R. Newman, *The Historical Archaeology of Britain, c.1540-1900* (Sutton, 2001) and D.W. Crossley, *Post Medieval Archaeology in Britain* (Leicester University Press, 1990). An excellent illustration of the light that can be thrown on town defences by pictorial sources is P. Boughton, *Picturesque Chester: The City in Art* (Phillimore, 1997).

6

REFLECTIONS

It is tempting, when drawing to a close discussion of a subject over which diverse opinions have been expressed, to conclude that progress can only be made by strengthening, through polemic debate, one or other ends of the spectrum of argument. In this context, such discussion could too easily be polarised between argument for the serious defensive functions of town walls on the one hand, and greater emphasis on issues of symbolism and status on the other. This book has hopefully highlighted that perpetuation of such a debate would not actually be very meaningful or helpful. In short, it limits the varied framework of interpretation that the subject deserves and hinders any ambition towards a multi-faceted explanation appropriate to the spatial, chronological and social diversity of the phenomenon of urban defence. Rather than attempting to provide a final word on an argument centred on what is essentially a false dichotomy – i.e. whether the walls of towns were defensive or symbolic – this book has attempted to stress the enormous range of functions and meanings that town defences had to different individuals and social groups. To some they were, indeed, symbols of power, pride and prosperity; to others who lived both within and beyond them, they were monuments of oppression (perhaps representing the dominance of a colonial authority) and repression (for example, symbolising seigneurial control over tenants) or just rather inconvenient; and to others still they might on occasion provide real and much-needed protection.

First and foremost however, we should remember that, at least in an English context, kings regarded themselves as overlords of all fortifications, whether castles or town walls. In the urban context this is emphasised by the character of murage grants and by the frequency with which kings instructed towns to improve, or even directly funded defences that they clearly regarded as parts of the fabric of their kingdom. At the other end of the social scale, we should question what an urban 'community' actually comprised. One may doubt, without being overtly cynical, whether the richer classes and families above a certain level of prosperity maintained defences with the genuine motivation of

protecting the entire community as opposed to furthering the interests of privileged sectors within it. Even when the urban community made provision for
defence, at a practical level this was commonly manned by sectors of the
townscape (wards), so that overall defence was far less the product of a single
concerted activity but rather the accumulation of various contributions.
Another manifestation of this delegated responsibility for urban defence is the
ad hoc 'back dyking' of individual plots in Scottish burghs.

There is also a distinct impression that for much of the medieval period
considerable tension existed between the perceived need for overall upkeep of
defences on the one hand and the individual interests of those with properties
adjacent to walls on the other. Also notable is how the topographical development of walled towns led to fragmentation in the maintenance of, and
provision of access to, the walls themselves. Plentiful evidence exists, in particular, for the virtual privatisation of sectors of walled circuits by varied ecclesiastical bodies, and for the channelling of funds and work on walls through such
institutions who might, *de facto*, control separate stretches. Another central
theme of significance is that, far from representing distinct 'lines' that rigidly
defined urban zones, town walls were components within multi-layered 'zones'
of defence and jurisdiction, with the town's actual limits frequently defined by
insubstantial outlying bars on the approach roads and the boundaries of extramural portions of wards and parishes.

It is a truism, which deserves far greater critical appraisal, that whereas the
medieval castle was a private concern under a single lord, town walls reflected
the interests and ambitions of entire communities. This is one way of concep-
tualising traditions of medieval fortification and is helpful in that it characterises
some opposing essential qualities. In practice, however, the distinction between
'private' and 'public' fortification in the medieval world was not this simple,
and it reflects the standpoints from which we have studied medieval fortification rather than recognising the social variations in its character. We must also
recognise that, in certain contexts, the defensive functions of castles might be
deployed for wider communal purpose to a greater extent that we might
imagine. The outer enclosures of castles were in some cases available as refuges
for surrounding populations in time of threat, particularly in relatively exposed
and frontier regions. Also significant is the fact that in the eleventh or twelfth
centuries, an outer bailey and an enclosed seigneurial borough (or a settlement
which could potentially grow to become one) may have been essentially the
same thing. Therefore, just as it is possible to identify elements of communality
in the supposedly 'private' castle, so also it is possible to note elements of
private interest in the supposedly 'communal' defended town.

From time to time, this book has also noted some of the main ways in which
traditions of urban defence in Britain were different from those in much of
Western Europe: the generally lesser extent of defended areas; the lower
frequency with which they were extended; the smaller populations they

enclosed; and the earlier dates at which serious investment in them tailed off. The sheer variety of enclosed communities in Britain also stands out; these ranged from clusters of houses crammed into baileys under the shadow of castles to great cities with walled extensions and intra-mural precincts and enclosures. These observations of course reflect deep-rooted differences in the process of urbanism. What is crucial, however, is that British town walls are not dismissed merely as the poorer, less sophisticated – and basically less interesting – equivalents of their continental cousins, but that their distinctive characteristics are appreciated. Of particular significance is the telling input of royal power and the often conflicting interests of a wide range of urban stakeholders including lords, religious bodies, and various coteries of privileged citizens, whose specific influences might far outweigh the general influence of a supposed 'community'.

Paradoxically, this book has hopefully not given the impression that town walls represent a discrete phenomenon or an area of study independent of urban archaeology and history in general. The text has endeavoured to make abundantly clear that the town wall was but one manifestation of the activities of complex urban societies. In a sense, this book has necessarily taken walls out of towns; in another context, a more integrated approach would be to take the town as a whole, both archaeologically and historically, and consider the walls as one component of it. In another sense this book is also something of an appeal to both urban archaeologists and historians to recognise the full potential of town defences in their own broader-based studies. It seems appropriate to end this book with a sentiment familiar to medieval writers: to bring it to a close in order to leave plenty more to be written by those who follow.

GAZETTEER OF SURVIVING
REMAINS

For those seeking to research these places in more detail a crucial starting point is the annotated gazetteer in H.L. Turner's *Town Defences in England and Wales* (John Baker, 1970). This provides a variety of information, including summaries of key documentary evidence for the building of defences at individual towns, including murage grants and other sources of finance. This work also provides summaries of physical characteristics of the major surviving remains, and discusses the political and military circumstances of building works. This basic list has been added to in other articles and books, including C.M. Heighway, *The Erosion of History: Archaeology and Planning in Towns* (CBA Urban Research Committee, 1972), M.W. Barley 'Town defences in England and Wales after 1066', in M.W. Barley (ed.), *The Plans and Topography of Medieval Towns in England and Wales* (CBA Research Report No. 14, 1976), and J. Bond 'Anglo-Saxon and medieval defences', in J. Schofield and R. Leech (eds), *Urban Archaeology in Britain* (CBA Research Report No. 61, 1987).

Indispensable lists of published material relating to town defences (as well as castles and artillery defences) are provided in three bibliographies: J.R. Kenyon, *Castles, Town Defences and Artillery Fortifications in Britain: A Bibliography* (Volumes 1-3) and published by the Council for British Archaeology as Research Reports numbers 25 (1978), 53 (1983) and 72 (1990). Other published gazetteers of castle sites contain valuable information on walled towns and other fortified settlements associated with castles; in particular see D. Renn *Norman Castles in Britain* (John Baker, 1968) and D.J.C. King, *Castellarium Anglicanum* (2 volumes, Kraus, 1983). For town defences featuring artillery fortification, a valuable gazetteer of sites is provided in A.D Saunders, *Fortress Britain* (Beaufort, 1989).

Information on European walled towns can also be found on the web-site of the Walled Towns Friendship Circle (www.walledtowns.com).

While these various sources form the basis for the following listing, the gazetteer may not necessarily include every formerly defended small town that has lost every trace of its defences. This gazetteer is intended primarily for those readers who wish to be directed to sites where they can see more of the town defences of England and Wales at first-hand. Essentially, it relates to visible remains and entries are not supplemented by excavated or documentary data. Summary entries are provided for those towns where appreciable evidence of medieval defences survive, either as masonry structures or major earthworks. In line with one of the major themes of this book, the gazetteer alerts the general reader and traveller to the widely surviving fabric of town walls of note at places other than the obvious 'gems' such as Chester, Southampton and York.

The main entries are accompanied by brief annotated listings of other towns and settlements which appear to have been fortified but preserve little or no observable remains of defences. In these cases, the evidence of excavation, ancient maps, antiquarian accounts or historical documents has proved suffi-cient to demonstrate the former existence of town defences. In addition, even in those cases where no physical fabric of town defences survives, it should be noted that street patterns may preserve something of their former alignment. This gazetteer is also restricted to town defences of the later medieval period and excludes Roman or early medieval walled towns that did not see continued or renewed occupation, as well as fortifications only of the seven-teenth century and later. Coastal artillery forts defending the seaward approaches to towns (for example Dartmouth) are also excluded. It should be noted that the counties within which the places lie are listed in the index. Finally, readers should note that an entry in this list does not indicate that public access is assured.

THE SOUTH WEST

Barnstaple: The curving line of the town defences is clearly marked in the street pattern; however, the only surviving above-ground fragment of the circuit is the jamb of one of the gates, preserved in Youings, on the corner of High Street and Boutport Street.

Bath: Vestiges of the East Gate, smallest of the four medieval gates, survive in Boatstall Lane, near Pultney Bridge.

Bristol: A single medieval gate survives, with the medieval church of St John the Baptist (St John on the Wall) above. The tripartite structure is not original, with two pedestrian arches either side of the central arch being nineteenth-century insertions. The central arch exhibits a portcullis groove and the passage is fan vaulted. The external face features seated statues of Brennus and Belinus, the legendary founders of Bristol; the arms of Charles II, the city and the Society of Merchant Venturers are also displayed. Very fragmentary remains of walls elsewhere.

Cricklade: Discontinuous remains of the ditched and embanked circuit of the Anglo-Saxon *burh* can be traced; St Mary's church is on the site of the north gate.

Exeter: One of the best-preserved medieval and Roman circuits in England, though lacking any of its gates. Fabric survives for approximately 70 percent of the sub-rectangular perimeter, which in the northern corner is coincident with the castle defences. Visible fabric contains masonry of many periods, from the Roman to the modern, and in many places these phases can be readily distinguished through the use of different building stones. The wall is massive but generally lacks details such as the medieval wall-tops. Northernhay Gardens, landscaped from the outer defences in the post-medieval period contain particular points of interest. On the north-west side, a projecting plinth marks the approximate Roman building line at ground level and Roman masonry is preserved to almost its full height. An unusual narrow rectangular medieval tower (Aethelstan's Tower) with a later medieval extension and modern piercings at ground level, marks the junction of the city wall and the castle wall. Nearby, 'fossilised' early-medieval crenellations sandwiched between Norman and Roman work are visible, above the massive bank added to the defences in the Norman period. Also in this area, a semi-circular bastion has been modified into a gazebo complete with 'improved' arrow loop. Three semi-circular bastions are preserved on the east side of the circuit, though heavily rebuilt. The bank formerly backing the town wall is now almost entirely missing, other than a short stretch principally in the garden of the Bishop's Palace.

Gloucester: A short stretch of the Roman circuit, reused in the medieval period, can be identified in King Street. The foundations of the excavated East Gate can be viewed under a protective glass covering.

Langport: A simple tunnel-vaulted arch is surmounted by the medieval guild or corporation chapel known as the 'hanging chapel', marking one of the entrances into the former *burh*; no other tangible traces of defences can be identified.

Launceston: Various fragments survive from the walled circuit formerly linked to the castle bailey defences. Of the medieval gates, only the South Gate survives; this rectangular structure features two entrances (one for road traffic and the other for pedestrians) with two storeys of chambers above.

Ludgershall: A length of rampart and ditch can be traced along the rear edges of properties and gardens in the north-east part of the medieval settlement, although it is not clear whether this represents vestiges of borough defences or an outwork of the castle.

Lydford: The neck of this promontory *burh* is cut off by a broad surviving bank; the present village features the remains of the stannary prison/tower and an earlier Norman fort, as well as a substantially intact late Saxon street network, with narrow lanes running off a central spinal street.

Lyng: The course of the bank formerly defending the landward approach to the late Saxon *burh* is partly traceable in the modern topography.

Malmesbury: The line of the circuit, following a rocky promontory above the River Avon, is marked in several places by masonry terraced into the natural contours, though little or none of the surviving fabric is medieval in date.

Old Sarum: The Saxon *burh* appears to have lain within the univallate defences of a late prehistoric hillfort, which also formed the focus of the post-Conquest borough containing the Bishop of Salisbury's castle/palace and the cathedral.

Plymouth: By the later medieval period the harbour was defended by a quadrangular fortification, of which part of a single fragmentary tower is visible. In the sixteenth and seventeenth centuries a circuit of defences was extended around part of the town itself, including major works of the Civil War.

Salisbury: A surviving stretch of the town bank can be identified in the north-east part of the town, which seems never to have been fully walled. The medieval gates (North Gate, Harnham Gate and St Ann's Gate) were associated with the cathedral close, which preserves an enclosure wall, crenellated in places; none of the city gates survive.

Totnes: The course of the late Saxon and medieval wall line is traceable in the well-preserved street and tenement pattern; fragments of the simple North Gate survives, as well as the more substantial east gate incorporated into a much later building.

There are no significant above-ground remains of former medieval town defences or gates at Bridgwater, Devizes, Dorchester, Ilchester, Ilfracombe, Kingsbridge, Melcombe, Shaftesbury and Taunton, Teignmouth, Tetbury, Wilton and Winchcombe; it is also possible that Dunster, Fowey, Newent and Newnham possessed enclosing defences. The cathedral precinct and bishop's palace at Wells were fortified, but it is unclear whether the town (which received a murage grant) was walled. At Trematon a Norman borough was probably contained within the bailey or outer bailey of the castle.

THE SOUTH

Oxford: The only substantial upstanding remains, comprising the inner wall on the north-east corner of the medieval circuit, lie in the grounds of New College; these, though, are of outstanding quality in their preservation and architectural detail. The angle is marked by a D-shaped projecting bastion, and the walls striking from it feature two complete half-round bastions to the south and two to the west. On the western part of the circuit can also be identified another bastion knocked through to form an entrance to New College in the eighteenth century, and a medieval bell-tower on the site of another demol-ished bastion. Architectural details of particular note on the wall include a continuous series of crenellations (some infilled, some with merlons pierced with simple vertical loops, most complete with coping stones), an intact wall-walk complete with stairs leading to bastions on either side, and blocked posterns. All the towers on the north side have loops on two levels and are open backed; one on the east side has upper loops only and the other is partly rebuilt. Landscaping of the College gardens may preserve vestiges of an internal bank.

Portchester: Late Roman Saxon Shore fort, adapted as a *burh* and castle; the adjacent settlement in the medieval period was not separately defended.

Portsmouth: While nothing of the medieval defences is visible, numerous remains of artillery fortification from the early Tudor to the early modern periods are preserved.

Southampton: The defences are extremely well preserved, and while the wall itself cannot be walked, the circuit is punctuated with features of great archi-tectural interest, many representing unique survivals in a British context. Evidence for the development of early artillery fortification is especially signif-icant. The circuit is approximately rectangular, its west side built originally along the River Test, which no longer reaches the town wall, with the castle placed approximately centrally on this side. The south-east corner is marked by God's House Tower (now a museum), an important and early example of a purpose-designed artillery platform and armoury, projecting from the angle, and with a later gateway providing access to the quay. Four other gates are preserved: on the east side is Friary Gate; to the south is Watergate; to the west, Westgate is a relatively simple tower; and on the north side, Bargate is a somewhat isolated feature, the walls directly to either side having been destroyed. The most impressive of the gates, Bargate has an elaborate machico-lated façade fronting a multi-phase structure; the gate has two storeys, a large upper chamber being lit by three windows on the side facing the town. The circuit is punctuated by numerous rounded towers, with larger towers at the angles, including Arundel Tower at the north-west and Polymond to the north-east. Unique in Britain is the projecting arcading external to the wall with blockings pierced by 'keyhole' type gunports, demonstrating the incor-poration of merchant houses into the circuit.

Wallingford: Probably the best surviving example of Anglo-Saxon town defences in England. A substantial embankment and external ditch formerly embraced the town on three sides, forming a rectangular enclosure adjacent to the Thames, which defines the remaining (eastern) side. This earthwork survives as a more or less continuous feature to the south and west of the town, particularly in the open zones known as the Bullcroft and Kinecroft; on the northern side it was disrupted by an expansion of the Norman and later castle, the earthworks of which are preserved remarkably clearly under pasture in Castle Meadows.

Wareham: The town is surrounded on three sides by the earthwork defences of the Saxon *burh*, still forming an impressive and elevated rampart; the remaining (south) side of the circuit was provided by the River Frome.

Winchester: Considerable remains of a rectangular circuit of Roman origin, with a castle inserted on the west side and a bishop's palace (Wolvesey Palace) in the south-east corner. The finest surviving feature is the magnificent West Gate, now an isolated structure; this has a machicolated top above armorial panels and gunports. The King's Gate, leading into the cathedral precinct on the south side of the circuit, is a plainer structure of three arches with St Swithun's chapel above. The surviving wall is best preserved on the east side where it defined the precinct of Wolvesey Palace; this stretch has surviving crenellations and the earthwork of a substantial bank behind.

There are no significant above-ground remains of former medieval town defences or gates at Abingdon, Banbury, Bedford, Bridport, Brighton; Buckingham, Charmouth, Christchurch, Cirencester, Dorchester, Dunstable; Farnham; Guildford, Hertford, Huntingdon, Poole, and Weymouth; it is likely but not certain that Henley-on-Thames, Newbury and Woodstock possessed defences, and Yarmouth may have been gated in the late medieval period. The following places seem to have had settlements enclosed within the baileys or outer baileys of castles: Ascot Doilly, Ashley, Anstey, Benington, Pirton and Therfield; more doubtful examples are Arlesey, Bletsoe, Cainhoe, Meppershall, Thurleigh, Totternhoe, Yielden. Fastendich and Old Dashwood Hill are possible examples of enclosed medieval villages.

THE SOUTH EAST

Canterbury: Over half of the approximately oval circuit survives, the scale of the surviving walls and towers making it one of the most magnificent in Britain. While the circuit is Roman in origin, most of the visible fabric is medieval in date, and short stretches of the circuit are the product of post World War II reconstruction. The best preserved stretch is the south-east part, which can be walked at parapet level, where the walls run through the public park known as Dane John Gardens. Here, the crenellations and wall-walk are intact, and a series of open-backed interval towers feature 'keyhole' type gunports, although the towers and wall above the bus station are modern. Several later rectangular towers can also be identified in the northern part of the circuit. On the north-west side of the circuit much of the wall is hidden by development and a number of towers are built into later houses; on the west and south-west the circuit is vanished entirely. Features of particular interest include the stretch of walling incorporated into the nave of St Mary Northgate, which contains 'fossilised' crenellations, the tower on the east side which is converted into the Zoar Chapel, and the vestiges of a Roman gate (Queningate) adjacent to a rectangular bastion on the north-east corner. Of the medieval gates only the West Gate survives, though one of the most impressive in Britain. This comprises drum towers rising from battered ashlar plinths that flank a single vaulted gate passage with portcullis slot; external architectural details include 'keyhole' type gunports (asymmetrically placed in the towers) and machicolations; the side facing in towards the town is more domestic in character.

Chichester: The irregular ten-sided circuit, based on Roman foundations, survives substantially intact, accessible and walkable, although the flint-faced remains are somewhat featureless and none of the gates survive. The best-preserved and most dramatic remains are on the south-west side of the town, where two semi-circular bastions can be identified as well as a rectangular projection from the circuit with blocked-up windows, marking the position of the Deanery. The south-west corner, near the Bishop's Palace Gardens is largely rebuilt in brick, and the stretch either side of the West Gate is missing. A promenade along the wall-top exists for most of the northern and eastern part of the circuit, carried on arches over cuttings made through the wall for

Chapel Street to the north and East Row to the east. A bastion that has become detached from the main circuit can also be identified in a garden on the north side. While the wall is extant on the south-east side, it is inaccessible and obscured and disturbed by gardens and houses built against it, including a summer house on the wall-top. A shorter length of wall-top walkway lies on the south side inside Market Avenue, where another semi-circular bastion can be seen, with a modern structure on top of it.

Colchester: While discontinuous and, for most of its length, not a visually impressive monument, Colchester's town wall is especially significant for the volume of Roman work it contains. Approximately two thirds of the wall survives. The north-east part of the circuit, including the length running through Castle Park, is relatively featureless, the masonry comprising the wall's rubble core, splaying out sharply and containing only occasional traces of Roman tile and later buttresses. A well-preserved stretch is visible in the south-east corner, along the line of Priory Street, where three semi-circular medieval bastions have been added, although the wall itself is patched with later brickwork. None of the medieval gates survive, although a small part of the arch of Duncan's Gate can be seen on the north-east part of the wall, and a pedestrian arch and foundations of the Roman Balkerne Gate, on the west side of the circuit, are visible. The tile courses and layers of Septaria stone running through the Roman wall are most apparent on the well-preserved stretch to the north, along Balkerne Hill. A section through the wall is visible where North Hill cuts through the circuit near the north-west corner.

Chipping Ongar: The line of a ditch and traces of a rampart can be traced forming a sub-rectangular settlement enclosure attached to, and immediately east of, the Norman motte and bailey castle.

Hastings: Some walling survives on the south side of the town: one stretch between East Street and Winding Street, and a shorter length between Pleasant Row and East Bourne Street. Much of the surviving fabric represents a battered retaining wall, with occasional stretches of thinner parapet walling surviving, including the lower portion of a circular opening that may be a gunport.

Lewes: Parts of the wall survive on the town's western side, though much disturbed and lacking discernible architectural features. On the north side of Southover Road, a short section of flint-faced walling survives along a raised walkway, while a substantial but largely rebuilt stretch runs between Westgate Street and Pipe Passage. Possible fragments are also built into a house adjacent to the Westgate chapel.

London: Numerous fragments of the medieval city wall, built on the Roman line, are preserved, mostly built into later structures; a series of panels set up by the Museum of London describe the main extant remains. The lower parts of an excavated postern lie at the south end of Tower Hill underpass; the most impressive surviving section of the wall lies almost adjacent, comprising Roman work (with tile layers) to sentry walk level, and medieval masonry above. A substantial stretch with intact medieval arrow loops and embrasures, socket holes for a timber platform and the scars of stairs can be viewed from a public open space off Cooper's Row. Moving counter-clockwise around the circuit, of the other visible fragments, most notable are the section off Vine Street (that can be viewed through glass panels on the side of a building), the section visible as a mosaic in the subway under Duke's Place near Aldgate, and by All Hallows church, London Wall. The most impressive parts of the city's surviving northern defences are in the vicinity of the Museum of London. Later medieval decorative brickwork is visible in the section preserved in the gardens at St Alphege and a number of rounded medieval bastions lie in and around the gardens adjoining the museum and St Giles Cripplegate.

Pleshey: A well-preserved rampart, largely obscured by hedgerows and vegetation, forms a semi-circular enclosure embracing the settlement attached to a substantial motte and bailey castle.

Rochester: Impressive remains of the wall can be traced on the east part of the circuit, and other fragments survive on the north side. At the north-east corner lies a semi-circular bastion with arrow loops at ground level; another can be identified at the south-east corner, though largely obscured by vegetation.

Rye: The principal surviving vestiges of the town's defences is Landgate, a monumental structure featuring two round towers flanking a single entrance. The towers rise from plinths with double offsets, incorporate numerous but largely rebuilt arrow loops, and are accessed from doors on either side of the entrance, marked by a portcullis slot. The western tower features a small octagonal tower rising above the roof level. The upper portion of the front features a triangular arrangement of three windows and a row of projecting corbels, and a probable drawbridge rebate. The back of the tower features a single offset window in its upper portions. The remains of the town wall are less impressive. The principal surviving stretch is along the north side of the town, along Cinque Ports Street. The wall is rebuilt in brick in its upper part with a rectangular projecting structure rebuilt in its upper parts representing a former bastion. Other disturbed sections of wall are visible between the curving lines of Wish Ward and The Mint, including a length with facing stones built into a shop. A short length, built on the natural rock, is visible in the bottom floor of The Old Borough Hotel. While no evidence of the Strand

Gate is standing, the coat of arms of the Cinque Ports that formerly decorated its outer face, is visible on the corner of Mermaid Street and Traders Passage. The 'quatrefoil' tower at the south-east corner of the circuit known as Ypres Tower seems to have functioned as something of a 'town castle' rather than a private fortification.

Sandwich: The town preserves two gatehouses on the riverside of the medieval town. Fishergate, near the quay, is the simpler of the two, comprising a rectangular structure with the upper portion substantially rebuilt. The building known as the 'Barbican' consists of the lower portions of two flanking gate towers, with decorative flint and stone chequered stone exteriors, linked by a modern structure across the top. On the landward side, an impressive rampart and ditch lies along the line of The Bulwark, Millwall, Ropewalk and The Butts, and at the north-east corner of the circuit the remains of flint masonry represents the vestige of a late medieval artillery fortification.

Tonbridge: Very eroded earthworks of a rampart and ditch are visible as discrete detached lengths, forming parts of a semi-circular earthwork embracing a settlement attached to the castle.

(New) Winchelsea: The town's three gates all survive, though the settlement itself has withered away and much of the former walled area is now an open greenfield site. The largest and most impressive of these is the Strand Gate, standing on the route to the former harbour and comprising four small circular towers around a single gate passage within which a double portcullis groove can be identified. Newgate preserves a single entrance flanked by three-sided projecting towers; Pipewell Gate is a simple rectangular structure. The most significant remaining parts of the wall are a featureless fragment near Pipewell Gate and another on the north-east part of the circuit; in other places a bank and ditch can be identified.

There are no significant above-ground remains of former medieval town defences or gates at Arundel, Burpham, Dover, Saffron Walden, St Albans, Southwark, Old Winchelsea and Tilbury; it is likely but not certain that Southwold, Staines and Queensborough possessed defences, or that they were at least intended. Mount Bures and Rayleigh had settlements enclosed within the baileys or outer baileys of castles.

EAST ANGLIA

Bury St Edmunds: The great Benedictine abbey lay within a large fortified precinct with two impressive gatehouses; although the adjacent planned town was also provided with defences, no physical traces of these survive.

Castle Acre: A well-preserved rampart forms a sub-rectangular settlement enclosure attached to the great castle of the de Warenne family. Only a fragment of the wall encompassing this settlement survives, adjoining the south-west corner of the bailey enclosure. Bailey Gate, a flint structure with two round towers and a single arch with portcullis grooves, marks the north entrance to the settlement.

Framlingham: Traces survive of a ditch formerly enclosing the town appended to the castle.

King's Lynn: Remains are vestigial and widely dispersed around the town. The most important survival is the South Gate, spanning London Road: this is a three-storey rectangular structure of brick and stone with polygonal corner turrets and circular gunports, and has an original carriageway with later pedestrian side entrances. The vaulting inside demonstrates an unusual building sequence whereby an original ribbed vault was abandoned and replaced with a barrel vault. Only a short and discontinuous stretch of the wall survives, in the north-east of the town, along Kettlewell Lane and Wyatt Street. The circuit, which formed a partial enclosure against the River Ouse, was not of masonry construction along its entire length. The northern stretch of the surviving wall features a series of external buttresses and well-preserved internal arcades with pointed brick-built arches, with each recess containing a single stone-built loop. The more poorly preserved southern stretch displays a mishmash of masonry, including cobbles of reused medieval ship's ballast, although outlines of arcades and loops can be identified; an impressive fragment is built into the Hob in the Well public house on the corner of Littleport Street and Wyatt Street. Another part of the circuit is visible as a landscaped watercourse and earthwork in the area of gardens known as The Walks; the feature known as the North Guanock Gate is a heavily restored postern. Another fragment of walling lies at the north end of North Street, near the Alexandra Dock.

Norwich: Substantial remains of the town wall enclosing an unusually large circuit with a great castle at its centre exist. All the gates have been demolished, however, and the scattered nature of the remains render it difficult to follow the walled perimeter. By some measure the most impressive remains lie to the south-east of the historic city. The bases of two boom towers, one on either side of the River Wensum, can be identified where Carrow Road crosses the river. From near this point the wall runs sharply uphill and along the line of Carrow Hill, incorporating two towers. The uppermost of these is the Black (or Wilderness) Tower, a massive circular structure preserving a door providing access to an intact stretch of wall-walk. The adjacent stretch of wall preserves the wall's characteristic features, some or all of which can be identified in most other surviving sections. These comprise a brick-built internal arcade, with the arches supporting a broad wall-walk and sheltering recessed embrasures for brick-faced arrow loops. Nearby, a re-entrant angle can be seen on the corner of Ber Street and Bracondale. West and north of this stretch, the curving wall can be traced along the lines of: Queen's Road (a short stretch with a tower); Chapelfield Road (two discontinuous stretches with a number of bastions); Grapes Hill (a thin and featureless scrap); and Barn Road (an impressive series of arcades). Other remains to the north of the Wensum indicate that the medieval suburb here was walled. Remains run from Oak Street to Bakers Road (including one stretch preserving a cruciform loop unique in the circuit); Magpie Road (a stretch with arcades); and Bull Close Road (terminating at a polygonal tower with a substantially surviving ribbed vault). In the bend of the Wensum marking the north-east corner of the circuit, the Cow Tower is a remarkable example of a free-standing artillery platform, comprising a brick-built tower, with very early gunports. To the south of this the River Wensum continued the circuit, including the formerly fortified Bishop Bridge.

Great Yarmouth: Defining an irregularly shaped enclosure running alongside the River Yare, the town wall is one of the most intact in Britain. Many parts are obscured by development, however, and none of the gates survive. The most impressive remains lie along the south-east part of the circuit along Blackfriars Road, where architectural details of the wall's interior and exterior are particularly clear. Particularly notable is the brick-built internal arcading supporting the wall-walk, with single brick-faced arrow loops piercing the wall beneath each arch. The rampart running along the back of the wall in some places appears to be a Tudor reinforcement, and other additions for the provision of artillery can be noted, including a triangular earthen bastion. The wall is punctuated by many D-shaped towers, many with decorative chequer work in their upper portions, and by some larger examples at important points. Especially impressive are the South-East Tower (displaying two tiers of loops along with the immediately adjoining wall), and North-West Tower (now an isolated feature following the demolition of the wall to either side). King Henry's Tower, on the north-east corner, is unique in the circuit on account of its octagonal plan.

New Buckenham: Slight vestiges remain of a town ditch linked to the outer defences of the castle.

Thetford: A length of bank and ditch survives from a crescentic earthwork enclosing an area of the town south of the Little Ouse.

There are no significant above-ground remains of former medieval town defences or gates at Bungay, Caistor, Cambridge, Dunwich, Harwich, Ipswich, Southwold, Tempsford and Witham. It is likely but not certain that Swavesey possessed defences. At Castle Camps and Ongar, settlements were contained within the outer baileys of castles.

THE WEST MIDLANDS AND WELSH MARCHES

Bridgnorth: The North Gate is heavily rebuilt and the only major survival.

Caus: The fortified borough lay within the earthwork defences of a late prehistoric hillfort; though damaged in places, these still survive to massive proportions, and the entrances through them at two former gates can be clearly identified.

Coventry: Two of town's gates survive, although neither were principal entrances to the medieval town. The gate passage through the rectangular structure of Swanswell (or Priory) Gate was blocked in the nineteenth century when it was modified as a dwelling; the crenellations are the product of twentieth-century restoration, although the scar of the town wall can be discerned, along with blocked doorways. Cook Street Gate is a slighter and simpler rectangular structure with a single gate passage and restored crenellations. Although the only substantially surviving stretch of the wall lies in Lady Herbert's Garden between the two surviving gates, other shorter sections can be seen off Upper Well Street and along a footpath between the ring road flyover between Cox Street and Gosford Street.

Hereford: Long but quite featureless stretches of wall lie along the line of the ring-road; on the west side of the city low and discontinuous remains run from the river to near West Street; parts of two rounded bastions survive.

Ludlow: Only one of the medieval gates (Broadgate) survives, on the south side of the former circuit. While largely obscured by later buildings, this comprised two drum towers either side of a single arch, where a portcullis groove and two opposing squints can be identified. The western tower is heavily rebuilt and contains little external medieval fabric; the eastern one is less encumbered and features two arrow loops one above the other. Fragments of walling can be identified on the south side; the best-preserved section runs westwards from the gate, but is much built into and retains no identifiable architectural features.

Richard's Castle: Vestiges of a rampart and ditch embracing a former borough attached to the motte and bailey castle can be identified, best preserved on the north-east side of the site.

Shrewsbury: Remains of the town wall are minimal: a short stretch of revetment wall lies along Town Walls; a single mural tower nearby is converted into a dwelling; and a small postern can be identified at the end of St Mary's Water Lane.

Warwick: Two of the medieval town gates survive, both surmounted by medieval chapels: the West Gate, featuring a particularly long tunnel partly cut out of the natural rock, has the chapel of St James above, and the East Gate the chapel of St Peter, although substantially rebuilt in the late eighteenth century. Slight traces of the town walls, including remains of at least one bastion.

Worcester: Vestiges survive of the medieval walled cicuit that replaced the Anglo-saxon *burh* defences. Along the eastern ring road (City Walls Road) there survive stretches of masonry including the battered base of a mural tower. The best impression is, however, on the riverside, next to the Cathedral, where surviving wall fabric extends from the (destroyed) castle site northwards towards the Severn Bridge, and includes the remains of a water gate. This area was landscaped as a promenade in the early nineteenth century.

There are no significant above-ground remains of former medieval town defences or gates at Bewdley, Chirbury, Clare, Clifford, Clun, Crickhowell, Droitwich, Eddisbury, Henley-in-Arden, Knighton, Lichfield, Oswestry, Overton, Runcorn, Stafford, Tamworth, Tewkesbury, Towcester, Trelwall and Whitchurch; it is likely but not certain that Ellesmere, Halesowen, Stourbridge and Stow-on-the-Wold possessed gates or defences; Leintwardine lay within Roman defences, but these do not seem to have been used in the medieval period. At Ashperton, Boteler's Castle, Eardisley, Kilpeck, Longtown, Holdgate, More, Pontesbury, Tutbury, West Felton and Whittington, settlements were contained within the baileys or outer baileys of castles; less certain examples are Castle Church (Stafford), English Bicknor, Ewyas Harold and Wigmore.

THE EAST MIDLANDS
Castleton: Stretches of a town bank and vestiges of a ditch can be identified, forming parts of a sub-rectangular circuit enclosing a small grid-plan town beneath Peveril Castle.

Leicester: The prominent landmark known as the Jewry Wall, is a fragment of the Roman baths complex and not part of the city's defences, all traces of which have entirely vanished from the present townscape.

Lincoln: The Newport Arch, lying at the end of Bailgate, was the north gate to the Roman city. One of the medieval town gates (the 'Stonebow') survives, although its medieval character has been obscured by modern renovation; the city's Guildhall lies inside, with the council chamber over the arch. A fragment of the south gate survives in Steep Hill.

Stamford: Some short lengths of walling remain, widely dispersed through the town, in addition to the heavily rebuilt lower portions of a bastion and a postern incorporated into a garden.

There are no significant above-ground remains of former medieval town defences or gates at Bolsover, Boston, Chesterfield, Derby, Grimsby, Newark, Northampton, Oakham, Nottingham and Peterborough; Barton-upon-Humber may also have possessed enclosing defences. At Castle Bytham, Castle Carlton and Bourne, settlements were contained within the baileys or outer baileys of castles, although the evidence in the field is not clear; more doubtful examples are Belvoir and Kingerby. Kempsey is a rare example of an enclosed medieval village without a castle, and Marholm another possible candidate.

YORKSHIRE

Beverley: One town gate (North Bar) survives: a three-storey brick-built square structure with a single arch and evidence of portcullis grooves. Architectural detailing includes crow-stepped battlements a with decorative string course below, and three ogee-headed blind windows, giving the structure a particularly ornate external appearance. The only visible signs of the ditch are on the south side of the town, where an earthwork can be seen running through allotments and open land near Kitchen Lane.

Kingston-upon-Hull: The consolidated remains of part of Beverley Gate and the adjoining town wall, as revealed by excavation, are displayed in a pedestrianised development in the Prince's Quay area of the town, between Prince's Dock Street and Carr Lane. The remainder of the wall has vanished entirely, though parts of its former course are marked by coloured paving.

Richmond: Two short stretches of walling survive, as well as two small gates: the single arched Cornforth Bar, and a postern gate in Friars' Wynd formerly providing access to and from the Franciscan Friary.

York: Representing one of the longest, most impressive and intact circuits in Britain, the city's defences are especially remarkable for the architecture of four surviving town gates, all rectangular structures with bartizan towers at the angles, but exhibiting many architectural differences. Much of the fabric of the walls has been rebuilt in the post-medieval period including the upper portions of virtually all the towers, which are a mixture of rounded, rectangular and polygonal forms. The remains are usefully divided into three lengths: a right angled stretch to the south-east built across a loop of the Foss; a three-sided stretch to the west adjoining the Ouse; and a right-angled stretch to the north, linking the Ouse and incorporating two sides of the former Roman fort. The stretch to the south-east is the shortest, incorporating Walmgate Bar, the only one of York's gates with a surviving barbican. The wall following Paragon Street, Barbican Road and Foss Island Road is walkable. The northern terminus of this section is marked by the Red Tower, built on the edge of the former Foss pool, and the western limit is marked by the Fishergate Postern. On the west side of the city, the wall runs from the Old Baile (one of York's two Norman castles – the other, known as Clifford's Tower, lies between the Ouse and the Foss) to the North Street Postern, forming a three-sided enclosure. The gate here is Micklegate Bar. The walling on the northern side of the city is perhaps the most architecturally rewarding, and the wall-walk affords dramatic views over the cathedral and townscape. The Lendal Tower, marking the western extremity of this stretch of wall, is one of the boom towers for a chain that ran across the Ouse. The Multangular Tower marks the west angle of the Roman fortress, rebuilt in its upper portions in the medieval period with each of its nine faces incorporating a cruciform arrow slit. Near this is the excavated 'Anglian Tower', an early medieval or late Roman tower within the line of the medieval wall. The gates on this stretch are Bootham Bar and Monk's Bar.

There are no significant above-ground remains of former medieval town defences or gates at Doncaster, Hedon, Knaresborough, New Malton, Scarborough, Tadcaster and Wakefield, while Pontefract and Ripon may also have posessed defences of some description that have left no traces. At Almondbury, Barwick-in-Elmet, Skelton and Whorlton, settlements were contained within the baileys or outer baileys of castles; other castles with large outer enclosures that may have embraced settlements are Harewood (Rougemont Castle), Helmsley, Middleham, Mount Ferrant, Northallerton, Skipton, Thirsk and Tickhill.

THE NORTH WEST

Carlisle: The only parts of the city wall extant are two stretches linked to the defences of the castle. The city wall on east side strikes south from the castle's Queen Mary's Tower, a re-entrant angle being marked by a blocked round-headed postern; the wall shows episodes of repair and features a small turret and later buttresses, as well as sections of an intact parapet walk. On the west side, a straight length of wall runs south from the corner of the castle's outer ward and continues along the long but relatively featureless line of West Walls, where a blocked postern can be seen. This stretch features the unusual Tile (or Richard III's) Tower, a projecting rectangular structure, the lower part in masonry and the upper portions in brick, and containing three gunports at ground-floor-level which appear to be later modifications. This stretch of wall ends at the remains of the Citadel, an artillery strongpoint added by Henry VIII to guard the southern side of the walled city, which was rebuilt in the early nineteenth century as the city's Assize Courts.

Chester: One of the most impressive walled circuits in Britain, especially remarkable for the fact that virtually all the wall is walkable and continuous, the original medieval gates having been replaced with traffic-friendly arches. Set within a loop of the River Dee, the circuit is approximately rectangular, with the castle set in the southern part. The north and east walls preserve most features of interest, although a length of the Roman quay wall, built of massive sandstone blocks, is visible below the city wall on the west side of the circuit on the edge of the racecourse. The most impressive of the surviving towers is the Water Tower on the north-west corner of the city, built on a spur off the main circuit and formerly set within the river, which has since silted up. Impressive towers survive on the north-east corner (Pheonix or King Charles Tower), the north side (Pemberton's Tower), and the north-west corner (Bonewaldesthorne's Tower). The stretch of walling immediately east of Northgate preserves vestiges of the wall around the Roman fortress, visible in the bowed out appearance of the wall in its lower parts above the eighteenth-century canal cutting. The vestiges of the bank behind the wall is most apparent in the north-east corner. Damage inflicted on the city wall during the Civil War can be noted in several places, most notably in the 'Roman Gardens' near Newgate on the east side of the circuit, where a large patch of unweathered stonework marks the position of a large breach.

There are no significant above-ground remains of former medieval town defences or gates at Lancaster, Macclesfield, Manchester, Penrith, Stockport or Thelwall. Askham, Great Orton, Melmerby, Milburn, Salkeld and Temple Sowerby are all likely examples of enclosed or gated medieval villages.

THE NORTH EAST

Alnwick: One of the town's original four gates (Hotspur Gate) spanning Bondgate survives, this featuring semi-octagonal projections either side of a single arch. Architectural details comprise slit windows, corbels once carrying machicolation, and the barest vestiges of a lion on the external face, and two windows on the internal face. Pottergate Tower is the eighteenth-century rebuild of a tower or another gate, incorporating traces of medieval masonry.

Medieval Town Walls

Berwick-upon-Tweed: By some measure the best-preserved example of town defences in Britain designed for post-medieval artillery warfare. Vestiges of the original medieval walled circuit, linked to the castle, can be identified; these pale into insignificance however, when compared to the Elizabethan enceinte, comprising five large angled bastions linked with a massive stone-faced rampart. Although not entirely finished, these works are of European significance in terms of their design, unity and scale.

Durham: Stretches survive of the enclosure wall built within the loop of the River Wear, although in largely featureless condition; on the south side the remains of Water Gate were rebuilt in the eighteenth century, and a rounded bastion off Sadler Street survives.

Hartlepool: Considerable, but relatively featureless remains of the medieval wall on the harbour side of the settlement exist; one gate (Sandwell Gate) survives, preserving a shouldered arch with turrets or buttresses to either side.

Newcastle: Impressive surviving remains of the town walls in places, although none of the medieval gates survive. The best preserved stretch is from St Andrew's church, along the line of Stowell Street to Westgate Road, forming part of the west side of the medieval circuit. Here, four main mural towers and two smaller turrets survive, along with a length of landscaped ditch and a blocked postern. The tower on the angle of this section (Heber Tower) is particularly impressive, featuring projecting corbels, arrow loops and a garderobe shoot. The interior of part of this section is visible along the back lane West Walls. Elsewhere, the wall survives in fragments only: Plummer Tower lies on Croft Street; Wall Knot Tower and a short stretch lie on City Road; and another section runs along Orchard Street/Hanover Square.

Warkworth: A small plain rectangular gate, featuring a parallel guard chamber, lies on the nearside of the bridge controlling access into the town. There are also nearby fragments of associated walling although it is unsure whether these formed part of a former circuit, or whether the loop of the river within which the town lay provided a natural barrier.

Morpeth possessed town gates but probably no surrounding defences; at Wark-on-Tweed a medieval settlement was enclosed within the outer bailey of the castle.

SOUTH WALES

Brecon: Fragments of the town wall exist in two places on the southern part of the circuit. Along Captains Walk, a substantial earthwork can be identified to the rear of lawns in school grounds, fronted in places with the town wall (largely rebuilt), which features a battered plinth that may be original. The vestiges of a simple rubble-built gatehouse lie where this stretch of wall meets the River Usk, near the south-west corner of the circuit. On the south-east side, a small section of wall survives on top of an apparently natural mound in the grounds of Watton Mount.

Cardiff: Two fragments of the town wall survive, both adjacent to the castle. Near the south-east corner of the reconstructed castle wall runs a short stretch; only the lower portion is medieval, separated from later reconstruction by a layer of tiles. Attached to a short length of town wall running from the opposite (west) side of the castle defences is the West Gate, entirely rebuilt from vestigial remains in 1921.

Cardigan: At least two insignificant stretches of the wall survive on the east side of the town: a bulging and much repaired fragment behind a property off Pwllhai; and a short stretch behind St Mary's Street.

Chepstow: The medieval Portwall built across the landward approach to the town survives for much of its length. Along more than one kilometre of wall lie seven towers, six of them semicircular and open-backed, and the other, at the end nearest the castle, of rectangular plan. Parts of the wall preserve crenellations as well as numerous putlog holes, and a wall-walk runs along much of its length, being carried around the towers. The Town Gate, with a single simple passageway through the Portwall has a rectangular plan, although its external appearance is modified through episodes of post-medieval rebuilding and modern restoration.

Cowbridge: Considerable remains survive of an irregular pentagonal circuit, unusually never linked to a castle. The south-west corner survives virtually intact, with a projecting circular tower with a battered base and upper portion rebuilt as a summer house at the angle; other short discontinuous stretches are built into later structures and boundary walls. The South (or Mill) Gate is a very simple two-storey square structure with a single gate passage, a murder hole and portcullis provision, and later buttresses on its outer face.

Dolforwyn: Traces of defensive earthworks surrounding the hilltop castle-borough.

Dryslwyn: A deserted castle-town perched on a prominent hilltop overlooking the Towy valley; the earthworks of a former town wall and massive outer ditch can be clearly identified appended to the castle defences, as can the foundations of a small and simple rectangular gatehouse on the west side of the circuit.

Kenfig: Stretches of the rampart and ditch forming a quadrangular enclosure around the deserted borough attached to the castle can be identified within the dunefield that otherwise mantles the site, which is overshadowed and disturbed by industrial development.

Kidwelly: The fortified town lay in the southernmost of three bailey enclosures attached to the castle. A stretch of town wall, rough and robbed of facing stones but containing putlog holes, is visible running west from the direction of the castle on the north side of the circuit, and a rampart can be traced elsewhere. On the south side of the town, an impressive gatehouse, featuring a drop arch and portcullis groove, has chambers to either side of the portal and contains two upper storeys.

Monmouth: While neither the town wall nor the four town gates survive, the town preserves the only surviving medieval bridge gate in Britain, this rising from one of the bridge piers on the opposite side of the river to the town and incorporating fine architectural detailing including machicolation.

Montgomery: No standing masonry or gates survive, although lines of buried and partly overgrown foundations defining part of the rectilinear perimeter of the castle-borough are traceable.

Pembroke: The principal surviving feature of the town defences is Barnard's Tower, a large circular structure with a battered base, projecting from the north-east corner of the circuit, built around a narrow rocky ridge on the opposite side of which lies the castle. Parts of four half-round towers (Round Turret, Goose Lane Tower, Gazebo Tower and Gun Tower) can be identified in various states of preservation, as can several sections of the town wall, especially on the southern side of the circuit along the mill pond. The wall is noticeably thin, and in places clearly built as a revetment against the natural slopes. A fragment of the town wall alongside a house on the corner of Westgate Street, at the west end of the circuit, includes the springing for an arch, presumably that of the West Gate.

Swansea: Only a single fragment of the town wall survives; part of the east wall lies between The Strand and High Street, comprising the southern half of a polygonal projecting tower, partly rebuilt but incorporating putlog holes and one splayed arrow loop, and a short adjoining stretch of curtain.

Tenby: Magnificent remains, built to enclose the landward side of the town. The wall is best preserved along South Parade and White Lion Street; two sea walls ran along the cliffs to link this wall to the castle, but these do not survive. The most impressive feature is the 'Five Arches', originally the south-west gate into the town, which is unique in Britain on account of its D-shaped plan.

Seven towers survive, including rounded and rectangular forms. Stretches of the walls contain well-preserved arrow slits, gun-ports of the 'keyhole' type (some apparently developed from arrow loops), blocked crenellations, putlog holes and joist holes for hourding. In places, the back of the wall preserves an arcade. On the south side of the town, a tower (Brechmaenchine Tower) in the garden of a house off Rock Street is the only medieval feature on the wall running along the cliffs; it is D-shaped, rubble-built and features a parapet and blocked crenellations.

There are no significant above-ground remains of former medieval town defences or gates at Abergavenny, Bangor, Caerphilly, Carmarthen, Haverfordwest, Hay on Wye, Laugharne, Llan Faes, Llanidloes, Neath, Newport (Gwent), New Radnor, Overton, Rhayader, Trelech and Usk. Less certain examples include possible earthwork circuits at Bala, Holt, Newcastle Emlyn, Newport (Pembrokeshire), Newtown (Montgomeryshire) and Rhyader, and village enclosures at Buddurge and Penmark. At Caerleon, Caerwent and Loughor medieval boroughs lay entirely or partly within the lines of Roman defences, though these works seem not to have been refurbished. At Bere, Cefnllys, Deganwy, Knighton, Knucklas, Newtown (Dynevor), St Clears, Skenfrith, Whitecastle and Painscastle boroughs were probably contained within the baileys or outer baileys of castles; other possible examples are Colwyn and Glascwm.

NORTH WALES

Beaumaris: A fragment of the town wall appended to the Edwardian castle (which is earlier) can be seen.

Caernarfon: Internationally famous for its great Edwardian castle, the town also features a remarkably intact walled circuit contemporary with and linked to the royal fortress. The compact, approximately rectangular circuit features eight substantially surviving interval towers and two gates. The West (also Water or Golden) Gate provided access to and from the Menai Strait; it is a twin-towered form and features a small projecting rectangular barbican, although the windows and crenellations are nineteenth-century additions. Only the lower parts of the East (or Exchequer) Gate are medieval; this was also twin-towered but has been extensively restored from the eighteenth century. The defences are best preserved on the north and east sides; in places the bank in front of the wall can be traced, as can vestiges of crenellations. The Chapel of St Mary lies directly inside the north-west angle, the tower here being used as a vestry. No parts of the wall-walk have open public access; the best views of the wall are from the castle's north-east tower.

Conwy: One of the most impressive walled circuits entirely of medieval date around a small town anywhere in Europe. Especially remarkable for the fact that development is largely contained within the walls to give a still vivid impression of the appearance of a bastide, and notable also for the single-phase nature of the works. The irregular quadrilateral circuit linked to the castle features 21 half-round towers and three original gates. On the west side, Upper Gate was the main entrance and the most architecturally complex, still with vestiges of a barbican pieced with arrow loops; the entrance features a draw-bridge rebate, portcullis slot, drawbar holes and squints. On the north side, Mill Gate is notable for the fact that one of its two towers is D-shaped and the other round. The least well preserved is the double-towered Lower Gate, on the east side of the circuit, which leads onto the River Conwy.

The circuit is least well-preserved on the east (river) side, where it has been disturbed by later buildings. For most of the rest of its length the wall preserves its crenellations, characterised by a vertical loop through individual merlons. The towers are mainly of similar design: 'gap-backed', each provided with steps into the town, though few have surviving battlements. Many of the gates and towers show clear evidence of 'helicoidal' arrangements of putlog holes, showing the position of scaffolding. Around the circuit, particular features of interest include the series of twelve privies perched on the wall-top immediately west of Mill Gate, and the spur-work projecting into the River Conwy, from which a terminal tower has been eroded. The entire ensemble is best viewed from the tower on the extreme west corner of the circuit, built on a rocky eminence and providing unbroken views along the ditches and walls to either side.

Denbigh: The area within the triangular walled circuit is largely open, the town having migrated downhill to its present position, which partly accounts for the excellent state of the walls' preservation. The Exchequer Gate, immediately north of the castle, survives as excavated foundations only; it is partly obliterated by a road, but seems to have been of similar twin-towered form to the Burgess Gate. Lying on the north side of the defences, the Burgess Gate is a spectacular example of military architecture, comprising a vaulted passage flanked by twin towers with rectangular bases but rounded upper parts. The first floor level comprises two rooms, the larger with a fireplace; these rooms are lit by three windows on the south (town) side. Other architectural details of note include the chequer-work pattern in the upper parts of the towers and a single triangular-headed window centrally above the gate; within the gate passage can be identified a portcullis slot, three groups of murder holes, and squints. The section of wall running east of the Burgess Gate is poorly preserved, although the north-east portion of the town defences is remarkably intact, with wall-walk preserved. Structures of note in this section include the half-round north-eastern tower (with adjacent garderobe shoot); the multi-phase Countess

Tower (with a fireplace and dovecot); and the Goblin Tower (a hexagonal structure projecting from a salient added to the town wall and containing a deep well).

Rhuddlan: Extremely slight traces of the Edwardian borough's earthwork defences can be identified.

There are no significant above-ground remains of former medieval town defences or gates at Aberystwyth, Flint or Ruthin.

APPENDIX:
THE RESEARCH AGENDA

The concluding discussion in Chapter 5 has highlighted the importance of surviving urban defences within the context of modern built environments and the heritage industry. But as well as an amenity and conservation dimension to the future of town walls, there needs to be a continuing academic agenda. The following list attempts a series of important avenues for future work, but is not exhaustive. The suggestions are constrained by practical limitations and are not a theoretical 'wish list'; the latter would undoubtedly include an appeal for massive excavations on the defences of many towns, which in present circumstances are most unlikely to occur. Archaeologists do, however, need to make maximum capital from those opportunities for intervention that do arise.

The following is considered a working list of priorities, but in no particular order.

Municipal records: We should not neglect the fact that numerous towns with clear evidence of walls have no surviving murage grants (such as Launceston), while others apparently have no direct documentary evidence whatsoever for the origins of walls, even of monumental proportions, such as those at Chepstow. In short, the history of medieval town walls is far more than the history of murage tax. It is important, therefore, that historians amplify the general picture from murage grants (recorded centrally in royal records) with detailed transcription and analysis of municipal documents (available in local archives). This could further amplify issues of chronology, building works, labour, materials, prices and individual structures at the level of individual towns. The immense potential for this type of work has been highlighted by a detailed study by Stoyle of the later and post-medieval periods for Exeter.[1]

Other prime candidates, of medieval towns with records holding potential for further study at a similar level of detail include Bristol and Coventry.

Shrunken and deserted boroughs: Those medieval towns with walls that have become entirely deserted, shifted to new sites or shrunken in extent, hold particular potential for further study for two reasons. First, it is easy to under-estimate their original significance in their contemporary settlement hierarchy. Second, given their relative undeveloped status, shrunken and deserted medieval boroughs contain a great resource for archaeological study, in terms of topography and excavation, with massive potential to reveal relationships between defences and tenements, street patterns and immediately extramural features. Among a list of sites with particularly obvious potential in this regard are: Kenfig, Kilpeck, Richard's Castle and New Winchelsea.

Urban archaeological data: In an era when urban excavation is dominated by small-scale developer-funded work, it is increasingly crucial that results, whether positive or negative, are adequately collated and available for research. Volumes such as those produced for Hereford, Leicester, Lincoln and Oxford show that, collectively, excavations on a town's defences can prove extremely illuminating about urban development in general.[2] Urban archaeological databases and related GIS technologies are important tools in this regard. Given the physical properties of town walls as long, narrow sinuous features whose remains are likely to survive in many different but related places within an historic townscape, it is vital that interventions, even if very small in scale, are fully catalogued, interpreted in the context of the town's defences as a whole, and the results ultimately disseminated in the public domain rather than remaining in the archives of archaeological practitioners. Outstanding examples of cities very much in need of synthetic work bringing together the results of numerous small-scale excavations of complex, extensive and multi-phase defences are Bristol and London.

Fabric analysis: As in other fields of architectural study, close scrutiny and recording of the fabric of town walls reveals how new and important messages can emerge from apparently familiar structures that have been visible for a very long time. Analysis of building stones, phases of construction and rebuildings can illuminate the chronology and character of wall evolution in a manner unachievable through any other means. While surveys at places such as Carlisle, Newcastle and York are fully published, others, for instance the extremely thorough surveys at Exeter and Tenby, remain in the realm of 'grey literature'; many other places still require basic recording work.[3]

Small towns: While the small towns of Roman Britain have received much academic attention, those of medieval Britain still tend to be overshadowed by larger and more famous centres. The defences of such places have similarly been neglected, yet tell us much about the spread of defensive aspirations down the hierarchies of settlement, status and wealth. Question marks also still remain over whether many smaller boroughs were indeed provided with defences in the post-Conquest period. Towns such Langport, Oakham and Tickhill deserve attention in this regard, for instance.

Topographies of defence:. While some towns and cities have had a defended perimeter defined in Roman times and surviving through the medieval and modern periods, the topography of other places has been more complex. In such cases, enceintes have either been extended or replaced so that a succession of defended plans occurs through time. Here, town defences do not represent continuity so much as evolution. The analyses of Rhuddlan and York – to take towns of very different size and status – have been revealing examples of evolution of successive and differently located perimeters. Defences can thus illuminate not only the enclosure of communities, but also their growth. Other places deserving of further attention in this regard include Bristol, Lincoln Northampton and Norwich.

Urban frameworks and defence: Larger towns were subdivided into wards, which commonly also had extramural portions. One of the functions of wards related to organisation of manpower for the urban militias generally and for guarding the walls in particular. The small number of case studies discussed above reveal that our understanding of the origins and evolution of wards, which sometimes began in the late Anglo-Saxon period, is far from complete. Synthesis of available data, in documentary and cartographic form, would contribute considerably to our knowledge of urban defences and their workings, and has great potential to inform more generally about the development of town plans and the growth of suburbs.

Environmental evidence: While the popular perception of town defences is one of stone walls and gates, or possibly earthen ramparts and timber palisades, such features were always accompanied by at least one surrounding ditch. These features have become an even greater casualty of urban development than walls and gates themselves, and virtually none survive at ground level. Where portions of ditch systems may survive as filled-in features, however truncated by later structures, they are potentially great resources of artefactual and environmental data that could illuminate contemporary society and economy as well as the chronology of the infilling and abandonment of originally important features. In particular, archaeological analysis of waterlogged ditch deposits presents us with one of our best chances of revealing the relationship between lifestyle and defences and, crucially, this can be achieved by small-scale excavation of the sort now very common.

The European dimension: A recurrent, but deliberately under-explored theme of this book, has been the contrast between the scale and incidence of walled towns in Britain and much of Europe. Remarks made about this have been, of necessity, brief and simple. It would, of course, be a valuable exercise to extend to all parts of Europe an exploration of the subjects dealt with here on a British level (and even here, incompletely, given our almost total exclusion of Ireland). This exercise would, from a British standpoint, no doubt reveal many chronological, national, regional and local variations, further illuminating the defensive and social roles of urban defences, and highlight more clearly the nature of the British experience within the wider whole. In short, it is necessary to examine the European material further to help understand Britain, while other avenues for study demand a more international approach than is often the case within the world of medieval archaeology, which is so often compartmentalised along national lines. One area with enormous comparative potential, for instance, is the study of *bastide* planning on both sides of the English Channel in the later medieval period.

GLOSSARY

Bailey	dependent castle enclosure of a motte, ringwork or donjon
Barbican	an outwork from the gate of a town or castle comprising a defended passage
Bartizan	a turret corbelled out from the angle of a wall
Burgh	a borough, in a Scottish context
Burghal Hidage	list of *c.*900 containing the names of royal defended centres within and around Wessex
Burh	enclosed site of Anglo-Saxon date, sometimes domestic but often urban in character
Ceaster	Anglo-Saxon place name element derived from the Latin *castrum* (fortress)
Danelaw	area of England subject to Danish control and law in the ninth and tenth centuries
Five boroughs	a series of urban or quasi-urban fortified centres (Derby, Leicester, Lincoln, Nottingham and Stamford), forming the basis of the ninth-century Danish confederacy known as the Danelaw
Hide	land unit, originally relating to an actual area, but eventually more applied as a notional unit for the assessment of tax and military service
Merlon	the upstanding component of crenellations, sometimes incorporating an arrow slit
Motte	artificial mound, usually of earthen construction, providing the basis for a fortified and/or domestic castle superstructure
Murage	tax raised on goods entering a town for sale, the proceeds to be applied to the building and maintenance of walls
Ringwork	fortification comprising a bank with timber or stone walls and gatehouse, and an external ditch, enclosing a series of internal domestic structures
Vicus	small Roman civilian settlement, usually attached to a military establishment, leading etymologically to the Old English *–wic*, a trading settlement of the eighth or ninth century
Ward	administrative subdivision of a town with legal and financial functions; also the basis of organised manpower for urban militia: watch and ward

NOTES

CHAPTER 1

1   See for instance Heighway 1972, 9
2   See Smith 1985
3   Gooder 1967, 5
4   Giles 2000
5   See Lilley 1999; 2000b
6   Bradley 1995, 41-46
7   Higham and Barker 1992
8   Carter 1969, 4
9   Henderson 2001, 93
10 Shoesmith 1982, 17
11 Barlow *et al.* 1976, 434
12 Norris and Kain 1982; Hopkinson 2000
13 Wacher 1975, 408
14 Brooks 1984; 1989; Tatton Brown 1984, 5-12
15 Brooks 1977
16 Brooks 1984
17 RCHME 1972; Hall 1994
18 Barlow *et al.* 1976, 272-7; Yorke 1982; Keene 1985, 42-8; James 1997, 41-2, 56, 65-7
19 White and Barker 1998
20 Morton 1992, 30-1; Andrews 1997, 22-30

21 Clarke and Ambrosiani 1991; Schofield and Vince 2003, 23-6
22 Hill 1969
23 Keen 1984, 230-3
24 Baker and Holt 1996; see also Carver 1980, 53-11; Brooks 1996; Whitelock 1955, 498
25 Vince 1990, 87-90
26 Gould 1968-9
27 Shoesmith 1982, 74-7
28 Haslam 1987
29 Hill and Worthington 2002
30 Blair 1988; 2000
31 Hall 1989; 2001; Vince 2001
32 Jones *et al.* 2003, 170

CHAPTER 2

1   Beresford 1967; Dyer 2002; 2003
2   Macrory 1980
3   See for instance Silvester 1997
4   Turner 1970, 23
5   Darby 1977, 289-95
6   Ayers 1994, 51
7   Frere *et al.* 1982, 34, 40
8   Chapman 1998-9, 33-7

9   Butler 1976; Pounds 1990, 215–21; Creighton 2003
10 RCHME 1977, xli
11 Drage 1987; English 1995
12 Biddle and Hill 1971, 82
13 Hassall 1976, 253–4
14 Jones *et al.* 2003, 170–2
15 Buckley and Lucas 1987, 45, 59
16 Everson and Jecock 1999, 99–101
17 Grenville 1997, 175–9
18 Stell 1988
19 Mallory and McNeill 1991, 286–7
20 Higham and Saunders 1997; Creighton 2005
21 Higham 1999
22 Higham *et al.* 1985
23 Manley 1987; Quinnell and Blockley 1994, 212–3
24 Murphy 2000, 198–201
25 Rhys 1908, 50–1, 73
26 Owen-John 1985, 66–115
27 Lilley 2000b
28 Griffiths 1994, 309–10; Spurgeon 2001, 177–8
29 Soulsby 1983, 19, 36, 170–72
30 Soulsby 1983, 77
31 Butler 1989; 1995; Butler and Knight 2004
32 Simpson 1972, 7–10
33 Kellett 1969, 4; see also Dennison 1998 101–2
34 Stell 1988, 62
35 Stones 1987, 9–10; Cameron and Stones 2001, 304–5
36 Stell 1999, 63
37 RCAHMS 1951; Adams 1978, 38
38 RCAHMS 1963, 304–5
39 RCAHMS 1967, 280
40 Bowler *et al.* 1995, 917–20; Yeoman 1995, 65
41 Bowler *et al.* 1995, 927–8; Spearman 1988, 51–2
42 Stell 1988, 62; 1999, 64
43 Bond 2001, 67–8; Creighton 2002, 212–4
44 See Baker 1982
45 Compare Hill and Klemperer 1985 and Jecock and Corbett 2001
46 Liddiard 2000, 58
47 Creighton 2004b
48 Barley 1957
49 Beresford 1967
50 Owen 1992
51 Silvester 1997; Jones 1998
52 Torrance 1959
53 Shoesmith 1992; Dalwood 1996
54 Williams 1977, 5, 241; Beresford and St Joseph 1979, 222
55 Webster 1989, 97–8
56 Rowley 1986, 108–11; Murphy 2000
57 Higham and Barker 2000, 11–12, 149
58 Lilley 1995; Murphy 1997
59 Beresford 1967, 541; Renn 1968a, 214
60 Griffiths 1978, 49
61 Jones *et al.* 1997
62 Gooder *et al.* 1966, 89
63 See Ballard 1913; Ballard and Tait 1923
64 Crow and Olson 1966, 147
65 Scarfe 1971
66 West 1971a
67 RCAHMW 1937, cxlviii–cxlix, 4
68 VCH Oxon. IV 1979, 301
69 Turner 1970, 122, 201, 209; Allmand 1989, 225
70 Smith 1970, 73
71 See Fox 1991
72 VCH Stafford VI 1979, 199
73 Anderson 1921, 21
74 Morris and Hoverd 1994, 47–54
75 VCH 1962, 88–9; Rogers 1969, 4–6
76 RCHME 1959, xliii; Lobel 1975b, 12
77 See Miller *et al.* 1982, 39–41; VCH East Yorks. VI 1989, 178–9
78 Lancaster 1975, 5–6
79 Shoesmith 1982, 19
80 Brooke and Keir 1975, 174–5

81 Urry 1967, 185 ff

82 Gelling 1953, 44

83 Leach 1984, 60

84 Carter 1969, 4

85 VCH East Yorks VI 1989, 178-9

86 Keene 2001

87 Barron 1989, 45-6; Schofield 1984, 40, 70

88 See Nicholas 1997a, 92-3

89 Barley 1969

90 Carrington 1994, 65-8; Thacker 2000, 21-2

91 Lobel 1975a, 4-7; Sivier 2002, 82-3

92 Hebditch 1968, 135; Leech 1997, 28

93 James 1997, 56, 67

94 Barlow et al. 1976, 237; Keene 1985, 48

95 Keene 1976, 76-8; Jones et al. 2003, 186-8

96 Urry 1967, 186

97 Lobel 1969a, 7; Heighway 1983, 7

98 Morris 1895, 242-3

99 Lilley 1995, 34-6

100 Soulsby 1983, 10-11, 66, 97, 102-3; Clarke and Bray, 2003

101 Campbell 1975, 11

102 VCH Durham II 1928, 65, 91-3

103 Spurgeon 1977, 42

104 Smith 1970, 85-6

105 Teasdale 1999, 40

106 Beresford and St Joseph 1979, 241; Chambers 1937

107 Beresford and St Joseph 1979, 235-7; Soulsby 1983, 121

108 Bishop 1992

109 Griffiths 1994, 309-10

110 Carter 1969, 3

111 Taylor 1974

112 Kelly 1979, 112; Higham and Barker 1992, 173

113 Morris 1901, 200; Carr 1982, 238

114 Beresford 1967, 49-50, 534-5

115 Taylor 1974

116 Carr 1982, 239

117 Carter 1969

118 Beresford 1967; Bernard 1993

119 Trabut-Cussac 1954; Salch 1978

120 Coulson 1982; Thompson 1998, 108-14

121 Elder 2003, 11

122 Brooks and Whittington 1977

123 RCHME 1972, 13

124 Jones et al. 2003, 170

125 Buckley and Lucas 1987, 59

126 Butler 1987, 171; Carrington 1994, 64-8

127 VCH Oxon. IV 1979, 301

128 Barlow et al. 1976, 279

129 VCH Northants II 1906, 148

130 Burrow 1977

131 Stoyle 2003, plate 11

132 Keene 1985, 42-8

133 Kenyon 1981; Saunders 1989; Schmidtchen 1990; Kenyon 1994

134 Saunders 1976, 22

135 Renn 1968b

136 O'Neil 1951; Renn 1964; Saunders 1966, 136-7; 2000

137 Saunders 1976, 27-9

138 RCHME 1972, 51

139 Garfi 1993, 73-4

140 Tatton-Brown et al. 1982, 114

141 McCarthy et al. 1990, 65-8, 162

142 Saunders 1985; Youngs et al. 1986, 158-9; Ayers 1994, 79

143 Hudson and Tingey 1910, 216 ff.; Ayers 1994, 65

144 Saunders 1985; Youngs et al. 1986, 158-9

145 Quoted in Saunders 1985, 109

146 Kenyon 1981, 212-14; Saunders 2000

147 VCH Hants. 1912, 361

148 Pye and Woodward 1996, 2

149 See O'Neil 1935

CHAPTER 3

1   Beresford and St Joseph 1979, 201

2   Penn 1980, 58; Youngs and Clark 1981
3   Henderson 1999, map 61.8
4   See Cameron 1961, 194
5   Jones et al. 1997, 184
6   Room 1992, 122-4
7   Ekwall 1954, 90-93, 188-90
8   Brooke and Keir 1975, 161; Heighway 1983, 7-8
9   1897, 180ff; see also Williams 1992; Renn 1993
10 Soulsby 1983, 36-7
11 Gover et al. 1940, 21
12 Neale 2000, 173
13 Higham and Barker 2000, 148
14 See Neale 2000
15 See Burrow 1977, 71
16 Blaylock 1995, 46; 1998
17 RCHME 1972, 135
18 Garfi 1993, 19; see also Thomas 1993
19 Frere et al. 1982, 21, 84-5
20 Wheeler 1921; see also Crummy 1977, 92-3
21 Hoare et al. 2002
22 Ayers 1994, 65
23 Miller et al. 1982, 40-1
24 VCH East Yorks. I 1967, 412-3; Hull City Council 1990, 39-40; Evans 1997, 37-9
25 Wight 1972; Foreman 1989
26 Howes and Foreman 1999, 4-14
27 Barron 1989, 46
28 Schofield 1984, 129
29 Taylor 1974, 345-6
30 Henderson 2001
31 Schofield 1984, 70-3; Lyle 1994, 77; Elder 2003, 13
32 Hughes 1994, 133
33 Faulkner 1975, 58-62
34 Stoyle 2003, 14-20
35 Wedlake 1965-6, 89-90
36 Stocks and Stevenson 1923, 389, 412, 472
37 Stoyle 2003, 38-42
38 RCHME 1972, 39
39 Stocks and Stevenson 1923, 12
40 Cook 1998, 42
41 Rowlands 1993
42 Boughton 1997, 52
43 King and Cheshire 1982, 79-80; Ludlow 1991, 30
44 Radley 1972; Buckland 1984; see also Ottaway 1993, 109-11; Tweedle et al. 1999, 189-90
45 Steane 2001a, 2
46 Saunders 1976, 21; Flight and Harrison 1986
47 Hughes 1994, 135
48 Taylor 2003, 56-7
49 Burgess 1976, 59
50 Neale 2000, 173
51 Stoyle 2003, 32
52 Garfi 1993, 69-71; see also Thomas 1993
53 See Palliser 1987, 58
54 West 1971b
55 LeQuesne 1999, 154
56 Markuson 1980, 71-3, 80
57 Daniels 1986, 70-2
58 Poulton and Riall 1998
59 O'Neil and Foster-Smith 1940
60 Barker 1961; see also Radford 1957-8
61 Green 1970, 116
62 Colyer 1975, 260-2
63 Platt and Coleman-Smith 1975, 142-3
64 Hughes 1994, 134
65 Lawler 1998, 172-3
66 Cunliffe 1962, 6
67 For Boston, see Wilson and Hurst 1958, 200; for Hastings, Martin et al. 1995, 10
68 Schofield 1975-6, 181-2; Webster and Cherry 1974, 207
69 Ponsford 1971, 9
70 Owles 1973, 167
71 Carver 1977-8, 68
72 Hurst 1965, 132-143
73 Brooks 1965-6, 19-20

74 Streeten 1976

75 Haslam 1977-8

76 Leach 1984, 72

77 Jones *et al.* 1997, 86-8

78 Milne 2001, 35

79 Clarke and Bray 2003

80 Curnow and Thompson 1969, 117-9

81 Higham and Barker 1992

82 Shoesmith 1982, 56

83 Klingelhofer 1976-7, 89-90

84 Quinnell and Blockley 1994, 89

85 Miles 1996, 117-20

86 Brown *et al.* 1963, 323, 371

87 Hunter and Jope 1951; Durham *et al.* 1983

88 Palmer 1976, 150

89 Gaimster *et al.* 1990, 53

90 Bowler *et al.* 1995, 918-20

91 Youngs *et al.* 1987, 147; Hull City Council 1990; Evans 1994

92 Tatton-Brown 1978, 153

93 Harrison 1972, 130-1

94 Stoyle 2003, 73-4

95 Barton 1964, 185-6

CHAPTER 4

1 See Liddiard 2003

2 Lopez 1963, 27

3 Rosenau 1983, 26-32; see also Perbellini 2000a

4 Delano-Smith and Kain 1999, 11

5 Zeune 2000, 40

6 Delano-Smith and Kain 1999, 47

7 Ralph 1986

8 Alldridge 1981, 25-8; Palliser 1980, 7

9 Davis 1969

10 Steane 2001b, 226-32

11 Crow and Olson 1966, 144-5

12 Pearsall 1992, 96-7

13 Lilley 2000a, 255

14 Hurst 1899, 71

15 Schofield 1984, 69

16 Stewart and Cooke 1990

17 Jones *et al.* 2003, 304-6

18 Platt 1973, 185

19 Soulsby 1983, 115-16

20 Brodie *et al.* 2002, 12

21 Pugh 1968, 103-09

22 RCHME 1972, 95

23 Little and Easterling 1927, 15

24 Carrington 1994, 70

25 Nolan *et al.* 1989, 29

26 Keene 1985, 44

27 Daniels 1986, 71-2; 1991, 47-8

28 Palmer 1976, 159

29 Gooder *et al.* 1966, 95

30 Nenk *et al.* 1993, 224

31 BaRAS 2000, 24-5

32 Phythian-Adams 1979, 254-7

33 Conzen 1969

34 See Whitehand 1981, 15

35 Lobel 1969a, 7-8

36 Rawcliffe 1995, 48

37 Gilchrist 1992, 113-6; 1995, 40, 116

38 Salter 1936, 87-8

39 Jackson-Stops 1979, 153

40 RCHME 1939, 84-91, 159-61

41 Paterson 2000, 163, 169-70

42 Higham and Barker 1992, 244-67

43 Clay 1914, 66-8

44 Schofield 1984, 69

45 Kingsford 2000, 299

46 Hinton 2003, 104

47 Barrow 1992, 94

48 Creighton 2002, 147

49 Morris 1989, 214-17

50 Nenk *et al.* 1993, 280

51 Barlow *et al.* 1976, 276-7

52 Keene 1985, 114-15

53 Urry 1967, 185; Frere *et al.* 1992, 88-9

54 Haslam 1988

55 See Blair 1994, 163-7; Dodd 2003, 152-164; Parsons 2003

56 Morris 1989, 217-8; Palliser 1995, 116

57 VCH Oxon. IV 1979, 301; Turner

1970, 29, 121; 1990

58 Maitland 1897, 178-90

59 Turner 1970, 30

60 Smith 1970, 62

61 Kings Lynn Council, C6/3m.10v;
the authors are grateful to Dr
Robert Liddiard for this reference

62 Bateson 1906, 713-27

63 Allmand 1989, 226

64 Tatton-Brown 1984, 15

65 Calendar of Patent Rolls 1216-25,
238-9

66 Calendar of Patent Rolls 1216-25,
169

67 Rowe and Draisey 1989

68 Allmand 1989, 229

69 Oxley 1986, 63, 111

70 Allmand 1989, 229

71 Turner 1970, 89

72 Allmand 1989

73 Toulmin Smith 1907, 162

74 Saunders 2000, 54

75 Penn 1980, 79-82

76 Turner 1970, 32-3

77 Keene 1985, 42-8

78 Stoyle 2003, 64-8

79 For a recent discussion of the parish
phenomenon, see Pounds 2000

80 Morris 1895

81 Lobel 1969b, 7

82 Brand 1789, 6-7

83 Hudson 1891

84 Kermode 2000, 442-3, 546-7

85 Rowe 1977

86 Harding 1973, 41-2

87 Turner 1990

88 Brooke and Keir 1975, chapter 7;
Vince 1990, 91-2; Milne 2001, 129

89 Barron 1989, 34-37

90 Williams 1963

91 Stubbs 1913, 312-14

92 Urry 1967, 92-104

93 Kowaleski 1980

94 Wilkinson 1931; Kowaleski 1995,

337-40

95 Allan et al. 1984

96 Jenkins 1806, 22

97 Pers. comm. Dr M. Stoyle

98 Stoyle 2003, 27-32

99 RCHME 1972, 12-13, 15-18, 34-6

100 Darby 1977, 293-4

101 Burgess 1976.

102 Phythian-Adams 1979, 158-9, 323-4.

103 Stubbs 1913, 181-4, 362-5, 463-9.

104 VCH 2003, 28

105 Morris 1895, 222; VCH 2003, 40

106 Barlow et al. 1976, 426

107 See Harvey 1984, for what follows

108 RCHME 1972, 35-5

109 Boughton 1997, 59

110 James 1987, 57

111 Stoyle 2003, 51-64

112 McCarthy et al. 1990, 214-9;
RCHME 1972, 28; see also Macivor
2001, 111-4

113 Potter 1976, 31-35, 91-93, 141-143

114 France 1999, 110-12; see also Jones
1999

115 For example, Bradbury 1992

116 For example Duffy 1979

117 McCarthy et al. 1990, 136-7

118 Shoesmith 1982, 20

119 Atkin and Howes 1993, 21

120 Turner 1970, 80

121 Hughes 1994

122 Poole 1955, 483-6; Powicke 1962, 8-12

123 See McKisack 1959

124 Platt 1973, 109

125 See Platt and Coleman-Smith 1975

126 Hughes 1994, 129

127 Ditchfield 1924; Renn 1979

128 O'Neil 1960; Saunders 1976; 2000

129 Kenyon 1981, 205-40

130 Higham 1987; 1999, 141-2; 2000

131 Griffiths 2000, 702-4

132 Smith 1985

133 Coulson 1995

134 Coulson 1995, 137-8

135 Palliser 1995

136 See Clark and Ambrosiani 1991

137 Keynes and Lapidge 1983, 101-02

138 Vince 1990, 26 and pers. comm.;
Haslam 1984, passim

139 Barlow *et al.* 1976, 279

140 Salter 1926, vi

141 Ravenhill and Rowe 2000, 44-5

142 Lobel 1975a

143 See, for example, Ballard 1913;
Stubbs 1913, 258-262; Ballard and
Tait 1923; Douglas and Greenaway
1953, 944 ff

144 Campbell 2000, 72-3

145 Williams 1963

146 Vince 1990, 40-1

147 Turner 1970, 157

148 Reynolds 1977; 1994

149 Ballard 1913, 92-3; Ballard and Tait
1923, 120-1

150 Finch 2002, 107

151 Lobel 1969a, 7

152 Rosser 2000, 343-4

153 Lancaster 1975,

154 Gooder 1967, 5, 12, 22; Coss 1974.

155 Owen 1945; Barley 1969

156 Carter 1969, 5; Smith 1977, 21-3;
Griffiths 1994, 303

157 Hebditch 1968; Burchill 1996;
BaRAS 2000, 18-26

158 Taylor 1983

159 Bonney 1990, 41-9; Roberts 1994,
61-3

160 Demidowicz 2002

161 Herring 2003; Liddiard 2000

162 Turner 1970, 158

163 Reynolds 1977, ix-x; see also
Schlederman 1970-1

164 Dobson 2000, 275; Schofield and
Vince 2003, 27

165 Nicholas 1997a

166 Kermode 2000, 441, 451

167 Astill 2002

168 Ellis *et al.* 2000

169 Beresford 1967

170 Palliser 2000; Bond 1987

171 McNeill and Pringle 1997

CHAPTER 5

1 See for instance Dobson 1977, 6-7

2 Colvin *et al.* 1982

3 Mayhew 1984, 111-16

4 Stoyle 2003, 75-6

5 Stoyle 2003

6 RCHME 1972, 36

7 Gooder 1967, 30

8 Hearnshaw and Hearnshaw 1907,
576

9 Skelton 1970; De Boer 1973

10 McCarthy *et al.* 1990, 171

11 Harvey 1981; Delano-Smith and
Kain 1999, 194-200

12 Toulmin Smith 1907

13 Hindle 1988, 61-6

14 Smith 1988

15 Stoyle 2003, 7

16 Hyde 1994

17 Davey 1987, 72

18 Stoyle 2003, 103

19 Hutton and Reeves 1998, 201-2

20 O'Neil 1960, 111

21 RCHME 1964

22 Saunders 1989, 75-6

23 Saunders 1973, 232-5; Stoyle 1998

24 Kent 1988, 206-7

25 Courtney and Courtney 1992, 61-8

26 Carrington 1994, 88-90

27 Morris 1924; Barratt 2003

28 Stoyle 1995; Henderson 2001, 85-9

29 Atkin 1991; 1993; Atkin and Howes
1993

30 Stoyle 1997

31 Jennings 2003, 68-9

32 Schofield and Vince 2003, 52

33 Hare 1984, 75-9; Blaylock 1995, 46

34 Boughton 1997

35 Sabine 1937, 36-7

36 VCH Staffordshire VI 1979, 199

37 Leach 1984, 63

38 Schofield 1984, 145

39 O'Leary 1981, 15

40 Teasdale 1999, 40

41 Cullen 1988, 4

42 Dawson 1995, 204

43 Besant 1902, 98-9

44 Quoted in Buckley and Lucas 1987, 62-4

45 Boughton 1997, 51

46 Pers comm. Dr Andy Russel

47 Hoskins 1963, 90

48 Taylor 2003, 54-5

49 Brewis 1934, 6

50 Saunders and Smith 2001, KD 29

51 Gooder et al. 1966, 98-9

52 RCHME 1972, 28 ff.; Hall 1996, 17-19

53 RCHME 1972, 4; Boughton 1997, 55

54 RCHME 1939, 160

55 Boughton 1997; LeQuesne 1999

56 Wood 1970, 5; RCHME 1972, 33

57 Curr 1984, 37

58 Elder 2003, 21

59 Amiel et al. 2000

60 Bruce 1995; Bruce and Jackson 1999

61 Perbellini 2000b; 2003

62 Insall 1968; Wood 1970

63 Taylor 1970; 1995

64 Tatton-Brown et al. 1982, 118

65 Stoyle 2003, 182-3

66 Heighway 1972, 10-12

67 Brindle 2003

68 Macivor 1972

69 For example Chapman et al. 1985; Blaylock 1998; Elder 2003

70 See Snyder and Blakely 1997

APPENDIX

1 Stoyle 2003.

2 For Hereford, see Shoesmith 1982; for Leicester, Buckley and Lucas 1987; for Lincoln, Jones et al. 2003; and for Oxford, Dodd 2003.

3 For Exeter, see Blaylock 1995; for Tenby, Garfi 1993

BIBLIOGRAPHY

Adams, 1978: *The Making of Urban Scotland*. London: Croom Helm.

Allan, J., Henderson, C., and Higham, R.A., 1984: Saxon Exeter. In Haslam, J. (ed.), *Anglo-Saxon Towns in Southern England*. Chichester: Phillimore, 385-411.

Alldridge, N.J., 1981: Aspects of the topography of early medieval Chester. *Journal of the Chester Archaeological Society* 64, 5-31.

Allmand, C., 1989: Taxation in medieval England: the example of murage. In Bourin, M. (ed.), *Villes, Bonnes Villes, Cités at Capitales: Études d'Histoire Urbaine (XIIe - XVIIIe Siècle) Offertes à Bernard Chevalier*. Caen: Paradigme, 223-230.

Amiel, C., Martinat, J., Piniès, J., Poisson, O., Satgé, P. and Signoles, A., 2000: *De la Place Forte au Monument: La Restauration de la Cité de Carcassonne au XIXe Siècle*. Paris: Éditions du Patrimoine.

Anderson, R.C. (ed.), 1921: *Letters of the Fifteenth and Sixteenth Century from the Archives of Southampton*. Southampton: Publications of the Southampton Records Society No. 12.

Andrews, P. (ed.), 1997: *Excavations at Hamwic. Volume 2: Excavations at Six Dials*. London: CBA Research Report No. 109.

Astill, G., 2002: Windsor in the context of medieval Berkshire. In Keen, L. and Scarff, E. (eds), *Windsor. Medieval Archaeology, Art and Architecture of the Thames Valley* (British Archaeological Association Conference Transactions 25), 1-14.

Aston, M. and Bond, C.J., 2000: *The Landscape of Towns*. Stroud: Sutton.

Atkin, M., 1991: The Civil War defences of Gloucester. *Fortress* 10, 32-38.

Atkin, M., 1993: David Papillon and the Civil War defences of Gloucester. *Transactions of the Bristol and Gloucestershire Archaeological Society* 111, 147-163.

Atkin, M. and Howes, R., 1993: The use of archaeology and documentary sources in identifying the Civil War defences of Gloucester. *Post-Medieval Archaeology* 27, 15-41.

Ayers, B., 1994: *English Heritage Book of Norwich*. London: Batsford/English Heritage.

Baker, D., 1982: Mottes, moats and ringworks in Bedfordshire: Beauchamp Wadmore revisited. *Château Gaillard* 9–10, 35–54.

Baker, N. and Holt, R., 1996: 'The city of Worcester in the tenth century'. In Brooks, N. and Cubbitt, C. (eds), *St Oswald of Worcester. Life and Influence*. Leicester: Leicester University Press, 129-146

Baker, N. and Holt, R., 2004: *Urban Growth and the Medieval Church: Gloucester and Worcester*. Aldershot: Ashgate

Ballard, A., (ed.), 1913: *British Borough Charters, 1042-1216*. Cambridge: Cambridge University Press.

Ballard, A. and Tait, J., 1923: *British Borough Charters, 1216-1307*. Cambridge: Cambridge University Press.

BaRAS, 2000: *Archaeological Excavation of a Medieval Watergate, Temple Quay, Bristol*. Bristol: City of Bristol Museum and Art Gallery Report No. 677.

Barker, P.A., 1961: Excavations on the town wall, Roushill, Shrewsbury. *Medieval Archaeology* 5, 181-210.

Barley, M.W., 1957: Cistercian land clearances in Nottinghamshire: three deserted villages and their moated successor. *Nottingham Medieval Studies* 1, 75-89.

Barley, M.W., 1969: Nottingham. In Lobel, M.D (ed.), *Historic Towns: Maps and Plans of Towns and Cities in the British Isles, with Historical Commentaries, from Earliest Times to 1800* Vol. 1. London: Lovell, 1–8.

Barley, M.W., 1976: Town defences in England and Wales after 1066. In Barley, M.W. (ed.), *The Plans and Topography of Medieval Towns in England and Wales*. London: CBA Research Report No. 14, 57–71.

Barley, M.W. (ed.), 1977: *European Towns: their Archaeology and Early History*. London: Academic Press.

Barlow, F., Biddle, M., von Feilitzen, O. and Keene, D.J. (eds), 1976: *Winchester Studies I. Winchester in the Early Middle Ages: An Edition and Discussion of the Winton Domesday*. Oxford: Clarendon Press.

Barratt, J., 2003: *The Great Siege of Chester*. Stroud: Tempus.

Barron, C., 1989: The late Middle Ages: 1270-1520. In Lobel, M.D. (ed.), *The City of London from Prehistoric Times to c.1520* (The British Atlas of Historic Towns, Vol. III). Oxford: Oxford University Press/Historic Towns Trust, 34-56.

Barrow, J., 1992: Urban cemetery location in the high Middle Ages. In Bassett, S. (ed.), *Death in Towns: Urban Responses to the Dying and the Dead, 100-1600*. Leicester: Leicester University Press, 78-100.

Barton, K.J., 1964: The excavation of a medieval bastion at St Nicholas's Almshouses, King Street, Bristol. *Medieval Archaeology* 8, 184-212.

Bateson, M., 1906: The burgesses of Domesday and the Malmesbury wall. *English Historical Review* 21, 709-722.

Beresford, M.W., 1967: *New Towns of the Middle Ages*. London: Lutterworth Press.

Beresford M.W. and St Joseph, J.K.S., 1979: *Medieval England: An Aerial Survey*, 2nd ed. Cambridge: Cambridge University Press.

Bernard, G. 1993: *L'Aventure des Bastides*. Toulouse: Editions Privat.

Besant, W., 1902: *London in the Eighteenth Century*. London: A & C Black.

Biddle, M. and Hill, D., 1971: Late Saxon planned towns. *Antiquaries Journal* 51, 70–85.

Bishop, M.C., 1992: The White Wall, Berwick-Upon-Tweed. *Archaeologia Aeliana* (Fifth Series), 117-119.

Blair, J., 1988: Introduction: from minster to parish church. In Blair, J. (ed.), *Minsters and Parish Churches: The Local Church in Transition 950-1200*. Oxford: Oxford University Committee for Archaeology Monograph No. 17, 1-19.

Blair, J., 1994: *Anglo-Saxon Oxfordshire*. Oxford: Oxfordshire Books.

Blair, J., 2000: Small towns 600-1270. In Palliser, D.M. (ed.), *The Cambridge Urban History of Britain, Vol. I*. Cambridge: Cambridge University Press, 245-270.

Blaylock, S.R., 1995: *Exeter City Wall Survey*. Exeter: Exeter Archaeology.

Blaylock, S.R., 1998: *Exeter City Wall*. Exeter: Devon Archaeological Society and Exeter Archaeology

Bond, J., 1987: Anglo-Saxon and medieval defences. In Schofield, J. and Leech, R. (eds), *Urban Archaeology in Britain*. London: CBA Research Report No. 61, 92-115.

Bond, J., 2001: Earthen castles, outer enclosures and the earthworks at Ascott d'Oilly Castle, Oxfordshire. *Oxoniensia* 66, 43-69.

Bonney, M., 1990: *Lordship and Urban Community: Durham and its Overlords 1250-1540*. Cambridge: Cambridge University Press.

Bowler, D., Cox, A. and Smith, C., 1995: Four excavations in Perth, 1979-84. *Proceedings of the Society of Antiquarians of Scotland* 125, 917-999.

Boughton, P., 1997: *Picturesque Chester: The City in Art*. Chichester: Phillimore.

Bradley, J., 1995: *Walled Towns in Ireland*. Dublin: Country House.

Bradbury, J., 1992: *The Medieval Siege*. Woodbridge: Boydell.

Brand, 1789: *History and Antiquities of the Town and County of Newcastle-upon-Tyne* (2 Vols.). London.

Brewis, P., 1934: The west walls of Newcastle upon Tyne. Between Durham and Ever Towers. *Archaeologia Aeliana* 11 (Fourth Series), 1-20.

Brindle, S., 2003: Ancient monument casework in London. *Greater London Archaeology Advisory Service Annual Review* (April 2002-March 2003), 11-12.

Britnell, R., 1996: *The Commercialisation of English Society 1000-1500* (second edition). Manchester: Manchester University Press.

Britton, J., 1814: *The Architectural Antiquities of Great Britain, Vol. IV*. London: Longman, Hurst, Rees, Orme and Brown.

Brodie, A., Croom, J. and O'Davies, J., 2002: *English Prisons: An Architectural History*. Swindon: English Heritage.

Brooke, C. and Kier, G., 1975: *London 800-1216: The Shaping of a City*. London: Secker and Warburg.

Brogiolo, G.P., Gauthier, N. and Christie, N.J., 2000: *Towns and their Territories between Late Antiquity and the Early Middle Ages*. Leiden: Brill.

Brooks, N.P., 1965–66: Excavations at Wallingford Castle, 1965: an interim report. *Berkshire Archaeological Journal* 62, 17–21.

Brooks, N.P., 1977: The ecclesiastical topography of early-medieval Canterbury. In. Barley,

M.W. (ed.), *European Towns: Their Archaeology and Early History*. London: Council for British Archaeology for Academic Press, 487-498.

Brooks, N.P., 1984: *The Early History of the Church at Canterbury*. Leicester: Leicester University Press.

Brooks, N.P., 1989: The creation and early structure of the kingdom of Kent. In Bassett, S.R. (ed.), *The Origins of Anglo-Saxon Kingdoms*. London: Leicester University Press, 55-74.

Brooks, N.P., 1996: The administrative background to the burghal hidage. In Hill, D. and Rumble, A. (eds), *The Defence of Wessex: The Burghal Hidage and Anglo-Saxon Fortifications*. Manchester: Manchester University Press, 128-150.

Brooks, N.P. and Whittington, G., 1977: Planning and growth in the medieval Scottish burgh: the example of St Andrews. *Transactions of the Institute of British Geographers* (New Series) 2.1, 278-295.

Brown, R.A., Colvin, H.M. and Taylor, A.J., 1963: *The History of the King's Works, Volumes I and II: the Middle Ages*. London: HMSO.

Bruce, D.M., 1995: Sustainable tourism in Chepstow and Conwy. *Context* 46 (June edition), 13-14.

Bruce, D.M. and Jackson, M.J., 1999: Measuring Sustainability in Tourism – Lessons from a Study of Chepstow for other European Walled Towns. In Foley, M., McGillivray, D. and McPherson, G. (eds), *Leisure, Tourism and Environment: Sustainability and Environmental Policies*. Brighton: LSA Publication No.50 (Part 1), 141-155.

Buckley, R. and Lucas, J., 1987: *Leicester Town Defences: Excavations 1958–1974*. Leicester: Leicestershire Museums, Art Galleries and Records Service.

Buckland, P.C., 1984: The Anglian Tower and the use of Jurassic limestone in York. In Addyman, P.V. and Black, V.E. (eds), *Archaeological Papers from York Presented to M.W. Barley*. York: York Archaeological Trust, 51-57.

Burchill, R., 1996: Excavations on the Marsh Wall, King Street, Bristol. *Bristol and Avon Archaeology* 14, 11-16.

Burgess, L.A., (ed.), 1976: *The Southampton Terrier of 1454*. Southampton: Southampton Records Series No. 15.

Burrow, I., 1977: The town defences of Exeter. *Transactions of the Devonshire Association* 109, 13-40.

Butler, L.A.S., 1976: The evolution of towns: planted towns after 1066. In Barley, M.W. (ed.), *The Plans and Topography of Medieval Towns in England and Wales*. Oxford: BAR No. 14, 32–48.

Butler, L.A.S., 1987: Medieval urban religious houses. In Schofield, J. and Leech, R. (eds), *Urban Archaeology in Britain*. London: CBA Research Report No. 61, 167-176.

Butler, L., 1989: Dolforwyn Castle, Montgomery, Powys. First report: the excavations 1981-1986. *Archaeologia Cambrensis* 138, 78-98.

Butler, L., 1995: Dolforwyn Castle, Montgomery, Powys. Second report: the excavations 1987-1990. *Archaeologia Cambrensis* 144, 133-203.

Butler, L. and Knight, J., 2004: *Dolforwyn Castle. Montgomery Castle*. Cardiff: Cadw.

Calendar of Patent Rolls 1216-1225. 1901. London: HMSO.

Cameron, K., 1961: *English Place Names*. London: Batsford.

Cameron, A.S. and Stones, J.A. (eds), 2001: *Aberdeen: An In-Depth View of the Past: Excavations at Seven Major Sites Within the Medieval Burgh*. Edinburgh : Society of Antiquaries of Scotland Monograph No. 19.

Campbell, J. 1975: Norwich. In Lobel, M.D. (ed.), *The Atlas of Historic Towns, Volume II*. London: Scolar Press/Historic Towns Trust, 1-25.

Campbell, J., 2000: Power and authority 600-1300. In Palliser, D.M. (ed.), *The Cambridge Urban History of Britain, Vol. I*. Cambridge: Cambridge University Press, 51-78.

Carr, A.D., 1982: *Medieval Anglesey*. Llangefni: Anglesey Antiquarian Society.

Carrington, P., 1994: *English Heritage Book of Chester*. London: English Heritage/Batsford.

Carter, H., 1969: Caernarvon. In Lobel, M.D. (ed.), *Historic Towns: Maps and Plans of Towns and Cities in the British Isles, with Historical Commentaries, from Earliest Times to 1800, Volume I*. London: Lovell Johns-Cook, Hammond and Kell Organization, 1-8.

Carver, M.O.H., 1977-78: Two town houses in medieval Shrewsbury: the excavation and analysis of two medieval and later houses built on the town wall of Shrewsbury. *Transactions of the Shropshire Archaeological Society* 61 (entire volume).

Carver, M.O.H. (ed.) 1980: 'Medieval Worcester: an archaeological framework'. *Transactions of the Worcestershire Archaeological Society* (Third Series) 7 (entire volume).

Carver, M.O.H., 1987: *Underneath English Towns: Interpreting Urban Archaeology*. London: Batsford.

Chambers, G.E., 1937: The French bastides and the town plan of Winchelsea. *Archaeological Journal* 94, 177-206.

Chapman, A., 1998-9: Excavation of the town defences at Green Street, Northampton, 1995-06. *Northamptonshire Archaeology* 28, 25-60.

Chapman, H., Hall, J. and Marsh, G., 1985: *The London Wall Walk*. London: Museum of London.

Christie, N.J. and Loseby, S.T. (eds), 1996: *Towns in Transition: Urban Evolution in Late Antiquity and the Early Middle Ages*. Ashington: Ashgate.

Clarke, H. and Ambrosiani, B. (eds), 1991: *Towns in the Viking Age*. Leicester: Leicester University Press.

Clarke, S. and Bray, J., 2003; The Norman town defences of Abergavenny. *Medieval Archaeology* 47, 186-189.

Clay, R.M., 1914: *The Hermits and Anchorites of England*. London: Methuen.

Colvin, H.M., Summerson, J., Biddle, M., Hale, J.R. and Merriman, M., 1982: *The History of the King's Works, Volume IV (Part II) 1485-1660*. London: HMSO.

Colyer, C., 1975: Excavations at Lincoln 1970-1972: the western defences of the lower town. *Antiquaries Journal* 55, 227-266.

Conzen, M.R.G., 1969: *Alnwick, Northumberland: a Study in Town-Plan Analysis*. London: Philip.

Cook, M., 1998: *Medieval Bridge*. Princes Risborough: Shire.

Coss, P.R., 1974: Coventry before incorporation: a re-interpretation. *Midland History* 2.3, 137-151.

Coulson, C., 1982: Hierarchism in conventual crenellation: an essay in the sociology and metaphysics of medieval fortification. *Medieval Archaeology* 26, 69–100.

Coulson, C., 1995: Battlements and the bourgeoisie: municipal status and the apparatus of urban defence in later-medieval England. In Church, S. and Harvey, R. (eds), *Medieval Knighthood* 5. Woodbridge: Boydell, 119-195.

Courtney, P. and Courtney, Y., 1992: A siege examined: the Civil War archaeology of Leicester. *Post-Medieval Archaeology* 26, 47–90.

Creighton, O.H.. 2002: *Castles and Landscapes*. London and New York: Continuum.

Creighton, O.H. and Higham, R.A., *Medieval Castles*. Princes Risborough: Shire.

Creighton, O.H., 2003: Castles, lordship and settlement in Norman England and Wales. *History Today* 53.4, 12-19.

Creighton, O.H., 2004: 'The Rich Man in His Castle, the Poor Man at His Gate': Castle Baileys and Medieval Settlements in England. *Château Gaillard, Etudes de Castellologie Medievale* 21 (University of Caen).

Creighton, O.H,. 2005: Castles and castle-building in town and country. In Dyer, C. and Giles, K. (eds), *Medieval Town and Country 1100-1500*. Oxford: Society for Medieval Archaeology Monograph.

Crossley, D.W., 1990: *Post Medieval Archaeology in Britain*. Leicester: Leicester University Press.

Crow, M.M. and Olson, C.C., 1966: *Chaucer Life-Records*. Oxford: Clarendon.

Crummy, P., 1977: Colchester: The Roman fortress and the development of the Colonia. *Britannia* 8, 65-105.

Cullen, Hon. Lord, 1988: *The Walls of Edinburgh: A Short Guide*. Edinburgh: The Cockburn Association.

Cunliffe, B., 1962: The Winchester city wall. *Proceedings of the Hampshire Field Club and Archaeological Society* 22, part 2, 51-81.

Curnow, P.E. and Thompson, M.W., 1969: Excavations at Richard's Castle, Herefordshire, 1962–1964. *Journal of the British Archaeological Association* (Third Series) 32, 105–127.

Curr, G.G., 1984: Who saved York walls? The Role of William Etty and the Corporation of York. *York Historian* 5, 25-38.

Curry, A. and Hughes, M. (eds), 1994: *Arms, Armies and Fortifications in the Hundred Years War*. Woodbridge: Boydell.

Dalwood, H., 1996: *Archaeological Assessment of Kilpeck, Hereford and Worcester*. Unpublished report, Central Marches Historic Towns Survey, Herefordshire and Worcester County Council.

Daniels, R., 1986: The medieval defences of Hartlepool. *Durham Archaeological Journal* 2, 63-72.

Daniels, R., 1991: Medieval Hartlepool: evidence of and from the waterfront. In Good, G.L., Jones, R.H. and Ponsford, M.W. (eds), *Waterfront Archaeology: Proceedings of the Third International Conference, Bristol, 1988*. London: CBA Research Report No. 74, 43-50.

Darby, H.C., 1977: *Domesday England*. Cambridge: Cambridge University Press.

Davey, P.J., 1987: The post-medieval period. In Schofield, J. and Leech, R. (eds), *Urban Archaeology in Britain*. London: CBA Research Report No. 61, 69-80.

Davis, R.H.C., 1969: An Oxford charter of 1191 and the origins of municipal freedom. *Oxoniensia* 33, 53-65.

Dawson, K., 1995: *Town Defences in Early Modern England*. University of Exeter: Unpublished Geography PhD Thesis.

De Boer, G., 1973: The two earliest maps of Hull. *Post-Medieval Archaeology* 7, 79-87.

Delano-Smith, C. and Kain R.J.P., 1999: *English Maps: a History*. London: British Museum, Studies in Map History, Volume 2.

Demidowicz, G., 2002: The Hersum Ditch, Birmingham and Coventry: a local topographical term? *Transactions of the Birmingham and Warwickshire Archaeological Society* 106, 143-150.

Dennison, E.P., 1998: Power to the people? The myth of the medieval burgh community. In Foster, S., Macinnes, A. and MacInnes, R. (eds), *Scottish Power Centres from the Early Middle Ages to the Twentieth Century*. Glasgow: Cruithne Press, 100-131.

Ditchfield, P.H., 1924: The walls of Rye and Winchelsea. *Journal of the British Archaeological Association* 30, 120-131.

Dobson, R.B., 1977: Urban decline in late medieval England. *Transactions of the Royal Historical Society* 27 (Fifth Series), 1-22.

Dobson, B., 2000: General survey 1300-1540. In Palliser, D.M. (ed.), 2000: *The Cambridge Urban History of Britain, Vol. I*. Cambridge: Cambridge University Press, 273-290.

Dodd, A., 2003: *Oxford Before the University: The Late Saxon and Norman Archaeology of the Thames Crossing, the Defences and the Town*. Oxford: Oxford Archaeological Unit (Thames Valley Landscapes Monograph No. 17).

Douglas, D.C. and Greenaway, G.W. (eds), 1953: *English Historical Documents, II, 1042-1189*. London: Eyre and Spottiswoode.

Drage, C., 1987: Urban castles. In Schofield, J. and Leech, R. (eds), *Urban Archaeology in Britain*. London: CBA Research Report No. 61, 117-132.

Duffy, C., 1979: *Siege Warfare: The Fortress in the Early Modern World, 1494-1660*. London: Routledge & Kegan Paul.

Durham, B., Halpin, C. and Palmer, N., 1983: Oxford's northern defences: archaeological studies 1971-1982. *Oxoniensia* 48, 13-40.

Dyer, C., 2002: Small places with large consequences: the importance of small towns in England, 1000-1540. *Historical Research* 75 (no. 187), 1-24.

Dyer, C., 2003: The archaeology of medieval small towns. *Medieval Archaeology* 47, 85-114.

Ekwall, E., 1954: *Street-Names of the City of London*. Oxford: Clarendon Press.

Elder, J., 2003: *City Wall Trail*. Canterbury: Canterbury City Council.

Ellis, P. (ed.), 2000: *Ludgershall Castle, Wiltshire: a Report on the Excavations by Peter Addyman, 1964–1972*. Devizes: Wiltshire Archaeological and Natural History Society Monograph No. 2.

English, B., 1995: Towns, mottes and ring-works of the Conquest. In Ayton, A. and Price, J.L. (eds), *The Medieval Military Revolution*. London and New York: Tauris, 45-61.

Evans, D.H., 1994: *Excavations at the Beverley Gate, and Other Parts of the Town Defences of Kingston upon Hull*. Hull: Humberside SMR, Unpublished Report.

Evans, D.H., 1997: Archaeological work in the medieval port of Kingston-upon-Hull. *Lübecker Kolloquium sur Stadtarchäologie im Hanseraum* I, 25-49.

Everson, P. and Jecock, M., 1999: Castle Hill and the early medieval development of Thetford in Norfolk. In Pattison, P., Field, D. and Ainsworth, S. (eds), *Patterns of the Past: Essays in Landscape Archaeology for Christopher Taylor*. Oxford: Oxbow, 97–106.

Faulkner, P.A., 1975: The Surviving Medieval Buildings. In Platt, C. and Coleman-Smith (eds), *Excavations in Medieval Southampton, 1953-1969, Volume I, The Excavation Reports*. Leicester: Leicester University Press, 56-124.

Finch, J., 2002: Regionality and medieval landscapes. In Perring, D. (ed.), *Town and Country in England: Frameworks for Archaeological Research*. York: CBA Research Report No. 134, 107-115.

Flight, C. and Harrison, A.C., 1986: The southern defences of medieval Rochester. *Archaeologia Cantiana* 103, 1-26.

Foreman, M., 1989: The defences of Hull. *Fortress* 2, 36-45.

Fox, R., 1991: Portsmouth's ramparts revisited. *Fortress* 11, 29-38.

France, J., 1999: *Western Warfare in the Age of the Crusades, 1000-1300*. London: UCL Press.

Frere, S.S., Stow, S. and Bennett, P., 1982: *The Archaeology of Canterbury, Volume II: Excavations on the Roman and Medieval Defences of Canterbury*. Maidstone: Canterbury Archaeological Trust and Kent Archaeological Society.

Gaimster, D. R. M., Margeson, S. and Hurley, M., 1990: Medieval Britain and Ireland in 1989. *Medieval Archaeology* 34, 162-252

Garfi, S., 1993: *Tenby Town Walls Archaeological Recording Project for Pembrokeshire District Council and Cadw*. Unpublished Report: NMR, Aberystwyth.

Gelling, M., 1953: *The Place names of Oxfordshire, Part One*. Cambridge: Cambridge University Press.

Gilchrist, R., 1992: Christian bodies and souls: the archaeology of life and death in late medieval hospitals. In Bassett, S. (ed.), *Death in Towns: Urban Responses to the Dying and the Dead, 100-1600*. Leicester: Leicester University Press, 101-118.

Gilchrist, R., 1995: *Contemplation and Action: The Other Monasticism*. London: Leicester University Press.

Giles, K., 2000: *An Archaeology of Social Identity; Guildhalls in York, c.1350- 1630*. Oxford: British Archaeological Reports 315.

Gooder, E., 1967: *Coventry's Town Wall*. Coventry: Coventry and North Warwickshire History Pamphlets No. 4.

Gooder, E., Woodfield, C. and Chaplin, R., 1966: The walls of Coventry. *Transactions of the Birmingham Archaeological Society* 81, 88-138.

Gould, J., 1968-9: Third report on excavations at Tamworth, Staffs., 1968 – the western entrance to the Saxon borough. *Transactions of the South Staffordshire Archaeological and Historical Society* 10, 32-42.

Gover, J.E.B., Mawer, A. and Stenton, F.M, 1940: *The place names of Nottinghamshire*. Cambridge: Cambridge University Press.

Green, C., 1970: Excavations on the town wall, Great Yarmouth, Norfolk, 1955. *Norfolk Archaeology* 35, 109-117.

Green, J.R., 1893: *A Short History of the English People*. London: MacMillan.

Grenville, J., 1997: *Medieval Housing*. London: Leicester University Press.

Griffiths, R.A., 1978: *Boroughs of Medieval Wales*. Cardiff: University of Wales Press.

Griffiths, R.A., 1994: *Conquerors and Conquered in Medieval Wales*. Stroud: Sutton.

Griffiths, R.A., 2000: Wales and the marches. In Palliser, D.M. (ed.), 2000: *The Cambridge Urban History of Britain, Vol. I*. Cambridge: Cambridge University Press, 681-714.

Grose, F., 1801: *Military Antiquities Respecting a History of the English Army from the Conquest to the Present Day*. London: Egerton and Kearsley.

Hall, R.A., 1989: The five boroughs of Danelaw: a review of present knowledge. *Anglo-Saxon England* 18, 149-206.

Hall, R.A., 1994: *English Heritage Book of Viking Age York*. London: English Heritage/Batsford.

Hall, R.A., 1996: *English Heritage Book of York*. London: English Heritage/Batsford.

Hall, R.A, 2001: Anglo-Scandinavian urban developments in the East Midlands. In Graham-Campbell, J. *et al.* (eds), *Vikings and the Danelaw*. Oxford: Oxbow, 143-155.

Harding, A., 1973: *The Law Courts of Medieval England*. London: George Allen and Unwin.

Hare, M., 1984: The Watergate at Portchester and the Anglo-Saxon porch at Titchfield: a reconsideration of the evidence. *Proceedings of the Hampshire Field Club and Archaeological Society* 40, 71-80.

Harrington, P., 2004: *English Civil War Archaeology*. London: Batsford.

Harrison, A.C., 1972: Rochester East Gate, 1969. *Archaeologia Cantiana* 87, 121-157.

Harvey, J., 1984: *English Medieval Architects: A Biographical Dictionary Down to 1550* (revised edition). Gloucester: Sutton.

Harvey, P.D.A., 1981: The Portsmouth map of 1545 and the introduction of scale-maps into England. In Webb, J., Yates, N. and Peacock, S. (eds), *Hampshire Studies: Presented to Dorothy Dymond*. Portsmouth: Portsmouth City Records Office, 33-49.

Haslam, J., 1977-78: The excavation of the defences of Devizes. *Wiltshire Archaeological Magazine* 72-73, 59-65.

Haslam, J. (ed.), 1984: *Anglo-Saxon Towns in Southern England*. Chichester: Phillimore.

Haslam, J., 1987: Market and fortress in England in the reign of Offa. *World Archaeology* 19.1, 76-93.

Haslam, J., 1988: Parishes, churches, wards and gates in eastern London. In Blair, J. (ed.), *Minsters and Parish Churches: The Local Church in Transition 950-1200*. Oxford: Oxford University Committee for Archaeology Monograph No. 17, 35-43.

Hassall, T.G., 1976: Excavations at Oxford Castle, 1965–1973. *Oxoniensia* 41, 232–308.

Haslam, J., 1987: Market and fortress in England in the reign of Offa. *World Archaeology* 19.1, 76-93.

Hearnshaw, F.J.C. and Hearnshaw, D.M., 1907: *The Court Leet Records of Southampton, 1603-*

24, Vol. I, Part 3. Southampton: Cox and Sharland, Southampton Record Society Publications No. 4.

Hebditch, M., 1968: Excavations on the medieval defences, Portwall Lane, Bristol, 1965. *Transactions of the Bristol and Gloucestershire Archaeological Society* 87, 131–143.

Heighway, C., 1972: *The Erosion of History: Archaeology and Planning in Towns.* London: CBA Urban Research Committee.

Heighway, C., 1983: *The East and North Gates of Gloucester and Associated Sites.* Bristol: Western Archaeological Trust Excavation Monograph No. 4.

Henderson, C., 1999: The city of Exeter from AD 50 to the early nineteenth century. In Kain, R. and Ravenhill, W. (eds), *Historical Atlas of South-West England.* Exeter: Exeter University Press, 482–498.

Henderson, C., 2001: The development of the South Gate of Exeter and its role in the city's defences. *Proceedings of the Devon Archaeological Society* 59, 45–123.

Herring, P., 2003: Cornish medieval deer parks. In Wilson-North, R. (ed.), *The Lie of the Land Aspects of the Archaeology and History of the Designed Landscape in the South West of England.* Exeter: Mint Press, 34–50.

Higham, R.A., 1987: Public and private defence in the medieval south west: town, castle and fort. In Higham, R.A. (ed.), *Security and Defence in South-West England Before 1800.* Exeter: Exeter Studies in History No. 19, 27–49.

Higham, R.A. 1999: Castles, fortified houses and fortified towns in the middle ages. In Kain, R. and Ravenhill, W. (eds), *Historical Atlas of South-West England.* Exeter: Exeter University Press, 136–143.

Higham, R.A., 2000: The study and interpretation of British town walls: medieval urbanism and urban defences in south west England. In Perbellini, G. (ed.), *The Town Walls in the Middle Ages: Les Enceintes Urbaines Au Moyen Âge.* The Hague: Europa Nostra IBI Bulletin 53, 43–52.

Higham, R.A. and Barker, P., 1992: *Timber Castles.* London: Batsford.

Higham, R.A. and Barker, P., 2000: *Hen Domen, Montgomery. A Timber Castle on the English-Welsh Border: A Final Report.* Exeter: University of Exeter Press.

Higham, R.A., Goddard, S. and Rouillard, M., 1985: Plympton Castle, Devon. *Proceedings of the Devon Archaeological Society* 43, 59–75.

Higham, R.A. and Saunders, A., 1997: Public and private defence in British medieval towns. In Perbellini, G. (ed.), *The Defence of Rural Sites/Urban Fortified Houses: Les Defenses des Exploitations Rurales/Les Maison Urbaines Fortifies.* The Hague: Europa Nostra IBI Bulletin 50, 117–128.

Hill, C. and Klemperer, W., 1985: The deserted medieval settlement at Stafford Castle. *Medieval Village Research Group Annual Report* 33, 19–22.

Hill, D., 1969: The Burghal Hidage: the establishment of a text. *Medieval Archaeology*, 13, 84–92.

Hill, D., 1981: *An Atlas of Anglo-Saxon England.* Oxford: Basil Blackwell.

Hill, D. and Rumble, A. (eds), 1996: *The Defence of Wessex: The Burghal Hidage and Anglo-Saxon Fortifications.* Manchester: Manchester University Press.

Hill, D. and Worthington, M., 2002: *Offa's Dyke. History and Guide.* Stroud; Tempus.

Hindle, B.P., 1988: *Maps for Local History*. London: Batsford.

Hindle, B.P., 1990: *Medieval Town Plans*. Princes Risborough: Shire.

Hinton, D.A., 2003: Medieval Anglo-Jewry: The Archaeological Evidence. In Skinner, P. (ed.), *The Jews in Medieval Britain: Historical, Literary and Archaeological Perspectives*. Woodbridge: Boydell, 97-111.

Hoare, P.G., Vinx, R., Stevenson, C.R. and Ehlers, J., 2002: Reused bedrock ballast in King's Lynn's 'Town Wall' and the Norfolk port's medieval trading links. *Medieval Archaeology* 46, 91-105.

Hooper, N. and Bennett, M., 1996: *Cambridge Illustrated Atlas of Warfare in the Middle Ages 768-1487*. Cambridge: Cambridge University Press.

Hopkinson, M.F., 2000: Living in defended spaces: past structures and present landscapes. *Landscapes* 1.2, 53-77.

Hoskins, W.G., 1963: *Two Thousand Years in Exeter*. London: Phillimore.

Howes, A. and Foreman, M., 1999: *Town and Gun: The 17th-Century Defences of Hull*. Hull: Kinston Press/Kingston upon Hull Museums and Galleries.

Hudson, W., 1891: *The Wards of the City of Norwich, their Origin and History*. London: Jarrold and Sons.

Hudson, W. and Tingey, J.C., 1910: *The Records of the City of Norwich*. Norwich: Jarrold and Sons.

Hughes, M. 1994: The fourteenth-century French raids on Hampshire and the Isle of Wight. In Curry, A. and Hughes, M. (eds), *Arms, Armies and Fortifications in the Hundred Years War*. Woodbridge: Boydell, 121-143.

Hull City Council 1990: *Beverley Gate: The Birthplace of the English Civil War*. Hull: Hull City Council/Hutton Press.

Hunter, A.G. and Jope, E.M., 1951: Excavations on the city defences in New College, Oxford, 1949. *Oxoniensia* 16, 28-41.

Hurst, H., 1899: *Oxford Topography: An Essay*. Oxford: Oxford Historical Society.

Hurst, J.G., 1965: Excavations at Barn Road, Norwich, 1954-55. *Norfolk Archaeology* 33, 131-179.

Hutton, R. and Reeves, W., 1998: Sieges and fortifications. In Kenyon, J. and Ohlmeyer, J. (eds), *The Civil Wars: A Military History of England, Scotland and Ireland 1638-1660*. Oxford: Oxford University Press, 195-233.

Hyde, R., 1994: *A Prospect of Britain: The Town Panoramas of Samuel and Nathaniel Buck*. London: Pavilion.

Insall, D.W., 1968: *Chester: A Study in Conservation*. London: HMSO.

Jackson-Stops, G., 1979: The building of the medieval college. In Buxton, J. and Williams, P. (eds), *New College Oxford 1379-1979*. Oxford: New College, 147-264.

James, E.M., 1987: A fresh study of the South Gate at King's Lynn, in the light of recent restoration work. *Norfolk Archaeology* 40, 55-72.

James, T.B., 1997: *English Heritage Book of Winchester*. London: Batsford/English Heritage.

Jecock, M. and Corbett, G., 2001: The earthwork and architectural survey. In Darlington,

J. (ed.), *Stafford Castle: Survey, Excavation and Research 1978-98. Volume I - The Surveys.* Stafford: Stafford Borough Council, 83-115.

Jenkins, A., 1806: *The History and Description of Exeter* (second edition). Exeter: Hedgeland.

Jennings, S.B., 2003: 'A miserable, stinking, infected town': pestilence, plague and death in a Civil war garrison, Newark 1640-1649. *Midland History* 28, 51-70.

Jones, C., Eyre-Morgan, G., Palmer, S. and Palmer, N., 1997: Excavations in the outer enclosure of Boteler's Castle, Oversley, Alcester, 1992–3. *Transactions of the Birmingham and Warwickshire Archaeological Society* 101, 1–98.

Jones, M.J., Stocker, D. and Vince, A., 2003: *The City by the Pool: Assessing the Archaeology of the City of Lincoln.* Oxford: Oxbow (Lincoln Archaeological Studies No. 10).

Jones, N.W., 1998: Excavations within the medieval town at New Radnor, Powys, 1991- 92. *Archaeological Journal* 155, 134-206.

Jones, R.L.C., 1999: Fortifications and sieges in Western Europe *c.*800-1450. In Keen, M. (ed.), *Medieval Warfare: a History.* Oxford: Oxford University Press, 163-185.

Keen, L., 1984: The towns of Dorset. In Haslam, J. (ed.), *Anglo-Saxon Towns in Southern England.* Chichester: Phillimore, 203-247.

Keene, D., 1976: Suburban growth. In Barley, M.W. (ed.), *The Plans and Topography of Medieval Towns in England and Wales.* Oxford: BAR No. 14, 71-82.

Keene, D., 1985: *Survey of Medieval Winchester,* 2 Vols. Oxford: Clarendon Press (Winchester Studies No. 2).

Keene, D., 2001: Roots and branches of power, 1000-1300. *The London Journal* 26.1, 1-8.

Kellett, J.H., 1969: Glasgow. In Lobel, M.D. (ed.), *Historic Towns: Maps and Plans of Towns and Cities in the British Isles, with Historical Commentaries, from Earliest Times to 1800, Volume I.* London: Lovell Johns-Cook, Hammond and Kell Organization, 1-13.

Kelly, R.S., 1979: Excavation on two sites in Conway, 1975. *Archaeologia Cambrensis* 128, 104-118.

Kent, P., 1988: *Fortifications of East Anglia.* Lavenham: Terence Dalton.

Kenyon, J.R., 1978: *Castles, Town Defences and Artillery Fortifications in Britain: A Bibliography. 1945-1974.* London: CBA Research Report 25.

Kenyon, J.R., 1981: Early artillery fortification in England and Wales. *Archaeological Journal* 138, 205-240.

Kenyon, J.R., 1983: *Castles, Town Defences and Artillery Fortifications in Britain: A Bibliography 2.* London: CBA Research Report 53.

Kenyon, J.R., 1990: *Castles, Town Defences and Artillery Fortifications in Britain: A Bibliography 3.* London: CBA Research Report 72.

Kenyon, J.R., 1990: *Medieval Fortifications.* Leicester: Leicester University Press.

Kenyon, J.R., 1994: Coastal artillery fortification in England in the late fourteenth and early fifteenth centuries. In Curry, A. and Hughes, M. (eds), *Arms, Armies and Fortifications in the Hundred Years War.* Woodbridge: Boydell, 145-149.

Kenyon, J. and Ohlmeyer, J. (eds), 1998: *The Civil Wars: A Military History of England, Scotland and Ireland 1638-1660.* Oxford: Oxford University Press.

Kermode, J., 2000: The greater towns 1300-1540. In Palliser, D.M. (ed.), *The Cambridge*

Urban History of Britain, Vol. I. Cambridge: Cambridge University Press, 441-465.

Keynes, S. and Lapidge, M., 1983: *Alfred the Great. Asser's Life of King Alfred and other Contemporary Sources.* Harmondsworth: Penguin Books.

King, D.J.C., 1983: *Castellarium Anglicanum,* 2 Vols. London: Kraus.

King, D.J.C. and Cheshire, M., 1982: The town walls of Pembroke. *Archaeologia Cambrensis* 131, 77-84.

Kingsford, C.L. (ed.), 2000: *John Snow: A Survey of London,* 2 Vols. Oxford: Oxford University Press.

Klingelhofer, 1976-77: Barrack Street excavations, Warwick, 1972. *Transactions of the Birmingham and Warwickshire Archaeological Society* 88, 87-104.

Kowaleski, M., 1980: Tax payers in late fourteenth-century Exeter: the 1377 Murage Roll. *Devon and Cornwall Notes and Queries* 34.6, 217-222.

Kowaleski, M., 1995: *Local Markets and Regional Trade in Medieval Exeter.* Cambridge: Cambridge University Press.

Lancaster, J.C., 1975: Coventry. In Lobel, M.D. (ed.), *The Atlas of Historic Towns, Volume II.* London: Scolar Press/Historic Towns Trust, 1-13.

Lawler, M., 1998: Investigating the town wall and burgage plots at South Quay and Castle Terrace, Pembroke. *Archaeologia Cambrensis* 147, 159-180.

LeQuesne, C., 1999: *Excavations at Chester: the Roman and Later Defences, Part 1.* Chester: Chester City Council/Gifford and Partners.

Leach, P. (ed.), 1984: *The Archaeology of Taunton, Excavations and Fieldwork to 1980.* Gloucester: Western Archaeological Trust Excavation Monograph No. 8.

Leech, R.H., 1997: The medieval defences of Bristol revisited. In Keen, L. (ed.), *'Almost the Richest City'. Bristol in the Middle Ages* (British Archaeological Association Conference Transactions 19), 18-30.

Liddiard, R., 2000: *'Landscapes of Lordship': Norman Castles and the Countryside in Medieval Norfolk, 1066–1200.* Oxford: BAR British Series No. 309.

Liddiard, R., 2003: Introduction. In R. Liddiard (ed.), *Anglo-Norman Castles,* Woodbridge: Boydell, 1-21.

Lilley, K.D., 1995: *The Norman Town in Dyfed.* University of Birmingham School of Geography Research Monograph No. 1.

Lilley, K.D., 1999: Urban landscapes and the cultural politics of territorial control in Anglo-Norman England. *Landscape Research* 24.1, 5–23.

Lilley, K.D.. 2000a: Decline or decay? In Slater, T.R. (ed.), *Towns in Decline AD 100-1600.* Aldershot: Ashgate, 235-265.

Lilley, K.D., 2000b: 'Non urbe, non vico, non castris': territorial control and the colonization and urbanization of Wales and Ireland under Anglo-Norman lordship. *Journal of Historical Geography* 26.4, 517–531.

Lilley, K.D., 2002: *Urban Life in the Middle Ages, 1000-1450.* Basingstoke: Palgrave.

Little, A.G. and Easterling, R.C., 1927: The Franciscans and Dominicans of Exeter. *History of Exeter Research Group* 3, 15.

Lloyd, D.W., 1992: *The Making of English Towns: 2000 Years of Evolution.* London: Victor

Gollancz/Peter Crawley.

Lobel, M.D., 1969a: Gloucester. In Lobel, M.D. (ed.), *Historic Towns: Maps and Plans of Towns and Cities in the British Isles, with Historical Commentaries, from Earliest Times to 1800, Volume I*. London: Lovell Johns-Cook, Hammond and Kell Organization, 1–14

Lobel, M.D., 1969b: Hereford. In Lobel, M.D. (ed.), *Historic Towns: Maps and Plans of Towns and Cities in the British Isles, with Historical Commentaries, from Earliest Times to 1800, Volume I*. London: Lovell Johns-Cook, Hammond and Kell Organization, 1–11.

Lobel, M.D., 1975a: Bristol. In Lobel, M.D. (ed.), *The Atlas of Historic Towns, Volume II*. London: Scolar Press/Historic Towns Trust, 1–27.

Lobel, M.D., 1975b: Cambridge. In Lobel, M.D. (ed.), *The Atlas of Historic Towns, Volume II*. London: Scolar Press/Historic Towns Trust, 1–23.

Lopez, R.S., 1963: The crossroads within the wall. In Handlin, O. and Burchard, J. (eds), *The Historian and the City*. Massachusetts: Massachusetts Institute of Technology Press, 27–43.

Ludlow, N., 1991: Pembroke castle and town walls. *Fortress* 8, 25–30.

Lyle, M., 1994: *English Heritage Book of Canterbury*. London: English Heritage/Batsford.

Macivor, I., 1972: *The Fortifications of Berwick-upon-Tweed*. London: HMSO.

Macivor, I., 2001: *A Fortified Frontier: Defences of the Anglo-Scottish Border*. Stroud: Tempus.

Macrory, P., 1980: *The Siege of Derry*. London: Hodder and Stoughton.

Maitland, F.W., 1897: *Domesday Book and Beyond*. Cambridge: Cambridge University Press.

Mallory, J.P. and McNeill, T.E., 1991: *The Archaeology of Ulster from Colonization to Plantation*. Belfast: Institute of Irish Studies.

Manley, J., 1987: *Cledemutha*: a Late Saxon *burh*. *Medieval Archaeology* 31, 13–46.

Markuson, K.W., 1980: Excavation on the Green Lane access site, Barnstaple, 1972. *Proceedings of the Devon Archaeological Society* 38, 67–90.

Martin, D., Martin, B. and Wittick, C., 1985: *An Archaeological Interpretative Survey of The Old Town Wall, Hastings, East Sussex* (University College London Field Archaeology Unit). Lewes: East Sussex SMR, Unpublished Report.

Mayhew, G., 1984: Rye and the defence of the narrow seas: a sixteenth-century town at war. *Sussex Archaeological Collections* 122, 107–126.

McNeill, T.E. and Pringle, M., 1997: A map of mottes in the British Isles. *Medieval Archaeology* 41, 220–222.

McCarthy, M.R., Summerson, H.R.T. and Annis, R.G., 1990: *Carlisle Castle: a Survey and Documentary History*. London: HMSO.

McKisack, M., 1959: *The Fourteenth Century 1307-1399*. Oxford: Clarendon Press.

Miles, T.J., 1996: Flint: excavations at the castle and on the town defences 1971-1974. *Archaeologia Cambrensis* 145, 67–151.

Miller, K., Robinson, J., English, B. and Hall, I., 1982: *Beverley: An Archaeological and Architectural Survey*. London: HMSO, RCHME Supplementary Series 4.

Milne, G., 2001: *Excavations at Medieval Cripplegate, London: Archaeology after the Blitz, 1946-*

68. Swindon; English Heritage.

Morris, J.E., 1901: *The Welsh Wars of Edward I. A Contribution to Medieval Military History Based on Original Documents*. Oxford: Clarendon Press.

Morris, R., 1895: *Chester in the Plantagenet and Tudor Reigns*. Chester: G.R. Griffith.

Morris, R., 1924: *The Siege of Chester 1643-46*. Chester: G.R. Griffith.

Morris, R.K., 1989: *Churches in the Landscape*. London: Dent.

Morris, R.K. and Hoverd, K., 1994: *The Buildings of Salisbury*. Stroud: Sutton.

Morton, A.D. (ed.), 1992: *Excavations at Hamwic. Volume 1: Excavations 1946-83, Excluding Six Dials and Melbourne Street*. London: CBA Research Report No. 84.

Murphy, K., 1997: Small boroughs in south-west Wales: their planning, early development and defences. In Edwards, N. (ed.) *Landscape and Settlement in Medieval Wales*. Oxford: Oxbow, 139-156.

Murphy, K., 2000: The rise and fall of the medieval town in Wales. In Slater, T.R. (ed.), *Towns in Decline AD 100-1600*. Aldershot: Ashgate, 193-213.

Neale, F. (ed.), 2000: *William Worcestre, The Topography of Medieval Bristol*. Bristol: Bristol Record Society Publications, Vol. 51.

Nenk, B.S., Margeson, S. and Hurley, M., 1993: Medieval Britain and Ireland in 1992. *Medieval Archaeology* 37, 240-313

Newman, R., 2001: *The Historical Archaeology of Britain, c.1540-1900*. Stroud: Sutton.

Nicholas, D., 1997a: *The Growth of the Medieval City from Late Antiquity to the Early Fourteenth Century*. Harlow: Longman.

Nicholas, D., 1997b: *The Later Medieval City*. Harlow: Longman.

Nolan, J., Fraser, R., Harbottle, B. and Burton, F.C., 1989: The medieval town defences of Newcastle upon Tyne: excavation and survey 1986-87. *Archaeologia Aeliana* (Fifth Series) 17, 29-78.

Norris, H. and Kain, R., 1982: Military influence of European town design. *History Today* 32, 10-15.

O'Leary, T.J., 1981: Excavation at Upper Borough Walls, Bath, 1980. *Medieval Archaeology* 25, 1-30.

O'Neil, B.H. St J., 1935: Dartmouth Castle and other defences of Dartmouth Haven. *Archaeologia* 85, 129-157.

O'Neil, B.H. St J., 1951: Southampton town wall. In Grimes, W.F. (ed.), *Aspects of Archaeology in Britain and Beyond*. London: H.W. Edwards, 243-257.

O'Neil, B.H. St J., 1960: *Castles and Cannon: A Study of Early Artillery Fortifications in England*. Oxford: Clarendon Press.

O'Neil, B.H. St J. and Foster-Smith, A.H., 1940: Montgomery town wall. *Archaeologia Cambrensis* 95, 217-228.

Ottaway, P., 1992: *Archaeology in British Towns: From the Emperor Claudius to the Black Death*. London: Routledge.

Ottaway, P., 1993: *Roman York*. London: Batsford/English Heritage.

Owen, A.E.B., 1992: Castle Carlton: the origins of a medieval 'new town'. *Lincolnshire*

History and Archaeology 27, 17–22.

Owen, L.V.D., 1945: The borough of Nottingham, 1066 to 1284. *Transactions of the Thoroton Society of Nottinghamshire* 49, 13–27.

Owen-John, H.S., 1985: *Annual Report, 1983-84*. Cardiff: Glamorgan-Gwent Archaeological Trust.

Owles, E., 1973: The West Gate of Ipswich. *Proceedings of the Suffolk Institute of Archaeology* 32, 164-167.

Oxley, J., 1986: *Excavations at Southampton Castle*. Southampton: Southampton City Museums.

Palliser, D.M., 1980: *Chester: Contemporary Descriptions by Residents and Visitors*. Chester: Chester Corporation.

Palliser, D., 1987: The medieval period. In Schofield, J. and Leech, R. (eds), *Urban Archaeology in Britain*. London: CBA Research Report No. 61, 54-68.

Palliser, D.M., 1995: Town defences in medieval England and Wales. In Ayton, A. and Price, J.L. (eds), *The Medieval Military Revolution*. London and New York: Tauris, 105-120.

Palliser, D.M. (ed.), 2000: *The Cambridge Urban History of Britain, Vol. I*. Cambridge: Cambridge University Press.

Palmer, N., 1976: Excavations on the outer city wall of Oxford in St Helen's Passage and Hertford College. *Oxoniensia* 41, 148-160.

Parker, H., 1882: *Some Account of Domestic Architecture in England*. Oxford and London: James Parker.

Parsons, D., 2003: Appendix I. The west tower of St Michael at the Northgate, Oxford. In Liddiard, R. (ed.), *Anglo-Norman Castles*. Woodbridge: Boydell, 85-89.

Paterson, C., 2000: The bell tower at Berwick-upon-Tweed. *Archaeologia Aeliana* (Fifth Series) 28, 163-175.

Pearsall, D., 1992: *The Life of Geoffrey Chaucer: A Critical Biography*. Oxford: Blackwell.

Penn, K.J., 1980: *Historic Towns in Dorset*. Dorchester: Dorset Natural History and Archaeological Society, Monograph No. 1.

Perbellini, G., 2000a: City walls and their symbolic significance. In Perbellini, G. (ed.), *The Town Walls in the Middle Ages: Les Enceintes Urbaines Au Moyen Âge*. The Hague: Europa Nostra IBI Bulletin 53, 7-18.

Perbellini, G. (ed.), 2000b: *The Town Walls in the Middle Ages: Les Enceintes Urbaines Au Moyen Âge*. The Hague: Europa Nostra IBI Bulletin 53.

Perbellini, G. (ed.), 2003: *The Evaluation of the Walled Towns: Kotor and Heraklion*. The Hague: Europa Nostra IBI Bulletin 56-7.

Perring, D. (ed.), 2002: *Town and Country in England: Frameworks for Archaeological Research*. York: CBA Research Report No. 134.

Pettifer, A., 1995: *English Castles: A Guide by Counties*. Woodbridge: Boydell.

Phythian-Adams, C., 1979: *Desolation of a City: Coventry and the Urban Crisis of the Late Middle Ages*. Cambridge: Cambridge University Press.

Platt, C., 1973: *Medieval Southampton: The Port and Trading Community, A.D. 1000-1600*.

London: Kegan Paul.

Platt, C., 1976: *The English Medieval Town*. London: Secker and Warburg.

Platt, C., 1978: *Medieval England. A Social History and Archaeology from the Conquest to AD 1600*. London: Routledge & Kegan Paul.

Platt, C. and Coleman-Smith, R., 1975: *Excavations in Medieval Southampton 1953-1969*. Leicester: Leicester University Press.

Ponsford, M.W., 1971: Nottingham town wall: Park Row excavations 1967. *Transactions of the Thoroton Society* 65, 5-32.

Poole, A.L., 1955: *From Domesday Book to Magna Carta 1087-1216* (second edition). Oxford: Clarendon Press.

Potter, K.R. (ed.), *Gesta Stephani*. Oxford: Clarendon Press.

Poulton, R. and Riall, N., 1998: Discussion: the town ditch and the origins and early development of Farnham. *Surrey Archaeological Collections* 85, 147-151.

Pounds, N.J.G., 1974: *An Economic History of Medieval Europe*. London and New York: Longman.

Pounds, N.J.G., 1990: *The Medieval Castle in England and Wales: a Social and Political History*. Cambridge: Cambridge University Press.

Pounds, N.J.G., 2000: *A History of the English Parish*. Cambridge: Cambridge University Press.

Powicke, M., 1962: *The Thirteenth Century 1216-1307* (second edition). Oxford: Clarendon Press.

Pugh, R.B., 1968: *Imprisonment in Medieval England*. Cambridge: Cambridge University Press.

Pye, A. and Woodward, F., 1996: *The Historic Defences of Plymouth*. Exeter: Exeter Archaeology Fortress Study Group South West.

Quinnell, H. and Blockley, M.R., 1994: *Excavations at Rhuddlan, Clwyd 1969-73. Mesolithic to Medieval*. London: CBA Research Reports No. 95.

Radford, C.A.R., 1957-8: The medieval defences of Shrewsbury. *Transactions of the Shropshire Archaeological and Natural History Society* 56, 15-20.

Radley, J., 1972: Excavations in the defences of the city of York: an early medieval stone tower and the successive earth ramparts. *Yorkshire Archaeological Journal* 44, 38-64.

Ralph, E., 1986: Bristol *circa* 1480. In Skelton, R.A. and Harvey, P.D.A (eds), *Local Maps and Plans from Medieval England*. Oxford: Clarendon Press, 309-316.

Ravenhill, M.H. and Rowe, M.M., 2000: *Early Devon Maps*. Exeter: Friends of Devon's Archives (Occasional Publications, No. 1).

Rawcliffe, C., 1995: *The Hospitals of Medieval Norwich*. Norwich: Centre of East Anglian Studies (Studies in East Anglian History No. 2).

Renn, D., 1964: The Southampton arcade. *Medieval Archaeology* 8, 226-228.

Renn, D., 1968a: *Norman Castles in Britain*. London: John Baker.

Renn, D., 1968b: The earliest gunports in Britain? *Archaeological Journal* 125, 301-303.

Renn, D., 1979: The castles of Rye and Winchelsea. *Archaeological Journal* 1979, 193-202.

Renn, D., 1993: Burhgeat and gonfanon: two sidelights from the Bayeux tapestry. *Proceedings of the Battle Conference on Anglo-Norman Studies* 16, 177–198.

Reynolds, S., 1977: *An Introduction to the History of English Medieval Towns*. Oxford: Clarendon Press.

Rhys, E. (ed.), 1908: *The Itinerary through Wales by Giraldus Cambrensis*. London: Dent.

Roberts, M., 1994: *Durham*. London: Batsford/English Heritage.

Rogers, J.H., 1969: Salisbury. In Lobel, M.D. (ed.), *Historic Towns: Maps and Plans of Towns and Cities in the British Isles, with Historical Commentaries, from Earliest Times to 1800, Volume I*. London: Lovell Johns-Cook, Hammond and Kell Organization, 1-9.

Room, A., 1992: *The Street Names of England*. Stamford: Paul Watkins.

Rosenau, H., 1983: *The Ideal City: Its Architectural Evolution in Europe*, (third edition). London: Methuen.

Rosser, G., 2000: Urban culture and the church, 1300-1540. In Palliser, D.M. (ed.), *The Cambridge Urban History of Britain, Vol. I*. Cambridge: Cambridge University Press, 335-369.

Rowe, M.M. (ed.), 1977: *Tudor Exeter. Tax Assessments 1489-1595 including the Military Survey 1522*. Exeter: Devon and Cornwall Record Society (New Series) No. 22.

Rowe, M.M. and Draisey, J.M. (eds), 1989: *The Receivers' Accounts of the City of Exeter, 1304-1353*. Exeter: Devon and Cornwall Record Society (New Series) No. 32.

Rowlands, M.L.J., 1993: Monnow bridge and gate, Monmouth. *Archaeologia Cambrensis* 142, 243-287.

Rowley, T., 1986: *The Landscape of the Welsh Marches*. London: Michael Joseph.

Royal Commission on Historical Monuments (England), 1939: *City of Oxford*. London: HMSO.

Royal Commission on Historical Monuments (England), 1959: *An Inventory of the Historical Monuments in the City of Cambridge* (2 Vols). London: HMSO.

Royal Commission on Historical Monuments (England), 1964: *Newark on Trent: The Civil War Siegeworks*. London: HMSO.

Royal Commission on Historical Monuments (England), 1972: *An Inventory of the Historical Monuments in the City of York, Volume II, The Defences*. London: HMSO.

Royal Commission on Historical Monuments (England), 1977: *The Town of Stamford*. London: HMSO.

Royal Commission on the Ancient and Historical Monuments of Wales, 1937: *Anglesey: An Inventory of the Ancient Monuments in Anglesey*. London: HMSO.

Royal Commission on the Ancient and Historical Monuments of Scotland, 1951: *An Inventory of the Ancient and Historical Monuments of the City of Edinburgh*. Edinburgh: HMSO.

Royal Commission on the Ancient and Historical Monuments of Scotland, 1963: *Stirlingshire: An Inventory of the Ancient Monuments*, 2 Vols. Edinburgh: HMSO.

Royal Commission on the Ancient and Historical Monuments of Scotland, 1967: *Peebleshire: An Inventory of the Ancient Monuments*, 2 Vols. Edinburgh: HMSO.

Sabine, E.L., 1937: *City cleaning in medieval London*. Speculum 12, 19-43.

Salch, C.L., 1978: *Atlas des Villes et Villages Fortifiés en France (Moyen Age)*. Strasbourg: Publitoal.

Salter, H.E., 1926: *Oxford City Properties*. Oxford: Clarendon Press (Oxford Historical Society Vol. 26).

Salter, H.E., 1936: *Medieval Oxford*. Oxford: Clarendon Press (Oxford Historical Society Vol. 100).

Saunders, A.D., 1966: Hampshire coastal defence since the introduction of artillery with a description of Fort Wallington. *Archaeological Journal* 123, 136-171.

Saunders, A.D., 1973: The coastal defences of Cornwall. *Archaeological Journal* 130, 232-236.

Saunders, A.D., 1976: The defences of Southampton in the later Middle Ages. In Burgess, L.A. (ed.), 1976: *The Southampton Terrier of 1454*. Southampton: Southampton Records Series No. 15, 20-34.

Saunders, A.D., 1985: The Cow Tower, Norwich: an East Anglian bastille? *Medieval Archaeology* 29, 109-119.

Saunders, A.D., 1989: *Fortress Britain: Artillery Forts in the British Isles and Ireland*. Liphook: Beaufort.

Saunders, A.D., 2000: Southampton: the introduction of gunpowder artillery to the town's defences. In Perbellini, G. (ed.), *The Town Walls in the Middle Ages: Les Enceintes Urbaines Au Moyen Âge*. The Hague: IBI Bulletin 53, 53-58.

Saunders, A. and Smith, V., 2001: *Kent's Defence Heritage*. Canterbury: Kent County Council.

Scarfe, N., 1971: Note on the historical records of Dunwich's defences. *Proceedings of the Suffolk Institute of Archaeology* 32.1, 34-37.

Schledermann, H., 1970-71: The idea of the town: typology, definitions and approaches to the study of the medieval town in northern Europe. *World Archaeology* 2, 115-127.

Schmidtchen, V., 1990: Castles, cannon and casemates. *Fortress* 6, 3-10.

Schofield, J., 1975-76: Excavations south of Edinburgh High Street, 1973-4. *Proceedings of the Society of Antiquaries of Scotland* 107, 155-241.

Schofield, J., 1984: *The Building of London: From the Conquest to the Great Fire*. London: British Museum Publications.

Schofield, J. and Leech, R. (eds), 1987: *Urban Archaeology in Britain*. London: CBA Research Report No. 61.

Schofield, J. and Vince, A., 2003: *Medieval Towns: The Archaeology of British Towns in their European Setting*. London: Continuum.

Shoesmith, R., 1982: *Hereford City Excavations. Volume 1, Excavations on and Close to the Defences*. London: CBA Research Report No. 46.

Shoesmith, R. (ed.), 1992: Excavations at Kilpeck, Herefordshire. *Transactions of the Woolhope Naturalists' Field Club, Herefordshire* 47, 162–209.

Silvester, R., 1997: New Radnor: the topography of a medieval planned town in mid-Wales. In Edwards, N. (ed.), *Landscape and Settlement in Medieval Wales*. Oxford: Oxbow, 157-164.

Simpson, G.G., 1972: *Scotland's Medieval Burghs: An Archaeological Heritage in Danger*. Edinburgh: Council of the Society of Antiquaries of Scotland.

Sivier, D., 2002: *Anglo-Saxon and Norman Bristol*. Stroud: Tempus.

Skelton, R.A., 1970: The military surveyor's contribution to British cartography in the sixteenth century. *Imago Mundi* 24, 77-83.

Smith, C., 1988: The excavation of the Exchequer Gate, Denbigh, 1982-83. *Archaeologia Cambrensis* 137, 108-112.

Smith, J.B., 1977: The foundation of Aberystwyth. In Jones, I.G. (ed.), *Aberystwyth 1277-1977: Eight Lectures to Celebrate the Seventh Centenary of the Foundation of the Borough*. Llandysul. Gomer Press, 14-27.

Smith, T.P., 1970: The medieval town defences of King's Lynn. *Journal of the British Archaeological Association* (3rd series) 33, 57-88.

Smith, T.P., 1985: Why did medieval towns have walls? *Current Archaeology* 8, 376-9.

Snyder, M.G. and Blakely, E.J., 1997: *Fortress America: Gated Communities in the United States*. Washington, D.C.: The Brookings Institution Press.

Soulsby, I., 1983: *The Towns of Medieval Wales: A Study of their History, Archaeology and Early Topography*. Chichester: Phillimore.

Spearman, R.M., 1988: The medieval townscape of Perth. In Lynch, M., Spearman, M. and Stell, G. (eds), *The Scottish Medieval Town*. Edinburgh: John Donald, 42-59.

Spurgeon, C.J., 1977: Aberystwyth castle and borough. In Jones, I.G. (ed.), *Aberystwyth 1277-1977: Eight Lectures to Celebrate the Seventh Centenary of the Foundation of the Borough*. Llandysul. Gomer Press, 28-45.

Spurgeon, C.J., 2001: The medieval town defences of Glamorgan. *Studia Celtica* 35, 161-212.

Steane, J., 2001a: Medieval Oxfordshire 1100-1540 (The Tom Hassall Lecture for 2000). *Oxoniensia* 66, 1-12.

Steane, J.M. 2001b: *The Archaeology of Power: England and Northern Europe AD 800-1600*. Stroud: Tempus.

Stell, G., 1988: Urban buildings. In Lynch, M., Spearman, M. and Stell, G. (eds), *The Scottish Medieval Town*. Edinburgh: John Donald, 60-80.

Stell, G., 1999: Recording Scotland's urban buildings. In Dennison, E.P. (ed.), *Conservation and Change in Historic Towns: Research Directions for the Future*. London: CBA Research Report No. 122, 60-68.

Stewart, J.O.R. and Cooke, J.J., 1990: *The Stonebow and Guildhall*. Lincoln: Ruddock and Sons.

Stocks, H. and Stevenson, W.H. (eds), 1923: *Records of the Borough of Leicester, Vol. IV, 1603-1688*. London: Cambridge University Press.

Stones, J.A. (ed.), 1987: *A Tale of Two Burghs: The Archaeology of Old and New Aberdeen*. Aberdeen: Aberdeen Art Gallery and Museums.

Stoyle, M.J., 1995: *Exeter in the Civil War*. Exeter: Devon Archaeology, 6.

Stoyle, M.J., 1997: 'Whole streets converted to ashes': property destruction in Exeter during the English Civil War. In Richardson, R.C (ed.), *The English Civil Wars: Local Aspects*. Stroud: Sutton, 129-144.

Stoyle, M.J., 1998: *Plymouth in the Civil War*. Exeter: Devon Archaeology, 7.

Stoyle, M.J., 2003: *Circled with Stone: Exeter's City Walls, 1485-1660*. Exeter: University of Exeter Press.

Streeten, A.D.F., 1976: Excavations at Lansdowne Road, Tonbridge, 1972 and 1976. *Archaeologia Cantiana* 92, 105-118.

Stubbs, W. (ed.), 1913: *Select Charters* (ninth edition). Oxford: Clarendon Press.

Tatton-Brown, T., 1978: The Sandown Gate at Sandwich. *Archaeologia Cantiana* 94, 153-155.

Tatton-Brown, T., 1984: The towns of Kent. In Haslam, J. (ed.), *Anglo-Saxon Towns in Southern England*. Chichester: Phillimore, 1-36.

Tatton-Brown, T., Bowen, J., Butcher, A. and Renn, D., 1982: The West Gate. In Frere, S.S., Stow, S. and Bennett, P., *The Archaeology of Canterbury, Volume II: Excavations on the Roman and Medieval Defences of Canterbury*. Maidstone: Canterbury Archaeological Trust and Kent Archaeological Society, 107-117.

Taylor, A.J., 1970: The walls of Conwy. *Archaeologia Cambrensis* 119, 1-9.

Taylor, A.J., 1974: *The King's Works in Wales 1277-1330*. London: HMSO.

Taylor, A.J., 1995: The town and castle of Conwy: preservation and interpretation. *Antiquaries Journal* 75, 339-363.

Taylor, A.J., 2003: *Conwy Castle and Town Walls* (fifth edition). Cardiff: Cadw.

Taylor, C.C., 1983: *Village and Farmstead: a History of Rural Settlement in England* London: Philip.

Teasdale, J.A., 1999: An archaeological investigation of the town wall between St Andrew's Street and St Andrew's churchyard, Newcastle upon Tyne. *Archaeologia Aeliana* (Fifth Series) 27, 29-43.

Thacker, A., 2000: The early medieval city and its buildings. In Thacker, A. (ed.), *Medieval Archaeology, Art and Architecture at Chester* (British Archaeological Association Conference Transactions 22), 16-30.

Thomas, A., 1992: *The Walled Towns of Ireland* (2 vols.). Dublin: Irish Academic Press.

Thomas, W.G., 1993: The walls of Tenby. *Archaeologia Cambrensis* 142, 1-39.

Thompson, M.W., 1998: *Medieval Bishops' Houses in England and Wales*. Aldershot: Ashgate.

Torrance, W.J., 1959: A contemporary poem on the removal of Salisbury Cathedral. *Wiltshire Archaeological Magazine* 57, 242-246.

Toulmin Smith, L. (ed.), 1907: *The Itinerary of John Leland in or about the years 1535-1543, Parts I and II*. London: George Bell and Sons.

Trabut-Cussac, J-P., 1954: Bastides ou forteresses? Les bastides de l'Aquitaine anglaise et les intentions de leurs fondateurs. *Le Moyen Age* 60, 81-135.

Tracy, J.D. (ed.), 2000: *City Walls: The Urban Enceinte in Global Perspective*. Cambridge: Cambridge University Press.

Turner, H.L., 1967: *An Architectural and Documentary Study of Town Defences in England and Wales 1200-1520*. Unpublished University of Oxford DPhil Thesis.

Turner, H.L., 1970: *Town Defences in England and Wales*. London: John Baker.

Turner, H.L., 1990: The Mural Mansions of Oxford: attempted identifications. *Oxoniensia* 55, 73-79.

Tweedle, D., Moulden, J. and Logan, E., 1999: *Anglian York: A Survey*. York: York Archaeological Trust (The Archaeology of York Vol. 7).

Urry, W., 1967: *Canterbury under the Angevin Kings*. London: University of London, Athlone Press.

VCH 1906: *The Victoria History of the Counties of England. A History of Northamptonshire, Vol. II*. London: Archibald Constable.
VCH 1912: *The Victoria History of the Counties of England. A History of Hampshire, Vol. V*. London: Archibald Constable.
VCH 1928: *The Victoria History of the Counties of England. A History of Durham, Vol. III*. London: St Catherine Press.
VCH 1954: *The Victoria History of the Counties of England. A History of the County of Oxfordshire, Vol. III*. London: Oxford University Press for the Institute of Historical Research.
VCH 1962: *The Victoria History of the Counties of England. A History of Wiltshire, Vol. VI*. London: Oxford University Press for the Institute of Historical Research.
VCH 1967: *The Victoria History of the Counties of England. A History of Yorkshire, East Riding, Vol. I*. London: Oxford University Press for the Institute of Historical Research.
VCH 1989: *The Victoria History of the Counties of England. A History of Yorkshire, East Riding, Vol. VI*. London: Oxford University Press for the Institute of Historical Research.
VCH 1979: *The Victoria History of the Counties of England. A History of the County of Oxfordshire, Vol. IV*. London: Oxford University Press for the Institute of Historical Research.
VCH 1979: *The Victoria History of the Counties of England. A History of the County of Staffordshire, Vol. VI*. London: Oxford University Press for the Institute of Historical Research.
VCH, 2003: *A History of the County of Chester, Vol. V, Part I, The City of Chester*. Woodbridge: Boydell.
Vince, A., 1990: *Saxon London: an Archaeological Investigation*. London: Seaby.
Vince, A., 2001: Lincoln in the Viking Age. In Graham-Campbell, J. *et al.* (eds), *Vikings and the Danelaw*. Oxford: Oxbow, 157-179.

Wacher, J., 1975: *The Towns of Roman Britain*. London: Batsford.
Webster, P., 1989: Dryslwyn Castle. In Kenyon, J.R. and Avent. R. (eds), *Castles in Wales and the Marches: Essays in Honour of D.J. Cathcart King*. Cardiff: University of Wales Press, 89-104.
Webster, L.E., and Cherry, J., 1974: Medieval Britain in 1973. *Medieval Archaeology* 18, 174-223.
Wedlake, W.J., 1965-66: The city walls of Bath, the church of St James, South Gate, and the area to the east of the church of St James. *Proceedings of the Somersetshire Archaeological and Natural History Society* 10, 85-107.
West, S.E., 1971a: The excavation of Dunwich town defences. *Proceedings of the Suffolk Institute of Archaeology* 32.1, 25-34.
West, S.E., 1971b: The excavation of the town defences at Tayfen Road, Bury St Edmunds, 1968. *Proceedings of the Suffolk Institute of Archaeology* 32.1, 17-24.

Wheeler, R.E.M., 1921: The Balkerne Gate, Colchester. *Transactions of the Essex Archaeological Society* (New Series) 15, 179-189.

White, R. and Barker, P.A., 1998: *Wroxeter: Life and Death of Roman City*. Stroud: Tempus.

Whitehand, J.W.R., 1981: Background to the urban morphogenetic tradition. In Whitehand, J.W.R. (ed.), *The Urban Landscape: Historical Development and Management*. London: Academic Press, Institute of British Geographers Special Publications No. 13, 1-24.

Whitelock, D. (ed.), 1955: *English Historical Documents c.500-1042*. London: Eyre and Spottiswoode.

Wight, J.A., 1972: *Brick Building in England from the Middle Ages to 1550*. London: John Baker.

Wilkinson, B., 1931: *The Medieval Council of Exeter*. Manchester: Manchester University Press (History of Exeter Research Group No. 4).

Williams, A., 1992: A bell-house and a *burhgeat*: lordly residences in England before the Norman Conquest. *Medieval Knighthood* 4, 221-240.

Williams, F., 1977: *Pleshey Castle, Essex (XII-XVI Century): Excavations in the Bailey, 1959-1963*. Oxford: BAR British Series No. 42.

Williams, G.A., 1963: *Medieval London: From Commune to Capital*. London: University of London, Athlone Press.

Wilson, D. M., and Hurst, J. G., 1958: Medieval Britain in 1957. *Medieval Archaeology* 2, 183-213

Wood, A.A., 1970: *Norwich City Walls*. Norwich: Norwich City Council.

Yeoman, P., 1995: *Medieval Scotland*. London: Batsford/Historic Scotland.

Yorke, B.A.E., 1982: The foundation of the Old Minster and the status of Winchester in the seventh and eighth centuries. *Proceedings of the Hampshire Field Club and Archaeological Society* 38, 75-84.

Youngs, S. M., and Clark, J,. 1981: Medieval Britain in 1980. *Medieval Archaeology* 25, 166-228.

Youngs, S. M., Clark, J., and Barry, T., 1986: Medieval Britain and Ireland in 1985. *Medieval Archaeology* 30, 114-198

Youngs, S.M., Clark, T. and Barry, T., 1987: Medieval Britain and Ireland in 1986. *Medieval Archaeology* 31, 110-191.

Zeune, J., 2000: German town walls: functionalism and symbolism. In Perbellini, G. (ed.), *The Town Walls in the Middle Ages: Les Enceintes Urbaines Au Moyen Âge*. The Hague: IBI Bulletin 53, 39-42.

INDEX